Cracknell's

Law Students' Companion

English Legal System

Cracknell's
Law Students' Companion

English Legal System

Fourth Edition

D. G. CRACKNELL, LLB
of the Middle Temple, Barrister

Series Editor
D.G.Cracknell, LLB
of the Middle Temple, Barrister

OLD BAILEY PRESS

OLD BAILEY PRESS LIMITED
The Gatehouse, Ruck Lane, Horsmonden, Kent TN12 8EA

First published 1963
Fourth Edition 1995

© Old Bailey Press Ltd 1995

ISBN 1 85836 004 8

British Library Cataloguing-in-Publication.

A CIP Catalogue record for this book is available from the British Library.

Printed and bound in Great Britain.

Contents

Preface

As an examination subject, the English Legal System takes many forms. In relation to some of the possible topics, if they are included within a particular course reference may be made to a wide range of source material, if only by way of illustration.

In preparing this work the aim has been to cover those topics which are most likely to fall within any English Legal System syllabus – and to reflect the law as at 1 January 1995.

Cases reported on or before 1 January 1995 have been taken into account and the statutes incorporate any relevant provisions (including any repeals, amendments or substitutions) passed *and brought into force* on or before that date. It follows that provisions, say, of the Judicial Pensions and Retirement Act 1993, the Criminal Justice and Public Order Act 1994 and the Police and Magistrates' Courts Act 1994 have been covered, as appropriate, only if they were in force on 1 January 1995.

To illustrate the policy adopted (and the danger of anticipating commencement dates), mention may be made of s11 of the Administration of Justice Act 1970. This provision was amended by the Social Security Act 1973, but as that amendment had not been brought into force on 1 January 1995 the section appears in its original and still current form. It must be said, though, that it now seems likely that all of the Acts (or the remaining provisions of them) mentioned in the previous paragraph will be brought into force within the next year or so.

The cases included are High Court decisions unless it is indicated otherwise.

Comments as to the scope of this work have been taken into account in preparing this edition (previous editions also covered Constitutional Law). Suggestions as to future editions would also be most gratefully received and they, too, would be carefully considered.

January 1995

Cases

Abbassy v Commissioner of Police of the Metropolis [1]
[1990] 1 WLR 385 (Court of Appeal)

The plaintiff motorist, an Iranian, was stopped by the police and asked four times about the ownership of the vehicle: on each occasion the reply was abusive. On being told that he would be arrested unless he could satisfy the constable as to the ownership of the Mercedes, the plaintiff said that British laws meant nothing to him. The constable then told him that he was being arrested for 'unlawful possession' and he was held in custody for some two hours before being released. In an action for, inter alia, wrongful arrest and false imprisonment the judge ruled that the arrest had been unlawful as the constable's explanation of the reason for the arrest had been insufficient and the plaintiff was awarded £5,000 by way of damages. The defendants appealed. *Held*, the judge had been wrong to withdraw from the jury the issue as to whether the arrest had been unlawful and the appeal would be allowed to that extent. 'Of course, in any case in which a jury has a part to play it is open to, and indeed the duty of, the trial judge if he is satisfied that there is no evidence on which the jury can reach a relevant conclusion to withdraw the matter from the jury. In cases of wrongful arrest, in which the issues have specifically and exceptionally been left for determination by a jury, the judge ought to be very slow to withdraw any particular issue from them ... The [constable's] evidence, which really cannot be refuted, was that she thought that the vehicle had either been stolen by the ... plaintiff or been driven away by him without the owner's consent or that he was a receiver of a vehicle that had been stolen by somebody else. Without any further investigation it would be quite impossible for an arresting officer to elect between these three possibilities ... I can see no mandate in the common law for a requirement that a constable exercising his powers of arrest without warrant should specify the particular crime for which the arrest is being made, provided that one or more of such alternatives present to his mind were arrestable offences. Nor does the arresting constable have to impart the information to the arrested person in the form of a technical statutory or common law definition. In my judgment, it is sufficient that commonplace words be used, the obvious meaning of which informs the person arrested of the offence or type of offence for which he is being arrested' (*per* PURCHAS LJ). (See also *Lewis v Chief Constable of the South Wales Constabulary*.)

Afzal v Ford Motor Co Ltd [1994] 4 All ER 720 (Court of Appeal) [2]

The cases before the court raised questions in relation to the automatic reference to arbitration of small claims in the county court. The defendant employers contended that there was no reasonable prospect of the particular plaintiffs receiving more than £1,000 by way of damages for minor personal injury, but in some cases damages limited to £3,000 were claimed in order to pre-empt reference to arbitration. *Held*, on the facts, the cases would be remitted for individual consideration by the district judge. 'The district judge cannot rescind an automatic reference to arbitration under CCR Ord 19, r3(1) merely because a question of law is involved or the facts are complex. Rule 3(2)(a) makes it clear that the question of law has to be one of difficulty and a question of fact one of exceptional complexity if the claim is to be regarded as one which should be tried in court ... The intentional overstatement of the amount involved in a claim to avoid a procedure which has been laid down by Parliament and incorporated in rules of the court is in our judgment a clear misuse of process' (*per* BELDHAM LJ).

Agricultural, Horticultural and Forestry Industry Training Board v Aylesbury Mushrooms Ltd [1972] 1 WLR 190 [3]

Under s1(4) of the Industrial Training Act 1964, before establishing an industrial training board the Minister of Labour was required to consult 'any organisation ... appearing to him to be representative of substantial numbers of employers engaging in the activities concerned ...'. In 1964 the minister proposed to set up a training board for the agricultural, horticultural and forestry industry. He consulted the National Farmers Union of which the Mushroom Growers Association was a specialist branch and, although he had intended to consult the association direct, a letter to them had never been received and they had not seen a press notice. The order was duly made and the association contended that they were not bound by it. *Held*, this contention would be upheld. 'I ... answer the question in the originating summons as follows: Whether before making an order establishing a training board ... the Minister was under a duty to consult the ... association – Yes. Whether the consultations held by the Minister with the National Farmers Union constituted a sufficient consultation ... – No. If it be held that the Minister was under a duty to consult the ... association, whether on the facts such consultation took place – No. If it be held that the Minister was under a duty to consult the ... association and failed to do so, what effect such failure had on the provisions of the [order]. The order has no application to mushroom growers as such' (*per* DONALDSON J). (But see *Bates v Lord Hailsham of St Marylebone*.)

Aiden Shipping Co Ltd v Interbulk Ltd, The Vimeira See Symphony Group plc v Hodgson.

Allen v Emmerson [1944] 1 KB 362 [4]

By statute, 'no theatre or other place of public entertainment' could operate without a licence. It was contended, inter alia, that the ejusdem generis rule applied and therefore that a licence was not required for a funfair. *Held*, this was not the case. 'No case was cited to us in which a genus has been held to be constituted, not by the enumeration of a number of classes followed by the words "or other", but by the mention of a single class (in this case "theatre") followed by those words' (*per* ASQUITH J). (But see *Powell v Kempton Park Racecourse Co Ltd*.)

American Cynamid Co v Ethicon Ltd [1975] AC 396 [5]
(House of Lords)

The plaintiffs owned a patent relating to the design and manufacture of surgical stitches. The defendants were about to market a product which, it was claimed, infringed that patent. The plaintiffs applied for an interlocutory injunction to restrain the launch pending trial of the action. *Held*, the injunction would be granted. Leaving aside the complicated scientific evidence which supported and denied the claim, there was a serious question to be tried and the balance of convenience favoured restraint upon a venture which had not yet been put into effect.

'The object of the interlocutory injunction is to protect the plaintiff against injury by violation of his right for which he could not adequately be compensated in damages recoverable in the action if the uncertainty were resolved in his favour at trial; but the plaintiff's need for such protection must be weighed against the corresponding need of the defendant to be protected against injury resulting from his having been prevented from exercising his own legal rights for which he could not be adequately compensated under the plaintiff's undertaking in damages if the uncertainty were resolved in the defendant's favour at trial. The court must weigh one need against another and determine where "balance of convenience" lies … unless the material available to the court at the hearing of the application for an interlocutory injunction fails to disclose that the plaintiff has any real prospect of succeeding in his claim for a permanent injunction at trial, the court should go on to consider whether the balance of convenience lies in favour of granting or refusing the interlocutory relief that is sought. As to that, the governing principle is that the court should first consider whether if the plaintiff were to succeed at the trial in establishing his right to a permanent injunction he would be adequately compensated by an award of damages for the loss which he would have sustained as a result of the defendant's continuing to do what was sought to be enjoined between the time of the application and the time of the trial. If damages in the measure recoverable at common law would be adequate remedy and the defendant would be in a financial position to pay them, no interlocutory injunction should normally be granted, however strong the plaintiff's claim appears to be at that stage … It is where there is doubt as to the adequacy of the respective remedies in damages available to either party or to both, that the question of balance of convenience arises. It would be unwise to attempt even to list all the various matters which may need to be taken into consideration in deciding where the balance lies, let alone suggest the relative weight to be attached to them. These will vary from case to case. Where other factors appear to be evenly balanced it is a counsel of prudence to take such measures as are calculated to preserve the status quo' (*per* LORD DIPLOCK).

Anton Piller KG v Manufacturing Processes Ltd   **[6]**
[1976] Ch 55 (Court of Appeal)

The plaintiffs, German manufacturers for the computer industry, suspected that the defendants, their English agents, were supplying confidential information to the plaintiffs' German competitors. Fearing that the defendants would destroy relevant documents or send them out of the jurisdiction, the plaintiffs applied ex parte for an order requiring the defendants to permit the plaintiffs to enter their premises in order to inspect, remove or make copies of such documents. *Held,* the court had inherent jurisdiction to make such an order and here it would be made as, in all the rare circumstances of the case, it was 'essential in the interests of justice' (*per* ORMROD LJ). 'In the enforcement of this order, the plaintiffs must act with due circumspection. On the service of it, the plaintiffs should be attended by their solicitor, who is an officer of the court. They should give the defendants an opportunity of considering it and of consulting their own solicitor. If the defendants wish to apply to discharge the order as having been improperly obtained, they must be allowed to do so. If the defendants refuse permission to enter or to inspect, the plaintiffs must not force their way in. They must accept that refusal, and bring it to the notice of the court afterwards, if need be on application to commit' (*per* LORD DENNING MR). (See also *Universal Thermosensors Ltd v Hibben.*)

Arab Bank plc v Mercantile Holdings Ltd [1994] 2 WLR 307   [7]

The question arose, inter alia, whether s151 of the Companies Act 1985 prohibited a foreign subsidiary of an English parent company from giving financial assistance for the acquisition of shares in the parent company. *Held*, applying the presumption that, in the absence of a contrary intention, s151 was not intended to have extra-territorial effect, s151 was to be construed as limited to those subsidiary companies which were English companies. (See also *R* v *Registrar General, ex parte Smith*.)

Arbuthnot Leasing International Ltd v Havelet Leasing Ltd   [8]
[1991] 1 All ER 591

The question was whether the court could permit a director of a company to appear as an advocate on its behalf. *Held*, 'First, RSC Ord 12, r1 is of statutory effect and prohibits a body corporate from taking a step in an action otherwise than through a solicitor. Second, the courts have an inherent power to regulate their own procedure and a judge in an individual case has, as part of that inherent power, the power to permit any advocate to appear for a litigant if the exceptional circumstances of the case so warrant. No limit can be placed on what might constitute sufficient exceptional circumstances. But third, subject to any exceptional circumstances that might require a particular individual in the interests of justice to be allowed to appear as advocate, the general practice of the court is that bodies corporate cannot appear by their directors but only by solicitors or counsel' (*per* SCOTT J).

Ashmore v Corp of Lloyd's [1992] 1 WLR 446 (House of Lords)   [9]

At the trial of an action for damages by certain 'names' the judge allowed an application by the defendants for the question of duty of care to be tried as a preliminary issue. The Court of Appeal allowed an appeal against this decision. *Held*, the judge's decision would be restored. 'Where a judge, for reasons which are not plainly wrong, makes an interlocutory decision or makes a decision in the course of a trial the decision should be respected by the parties and if not respected should be upheld by an appellate court unless the judge was plainly wrong ... The judge thought he would be assisted by an early deliberation of issues of law, whatever the result of that consideration. He deserved support ... the control of the proceedings rests with the judge and not with the plaintiffs. An expectation that the trial would proceed to a conclusion upon the evidence to be adduced is not a legitimate expectation. The only legitimate expectation of any plaintiff is to receive justice. Justice can only be achieved by assisting the judge and accepting his rulings' (*per* LORD TEMPLEMAN). (See also *Hicks* v *Chief Constable of the South Yorkshire Police*.)

Ashville Investments Ltd v Elmer Contractors Ltd   [10]
[1988] 3 WLR 867 (Court of Appeal)

There was a contract for the building of six warehouses and it provided that any dispute 'as to the construction of this contract ...' was to be referred to arbitration. The contractor commenced arbitration proceedings alleging mistake and misrepresentation; the owner sought a declaration that the arbitrator had no jurisdiction, inter alia, to hear and determine such issues. The judge upheld the arbitrator's jurisdiction; the owner appealed. *Held*, the appeal would be dismissed, in the light of the true construction of the arbitration clause. 'I think that it is necessary carefully to consider the role of precedent and the doctrine of stare decisis in a case such as this, in which a question of construction is in truth the fundamental issue between the parties. In my opinion the doctrine of precedent only involves this: that when a case has been decided in a court it is only the legal principle or principles on which that court has so decided that bind courts of concurrent or lower jurisdiction and require them to follow and adopt them when they are relevant to the decision in later cases before those courts. The ratio decidendi of a prior case, the reason why it was decided as it was, is in my view only to be understood in this somewhat limited sense ... I do not think that there is any principle of law to the effect that the meaning of certain specific words in one arbitration clause in one contract is immutable and that those same specific words in another arbitration clause in other circumstances in another contract must be construed in the same way. This is not to say that the earlier decision on a given form of words will not be persuasive, to a degree dependent on the extent of the similarity between the contracts and surrounding circumstances in the two cases. In the interests of certainty and clarity a court may well think it right to construe words in an arbitration agreement, or indeed in a particular type of contract, in the same way as those same words have earlier been construed in another case involving an arbitration clause by another court. But in my opinion the subsequent court is not bound by the doctrine of stare decisis to do so' (*per* MAY LJ).

Associated Provincial Picture Houses Ltd v Wednesbury [11] Corporation [1947] 2 All ER 680 (Court of Appeal)

Wednesbury Corporation granted permission for Sunday performances to be held in a cinema on condition that no children under the age of 15 years should be admitted to any entertainment, whether accompanied by an adult or not. By statute the corporation was entitled to impose such conditions as it thought fit but the proprietors of the cinema sought a declaration that this particular condition was ultra vires. *Held*, such a declaration would not be granted as it could not be said that, by imposing this condition, the Wednesbury Corporation had 'come to a conclusion so unreasonable that no reasonable authority could ever have come to it' (*per* LORD GREENE MR). (See also *Joyce* v *Sengupta*.)

Attorney General v Associated Newspapers Ltd [12] [1994] 2 WLR 277 (House of Lords)

The *Mail on Sunday* published particulars of a jury's deliberations in a fraud trial at the Central Criminal Court. The information was obtained from two members of the jury by an independent researcher. The newspaper, its editor and the journalist concerned were found to be in breach of s8 of the Contempt of Court Act 1981) by disclosing the jury's deliberations. *Held*, their appeals would be dismissed. 'To disclose is to expose to view, make known or reveal and in its ordinary meaning the word aptly described *both* the revelation by jurors of their deliberations *and* further disclosure by publication in a newspaper of the same deliberations, provided always – and this will raise a question of fact – that the publication amounts to *disclosure* and is not a mere republication of already known facts' (*per* LORD LOWRY). (See also *R* v *Thompson*.)

Attorney General v Guardian Newspapers Ltd (No 3) [13] [1992] 1 WLR 874

In the course of the trial of six defendants at Manchester Crown Court arising out of the widely-publicised collapse of a Manx company, and while other criminal proceedings were pending against some of these defendants at Manchester and in the Isle of Man, Henry J made an order under s4(2) of the Contempt of Court Act 1981 prohibiting the publication of reports of the present proceedings until all those trials had been concluded. The defendants published an article alleging that 'In big fraud cases, judges appear to be over-sensitive ... and clamping down unnecessarily on press reporting' and mention was made of Henry J's decision. *Held*, there had been no contempt of court as, on the facts, there had been no practical (as opposed to theoretical) risk that the course of justice would be seriously impeded. (But see *Attorney General* v *Times Newspapers Ltd* [1973].)

Attorney General v Hislop [1991] 1 All ER 911 (Court of Appeal)   **[14]**

Mrs Sutcliffe, wife of 'the Yorkshire Ripper', was suing *Private Eye* for libel. Three months before the trial of this action *Private Eye* published articles which, in effect, threatened to expose her to cross-examination as to her alleged knowledge of her husband's activities and abuse of the social security system. *Held*, even though *Private Eye* believed at the time of publication that the articles were true or that they would be able to cross-examine Mrs Sutcliffe on the matters contained in them, the articles gave rise to a substantial risk that the course of the proceedings would be seriously impeded or prejudiced and amounted to a contempt both at common law and under the Contempt of Court Act 1981. (But see *Attorney General* v *Guardian Newspapers Ltd (No 3)*.)

Attorney General v Jones [1990] 1 WLR 859 (Court of Appeal)   **[15]**

Under s42 of the Supreme Court Act 1981, the High Court may make a 'civil proceedings order' forbidding the institution of proceedings or the making of applications without leave, where a person has instituted vexatious civil proceedings, or made vexatious applications in any civil proceedings, whether in the High Court or any inferior court. *Held*, such an order could cover the making of a counterclaim and proceedings in the Court of Appeal on appeal from the High Court or any inferior court. 'For my part, I consider that s42 is ambiguous. From this it follows that it is both permissible and necessary to have regard to its purpose, to the mischief at which it is directed. This is that the compulsive authority of the state vested in the courts and the judiciary shall not be invoked without reasonable cause to the detriment of other citizens and that, where someone takes this course habitually and persistently, that person shall be restrained from continuing to do so, but shall nevertheless be as free as any other citizen to use those processes if he has reasonable cause for so doing. Given that purpose, there is no obvious or indeed any reason why the section should have been intended by Parliament to have regard only to proceedings in the High Court or in an inferior court to the exclusion of proceedings in the Court of Appeal' (*per* LORD DONALDSON OF LYMINGTON MR). (See also *Pepper* v *Hart* and *R* v *McFarlane*.)

Attorney General v Prince Ernest Augustus of Hanover   **[16]**
[1957] AC 436 (House of Lords)

The question was whether, in the light of a statute of 1705, the respondent was a lineal descendant of Princess Sophia and therefore a British subject. *Held*, he was as, inter alia, naturalisation had not been restricted by the preamble to the 1705 Act (for it was ambiguous) and there was no inherent absurdity in the 1705 Act at the time when it was passed. 'The contention ... was ... that, where the enacting part of a statute is clear and unambiguous, it cannot be cut down by the preamble ... I wish, at the outset, to express my dissent from it, if it means that I cannot obtain assistance from the preamble in ascertaining the meaning of the relevant enacting part. For words, and particularly general words, cannot be read in isolation; their colour and content are derived from their context. So it is that I conceive it to be my right and duty to examine every word of a statute in its context, and I use context in its widest sense ... as including not only other enacting provisions of the same statute, but its preamble, the existing state of the law, other statutes in pari materia, and the mischief which I can, by those and other legitimate means, discern that the statute was intended to remedy ... the elementary rule must be observed that no one should profess to understand any part of a statute or of any other document before he has read the whole of it ... the context of the preamble is not to influence the meaning otherwise ascribable to the enacting part unless there is a compelling reason for it ... Still less can the preamble affect the meaning of the enacting words when its own meaning is in doubt' (*per* VISCOUNT SIMONDS).

Attorney General v Sport Newspapers Ltd [1991] 1 WLR 1194   **[17]**

Suspecting that a girl might have been abducted by a man previously convicted of rape and assault, the police revealed his name and description but made it clear that details of his previous convictions were not to be published. In an article in their newspaper the respondents named the suspect, described him, inter alia, as a 'vicious evil rapist' and gave details of a rape committed by him. The man was subsequently convicted of the missing girl's murder and, following the trial, the Attorney General instituted proceedings for contempt of court. *Held*, the application would be dismissed as it had not been shown beyond reasonable doubt that the respondent's publication of their article possessed the necessary intention to prejudice the fair conduct of proceedings. 'On balance I conclude that the application has not shown beyond reasonable doubt that at the date of publication the second respondent [the respondents' editor] had the specific intention which must be proved against him. If proof of recklessness were enough, the answer might be different, but it is not' (*per* BINGHAM LJ). (But see *Attorney General v Hislop*.)

Attorney General v Times Newspapers Ltd   **[18]**
[1973] 3 WLR 298 (House of Lords)

Distillers made and sold the drug thalidomide the use of which had led to many children being born deformed. Proceedings were instituted and, while negotiations for a settlement were taking place, the *Sunday Times* published an article intended to show that Distillers had been guilty of negligence. *Held*, the article constituted a contempt of court as it gave rise to a real risk that the fair trial of the action (or the negotiation of terms for its settlement) would be prejudiced. (Distinguished in *Re Lonrho plc*; see also *Attorney General v Times Newspapers Ltd* [1991].)

Attorney General v Times Newspapers Ltd   **[19]**
[1991] 2 All ER 398 (House of Lords)

When interlocutory injunctions ('the Millett injunctions') were in force restraining two newspapers from publishing material from the book *Spycatcher* ('the confidentiality actions') three other newspapers published such material and the Attorney General brought proceedings for criminal contempt against them. The trial judge found in favour of the three newspapers and the Attorney General gave notice of appeal. Before the appeal was heard the *Sunday Times* began its serialisation of the book. The Attorney General alleged that such serialisation was contempt of court and subsequently his appeal in relation to the three newspapers was allowed. *Held*, the *Sunday Times* had indeed been in contempt of court. 'The purpose of the Millett injunctions was to prevent ... publication pending the trial of the confidentiality actions. The consequence of the publication of *Spycatcher* material by ... the *Sunday Times* before the trial of the confidentiality actions was to nullify, in part at least, the purpose of such trial, because it put into the public domain part of the material which it was claimed by the Attorney General in the confidentiality actions ought to remain confidential. It follows that the conduct of ... the *Sunday Times* constituted the actus reus of impeding or interfering with the administration of justice by the court in the confidentiality actions. Mens rea in respect of such conduct having been conceded ..., both the necessary ingredients of contempt of court were present' (*per* LORD BRANDON). (But see *Attorney General v Sport Newspapers Ltd*.)

Attorney General for Canada v Attorney General for Ontario [1937] AC 326 (Privy Council) [20]

The question arose whether the Dominion Parliament could, without provincial concurrence, pass legislation to implement an international convention regulating hours of work. *Held*, it could not. 'Within the British Empire there is a well-established rule that the making of a treaty is an executive act, while the performance of its obligations, if they entail alteration of the existing domestic law, requires legislative action ... unlike some other countries, the stipulations of a treaty duly ratified do not ... by virtue of the treaty alone, have the force of law' (*per* LORD ATKIN).

Attorney General of Hong Kong v Cheung Wai-bun [1993] 3 WLR 242 (Privy Council) [21]

The trial of the respondent, the manager of a bank, in relation to offences alleged to have been committed between 1979 and 1982 was eventually fixed for 28 April 1992. On 16 June 1992 the judge granted a permanent stay of the proceedings on the ground that the long delay had prejudiced their fairness, but the Attorney General appealed, contending that alleged further offences had concealed the original alleged offence. *Held*, the appeal would be dismissed. On the facts, it could not be said that the alleged further offences had contributed to the delay and the judge had applied the correct test (was the delay such that, on the balance of probabilities a fair trial could not be held?) when making his decision. (See also *Attorney General's Reference (No 1 of 1990)*.)

Attorney General's Reference (No 1 of 1990) [1992] 3 WLR 9 (Court of Appeal) [22]

The court was asked to consider the circumstances in which proceedings upon indictment may be stayed on the grounds of prejudice resulting from delay in their institution. *Held*, 'stays imposed on the grounds of delay or for any other reason should only be employed in exceptional circumstances. If they were to become a matter of routine, it would be only a short time before the public, understandably, viewed the process with suspicion and mistrust ... Still more rare should be cases where a stay can properly be imposed in the absence of any fault on the part of the complainant or prosecution. Delay due merely to the complexity of the case or contributed to by the actions of the defendant himself should never be the foundation for a stay ... no stay should be imposed unless the defendant shows on the balance of probabilities that owing to the delay he will suffer serious prejudice to the extent that no fair trial can be held, in other words that the continuance of the prosecution amounts to a misuse of the process of the court' (*per* LORD LANE CJ). (See also *Attorney General of Hong Kong* v *Cheung Wai-bun.*)

Balogh v St Albans Crown Court [1975] QB 73 (Court of Appeal) [23]

Being exceedingly bored with the proceedings, a casual clerk employed by defence solicitors planned to liven things up – he would put laughing gas into the court's ventilating system! One night he climbed on to the roof to establish where he would place the cylinder: next morning he brought the cylinder (which he had stolen) to court in a briefcase, awaiting his moment to carry out his plan. However, an officer apprehended him and he freely confessed his intention. He was sentenced to six months' imprisonment for contempt of court and he now appealed. *Held*, the appeal would be allowed. 'Mr Balogh had the criminal intent to disrupt the court but that is not enough. He was guilty of stealing the cylinder, but no more. On this short ground we think the judge was in error' (*per* LORD DENNING MR). (But see *R* v *Powell.*)

Barlow Clowes Gilt Managers Ltd, Re [1992] 2 WLR 36 [24]

The liquidators of two companies sought the court's direction as to whether they were at liberty to disclose to certain defendants connected with those companies transcripts of statements made to them (the liquidators) in confidence. *Held*, disclosure should not be made unless it was ordered by the Crown Court. 'In a criminal case, the defendant is under no obligation to assist the prosecution. With certain limited exceptions, he is entitled to the so-called "right of silence". But the prosecution is in a different position. Traditionally it is not regarded as a combatant. It has duties to be objective and balanced in the presentation of its case, and must not withhold from the defence matters, whether strictly evidence or not, which may prove helpful to the defence' (*per* MILLETT J). (See also *R* v *Banks.*)

Barrister (Wasted Costs Order) (No 1 of 1991), Re a See Ridehalgh v Horsefield.

Bates v Lord Hailsham of St Marylebone [1972] 1 WLR 1373 [25]

Under s56(1) of the Solicitors Act 1957 a committee was constituted and, by virtue of s56(2) it had power to make general orders prescribing solicitors' remuneration in respect of non-contentious business: s56(3) provided that, before any such order was made, the Lord Chancellor should cause the Council of the Law Society to be consulted. In May 1972 the Lord Chancellor announced that it was proposed to abolish scale fees for conveyancing; the Law Society received a draft of the proposed order in June of that year. Section 56(3) of the 1957 Act gave the Law Society one month in which to submit its observations, but the British Legal Association, a smaller organisation of solicitors which had registered itself as a trade union, asked the committee to delay its decision and to consult further and more widely within the profession. In July the Lord Chancellor said that he saw no reason why the making of an order should be postponed and on the same day the plaintiff, a member of the association's executive, sought an injunction to restrain the committee from making an order until, inter alia, the association had been given the opportunity to make representations. *Held*, the injunction would not be granted as, inter alia, the committee was not required to provide opportunities for representations by bodies other than the Council of the Law Society. 'Let me accept that in the sphere of the so-called quasi-judicial the rules of natural justice run, and that in the administrative or executive field there is a general duty of fairness. Nevertheless, these considerations do not seem to me to affect the process of legislation, whether primary or delegated ... Of course, the informal consultation of representative bodies by the legislative authority is a commonplace; but although a few statutes have specifically provided for a general process of publishing draft delegated legislation and considering objections ..., I do not know of any implied right to be consulted or make objections, or any principle on which the courts may enjoin the legislative process at the suit of those who contend that insufficient time for consultation and consideration has been given ...' (*per* MEGARRY J). (But see *Agricultural, Horticultural and Forestry Industry Training Board* v *Aylesbury Mushrooms Ltd*.)

Bennett v Horseferry Road Magistrates Court See R v Horseferry Road Magistrates' Court, ex parte Bennett.

Berry v R [1992] 3 WLR 153 (Privy Council) [26]

At a murder trial in the Circuit Court, Kingston, Jamaica, the jury returned after an hour's deliberations and said that they had a problem. After ascertaining that the problem was one of fact rather than law, the judge did not enquire further but gave general guidance. *Held*, the jury are entitled at any stage to the judge's help on the facts as well as on the law. To withhold that assistance constitutes an irregularity which, depending on the circumstances, could be material.

Birkett v James [1978] AC 197 See Roebuck v Mungovin.

Black-Clawson International Ltd v Papierwerke [27]
Waldhof-Aschaffenburg AG [1975] AC 591 (House of Lords)

The question was whether a claim was barred under s8(1) of the Foreign Judgments (Reciprocal Enforcement) Act 1933. This Act was passed following the report of a committee appointed by the Lord Chancellor. *Held*, in so far as s8(1) was ambiguous, reference could be made to the report to establish that Parliament had not intended to alter the common law. 'I think that we can take this report as accurately stating the "mischief" and the law as it was then understood to be, and therefore we are fully entitled to look at those parts of the report which deal with those matters. But the report contains a great deal more than that. It contains recommendations, a draft Bill and other instruments intended to embody those recommendations, and comments on what the committee thought the Bill achieved. The draft Bill corresponds in all material respects with the Act so it is clear that Parliament adopted the recommendations of the committee. But nevertheless I do not think that we are entitled to take any of this into account in construing the Act. Construction of the provisions of an Act is for the court and for no one else' (*per* LORD REID). (See also *Director of Public Prosecutions* v *Bull*.)

Bodden v Commissioner of Police of the Metropolis [28]
[1990] 2 WLR 76 (Court of Appeal)

A loudhailer was used to address a crowd of demonstrators outside Bow Street Magistrates Court: the demonstration related, apparently, to a trial to take place that morning. A magistrate sitting in another court was unable to hear a witness giving evidence before him: did s2 of the Contempt of Court Act 1981 empower this magistrate to deal with the interruption as a contempt of court? *Held*, it did. 'The mischief at which this ... is aimed is the wilful interruption of the proceedings in court, whether this results from acts done within the court or whether they are brought to a standstill by acts done outside ... The judge went on to consider the meaning of the word "wilfully" and, in my view, correctly concluded that, in the context of s12, it is necessary for there to be established, in addition to the deliberate commission of the acts causing the interruption, the mental element of intending they should interrupt the proceedings of the court ... In addition to an intention to interrupt the proceedings of the court, "wilfully" would, in my judgment, also include the state of mind of an interrupter who knew that there was a risk that his acts would interrupt the proceedings of the court but nevertheless went on deliberately to do those acts. In that sense, recklessness would be a sufficient state of mind ...' (*per* BELDAM LJ).

British Railways Board v Pickin [1974] AC 765 House of Lords [29]

The validity of a private Act of Parliament, the British Railways Act 1968, was challenged. It was alleged that there were false and misleading recitals in the preamble of the Act which made the Act ineffective to deprive the plaintiff of his land or proprietary rights. *Held*, the proceedings would be struck out as the courts have no power to disregard an Act of Parliament nor to examine proceedings in Parliament in order to ascertain whether the Act had been enacted by any irregularity. (See also *Manuel v A-G* [1982] 3 All ER 786.)

Bugg v Director of Public Prosecutions, Director [30] of Public Prosecutions v Percy [1993] 2 WLR 628

These two appeals arose out of a conviction of, and a dismissal of a charge for, entering a protected area without permission, contrary to the relevant by-laws, the Alconbury By-laws and the Forest Moor By-laws respectively. *Held*, the first appeal would be allowed and the second dismissed. WOOLF LJ explained that there were two different situations in which a defendant who was charged with breaching a by-law might seek to challenge the validity of the by-law. The first was where the by-law was on its face invalid because either it was outwith the power pursuant to which it was made or it was patently unreasonable (substantive invalidity), and the second was where there had been non-compliance with a procedural requirement with regard to the making of that bylaw, eg a failure to consult (procedural invalidity). As a matter of principle, a criminal court (as opposed to a civil court) could not investigate matters of procedural invalidity unless, perhaps, it was alleged that these had been an abuse of power because of mala fides on the part of the by-law maker. With regard to the by-laws in question, the Forest Moor By-laws did not state with sufficient certainty the area covered and were thus defective on their face. The Alconbury By-laws referred to the area covered as being marked by a perimeter fence. That had since been moved. In those circumstances it was quite wrong to prosecute someone for offences which involved proceedings beyond the boundary when that boundary was no longer correctly marked.

Bulmer (HP) Ltd v J Bollinger SA [31]
[1974] 3 WLR 202 (Court of Appeal)

The plaintiffs, two of the largest producers of cider in England, sought a declaration that they could use the word 'champagne'. The defendant French producers counter-claimed for an injunction to stop the plaintiffs using the name in connection with any beverage that was not a wine produced in the champagne region of France. After the United Kingdom joined the EEC the defendants amended their pleadings to include a claim for a declaration that the use of expressions such as 'champagne cider' and 'champagne perry' were contrary to EEC Regulations. They asked the judge to refer two questions of Community law to the European Court under article 177 for a preliminary ruling. Whitford J refused to make such a reference: the defendants appealed. *Held*, the appeal would be dismissed. A High Court judge is not obliged to refer a matter; he has a discretion and it is for him to decide when to exercise it. Here, the judge had considered all the relevant matters and had exercised his discretion correctly. LORD DENNING MR laid down guidelines as to the exercise of this discretion as follows: (i) The point must be conclusive of the case. (ii) If there is already a previous ruling on the same or substantially the same point, reference is not necessary. However, the European Court is not bound by its own decisions and therefore any English court may wish to submit a point for reconsideration if it considers it to have been wrongly interpreted before. (iii) A reference need not be made if the court considers the point to be reasonably clear and free from doubt. (iv) The court may decide that questions of fact should be decided first. As to the interpretation of the Treaty (and Regulations and Directives), LORD DENNING MR said English courts 'must follow the European pattern. No longer must they examine the words in meticulous detail. No longer must they argue about the precise grammatical sense. They must look to the purpose or intent. To quote the words of the European Court in the *Da Costa* case ([1963] CMLR 224) they must limit themselves to deducing from "the wording and the spirit of the treaty the meaning of the Community rules ..."'.

C v Director of Public Prosecutions [1994] 3 All ER 190 [32]

On an appeal by way of case stated to the Queen's Bench Divisional Court, the question was whether there was sufficient evidence to justify the justices' finding of fact that a boy aged 12 had known that what he was doing (interfering with a motor cycle) was 'seriously wrong'. *Held*, the rebuttable presumption that a child aged between 10 and 14 did not know that his act was seriously wrong was outdated and no longer part of the law of England. It was not apt, therefore, to answer the question framed in the case stated. 'All the cases cited to us were decided either in the Divisional Court or at trial at first instance, save two... which were decisions of the Court of Appeal, Criminal Division. It is clear on authority that the Divisional Court has the power to depart from its own previous decisions: *R v Greater Manchester Coroner, ex parte Tal* [1985] QB 67. The rule is that the court will follow a decision of a court of equal jurisdiction unless persuaded that it is clearly wrong ... In the present case all the earlier decisions proceeded upon the unargued premise that the presumption now in question was undoubtedly part of the fabric of English criminal law. To discard it, therefore, does not involve any disagreement with the express reasoning in the cases. I would hold that there is not the least impediment upon our departing from the earlier Divisional Court authorities so far as, by implication, they upheld the existence of this presumption (as they plainly did): to do so is no affront to any principle of judicial comity, far less the doctrine of precedent. The two cases in the Court of Appeal proceeded upon the same unargued premise ... No doubt in general this court is bound by decisions of the Court of Appeal, Criminal Division. But the question whether this presumption is or should remain part of our law has never, so far as has been ascertained, fallen from distinct argument as an issue requiring that court's specific determination. That being so, in my view this court is entitled to depart from the premise which lay behind the Court of Appeal's two decisions; to do so does not involve a departure from any adjudication which that court was required to make upon an issue in dispute before it' (*per* LAWS J). NB Leave was granted to appeal to the House of Lords. (See also *R v Metropolitan Stipendiary Magistrate, ex parte London Waste Regulation Authority* and *Re Hetherington, Gibbs v McDonnell*.)

C (Adult: Refusal of Treatment), Re [1994] 1 WLR 290   **[33]**

A prisoner developed gangrene in a foot. A consultant believed that amputation below the knee was required in order to save the prisoner's life. The prisoner sought an injunction restraining the hospital from carrying out an amputation, then or in the future, without his express written consent. *Held*, the relief sought would be granted. 'Can the High Court exercising its inherent jurisdiction (1) rule by way of injunction or declaration that an individual is capable of refusing or consenting to medical treatment and (2) determine the effect of a purported advance directive as to the future medical treatment? I would answer both questions affirmatively' (*per* THORPE J).

Cassell & Co Ltd v Broome [1972] AC 1027 (House of Lords)   **[34]**

When confronted by a question relating to exemplary damages, the Court of Appeal concluded that *Rookes* v *Barnard* [1964] AC 1129 had been decided by the House of Lords per incuriam (or that the decision was 'unworkable') and therefore that it was not binding, even on the Court of Appeal. *Held*, the decision in *Rookes* v *Barnard* had not been made per incuriam as all relevant authorities had been fully considered. Even if it had, it was not open to the Court of Appeal to decline to follow it on that ground (or because they found it unworkable). 'It is inevitable in a hierarchical system of courts that there are decisions of the supreme appellate tribunal which do not attract the unanimous approval of all members of the judiciary. ... But the judicial system only works if someone is allowed to have the last word and if that last word, once spoken, is loyally accepted ... the label per incuriam ... is relevant only to the right of an appellate court to decline to follow one of its own previous decisions, not to its right to disregard a decision of a higher appellate court or to the right of a judge of the High Court to disregard a decision of the Court of Appeal' (*per* LORD DIPLOCK).

Central Independent Television plc, Re   **[35]**
[1991] 1 WLR 4 (Court of Appeal)

At the point when the jury were about to retire to consider their verdict and to spend the night at a hotel, the judge said: 'I do not want to gag radio, or television, but I think it is an imposition on the jury that they should not be able to relax and watch television. It is highly unlikely there will be anything about the case tonight, but I do make a formal order there should not be, so that the jury can relax. Of course, it only applies to tonight, and the radio and television can publish whatever they like tomorrow.' The order was made under s4(2) of the Contempt of Court Act 1981 and certain television and radio bodies appealed against it under s159 of the Criminal Justice Act 1988. *Held*, the appeal would be allowed. 'There was, it seems, nothing in the broadcast reports of the case during its currency which gave rise to a fear that any reports broadcast ... would be other than fair and accurate. Indeed, we gather that there had been very little of interest either to the media or to the public happening on that day prior to the jury retiring to their hotel. There was therefore no ground on which the judge could have concluded that there was a substantial risk of prejudice to the administration of justice ... One appreciates the judge's concern here for the welfare of the jury, but had it been necessary to insulate them from the media, it would in this case, and in most others where such a risk exists, have been possible to overcome it by means other than action under s4(2). Where such an alternative is reasonably available, it should be used ...' (*per* LORD LANE CJ).

Chief Adjudication Officer v Foster [36]
[1993] 2 WLR 292 (House of Lords)

The question arose as to whether a severely disabled young woman, the appellant, was entitled to the severe disability premium, in addition to the statutory allowances, payable by virtue of the Social Security Act 1986 and regulations made under it. The social security commissioner had held that the regulation which would have defeated her claim was ultra vires but the Court of Appeal took the view that he had no jurisdiction to question the vires of the regulation and that in any case his decision as to vires had been mistaken. *Held,* in exercising his appellate function the commissioner has been entitled to determine any challenge as to vires, but the regulation was indeed intra vires and the appellant's claim to the premium therefore failed. 'Since the oral argument on the appeal your Lordships' House has ruled in *Pepper* v *Hart* that in certain circumstances the parliamentary history of a provision in a Bill and references to it in Hansard may be considered when that provision reaches the statute book and falls to be construed ... The significance of this, following as it does two other cases decided by your Lordships' House since *Pepper* v *Hart* (*Stubbings* v *Webb* and *Warwickshire CC* v *Johnson*) where the parliamentary material has been found decisive of a statutory ambiguity, is to illustrate how useful the relaxation of the former exclusionary rule may be in avoiding unnecessary litigation. Certainly in this case, if it had been possible to take account of the parliamentary material at the outset, it would have been clear that it refuted the appellant's contention and there would probably never have been any appeal to the Commissioner, let alone beyond him' (*per* LORD BRIDGE OF HARWICH).

Colchester Estates (Cardiff) v Carlton Industries plc [37]
[1984] 3 WLR 693

In proceedings concerning the recovery by the landlord of the cost of repairs, Nourse J was confronted by conflicting High Court decisions. *Held,* the later decision would be followed. 'There must come a time when a point is normally to be treated as having been settled at first instance I think that that should be when the earlier decision has been fully considered, but not followed, in a later one ... I would make an exception only in the case, which must be rare, where the third judge is convinced that the second was wrong in not following the first. An obvious example is where some binding or persuasive authority has not been cited in either of the first two cases' (per NOURSE J).

Connelly v Director of Public Prosecutions [38]
[1964] AC 1254 (House of Lords)

The appellant (and others) took part in an armed raid; one of the robbers shot and killed a man. There were two indictments against the appellant, ie, murder and robbery with aggravation. He was convicted of murder and the trial judge ordered the second indictment to remain on the file. On appeal, the conviction was quashed because of a misdirection and leave was then given for the second indictment to proceed and he was convicted of robbery with aggravation. He appealed against this conviction on grounds of, inter alia, autrefois acquit. *Held,* his appeal would be dismissed. 'The test is ... whether such proof as is necessary to convict of the second offence would establish guilt of the first offence or of an offence for which on the first charge there could be a conviction. Applying to the present case the law as laid down, the question is whether proof that there was robbery with aggravation would support a charge of murder or manslaughter. It seems to me quite clear that it would not. The crimes are distinct ... That the facts in the two trials have much in common is not a true test of the availability of the plea of autrefois acquit. Nor is it of itself relevant that two separate crimes were committed at the same time so that in recounting the one there may be mention of the other' (*per* LORD MORRIS OF BORTH-Y-GEST). (See also *Richards* v *R.*)

Crook, Re [1992] 2 All ER 687 (Court of Appeal) [39]

A freelance journalist was excluded from a trial at the Central Criminal Court while the judge heard applications by counsel as in chambers. He appealed against his exclusion. *Held*, his appeal would be dismissed. 'From the cases it is clear that the public can be excluded only when and to the extent that is strictly necessary, and also that each application must be considered on its own merits. It is not sufficient that a public hearing will cause embarrassment for some or all of those concerned ... The judge could not know until he was given further information whether it would be prejudicial to the administration of justice if that information was made public. It was wholly appropriate that information in these circumstances should in the first instance be given in the presence of defendants and counsel but in the absence of the public. ... If exclusion of the public is necessary, applying the strict standard required to justify it, it would not usually be right to make an exception in favour of the press' (*per* LORD LANE CJ).

Customs and Excise Commissioners v Cure and Deeley Ltd [40]
[1962] 1 QB 340

Section 33(1) of the Finance (No 2) Act 1940 empowered the commissioners to 'make regulations providing for any matter for which provision appears to them necessary for the purpose of giving effect to the provisions of ... this Act and of enabling them to discharge their functions thereunder ...' relating to purchase tax. The commissioners made a regulation covering failure to make a return, including a power to 'determine the amount of tax appearing to them to be due ...' *Held*, this particular regulation was ultra vires. '[This regulation] is ultra vires on at any rate three grounds, which ... are distinct in law though they overlap in so far as they may be different ways of expressing the result of certain facts. First, it is no part of the functions assigned to the commissioners to take on themselves the powers of a High Court judge and decide issues of fact and law as between the Crown and the subjects. Secondly, it renders the subject liable to pay such tax as the commissioners believe to be due, whereas the charging sections [of the Act] impose a liability to pay such tax as in law is due. Thirdly, it is capable of excluding the subject from access to the courts and of defeating pending proceedings ... There also exists, parallel to the third ground, a subsidiary repugnance between the regulation and that part of [the Act] which makes obligatory the reference of certain disputes to arbitration' (*per* SACHS J).

Da Costa en Schaake NV v Nederlandse Belastingadministratie See
Bulmer (HP) Ltd v J Bollinger SA.

Derby & Co Ltd v Weldon (No 3) [1989] 1 WLR 1244 [41]

Two of the defendants sought, inter alia, to have struck out a conspiracy claim, citing in support a recent Court of Appeal decision as to the essential elements of the tort of conspiracy. *Held*, taking into account the possible reversal of the recent decision by the House of Lords, the court, in the exercise of its discretion, would not strike out the claim.

Dimes v Grand Junction Canal See **R v Gough.**

Director General of Fair Trading v Buckland [42]
[1990] 1 WLR 920 (Restrictive Practices Court)

It was alleged that two companies had committed a contempt of the Restrictive Practices Court by breaching an order of that court relating to the supply of ready-mixed concrete. As a matter of law, could two specific directors of these companies be liable to a penalty, including imprisonment, for contempt of court? *Held*, such liability would arise only if the directors could be shown to be in contempt under the general law of contempt.

Director General of Fair Trading v Smiths Concrete Ltd [43]
[1991] 4 All ER 150 (Court of Appeal)

One of the appellants' unit managers entered into an agreement with three other companies in breach of orders made by the Restrictive Practices Court. The appellants had expressly forbidden their employees to enter into any such agreements and they had adequate procedures to ensure compliance with the Restrictive Trade Practices Act 1976. Nevertheless, the Restrictive Practices Court found the appellants vicariously liable for contempt of court. *Held*, this finding would be quashed as the manager had had no authority to enter into the agreement on the appellants' behalf. 'Proceedings for contempt of court are punitive rather than remedial and it follows from this that mens rea, or an intention on the part of the person proceeded against to omit or commit the act, the omission or commission of which constitutes disobedience of the injunctive order, must be established and the offence thereby proved beyond all reasonable doubt' (*per* LORD DONALDSON OF LYMINGTON MR).

Director General of Fair Trading v Stuart [44]
[1991] 1 WLR 1500 (Court of Appeal)

The district judge made an order against Mr Stuart under the Fair Trading Act 1973. How could he appeal against that order? *Held*, appeal lay to the circuit judge and it was not until that internal form of appeal had been exhausted that an appeal could be brought to the Court of Appeal.

Director of Public Prosecutions v Bull [1994] 4 All ER 411 [45]

A man was charged with an offence under s1(1) of the Street Offences Act 1959. At the conclusion of the prosecution case the magistrate upheld the submission that there was no case to answer as s1(1) applies only to female prostitutes. *Held*, this decision had been correct. In reaching this conclusion, their Lordships took account of Darling J's definition of 'common prostitute' in *R v De Munck* [1918] 1 KB 635, a view expressed in a current textbook and the report of the Wolfenden Committee on which the 1959 Act was based. In the light of this report MANN LJ said: 'It is plain that the "mischief" that the Act was intended to remedy was a mischief created by women.' (See also *Black-Clawson International Ltd v Papierwerke Waldhof-Aschaffenburg AG*.)

Director of Public Prosecutions v Hutchinson [46]
[1990] 3 WLR 196 (House of Lords)

The appellants had been convicted of entering without authority an airbase, contrary to one of the RAF Greenham Common By-laws 1985 made under the

Military Lands Act 1892. The statute provided that any such by-laws should not 'take away or prejudicially affect any right of common'. The airbase was subject to rights of common. *Held*, the appellants had been wrongly convicted as the by-laws in question were wider than was authorised by the statute. In all the circumstances, the invalidity of the particular by-law under which the appellant had been charged could not be cured by severance. 'Taking the simplest case of a single legislative instrument containing a number of separate clauses of which one exceeds the lawmaker's power, if the remaining clauses enact free-standing provisions which were intended to operate and are capable of operating independently of the offending clause, there is no reason why those clauses should not be upheld and enforced. ... The invalid clause may be disregarded as unrelated to, and having no effect on, the operation of the valid clauses, which accordingly may be allowed to take effect without the necessity of any modification or adaptation by the court ... Considering the Greenham by-laws as a whole it is clear that the absolute prohibition which they impose on all unauthorised access to the protected area is no less than is required to maintain the security of an establishment operated as a military airbase and wholly enclosed by a perimeter fence. By-laws drawn in such a way as to permit free access to all parts of the base to persons exercising rights of common and their animals would be by-laws of a totally different character' (*per* LORD BRIDGE OF HARWICH). (See also *R* v *Secretary of State for the Home Department, ex parte Leech*; but see *Dunkley* v *Evans*.)

Director of Public Prosecutions v Schildkamp See **R v Kelt**.

D'Souza v Director of Public Prosecutions [47]
[1992] 1 WLR 1073 (House of Lords)

A mother had been detained in hospital under the Mental Health Act 1983 and, without leave having been given under that Act, she had left the premises. Three uniformed police officers went to her home, intending to return her to the hospital. Entry having been refused, the officers broke into the premises and they were there attacked by the daughter. She was convicted of assaulting the officers in the execution of their duty and she appealed against the conviction. *Held*, her appeal would be allowed as, at the material time, the officers had not been acting in the execution of their duty. 'I turn now to the second question on the basis, which I regard as justified, that the patient was "unlawfully at large". Was she a person "whom the constables were pursuing"? ... I cannot find any evidence from which pursuit by the constables before the break-in can be inferred. The verb in the clause "whom he is pursuing" is in the *present continuous* tense and therefore, give or take a few seconds or minutes – this is a question of degree – the pursuit must be almost contemporaneous with the entry into the premises. There must, I consider, be an act of pursuit, that is a chase, however short in time and distance' (*per* LORD LOWRY).

Dunkley v Evans [1981] 1 WLR 1522 [48]

The West Coast Herring (Prohibition of Fishing) Order 1978 prohibited fishing for herring in an area defined in the schedule to the order as within a line drawn by reference to co-ordinates and coastlines. The order was made by the Minister of Agriculture Fisheries and Food under the Sea Fish (Conservation) Act 1967. The prohibited area included a stretch of sea adjacent to the coast of Northern Ireland, representing 0.8% of the total area covered by the order, to which the enabling power in the 1967 Act did not extend. Information laid against the respondents for fishing in a part of the prohibited area to which the enabling power did extend were dismissed on the ground that, by including the area to which the enabling power did not extend, the minister had acted ultra vires and, since textual severance was not possible, the whole order was invalid. The prosecutor appealed. *Held*, the appeal would be allowed and the case remitted to the magistrates to convict. 'It would have been competent for the court in an action for a declaration that the provisions of the order in this case did not apply to the area of the sea off Northern Ireland ... to make the declaration sought, without in any way affecting the validity of the order in relation to the remaining 99.2% of the area referred to in the schedule to the order ... Accordingly we hold that the [order] is not ultra vires the minister who made the order, save in so far as it affects the area of the sea [off Northern Ireland]' (*per* ORMROD LJ). (But see *Director of Public Prosecutions* v *Hutchinson*.)

Easton v Ford Motor Co Ltd [1993] 4 All ER 257 (Court of Appeal) [49]

When an employee sued to obtain a reward which he alleged was due to him under an employee suggestion scheme, the company's initial defence was that the suggestion was not novel. Five years later, the company sought to amend its defence by adding the contention that, in accordance with the rules, the suggestion committee's decision was final and could not be challenged. *Held*, the amendment would be allowed as no injustice would result. The action was not ready for trial ('there is more to be said for refusing an amendment when the action is in the course of trial or very nearly ready for trial': DILLON LJ), the application did not give rise to any need for new evidence and the delay in bringing the action to trial was largely the responsibility of the employee and his advisers.

Evans v Bartlam [1937] AC 473 (House of Lords) [50]

Judgment having been entered against him in default of appearance, the defendant applied to have the judgment set aside and for leave to defend. The application was dismissed by the master, but an appeal to the judge in chambers was successful. The Court of Appeal restored the master's order and the defendant appealed against this decision. *Held*, the appeal would be allowed. 'Appellate jurisdiction is always statutory; there is in the statute no restriction upon the jurisdiction of the Court of Appeal, and, while the appellate court, in the exercise of its appellate power, is no doubt entirely justified in saying that normally it will not interfere with the exercise of the judge's discretion except on grounds of law, yet, if it sees that, on other grounds, the decision will result in injustice being done, it has both the power and the duty to remedy it' (*per* LORD ATKIN).

Evans v Cross [1938] 1 KB 694 [51]

Section 48(9) of the Road Traffic Act 1930 defined 'traffic sign' as including 'all signals, warning sign-posts, direction posts, signs, or other devices for the guidance or direction of persons using roads ...' Did it include a white line painted on the road? *Held*, it did not. 'The word "device" refers to things ejusden generis with signals, warning sign-posts, direction posts and signs, and it cannot be said that this painted line was a sign-post or sign of that nature' (*per* LORD HEWART, LCJ). (But see *Allen* v *Emmerson*.)

Filmlab Systems International Ltd v Pennington [52]
[1994] 4 All ER 673

In the course of proceedings alleging, inter alia, breach of contract and infringement of copyright, the defendants made an application for discovery which the judge believed was 'wholly misconceived'. The plaintiffs sought a wasted costs order against the defendants' counsel. *Held*, on the facts, the application would be dismissed and it was only in exceptional circumstances that such an order would be made until after the trial. 'The plaintiff must show that there was an error and that it was one that no reasonable well-informed and competent member of the Bar could have made ... the test under [s51(6) of the Supreme Court Act 1981] must be the same whether the legal representative, against whom an order for costs is sought, is representing a legally aided client or not' (*per* ALDOUS J). (See also *Ridehalgh* v *Horsefield.*)

Francovich v Italian Republic Cases C-6/90 and C-9/90 [53]
[1992] IRLR 84 (European Court of Justice)

Council Directive No 80/987/EEC sought to ensure employees throughout the Community of a minimum level of protection in case of insolvency of the employer. To that end it provided, in particular, specific guarantees for the payment of unpaid remuneration. According to article 11 of the Directive, member states were bound to bring into force the laws, regulations and administrative provisions necessary to comply with the Directive by 23 October 1983. The Court had held in its judgment in Case 22/87 Commission v Italy [1989] ECR 143 that the Italian Republic had failed to comply with that obligation. The applicants had been employees of undertakings which had become insolvent leaving substantial arrears of salary unpaid. They therefore brought proceedings against the Italian Republic, before certain Italian courts, seeking payment of the compensation provided for by the Directive and those courts sought a ruling from the European Court. *Held*, Community law laid down, subject to certain conditions, the principle that member states were obliged to make good damage caused to individuals by infringements of Community law for which they were responsible. Here, those conditions had been fulfilled and it followed that Italy was liable to make good damage to the applicants arising from non-implementation of the Directive.

Furniss v Dawson [1984] 1 All ER 530 (House of Lords) [54]

The question was whether taxpayers had, by means of a series of prearranged steps, secured deferment of their capital gains tax liability. *Held*, applying to the facts of the case principles established in previous decisions, they had not succeeded in their objective. 'The law in this area is in an early state of development. Speeches in your Lordships' House and judgments in the appellate courts of the United Kingdom are concerned more to chart a way forward between principles accepted and not to be rejected than to attempt anything so ambitious as to determine finally the limit beyond which the safe channel of acceptable tax avoidance shelves into the dangerous shallows of unacceptable tax evasion. The law will develop from case to case. ... What has been established with certainty by the House in *WT Ramsay Ltd* v *IRC* [1981] 1 All ER 865 is that the determination of what does, and what does not, constitute unacceptable tax evasion is a subject suited to development by judicial process. ... Difficult though the task may be for judges, it is one which is beyond the power of the blunt instrument of legislation. Whatever a statute may provide, it has to be interpreted and applied by the courts; and ultimately it will prove to be in this area of judge-made law that our elusive journey's end will be found' (*per* LORD SCARMAN).

Geogas SA v Trammo Gas Ltd, The Baleares [55]
[1991] 3 All ER 554 (House of Lords)

Under s1 of the Arbitration Act 1979, in certain circumstances appeal lies to the High Court against an arbitrator's decision and, with the leave of either the High Court or the Court of Appeal, there is a further appeal to the Court of Appeal. Does an appeal lie to the House of Lords against a decision of the Court of Appeal to refuse or grant leave to appeal from the High Court to itself? *Held*, it does not as, whenever power is given to a legal authority to grant or refuse leave to appeal, the decision of that authority is final and conclusive and without appeal unless there is an express right of appeal from it.

Grey v Pearson (1857) 6 HL Cas 61 (House of Lords) [56]

When confronted with the construction of a will, their Lordships considered the principles to be applied. *Held*, 'in construing wills, and indeed statutes, and all written instruments, the grammatical and ordinary sense of the words is to be adhered to, unless that would lead to some absurdity or some repugnance or inconsistency with the rest of the instrument, in which case the grammatical and ordinary sense of the words may be modified so as to avoid that absurdity or inconsistency, but no further' (*per* LORD WENSLEYDALE). (But see *R* v *Judge of the City of London Court.*)

Griffiths v Jenkins [1992] 2 WLR 28 (House of Lords) [57]

The respondents were alleged to have fished in a private stream and stolen three trout: the justices dismissed the charges. The prosecutor appealed to the Divisional Court by way of case stated and, but for the fact that two of the justices had retired, the court would have remitted the case to the justices with a direction to continue the hearing. The Divisional Court ruled that it had no power to remit the case to a freshly constituted bench and the prosecutor appealed against this decision. *Held*, although the Divisional Court could have remitted the case to a different bench of justices, in the circumstances it would now be inappropriate to do so. Accordingly, the appeal would be dismissed. 'There is always power in the court on hearing an appeal by case stated under s6 of the Summary Jurisdiction Act 1857 to order a rehearing before either the same or a different bench when that appears to be an appropriate course and the court, in its discretion, decides to take it. It is axiomatic, of course, that a rehearing will only be ordered in circumstances where a fair trial is still possible ... It would be most unwise to attempt to lay down guidelines for the exercise of such a discretion and I have no intention of doing so' (*per* LORD BRIDGE OF HARWICH).

H v Ministry of Defence [1991] 2 WLR 1192 (Court of Appeal) [58]

The defendants admitted liability for negligence which led to the amputation of a major part of a soldier's penis. Damages remained to be determined and the soldier applied for trial by jury. The judge granted his application in view of the exceptional circumstances and the defendants appealed against this decision. *Held*, the appeal would be allowed. 'We have ... come to the conclusion that the judge's discretionary order was wrong and we think that the basis of the error was either a failure to appreciate the significance of the shift in emphasis created by the enactment of s69 of the Supreme Court Act 1981 ... or his acceptance of the submission that the retention of a judicial discretion necessarily involved the proposition that there must be some claims for compensatory damages in personal injury cases which were appropriate to be tried by jury or both. It follows that we are entitled, and indeed bound, to exercise a fresh discretion ... The policy should be that stated in *Ward* v *James* [1966] 1 QB 273, namely that trial by jury is normally inappropriate for any personal injury action in so far as the jury is required to assess compensatory damages, because the assessment of such damages must be based upon or have regard to conventional scales of damages. The very fact that no jury trial of a claim for damages for personal injuries appears to have taken place for over 25 years affirms how exceptional the circumstances would have to be before it was appropriate to order such a trial and the enactment of s69 of the 1981 Act strengthens the presumption against making such an order ... If, for example, personal injuries resulted from conduct on the part of those who were deliberately abusing their authority, there might well be a claim for exemplary damages and this could place the case in an exceptional category which, since it is not expressly contemplated by s69, would fall within the general judicial discretion with its bias against a trial by jury, but yet is not dissimilar to a claim for malicious prosecution or false imprisonment in respect of which there is a legislative intention that there shall be a jury trial, unless there are contraindications' (*per* LORD DONALDSON OF LYMINGTON MR). (See also *Racz* v *Home Office*.)

Hanlon v Law Society [1981] AC 124 (House of Lords)   **[59]**

In considering, inter alia, whether property subject to a property adjustment order under s24 of the Matrimonial Causes Act 1973 could be liable to a legal aid charge under s9 of the Legal Aid Act 1974 (see now s16 of the Legal Aid Act 1988) and relevant regulations and whether the Law Society had a discretion to postpone enforcement or transfer the charge to a replacement home (it had, provided the security was not endangered), questions arose as to the construction of the relevant provisions. *Held*, (1) 'The advent of new legislation bearing on existing social welfare legislation is to be expected from time to time. When it happens, a broad, flexible approach to the language of Parliament is most likely to achieve the purpose of the two sets of legislation. In such a situation, the courts will not exclude as aids to interpretation either regulations made pursuant to the earlier code or the subsequent legislation. As Harman LJ recognised in *Britt* v *Buckinghamshire County Council* [1964] 1 QB 77, where a statutory provision permits exceptions to be made to it by regulations, it is permissible to refer to the regulations as an aid to the interpretation of the provision.' (*per* LORD SCARMAN). (2) Can one have regard to punctuation at all? I take the view ... that it is right to do so ... Before 1850 Acts of Parliament were not punctuated; even after that punctuation was left to the draftsman and not scrutinised by Parliament. And sometimes a clause would be amended in debate but the punctuation might not be altered to take account of the amendment. Lord Esher MR proclaimed the old doctrine ... when he said "... it is perfectly clear that in an Act of Parliament there are no such things as brackets any more than there are such things as stops." But I respectfully adopt what Lord Jamieson said in *Alexander* v *Mackenzie* [1947] JC 155: "I am not prepared to hold that in construing a modern Act of Parliament a court may not have regard to punctuation. Bills when introduced in Parliament have punctuation, and without such would be unintelligible to the legislators, who pass them into law as punctuated. There appears to me no valid reason why regard should be denied to punctuation in construing a statute so passed, when effect may be given to it in a punctuated writing under the hand of a testator, as was held in *Houston* v *Burns* [1918] AC 337. While notice may, therefore, in my view be taken of punctuation in construing a statute, a comma or the absence of a comma must, I think, be disregarded if to give effect to it would so alter the sense as to be contrary to the plain intention of the statute." ... I consider that not to take account of punctuation disregards the reality that literate people, such as parliamentary draftsmen, punctuate what they write, if not identically, at least in accordance with grammatical principles. Why should not other literate people, such as judges, look at the punctuation in order to interpret the meaning of the legislation as accepted by Parliament?' (*per* LORD LOWRY).

Hastie and Jenkerson v McMahon [60]
[1990] 1 WLR 1575 (Court of Appeal)

An order had required that 'The plaintiffs serve on the defendant by 4.30 pm on 19 December 1988 a list of documents ...': they had caused a clearly legible list of documents to be transmitted by fax to the defendant's solicitors by 4.10 pm on 19 December 1988. *Held*, the plaintiffs had complied with the order: service by fax could be good service, subject to any requirement of the order requiring service of a particular document and any requirement of the Rules of the Supreme Court. Special considerations applied to writs and other documents used for initiating legal proceedings and nothing here applied to such documents.

Hetherington, Re, Gibbs v McDonnell [1989] 2 WLR 1094 [61]

When called upon to decide whether a gift for the saying of Masses established valid charitable trusts, the question arose whether the High Court was bound by the decision of the House of Lords in *Bourne* v *Keane* [1919] AC 815. *Held*, it was not so bound. 'The authorities ... clearly establish that even where a decision of a point of law in a particular sense was essential to an earlier decision of a superior court, but that superior court merely assumed the correctness of the law on a particular issue, a judge in a later case is not bound to hold that the law is decided in that sense. So therefore ... *Bourne* v *Keane* is not decisive of the case before me' (*per* SIR NICOLAS BROWNE-WILKINSON V-C). (See also *C* v *Director of Public Prosecutions*.)

Heydon's Case (1584) 3 Co Rep 8 [62]

The Barons of the Exchequer laid down rules as follows: 'That for the sure and true interpretation of all statutes in general (be they penal or beneficial, restrictive or enlarging of the common law) four things are to be discerned and considered: (1) what was the common law before the passing of the Act; (2) what was the mischief and defect for which the common law did not provide; (3) what remedy the Parliament hath resolved and appointed to cure the disease of the commonwealth; (4) the true reason of the remedy. And then the office of all the judges is always to make sure construction as shall suppress the mischief and advance the remedy, and to suppress subtle inventions and evasions for the continuance of the mischief and pro privato commodo, and to add force and life to the cure and remedy according to the true intent of the makers of the Act pro bono publico.' (See also *Grey* v *Pearson*.)

Hicks v Chief Constable of the South Yorkshire Police [63]
[1992] 2 All ER 65 (House of Lords)

Arising from the Hillsborough stadium disaster, the trial judge dismissed claims for damages under s1(1) of the Law Reform (Miscellaneous Provisions) Act 1934 for the benefit of the estates of two persons crushed to death on the ground that the plaintiffs had failed to prove pre-death pain and suffering. The Court of Appeal upheld the judge's finding. *Held*, the further appeal would be dismissed. 'The appellants must ... persuade your Lordships to reverse those concurrent findings [of fact] if they are to succeed ... In the circumstances I think it is sufficient to say that ... the conclusion of fact reached by [the trial judge] and the Court of Appeal was fairly open to them and it is impossible to say that they were wrong' (*per* LORD BRIDGE OF HARWICH). (See also *Ashmore v Corp of Lloyd's*.)

Hill (Gary) v Chief Constable of the South Yorkshire Police   [64]
[1990] 1 WLR 946 (Court of Appeal)

After being arrested for, and subsequently convicted of, being drunk and disorderly, a man brought an action in the county court claiming damages for, inter alia, false imprisonment, alleging that his arrest had been wrongful because he had not been informed of the reason for it as soon as practicable and that his detention had been wrongful because he had not been charged as soon as practicable. The registrar ordered trial by jury, but the judge allowed an appeal against that decision. *Held*, the judge's decision would be reversed. 'The effect of s66(3) of the County Courts Act 1984 is that if the court is satisfied that the pleadings clearly raise a claim in respect of false imprisonment, which is in issue, the court must order trial by jury. In this case the particulars of claim ... undoubtedly raised a claim of false imprisonment, and equally clearly this was put in issue by the defence ... the registrar's order was thus in my view correct' (*per* GLIDEWELL LJ).

Joyce v Sengupta [1993] 1 WLR 337 (Court of Appeal)   [65]

An issue of *Today*, the defendants' newspaper, had a banner headline 'Royal maid stole letters'. This statement was false and the maid, mainly to clear her name, instead of suing for libel (for which legal aid was not available), sued for malicious falsehood and she obtained legal aid to pursue her claim. The judge struck out her claim on the ground that it could not properly be based on malicious falsehood when it was in essence a case of libel. *Held*, the plaintiff's action would be reinstated. 'If the defendants consider legal aid should not have been granted in this case one course open to them is to take up the matter with the Legal Aid Board. This is commonly done by unassisted parties. Frequently an unassisted defendant goes to the board and asks for a legal aid certificate to be revoked when a legally assisted plaintiff has declined a reasonable offer. Further, if these defendants consider they have grounds for contending that the board misdirected itself or that the decision to grant legal aid was unreasonable in the Wednesbury sense (see *Associated Provincial Picture Houses Ltd v Wednesbury Corporation* [1948] 1 KB 223), an application for judicial review of the board's decision is another course open to them ... I mention these points only because it is important to appreciate that the defendants' submission raises two distinct questions, one of these questions is before us on this appeal and the other is not. One question is whether legal aid should have been granted. That question is not before us. The other question is whether, legal aid having been granted, this action should be permitted to continue even if, as the defendants assert, at most only modest damages will be recoverable. On this second question the fact that the plaintiff is legally aided is neither here nor there' (*per* SIR DONALD NICHOLLS V-C).

Kennedy v Spratt [1972] AC 83 (House of Lords)   [66]

In the context of two Northern Ireland statutes, a question arose as to the meaning of the expression 'sentenced to imprisonment'. The appeal was heard by five Law Lords, but one of them (Lord Upjohn) died before the speeches were delivered although, in accordance with precedent, Lord Reid adapted his speech (which he had prepared before his death) and read it as part of his own. *Held*, as the votes were equal, in accordance with standing orders and the ancient rule semper praesumiter pro negante, the appeal would be dismissed. Lord Upjohn's conclusion was disregarded although, as it happens, he would have dismissed the appeal.

Khan v Armaguard Ltd [1993] 3 All ER 545 (Court of Appeal)   **[67]**

In an action for damages for personal injury, the defendant employers admitted liability but had medical reports indicating that the plaintiff was a malingerer. They also had a video film of the plaintiff which, they said, was wholly inconsistent with his claim as to the extent of his injuries, but they applied under RSC Ord 38, r5, for this to be shown at the trial without prior disclosure to the plaintiff or his solicitors. *Held*, this application had properly been dismissed. 'The "cards-on-the-table" approach which now operates in my view requires that it should be very rare indeed in a personal injury case for an order for non-disclosure of a video film to be made ... It is ... in the interests of the parties, the legal aid fund, and the efficient dispatch of business by the courts, that cases should be disposed of by settlement at an early stage' (per ROSE LJ).

Kruse v Johnson [1898] 2 QB 91   **[68]**

Kent County Council made a by-law, under the Local Government Act 1888, providing that 'No person shall sound or play upon any musical or noisy instrument or sing in any public place or highway within fifty yards of any dwelling-house after being required by any constable or by an inmate of such house personally or by his or her servant to desist.' *Held*, the by-law was not invalid as being, inter alia, unreasonable. 'When the court is called upon to consider the by-laws of public representative bodies clothed with ... ample authority ... and exercising that authority accompanied by ... checks and safeguards ... I think ... such by-laws ... ought to be ... "benevolently" interpreted, and credit ought to be given to those who have to administer them that they will be reasonably administered ... I do not mean to say that there may not be cases in which it would be the duty of the court to condemn by-laws made under such authority as these were made as invalid because unreasonable. If, for instance, they were found to be partial and unequal in their operation as between different classes, if they were manifestly unjust, if they disclosed bad faith, if they involved such oppressive or gratuitous interference with the rights of those subject to them as could find no justification in the minds of reasonable men, the court might well say Parliament never intended to give authority to make such rules, and that they are unreasonable and ultra vires. But it is in this sense, and in this sense only, as I conceive, that the question of unreasonableness can properly be regarded' (*per* LORD RUSSELL OF KILLOWEN CJ).

Langley v North West Water Authority   **[69]**
[1991] 1 WLR 697 (Court of Appeal)

Mrs Langley tripped over the defendants' manhole cover and suffered personal injuries. She commenced proceedings, but her claim was settled and an order for costs was made against her solicitor personally for certain breaches of a code of practice issued by the county court in which the proceedings were brought. *Held*, the appeal against this order would be dismissed. A court has inherent jurisdiction to issue local practice directions (of which the code of practice was an example) and the court had inherent jurisdiction, by virtue of CCR Ord 38, r1, to order the solicitor to pay costs personally. On the facts, the court had correctly exercised this discretion. The authority of certain previous Court of Appeal decisions having arisen, LORD DONALDSON OF LYMINGTON MR said: 'The authority of a two-judge court should today be regarded as being the same as that of a three-judge court ... Any departure from previous decisions of this court is in principle undesirable and should only be considered if the previous decision is manifestly wrong. Even then it will be necessary to take account of whether the decision purports to be one of general application and whether there is any other way of remedying the error, for example by encouraging an appeal to the House of Lords.' (See also *Young* v *Bristol Aeroplane Co Ltd.*)

Law Debenture Trust Corp plc v Ural Caspian Oil Corp Ltd   [70]
[1993] 1 WLR 138

On an application to strike out a statement of claim, the question arose whether the principle of *Lumley* v *Gye* (1853) 2 E & B 216 could be extended beyond interference with contractual relations to interference with the remedies arising out of a broken contract. *Held*, the claim in question would not be struck out. NB This decision was reversed by the Court of Appeal: see [1995] 1 All ER 157. (See also *Lonrho plc* v *Tebbit.*)

Leslie (R) Ltd v Sheill [1914] 3 KB 607 (Court of Appeal)   [71]

The defendant, an infant, was allowed to borrow £400 from the plaintiff moneylenders by deceiving them as to his age. The jury found that the defendant had been guilty of fraud and judgment was given against him for the full amount of the money that he had received. The defendant appealed. *Held*, the appeal would be allowed. 'The claim ... is for the amount of principal and interest as damages sustained, because by his fraud the plaintiffs have been induced to make and act upon an unenforceable contract. As long ago as *Johnson* v *Pye* (1665) 1 Sid 258 it was decided that, although an infant may be liable in tort generally, he is not answerable for a tort directly connected with a contract which, as an infant, he would be entitled to avoid. "One cannot make an infant liable for the breach of a contract by changing the form of action to one ex delicto": *per* BYLES J, in *Burnard* v *Haggis* (1863) 32 LJCP 189 ... In the present case ... the money was paid over in order to be used as the defendant's own, and he has so used and I suppose, spent it. There is no question of tracing it, no possibility of restoring the very thing got by the fraud, nothing but a compulsion through a personal judgment to pay an equivalent sum out of his present or future resources, in a word nothing but a judgment in debt to repay the loan. I think this would be nothing but enforcing a void contract. So far as I can find the Court of Chancery never would have enforced any liability under circumstances like the present any more than a court of law would have done, and I think that no ground can be found for the present judgment ...' (*per* LORD SUMNER).

Levitt (Jeffrey S) Ltd, Re [1992] 2 WLR 975   [72]

In a case concerning the privilege against self-incrimination, counsel relied on an earlier decision of Ferris J, also in the High Court. *Held*, the earlier decision would not be followed. While VINELOTT J was reluctant not to follow a reasoned decision of a brother judge reached after full argument and embodied in a long and careful judgment, more particularly in a matter which affected the everyday practice of the court, he felt compelled to take this course, not least because certain statutory provisions, and a particular passage in a speech by Lord Reid, had not been drawn to Ferris J's attention.

Lewis v Chief Constable of the South Wales Constabulary   **[73]**
[1991] 1 All ER 206 (Court of Appeal)

The plaintiffs had been arrested on suspicion of burglary and taken to a police station. One had been told the reason for the arrest 10 minutes after it had occurred, the other some 23. They were detained for about five hours and then released. In an action for false arrest and wrongful imprisonment, they were awarded damages for unlawful detention of only 10 and 23 minutes respectively. They appealed, contending that, in view of s28(3) of the Police and Criminal Evidence Act 1984, they were entitled to compensation for the whole period of their detention. *Held*, their appeal would be dismissed. Arrest is a continuing act, so there is nothing inconsistent with the wording of s28(3) to say that from the moment when reasons were given the arrest became lawful. (See also *Abbassy v Commissioner of Police of the Metropolis*.)

Lim Poh Choo v Camden & Islington Area Health Authority   **[74]**
[1980] AC 174 (House of Lords)

Having been admitted to hospital for a minor operation, the plaintiff suffered irreparable brain damage, due to the defendants' negligence. Damages were awarded for pain, suffering and loss of amenities, loss of earnings, cost of future care and future inflation. Both parties appealed. *Held*, both appeals would be dismissed. 'It cannot be said that any of the time judicially spent on these protracted proceedings has been unnecessary. The question, therefore, arises whether the state of the law which gives rise to such complexities is sound. Lord Denning MR in the Court of Appeal declared that a radical reappraisal of the law is needed. I agree. But I part company with him on ways and means. Lord Denning MR believes it can be done by the judges, whereas I would suggest to your Lordships that such a reappraisal calls for social, financial, economic and administrative decisions which only the legislature can take' (*per* LORD SCARMAN). (But see *R v R (Rape: Marital Exemption)*.)

Litster v Forth Dry Dock Co Ltd See Morris Angel & Son Ltd v Hollande.

Loade v Director of Public Prosecutions [1989] 3 WLR 1281   **[75]**

Having been convicted by magistrates of using 'towards another threatening, abusive or insulting words or behaviour whereby another person was likely to believe that unlawful violence would be used or provoked', the appellants had appealed to the Crown Court. At the opening of their appeal they submitted that the information had been defective in so far as it had referred to the likely belief of 'another person' as opposed to the person towards whom the words or behaviour were allegedly used: the court rejected this submission but agreed to state a case to the High Court before proceeding with the appeal. Only if the rejection of the submission was a 'decision' of the Crown Court, within s28(1) of the Supreme Court Act 1981, did the High Court have jurisdiction to hear the case stated. *Held*, the High Court did not have such jurisdiction in a criminal case until the Crown Court proceedings had been concluded, ie, reached a final determination.

Lonrho plc, Re [1989] 3 WLR 535 (House of Lords)   **[76]**

The Al Fayed brothers having acquired House of Fraser plc (including Harrods) thereby frustrating Lonrho's attempt to acquire control of Harrods, the Secretary of

State appointed inspectors to inquire into the takeover. Having received the inspectors' report, the Secretary of State decided that he should not publish it at that stage and Lonrho sought judicial review of those decisions. The Court of Appeal reversed the Divisional Court's decision to grant the application, so Lonrho appealed to the House of Lords. While those further appeals were pending, the *Observer*, a newspaper owned by Lonrho, published extracts from the inspectors' report and Lonrho sent copies of the newspaper to, amongst others, four of the five Law Lords who were listed to hear the appeals. Did this amount to a contempt? *Held*, it did not. 'We think that it would be a novel extension of the law of contempt to hold that direct action taken by a litigant to secure the substance of a remedy which he was seeking in judicial proceedings amounted to a contempt in relation to those proceedings, and that the publication of extracts from the inspectors' report in the *Observer* special edition did not create any risk that the course of justice in the appellate proceedings challenging the lawfulness of the Secretary of State's decision to defer publication would be impeded or prejudiced' (*per* LORD BRIDGE OF HARWICH). (Distinguished: *Attorney General* v *Times Newspapers Ltd.*)

Lonrho plc v Tebbit [1992] 4 All ER 280 (Court of Appeal)   [77]

In an action for negligence, the defendants applied for the striking out of the statement of claim. *Held*, the summons had been correctly dismissed. 'There is an arguable case for Lonrho ... In these circumstances Lonrho's claim should not be struck out as disclosing no reasonable cause of action. Lonrho faces considerable difficulties, and others may arise on the facts as the evidence emerges at a trial, but I cannot say that Lonrho has no arguable case, or, in Lord Bridge's words [in *Lonrho plc* v *Fayed* [1991] 3 All ER 303], that the claim is obviously foredoomed to fail' (*per* DILLON LJ). (See also *Law Debenture Trust Corp plc* v *Ural Caspian Oil Corp Ltd.*)

Lord Advocate v Dumbarton District Council, Lord Advocate   [78]
v Strathclyde Regional Council [1989] 3 WLR 1346 (House of Lords)

In the course of improving the security fence at the Faslane submarine base, the contractors employed by the Ministry of Defence encroached upon a road. The question arose as to whether certain Scottish highways and planning statutes bound the Crown. *Held*, they did not: a statute binds the Crown only by express words or necessary implication to that effect.

McConnell v Chief Constable of the Greater Manchester Police   [79]
[1990] 1 WLR 364 (Court of Appeal)

In an action for damages for false imprisonment, the county court judge accepted the defendant's submission that a breach of the peace could take place on private premises. The plaintiff appealed. *Held*, the appeal would be dismissed. '... counsel for the plaintiff ... submits that, in order for there to be a breach of the peace on private premises, the authorities justify the proposition that it is necessary to find some disturbance which would affect members of the public, or at least one other person, outside the premises themselves ... In my judgment, there is no warrant for this restriction on the bounds of what may constitute a breach of the peace for the purposes of entitling a police officer, who genuinely suspects on good grounds that a breach of the peace may occur, to make an arrest' (*per* GLIDEWELL LJ). (See also *McLeod* v *Commissioner of Police of the Metropolis.*)

McLeod v Commissioner of Police of the Metropolis   **[80]**
[1994] 4 All ER 553 (Court of Appeal)

Arising out of a confrontation between a divorced couple in relation to furniture in which the police had intervened, a question arose in relation to police powers. *Held,* 'Parliament in s17(6) [of the Police and Criminal Evidence Act 1984] has now recognised that there is a power to enter premises to prevent a breach of the peace as a form of preventive justice. [There is] no satisfactory basis for restricting that power to particular classes of premises such as those where public meetings are held. If the police reasonably believe that a breach of the peace is likely to take place on private premises, they have power to enter those premises to prevent it. The apprehension must, of course, be genuine and it must relate to the near future' (*per* NEILL LJ). (See also *McConnell* v *Chief Constable of the Greater Manchester Police.*)

Manuel v A-G [1982] 3 All ER 786; affd [1982] 3 All ER 822   **[81]**
(Court of Appeal)

Fearing that the passing, by the United Kingdom Parliament, of the Canada Act 1982 could put at risk certain of their rights, the plaintiff Indian chiefs sought, inter alia, a declaration that the 1982 Act was ultra vires. *Held,* the action would be dismissed as, once an instrument is recognised as being an Act of Parliament, no English court can refuse to obey it or question its validity. (Followed: *British Railways Board* v *Pickin.*)

Mareva Compania Naviera SA v International Bulkcarriers SA,   **[82]**
The Mareva (1975) [1980] 1 All ER 213n (Court of Appeal)

The plaintiffs claimed unpaid hire and damages for the repudiation of a charterparty of the *Mareva* and sought ex parte the extension of an injunction restraining the defendants from removing out of the jurisdiction moneys standing to the credit of their account at a London bank. *Held,* the injunction would be continued. 'The court will not grant an injunction to protect a person who has no legal or equitable right whatever ... If it appears that the debt is due and owing, and there is a danger that the debtor may dispose of his assets so as to defeat it before judgment, the court has jurisdiction in a proper case to grant an interlocutory judgment so as to prevent him disposing of those assets. It seems to me that this is a proper case for the exercise of this jurisdiction ... until the trial or judgment in this action. If the [defendants] have any grievance about it when they hear of it, they can apply to discharge it. But meanwhile the [plaintiffs] should be protected. It is only just and right that this court should grant an injunction' (*per* LORD DENNING MR). (See also s37(1), (3) of the Supreme Court Act 1981 and *Practice Direction* [1994] 4 All ER 52 (guidelines in relation to Mareva injunctions and Anton Piller orders.)

Marr, Re [1990] 2 WLR 1264 (Court of Appeal)   **[83]**

Bankruptcy orders had been made against the appellants on the ground, inter alia, that s271(2A) of the Insolvency Act 1986 (the later provision) prevailed over s271(1) of the Act. *Held,* the appeals would be allowed as any such rule as had been applied by the judge (that where two sections of the same statute are repugnant the later provision prevails) was obsolete. 'Such a mechanical approach to the construction of statutes is altogether out· of step with the modern, purposive approach to the interpretation of statutes and documents' (*per* NICHOLLS LJ). Here, the overriding principle was to be found in s271(1) and s271(2A) was to be read subject to it.

Miliangos v George Frank (Textiles) Ltd [1976] AC 443   **[84]**
(House of Lords)

The question was whether an English court could give judgment for the amount of a debt expressed in the currency of a foreign country (here, Switzerland) if the proper law of the contract was the law of that country. A previous decision of the House of Lords (*Tomkinson* v *First Pennsylvania Banking and Trust Co* [1961] AC 1007) indicated that the answer was No. *Held*, the previous decision would not be followed and the answer would be Yes. 'It has to be reaffirmed that the only judicial means by which decisions of this House can be reviewed is by this House itself, under the declaration of 1966 [see *Practice Statement* [1966] 1 WLR 1234]. Whether it can or should do so is a difficult enough question, which I shall now examine ... Under [the declaration], the House affirmed its power to depart from a previous decision when it appears right to do so, recognising that too rigid adherence to precedent might lead to injustice in a particular case and unduly restrict the proper development of the law ... on the assumption that to depart from the *Tomkinson* case would not involve undue practical difficulties, that a new and more satisfactory rule is capable of being stated, I am of opinion that the present case falls within the terms of the declaration. To change the rule would ... avoid injustice in the present case. To change it would enable the law to keep in step with commercial needs and with the majority of other countries facing similar problems ... if once a clear conclusion is reached as to what the law ought now to be, declaration of it by this House is appropriate. The law on this topic is judge made; it has been built up over the years from case to case. It is entirely within this House's duty, in the course of administering justice, to give the law a new direction in a particular case where, on principle and in reason, it appears right to do so. I cannot accept the suggestion that because a rule is long established only legislation can change it – that may be so when the rule is so deeply entrenched that it has infected the whole legal system, or the choice of a new rule involves more far-reaching research than courts can carry out ... Questions as to the recovery of debts or of damages depend so much on individual mixtures of facts and merits as to make them more suitable for progressive solutions in the courts. I think that we have an opportunity to reach such a solution here. I would accordingly depart from the *Tomkinson* case ...' (*per* LORD WILBERFORCE).

Moodie v Inland Revenue Commissioners   **[85]**
[1993] 1 WLR 266 (House of Lords)

In relation to tax avoidance schemes, it appeared that there were conflicting House of Lords' decisions (*Inland Revenue Commissioners* v *Plummer* [1979] 3 WLR 689 and *WT Ramsay Ltd* v *Inland Revenue Commissioners* [1981] 2 WLR 449) as to the construction of the relevant statutory provisions. *Held*, the later decision would now be followed. 'The present appeals are heard after *Ramsay* and this House is bound to give effect to the principle of *Ramsay*. I do not consider that it is necessary to invoke the 1966 practice statement ... (see *Practice Statement* [1966] 1 WLR 1234). The result in *Plummer*'s case ... is inconsistent with the later decision in *Ramsay* ... Faced with conflicting decisions, the courts are entitled and bound to follow *Ramsay* because in *Plummer's* case this House was never asked to consider the effect of a [particular] scheme and because the *Ramsay* principle restores justice between individual taxpayers and the general body of taxpayers ... If it were necessary to invoke the 1966 practice statement I have no doubt that this would be an appropriate course to take but in my opinion it is sufficient to state that the decision in *Plummer's* case would have been different if the appeal had been heard after the enunciation by this House of the *Ramsay* principle ...' (*per* LORD TEMPLEMAN).

Morris Angel & Son Ltd v Hollande   [86]
[1993] 3 All ER 569 (Court of Appeal)

In an action to enforce a restraint of trade clause in a contract of employment, the court was required to consider the meaning of the Transfer of Undertakings (Protection of Employment) Regulations 1981 which had been enacted by Parliament to give effect to Council Directive (EEC) 77/187. *Held*, as LORD OLIVER OF AYLMERTON had explained in *Litster v Forth Dry Dock Co Ltd* [1990] 1 AC 546, if primary or subordinate legislation enacted to give effect to the United Kingdom's obligations under the EEC Treaty can reasonably be construed so as to conform with those obligations, a purposive construction will be applied even though perhaps it may involve some departure from the strict and literal application of the words which the legislature had elected to use.

Murphy v Brentwood District Council   [87]
[1990] 3 WLR 414 (House of Lords)

In *Anns v Merton London Borough* [1977] 2 WLR 1024 the House of Lords decided that a local authority which exercises statutory control over building operations is liable in tort to a building owner or occupier for the cost of remedying a dangerous defect in a building which results from the negligent failure by the authority to ensure that the building was erected in conformity with applicable standards prescribed by building by-laws or regulations. *Held*, this decision would be overruled. 'In my opinion it is clear that *Anns* did not proceed on any basis of established principle, but introduced a new species of liability governed by a principle indeterminate in character but having the potentiality of covering a wide range of situations, involving chattels as well as real property, in which it had never hitherto been thought that the law of negligence had any proper place. The practice statement of 26 July 1966 (see *Practice Statement* [1966] 1 WLR 1234) leaves it open to this House to depart from a previous decision of its own if it so chooses ... My Lords, I would hold that *Anns* was wrongly decided as regards the scope of any private law of duty of care resting on local authorities in relation to their function of taking steps to secure compliance with building by-laws or regulations and should be departed from' (*per* LORD KEITH OF KINKEL).

Murphy v Director of Public Prosecutions [1990] 2 All ER 390   [88]

Having been granted police bail and failed to surrender to a magistrates' court, a man contended that the magistrates had no jurisdiction in relation to an alleged offence under s6(1) of the Bail Act 1976 as the information was time-barred by virtue of s127(1) of the Magistrates' Courts Act 1980. *Held*, this contention was correct. 'Section 6(1) creates one offence of failing to surrender to custody. In the case of failure to surrender to the Crown Court the matter will, save possibly in rare cases, be dealt with as if it were a contempt and subject to no time limit. In the case of failure to surrender to a police station or to a magistrates' court where bail has been granted by the police the matter must be dealt with as a summary offence ... and will be subject to the time limit. The case of failure to surrender to a magistrates' court where bail has been granted by a magistrates' court ... will be dealt with by the magistrates' court as if it were a contempt and will be subject to no time limit' (*per* PARKER LJ).

National Westminster Bank plc v Daniel   [89]
[1993] 1 WLR 1453 (Court of Appeal)

By specially indorsed writ, the plaintiffs claimed against three defendants under a guarantee. Judgment in default of defence was entered against two of them and summary judgment under RSC Ord 14 was sought against the other. *Held*, the plaintiffs' application would be successful as, looking at the whole situation, there was no fair or reasonable probability of the defendant having a real or bona fide defence.

Nicholls v Brentwood Justices See **R v Brentwood Justices, ex parte Nicholls.**

Pepper v Hart [1992] 3 WLR 1032 (House of Lords)   [90]

The question having arisen whether the payment of reduced fees in respect of the sons of teaching staff at an independent school constituted a taxable benefit, for the purposes of certain provisions of the Finance Act 1976, accruing to the teachers concerned, the Appellate Committee decided to invite further argument, before a freshly constituted committee, as to whether reference could be made to the parliamentary proceedings which led to the passing of those provisions when construing them. *Held* (Lord Mackay of Clashfern LC dissenting), such reference could be made in certain circumstances and the previous position of the House would be relaxed to that extent. 'Under present law, there is a general rule that references to parliamentary material as an aid to statutory construction is not permissible (the exclusionary rule) ... This rule did not always apply but was judge-made ... The courts can now look at white papers and official reports for the purpose of finding the "mischief" sought to be corrected, although not at draft clauses or proposals for the remedying of such mischief ... Given the purposive approach to construction now adopted by the courts in order to give effect to the true intentions of the legislature, the fine distinctions between looking for the mischief and looking for the intention in using words to provide the remedy are technical and inappropriate. Clear and unambiguous statements made by ministers in Parliament are as much the background to the enactment of legislation as white papers and parliamentary reports. The decision in *Pickstone* v *Freemans plc* [1989] AC 66 which authorises the court to look at ministerial statements made in introducing regulations which could not be amended by Parliament is logically indistinguishable from such statements made in introducing a statutory provision which, though capable of amendment, was not in fact amended ... I therefore reach the conclusion ... that the exclusionary rule should be relaxed so as to permit reference to parliamentary materials where: (a) legislation is ambiguous or obscure, or leads to an absurdity; (b) the material relied on consists of one or more statements by a minister or other promoter of the Bill together if necessary with such other parliamentary material as is necessary to understand such statements and their effect; (c) the statements relied on are clear. Further than this, I would not at present go' (*per* LORD BROWNE-WILKINSON). (See also *Warwickshire County Council* v *Johnson*.) 'Any ambiguity [in the relevant provisions] should be resolved in favour of the taxpayer' (*per* LORD MACKAY OF CLASHFERN LC). (See also *R* v *Highbury Magistrates' Court, ex parte Di Matteo*.)

Pickering v Liverpool Daily Post and Echo Newspapers plc   [91]
[1991] 2 WLR 513 (House of Lords)

The question arose, inter alia, whether a mental health review tribunal (established by statute to give patients detained in secure mental hospitals under restriction orders the ability to apply for their release) was a 'court' within s19 of the Contempt of Court Act 1981. *Held*, it was a court for this purpose.

Pickstone v Freemans plc See **Pepper v Hart.**

Powell v Kempton Park Racecourse Co Ltd [92]
[1899] AC 143 (House of Lords)

Section 1 of the Betting Act 1853 prohibited the keeping of a 'house, office, room or other place' for betting with persons resorting thereto. Was Tattersall's ring on the racecourse such a 'place'? *Held*, it was not as the ejusdem generis rule applied and the words 'or other place' meant a place similar to a house, office or room. (See also *Evans v Cross.*)

Practice Statement [1966] 1 WLR 1234 (House of Lords) [93]

'Their Lordships regard the use of precedent as an indispensable foundation upon which to decide what is the law and its application to individual cases. It provides at least some degree of certainty upon which individuals can rely in the conduct of their affairs, as well as a basis for orderly development of legal rules.

Their Lordships nevertheless recognise that too rigid adherence to precedent may lead to injustice in a particular case and also unduly restrict the proper development of the law. They propose therefore to modify their present practice and, while treating former decisions of this House as normally binding, to depart from a previous decision when it appears right to do so.

In this connexion they will bear in mind the danger of disturbing retrospectively the basis on which contracts, settlements or property and fiscal arrangements have been entered into and also the especial need for certainty as to the criminal law.

This announcement is not intended to affect the use of precedent elsewhere than in this House.' (See, eg, *Murphy v Brentwood District Council*; see also *Moodie v Inland Revenue Commissioners.*)

R v Allen (1872) 1 CCR 367 (Court for Crown Cases Reserved) [94]

Section 57 of the Offences against the Person Act 1861 provided 'Whosoever, being married, shall marry any other person during the life of the former husband or wife ...' shall be guilty of bigamy. The word 'marry' in this context had two possible meanings: firstly, contracting a valid marriage; secondly, going through an actual marriage service. *Held*, the second interpretation would be adopted to avoid the absurd result that would occur by adopting the first (ie that no-one could ever be guilty of the offence).

R v Bailey [1993] 3 All ER 513 (Court of Appeal) [95]

Having been arrested and charged with robbery and, when interviewed by the police, exercised their right to silence, the appellants were remanded in custody and placed together in a cell which the police had 'bugged'. While there they made damaging admissions in the course of their conversation, which was recorded. At their trial, the judge so exercised his discretion under s78(1) of the Police and Criminal Evidence Act 1984 as to admit these recordings in evidence. *Held*, the judge had been entitled so to decide and the appellants' appeals against conviction would therefore be dismissed. 'We ... see no reason to decry the police's conduct ... nor to doubt the essential fairness of this evidence having been held admissible' (*per* SIMON BROWN LJ). (See also *R v Preston.*)

R v Banks [1916] 2 KB 621 (Court of Criminal Appeal)   [96]

At the appellant's trial for having had unlawful carnal knowledge of a girl under 16 years of age, counsel for the prosecution had asked the jury 'to protect young girls from men like the prisoner'. *Held*, the appeal against conviction would be dismissed. 'It has been properly said that counsel for the prosecution should not press for a conviction. In *R v Puddick* (1865) 4 F&F 497 CROMPTON J said that counsel should regard themselves as "ministers of justice" assisting in its administration rather than as advocates. Although the observation referred to may not have been in good taste, this court cannot say that it had the effect of misleading the jury and inducing them to find the appellant guilty' (*per* AVORY J). (See also *Re Barlow Clowes Gilt Managers Ltd*.)

R v Berry (No 2) [1991] 1 WLR 125 (Court of Appeal)   [97]

Berry applied to relist his appeal against his Crown Court conviction of making explosives for which he was sentenced to eight years' imprisonment. An earlier appeal against his conviction had been allowed by the Court of Appeal ([1984] 1 WLR 824) but, on appeal by the Crown on a point of law certified as of general public importance, the House of Lords ([1984] WLR 1274) directed that his conviction be restored. The grounds of the application were that the Court of Appeal should consider grounds of his original appeal which had been argued before, but not decided upon by, the Court of Appeal and which had not been decided by the House of Lords when disposing of the Crown's appeal on the certified question. *Held*, the application would be refused. 'The House of Lords regards itself we believe and, in our view, we say, with respect, rightly as giving a final judgment in the appeal before it. Having done so it makes its order. In the present case the order was in effect that the conviction of the applicant be restored. It was restored accordingly. It would be extraordinary and, in our opinion, unthinkable if the Court of Appeal (Criminal Division) were to be in a position thereafter to pronounce upon other grounds of appeal and thereby destroy the order of the House of Lords by again quashing the conviction' (*per* WATKINS LJ). NB The Court of Appeal subsequently heard an appeal against sentence, reducing the sentence from eight years' imprisonment to six, and the Home Secretary referred the whole case to the Court of Appeal under s17(1) of the Criminal Appeal Act 1968.

R v Blandford Justices, ex parte Pamment   [98]
[1990] 1 WLR 1490 (Court of Appeal)

Following the disruption of a hunt meeting, Pamment was charged with various offences and remanded in custody. Five days before the trial of the offences, Pamment applied to the Divisional Court for judicial review by way of an order of certiorari to quash the magistrates' decision to remand him in custody and an order for damages against them. Hearing this application after the trial, the Divisional Court granted the application, quashed the remand order and adjourned the claim for damages. The magistrates appealed. *Held*, the appeal would be dismissed as the Divisional Court's decision had been made 'in a criminal cause or matter' within s18(1)(a) of the Supreme Court Act 1981 and it followed that there was no right of appeal to the Court of Appeal against the Divisional Court's decision. (See also *R v McIlkenny*.)

R v Brentwood Justices, ex parte Nicholls [99]
[1991] 3 WLR 201 (House of Lords)

Three defendants were jointly charged with affray contrary to s3(1) of the Public Order Act 1986. One of them elected jury trial at the Crown Court, the others summary trial. *Held*, those who elected summary trial should have been tried summarily; in relation to the others, the magistrates should have inquired into the information as examining justices.

R v Bryce [1992] 4 All ER 567 (Court of Appeal) [100]

Having been arrested on suspicion of handling stolen goods, during a recorded interview, under caution, at the police station the appellant had made no comments. However, after the tape recorder had been switched off at his request, he had allegedly made a confession of which evidence was admitted at his trial. *Held*, the conviction would be quashed as a fresh caution should have been given before the unrecorded interview. 'If this interview was correctly admitted, the effect would be to set at nought the requirements of the Police and Criminal Evidence Act 1984 and the code in regard to interviews … In our judgment there would have to be some highly exceptional circumstances, perhaps involving cogent corroboration, before such an interview could be admitted without its having such an adverse effect on the fairness of the trial that it ought to be excluded under s78' (*per* LORD TAYLOR OF GOSFORTH CJ). (See also *R v King's Lynn Justices, ex parte Holland*.)

R v Canale [1990] 2 All ER 187 (Court of Appeal) [101]

Facing a charge of, inter alia, conspiracy to rob, the appellant was interviewed twice by the police and during these interviews he allegedly made certain admissions. These interviews were not contemporaneously recorded and the police otherwise failed to comply with the Code of Practice. However, a contemporaneous record was made of two subsequent interviews at which the alleged admissions were repeated. *Held*, as the interviews were the only effective evidence against the appellant, his conviction would be quashed. The police officers seemed to have displayed a cynical disregard to the rules. If the judge had appreciated the gravity of the breach he would have acted under s78(1) of the Police and Criminal Evidence Act 1984 to exclude evidence of the admissions. (See also *R v Bryce*.)

R v Chelmsford Crown Court, ex parte Chief Constable [102]
of Essex [1994] 1 WLR 359

During a Crown Court trial, the judge ruled that certain police evidence was inadmissible but should nevertheless be disclosed to the defence. After the trial, judicial review was sought of the order to disclose. *Held*, the application would be dismissed as the High Court had no power to review decisions of the Crown Court (a 'superior court') save where such power had been expressly granted by ss28 and 29(3) of the Supreme Court Act 1981 or another statute. (See also *R v Manchester Crown Court, ex parte Director of Public Prosecutions*.)

R v Chief Constable of the Kent County Constabulary,   [103]
ex parte L [1993] 1 All ER 756

L, aged 16, was charged with assault occasioning actual bodily harm, despite the fact that the criteria for administering a caution, set out in the code issued pursuant to s10(1) of the Prosecution of Offences Act 1985 and in guidelines issued by the Home Secretary, were made out in his case. L applied for judicial review by way of orders of certiorari to quash the decision of the police to prosecute him and that of the Crown Prosecution Service not to discontinue proceedings against him pursuant to its power under s23 of the 1985 Act, and mandamus to compel the Crown Prosecution Service to discontinue the proceedings. *Held*, his applications would be dismissed as, in view of the seriousness of the offence, the decision to continue the prosecution was not in any way flawed. 'I have come to the conclusion that, in respect of juveniles, the discretion of the CPS to continue or to discontinue criminal proceedings is reviewable by this court but only where it can be demonstrated that the decision was made regardless of or clearly contrary to a settled policy of the Director of Public Prosecutions evolved in the public interest ... Therefore, although the CPS decision may in principle be reviewed, in practice it is rarely likely to be successfully reviewed. I have confined my views as to the availability of judicial review of a CPS decision not to discontinue a prosecution to the position of juveniles ... My view as to the position of adults, on the other hand, in this respect is that judicial review of a decision not to discontinue a prosecution is unlikely to be available ... such review, if it exists, must ... be confined to very narrow limits. Juveniles and the policy with regard to them are in a special position ... I feel unable to say that, although there may be room for two views about the seriousness of the offence with which L is charged, the decision to continue the proceedings was in any way flawed. It was a proper exercise of discretion' (*per* WATKINS LJ). (See also *R v Commissioner of Police of the Metropolis, ex parte Blackburn*.)

R v Chief Constable of the Lancashire Constabulary,   [104]
ex parte Parker [1993] 2 WLR 428

When granting an application for search warrants under s9 of and Schedule 1 to the Police and Criminal Evidence Act 1984 in respect of the two applicants' homes, the circuit judge signed a two-page document headed 'Warrant to enter and search premises' and there was also a one-page document attached to it headed 'Schedule of application' setting out the articles to be sought. In searching the applicants' premises, the police used the original authorisation and a photocopy of the schedule and supplied the applicants only with a copy of the authorisation. By way of judicial review, the applicants sought, inter alia, an order of certiorari to quash the search warrants and the return of the documents seized. *Held*, there had been breaches of the requirements of s16(5)(b), (c) of the 1984 Act and the documents must be returned. Section 22(2)(a) of the 1984 Act does not authorise the retention by the police of material which has come into their hands by unlawful means and neither *R v Sang* nor s78 of the 1984 Act gives the police a general right to retain unlawfully seized material for use as evidence.

R v Commissioner of Police of the Metropolis,   [105]
ex parte Blackburn [1968] 2 WLR 893 (Court of Appeal)

As the result of his policy decision, the respondent commissioner failed to prosecute gaming clubs in London under the Betting, Gaming and Lotteries Act 1963. The applicant, a private citizen, complained that illegal gaming was being carried on and applied for an order of mandamus directing the respondent to reverse his policy. The respondent argued that he did not owe a duty to the public to enforce the law and had an absolute discretion not to prosecute. *Held*, as the respondent had given the court an undertaking which, in effect, secured for the applicant the relief that he sought, there were no grounds for considering further the granting of mandamus. 'Although the chief officers of police are answerable to the law, there are many fields in which they have a discretion with which the law will not interfere. For instance, it is for the Commissioner of Police of the Metropolis, or the chief constable, as the case may be, to decide in any particular case whether inquiries should be pursued, or whether an arrest should be made, or a prosecution brought. It must be for him to decide on the disposition of his force and the concentration of his resources on any particular crime or area. No court can or should give him direction on such a matter. He can also make policy decisions and give effect to them, as, for instance, was often done when prosecutions were not brought for attempted suicide. But there are some policy decisions with which, I think, the courts in a case can, if necessary, interfere. Suppose a chief constable were to issue a directive to his men that no person should be prosecuted for stealing any goods less than £100 in value. I should have thought that the court could countermand it. He would be failing in his duty to enforce the law ... the policy decision [here] was, I think, most unfortunate' (*per* LORD DENNING MR). (See also *R* v *Chief Constable of the County of Kent, ex parte L.*)

R v Cox [1993] 1 WLR 188 (Court of Appeal)   [106]

Aged 18 with one previous conviction, a young man, having pleaded guilty to theft and reckless driving, was sentenced to one month's and four months' detention concurrently for those offences. A pre-sentence report had noted that he had received an offer of part-time employment and had recommended a probation order. He appealed against this sentence. *Held*, the appeal would be allowed and the sentence varied. 'Standing back and applying it to all the known facts of this case, we have reached the conclusion that only a custodial sentence could be justified for this offence. [Counsel] submitted in particular that the learned judge's observation, "There is great public concern about driving of this sort", was irrelevant. We do not agree. The prevalence of offences of a particular class and public concern about them are relevant to the seriousness of an instant offence, as we made clear in *R* v *Cunningham*. That, however, is not the end of the matter. Section 1(2) [of the Criminal Justice Act 1991] enjoins the court not to pass a custodial sentence unless it is of the opinion that the criteria of seriousness are met. The court is not required to pass such a sentence even when they are ... We are of the view that, given the age and antecedent history of the appellant, [probation] would have been appropriate in the present case. Accordingly, if the appellant is willing to be placed on probation, we are prepared to quash sentences of detention and substitute for them concurrent probation orders' (*per* LORD TAYLOR OF GOSFORTH CJ).

R v Crampton (1991) 92 Cr App R 369 (Court of Appeal)   [107]

The appellant had been convicted of drugs offences. He had made admissions at interview in the police station 19 hours after his arrest when he might have been undergoing withdrawal. The defence contended that the confession was thereby rendered unreliable and should have been excluded by the trial judge either under s76(2)(b) of the Police and Criminal Evidence Act 1984 or through the exercise of his discretion under s78 of that Act. The police had relied on their own judgment to determine whether he was fit to be interviewed. They agreed that they would not have interviewed him if they had known he was withdrawing. *Held*, the appeal would be dismissed as their Lordships could see no reason on the evidence to conclude that the trial judge had come to a wrong conclusion on the facts in refusing to exclude the confession either under ss76 or 78 of the 1984 Act. It was in fact doubtful whether the mere holding of an interview at a time when the appellant was withdrawing was within s76(2)(b) as the words of the subsection seemed to postulate some words spoken by the police or some acts done by them which were likely to induce an unreliable confession.

R v Croydon Crown Court, ex parte Miller See Tucker v Director of Public Prosecutions.

R v Cunningham [1993] 1 WLR 183 (Court of Appeal) [108]

The applicant, aged 22 and without previous convictions, sought leave to appeal against the sentence of four years' imprisonment for robbery and two years' imprisonment concurrent for theft. *Held*, the application would be granted and the overall sentence reduced by one year. 'Does [s2(2)(a) of the Criminal Justice Act 1991] permit the sentencing judge to take the need for deterrence into account? In our judgment, it does. The purposes of a custodial sentence must primarily be to punish and to deter ... What s2(2)(a) does prohibit is adding any extra length to the sentence which by those criteria is commensurate with the seriousness of the offence simply to make a special example of the defendant. Prevalence of this kind of offence was also mentioned by the learned judge. Is that a legitimate factor in determining the length of the custodial sentence to be passed? Again, our answer is Yes ... the learned judge was right to regard the robbery as very serious and to bear in mind both the need for deterrence and the prevalence generally of offences of this kind. However, [counsel's] final ground of appeal is that the learned judge did not sufficiently have regard to the mitigating circumstances in the appellant's case, especially when compared with that of his co-accused ... who received the same sentence. We think there is merit in this argument' (*per* LORD TAYLOR OF GOSFORTH CJ). (See also *R v Cox*.)

R v Fisher [1969] 1 All ER 100 (Court of Appeal) [109]

On 28 October 1967 the appellant was arrested and on 2 January 1968 he was charged with being an accessory after the fact. On 5 March 1968 he was arraigned. The Criminal Law Act 1967 came into force on 1 January 1968 abolishing the offence. Counsel for the defence moved to quash the appropriate count on the indictment claiming that it disclosed no offence known to law. The chairman ruled against the appellant and he was tried and convicted. He appealed against that ruling. *Held*, the appeal would be dismissed. The offence existed at the time the act was committed and therefore the statutory provisions for its indictment and punishment remained in force. 'Without the clearest words we cannot think that Parliament intended that accessories after the fact to serious crime ... in the latter part of 1967 should not be guilty of any offence' (*per* O'CONNOR J).

R v Ford [1989] 3 WLR 762 (Court of Appeal) [110]

A black man was convicted of driving a conveyance taken without authority and reckless driving. At his trial, the Crown Court judge had declined to accede to an application for a multiracial jury: he appealed against conviction, inter alia, on that ground. *Held*, the trial judge had been right to refuse this application, although the man's appeal would be allowed on other grounds. 'It has never been suggested that the judge has a discretion to discharge a whole panel or part panel on grounds that would not found a valid challenge. Similarly, in the absence of evidence of specific bias, ethnic origins could not found a valid ground for challenge to an individual juror ... Responsibility for the summoning of jurors to attend for service in the Crown Court and the High Court is by statute clearly laid on the Lord Chancellor. That is clear from s2 of the Juries Act 1974 and from s5 ... It is not the function of the judge to alter the composition of the panel or to give any directions about the district from which it is to be drawn. The summoning of panels is not a judicial function, but it is specifically conferred by statute on an administrative officer' (*per* LORD LANE CJ).

R v Fulling [1987] 2 WLR 923 (Court of Appeal)   [111]

A woman was arrested for allegedly obtaining property by deception. While in police custody, for two days she exercised her right to say nothing in response to persistent questioning. An officer then told her that her lover had been having an affair with another woman for the last three years and, on hearing this, the accused confessed to the charge. At her trial, she contended that the confession was inadmissible under s76(2)(a) of the Police and Criminal Evidence Act 1984 because it had been obtained by oppression. *Held*, this was not the case, even if her account of the alleged disclosure by the police officer was correct, as such conduct does not amount to 'oppression' in this context. (See also *R v Mason*.)

R v Galbraith [1981] 1 WLR 1039 (Court of Appeal)   [112]

Having been convicted of affray, Galbraith maintained that the trial judge had been wrong to reject a submission made on his behalf that there was no case for him to answer. *Held*, on the facts, the case had properly been left to the jury to decide. 'This was eminently a case where the jury should be left to decide the weight of the evidence on which the Crown based their case. It was not a case where the judge would have been justified in saying that the Crown's evidence taken at its highest was such that the jury properly directed could not properly convict on it' (*per* LORD LANE CJ).

R v Gough [1993] 2 WLR 883 (House of Lords)   [113]

The appellant and his brother had been charged with robbery, but the brother had been discharged at the committal stage and the appellant indicted for allegedly conspiring with his brother to commit robbery. At the trial, one of the jurors was the brother's next door neighbour, but she had not connected him with the proceedings until he shouted out in court after the appellant's conviction. The Court of Appeal dismissed the appellant's appeal against conviction, believing that there had been no danger that the appellant might not have had a fair trial. *Held*, the Court of Appeal had applied the correct test and, on the facts, the appeal would be dismissed. 'I think it possible, and desirable, that the same test should be applicable in all cases of apparent bias, whether concerned with justices or members of other inferior tribunals, or with jurors, or with arbitrators ... Accordingly, having ascertained the relevant circumstances, the court should ask itself whether, having regard to those circumstances, there was a real danger of bias on the part of the relevant member of the tribunal in question, in the sense that he might unfairly regard (or have unfairly regarded) with favour, or disfavour, the case of a party to the issue under consideration by him; though, in a case concerned with bias on the part of a magistrates' clerk, the court should go on to consider whether the clerk has been invited to give the magistrates advice and, if so, whether it should infer that there was a real danger of the clerk's bias having infected the views of the magistrates adversely to the applicant' (*per* LORD GOFF OF CHIEVELEY). 'There is only one established special category and that exists where the tribunal has a pecuniary or proprietary interest in the subject-matter of the proceedings, as in *Dimes* v *Grand Junction Canal* (1853) 3 HL Cas 759' (*per* LORD WOOLF). (Applied in *R* v *Inner West London Coroner, ex parte Dallaglio*.)

R v Grafton [1992] 3 WLR 532 (Court of Appeal)   [114]

At his trial for allegedly causing grievous bodily harm with intent, two prosecution witnesses (including the alleged victim) gave evidence supporting the appellant's plea of self-defence. Prosecuting counsel decided to offer no further evidence and declined to take any further part in the proceedings, but the judge thought the case should continue and himself called the prosecution's remaining witness, a police officer. The appellant was convicted of the lesser offence of causing grievous bodily harm. *Held*, his appeal would be allowed and the conviction quashed. 'It is well established that the judge in a criminal trial has power to call a witness. It is, however, a power which should be used more sparingly and rarely exercised ... Here by calling the last witness, the judge was not only supplementing the prosecution: he was in effect taking it over. It cannot in our judgment be right that a judge can refuse to allow the prosecution to discontinue before their case is concluded if he believes the evidence already called raises a prima facie case' (*per* TAYLOR LJ).

R v Greater Manchester Coroner, ex parte Tal See C v Director of Public Prosecutions.

R v Greenwich London Borough Council, ex parte   [115]
Lovelace (No 2) [1992] 1 QB 155 (Court of Appeal)

With the assistance of legal aid, two members of a council's housing committee sought a declaration that a decision of the council reducing membership of the housing committee was ultra vires. The Divisional Court dismissed the application for judicial review with costs and an appeal to the Court of Appeal was similarly dismissed. The council sought payment of its costs from the Legal Aid Board under s18 of the Legal Aid Act 1988. *Held*, the council could recover from the board its costs in the Court of Appeal, but not the Divisional Court. Although the Divisional Court was here the court of first instance for the purpose of s18(4)(b) of the 1988 Act, the council had failed to show that it would suffer severe financial hardship unless the board paid the costs. The 'severe financial hardship' test did not apply to the council's costs in the Court of Appeal (the court which 'finally decided the proceedings') and, in all the circumstances, it was just and equitable that the board should pay them.

R v Harrow Crown Court, ex parte Dave [1994] 1 WLR 98   [116]

Having been convicted by justices of assault occasioning actual bodily harm, a woman appealed to the Crown Court. Dismissing the appeal, the Crown Court judge said simply: 'Over the course of three days we have had ample opportunity to hear and to assess the witnesses. It is our unanimous conclusion that this appeal must be dismissed.' The woman sought judicial review on the ground, inter alia, that the Crown Court should have given reasons for dismissing her appeal. *Held*, the application would be allowed. 'The weight of authority is now in favour of the conclusion that when the Crown Court sits in an appellate capacity it must give reasons for its decision. ... The appellant was entitled to know the basis upon which the prosecution case had been accepted by the court.

In the present case, that involved knowing the process by which the apparently powerful points in favour of the defence had been rejected. A refusal to give reasons may amount to the denial of natural justice' (*per* PILL J).

R v Highbury Corner Magistrates' Court, ex parte Di Matteo [117]
[1991] 1 WLR 1374

Following conviction of, inter alia, driving while disqualified, the stipendiary magistrate ordered the forfeiting of the applicant's car under s43(1) of the Powers of Criminal Courts Act 1973. *Held*, in principle, such an order could be made, but here it would be quashed as the magistrate had not considered the relevant matters set out in s43(1A) of the 1973 Act. 'In our judgment the words used in s43 should be given their natural and ordinary meaning, unless on a reading of the section there are two possible interpretations, in which case, this being a penal provision, the interpretation most favourable to a defendant should be adopted ... But we see no ambiguity in s43(1) when seeking to apply it to the facts of the present case' (*per* WATKINS LJ). (See also *Pepper* v *Hart* and *Arab Bank plc* v *Mercantile Holdings Ltd*.)

R v Highbury Corner Magistrates' Court, ex parte Ewing [118]
[1991] 3 All ER 192 (Court of Appeal)

The question was, inter alia, whether a person against whom a civil proceedings order had been made under s42(1) of the Supreme Court Act 1981 required leave under s42(1A)(a) to make an application for leave to apply for judicial review under RSC Ord 53, r3(1). *Held*, he did as 'civil proceedings' in s42(1A)(a) included such an application. 'Upon an application being made by someone to whom s42 applies for leave to apply for the judicial review of the decision, the matter should be placed before one of the judges who habitually deal with applications for leave under Ord 53, r3 and ... he should consider the matter on the footing that he is faced with an application under the s42 order and an application under Ord 53. If he decides that there is a case for giving leave under Ord 53, he will of course have no difficulty in deciding that it is a case in which he should also give leave under the s42 order, and he should give both leaves. If he decides that there is no case for giving leave under Ord 53, he equally will have no difficulty in refusing leave under the s42 order. It is at the next stage that things will be different according to whether or not he has given leave under the s42 order. If he refuses leave under the s42 order, that is the end of the matter, because there is no right of appeal from any such order ... If he gives leave, the respondent will be unable to attack the leave under s42 because that is final, but he may be able to attack the leave under Ord 53. At that stage the vexatious litigant, having obtained his leave under s42, will be treated in all respects as if he were not subject to the order' (*per* LORD DONALDSON OF LYMINGTON MR).

R v Horseferry Road Magistrates' Court, ex parte Bennett [119]
[1993] 3 WLR 90 (House of Lords)

Having been committed for trial in England in relation to offences alleged to have been committed there, a New Zealand citizen maintained that he had been forcibly returned to England from South Africa against his will. *Held*, the High Court had power, in the exercise of its supervisory jurisdiction, to inquire into the circumstances by which a person was brought within the jurisdiction and, if satisfied that it was in disregard of extradition procedures, could stay the prosecution and order the release of the accused. 'I ... affirm the power of the magistrates, whether sitting as committing justices or exercising their summary jurisdiction, to exercise control over their proceedings through an abuse of process jurisdiction. However, in the case of magistrates this power should be strictly confined to matters directly affecting the fairness of the trial of the particular accused with whom they are dealing, such as delay or unfair manipulation of court procedures. Although it may be convenient to label the wider supervisory jurisdiction with which we are concerned in this appeal under the head of abuse of process, it is in fact a horse of a very different colour from the narrower issues that arise when considering domestic criminal trial procedures ... this wider responsibility for upholding the rule of law must be that of the High Court and ... if a serious question arises as to the deliberate abuse of extradition procedures a magistrate should allow an adjournment so that an application can be made to the Divisional Court, which I regard as the proper forum in which such a decision should be taken' (*per* LORD GRIFFITHS). (See also *R v Telford Justices, ex parte Badham*.)

R v Inner West London Coroner, ex parte Dallaglio   [120]
[1994] 4 All ER 139 (Court of Appeal)

Following the *Marchioness* disaster on the Thames, the mothers of two of the victims sought judicial review of the coroner's refusal (a) to remove himself on the ground of apparent bias and (b) to resume the inquests. Earlier, the coroner had suggested that some of the victims' relatives were 'mentally unwell' and that one of them was 'unhinged'. *Held*, a new coroner should be appointed to consider whether or not to resume the inquests. '...one returns to the question whether in all the circumstances of the present case it appears that there was a real danger of bias on the part of the coroner. With considerable reluctance I am driven to the conclusion that there was such a danger' (*per* FARQUHARSON LJ). (Applied: *R v Gough*.)

R v Jefferson [1994] 1 All ER 270 (Court of Appeal)   [121]

When aged 15, a boy was interviewed by the police following a disturbance and he was eventually convicted of violent disorder. His father was present at the interview: he intervened robustly from time to time, sometimes joining in the questioning of his son and challenging his exculpatory account of certain incidents. The boy appealed contending, inter alia, that the judge had been wrong when he refused to exclude the interview under s76(2)(b) and/or s78 of the Police and Criminal Evidence Act 1984 on the ground that there had been a breach of the relevant code of practice. In other words, he maintained that, because of his conduct, his father had not been an 'appropriate adult' for the purpose of the code. *Held*, his appeal would be dismissed. Encouragement by an appropriate adult of a juvenile who is being fairly interviewed to tell the truth should not normally be stigmatised as a failure of the adult ... "to advise" him; nor should it have the consequence of turning him from an appropriate adult to an inappropriate adult for the purpose of these provisions ... The judge was, therefore, correct in ruling that he would not exclude evidence of anything said by [the boy] in the interviews under s76(2)(b) of the 1984 Act as likely to be unreliable, or under s78 of the Act as unfair' (*per* AULD J). (See also *R v Sang*.)

R v Judge of the City of London Court   [122]
[1892] 1 QB 273 (Court of Appeal)

A question arose as to the jurisdiction of the City of London Court, as conferred by Act of Parliament. *Held*, 'if the words of an Act are unambiguous and clear, you must obey those words, however absurd the result may appear ... If any other rule were followed, the result would be that the court would be legislating instead of the properly constituted authority of the country, namely, the legislature' (*per* LOPES LJ). (See also *Attorney General* v *Jones*.)

R v Kent [1977] 1 WLR 1365 (Court of Appeal)   [123]

The issue was whether the appellant had 'had with him' a firearm, contrary to s18(1) of the Firearms Act 1968. The marginal note to the section was 'Carrying firearm with criminal intent'. *Held*, this note was of no assistance in determining the scope of the section and, indeed, it was not necessary for the prosecution to establish that the appellant had been carrying the firearm. 'It used to be thought that one could have no regard to marginal notes in studying the meaning of an Act of Parliament. It is still law that one may not use a marginal note for the purpose of interpreting an Act, but the House of Lords made it clear in ... *Director of Public Prosecutions* v *Schildkamp* [1971] AC 1 that regard may be had to a marginal note, not to interpret the Act of Parliament, but as an indication of the mischief with which the Act is dealing. ... There can be no doubt but that the main subject with which a section such as s18 of the 1968 Act deals is that of carrying firearms with criminal intent, and the presence of a marginal note is a useful indication that this is the main subject. But that does not mean that the marginal note is of any value in determining the scope of the section, which is the problem with which the court at this moment is concerned' (*per* SCARMAN LJ).

R v King's Lynn Justices, ex parte Holland [1993] 1 WLR 324   [124]

At a committal hearing, the magistrates decided that they did not have jurisdiction to exclude evidence under s78(1) of the Police and Criminal Evidence Act 1984. *Held*, this was not the case, but they should exercise this discretion only in the clearest case and in exceptional circumstances. (See also *R* v *Bailey*.)

R v Leicester City Justices, ex parte Barrow   [125]
[1991] 3 WLR 368 (Court of Appeal)

The applicants sought the quashing of liability orders made by magistrates under the Community Charges (Administration and Enforcement) Regulation 1989 and a declaration that they had been entitled to the assistance of a friend in representing themselves. *Held*, the application would be successful. 'In my opinion there are in general no grounds for objecting to a litigant in person being accompanied by an assistant, who will sit beside him, take notes and advise sotto voce on the conduct of his case. If the court is open to the public, the assistant is entitled to be present in his own right provided that there is room; and, if the litigant wishes him as an assistant, he should be accorded priority over the public in general ... What I have said is in the context of civil proceedings, whether in the Court of Appeal, the High Court, the county court or before masters, district judges or magistrates ... The circumstances are also different when a civil court sits in chambers or in camera, as the public then has no right of access ... But the judge should consider whether this difference is a sufficient reason for excluding a person whom the litigant in person wishes to assist him ... The legal profession has, at present, monopoly rights of representing another as an advocate; the assistant can claim no right to do that, nor can the litigant claim a right to such representation ... I do not see that it can be in the interests of justice to prevent somebody giving ... assistance merely because the case is thought by the judge to be simple ... An assistant can be ordered to stay away from the litigant or to leave the court if he is disorderly ... If he wastes time unnecessarily, as by prompting the litigant to ask irrelevant questions or causing delay by long consultations, he should be warned;

and if this conduct persists his assistance should be terminated ... I also consider that there should be no need, in the ordinary way, for an application to be made to the court for a litigant in person to have an assistant. It should be sufficient for the litigant ... merely to introduce the person by name, and say that he is present as an assistant. That is in the ordinary way. If, however, the assistant is someone known to the court as likely to be disorderly or disruptive, the court can consider whether ... assistance should be allowed at all or at any rate a firm warning should be given' (*per* STAUGHTON LJ).

R v Liverpool City Magistrates' Court, ex parte Director   [126]
of Public Prosecutions [1992] 3 WLR 20

Questions arose as to (a) whether the procedure under s7(5) of the Bail Act 1976 calls for a formal hearing by a court consisting of at least two justices, (b) whether such procedure necessitates the giving of evidence on oath with the opportunity for cross-examination and for the person arrested to give evidence himself, and (c) whether such procedure could be adjourned. *Held*, the answer to all three questions was in the negative. In particular, a single justice may decide whether a bailed defendant should be remanded in custody or granted further bail on the same or varied conditions on the basis of an informal inquiry.

R v McFarlane [1994] 2 WLR 494 (Court of Appeal)   [127]

On the hearing of a charge of living on the earnings of prostitution, contrary to s30(1) of the Sexual Offences Act 1956, it appeared that the woman in question had been a 'clipper'. On appeal against conviction, the man contended that a clipper was not a prostitute. *Held*, the appeal would be dismissed. 'The words "prostitute" and "prostitution" are not defined in any statute. Our attention was drawn to dictionary definitions and to three decided cases ... In our judgment both the dictionary definitions and the cases show that the crucial feature in defining prostitution is the making of an offer of sexual services for reward ... There have been a number of statutes, from the Vagrancy Act 1824 through the Town Police Clauses Act 1847, up to and including the Street Offences Act 1959, whose object has been to prevent the nuisance of women soliciting and offering sexual favours in public places. If it were a defence to soliciting for prostitution under s1 of the 1959 Act that the accused woman was acting as a "clipper" and not as a "hooker", proof of such offences would be extremely difficult. It would be necessary to prove not merely the offer of sexual services in a public place, but that the services were actually provided, or were at the time of the offering intended to be provided. The mischief being simply the harassment and nuisance to members of the public on the streets, the distinction between "clippers" and "hookers" is immaterial' (*per* LORD TAYLOR OF GOSFORTH CJ). (See also *Heydon's Case*.)

R v McIlkenny [1992] 2 All ER 417 (Court of Appeal)   [128]

The judgment in this successful appeal by 'the Birmingham Six' was read by LLOYD, MUSTILL and FARQUHARSON LJJ by turns and it included the following: '(1) The Court of Appeal, Criminal Division is the creature of statute. Our powers are derived from, and confined to, those contained in the Supreme Court Act 1981, the Criminal Appeal Act 1968 and the Criminal Justice Act 1988. We have no inherent jurisdiction apart from statute ... Our function is to hear criminal appeals, neither more nor less.

(2) Just as we have no powers other than those conferred on us by Parliament, so we are guided by Parliament in the exercise of those powers. Thus by s2(1) of

the 1968 Act we are directed to allow an appeal against conviction if, but only if, (a) we think that the conviction is unsafe or unsatisfactory, (b) there has been a wrong decision on a question of law or (c) there has been a material irregularity. In all other cases we are obliged to dismiss the appeal. Where we allow an appeal, we are directly by s2(2) to quash the conviction. Where we quash the conviction, the order operates, by virtue of s2(3), as a direction to the trial court to enter a verdict of acquittal, except where a retrial is ordered under s7 of the 1968 Act. ... The task of deciding whether a man is guilty falls on the jury. We are concerned solely with the question whether the verdict of the jury can stand.

(3) Rightly or wrongly (we think rightly) trial by jury is the foundation of our criminal justice system. Under jury trial juries not only find the facts; they also apply the law. Since they are not experts in the law, they are directed on the relevant law by the judge. But the task of applying the law to the facts, and so reaching a verdict, belongs to the jury, and the jury alone. ...

(4) The primacy of the jury in the criminal justice system is well illustrated by the difference between the Criminal and Civil Divisions of the Court of Appeal. Like the Criminal Division, the Civil Division is also a creature of statute. But its powers are much wider. A civil appeal is by way of rehearing of the whole case. So the court is concerned with fact as well as law. It is true the court does not rehear the witnesses. But it reads their evidence. It follows that in a civil case the Court of Appeal may take a different view of the facts from the court below. In a criminal case this is not possible ... Hence it is true to say that whereas the Civil Division of the Court of Appeal has appellate jurisdiction in the full sense, the Criminal Division is perhaps more accurately described as a court of review ... We have no power to upset the verdict of a jury on a question of fact unless we think a conviction unsafe or unsatisfactory under all the circumstances of the case ...

(5) Another feature of our law, which goes hand in hand with trial by jury, is the adversarial nature of criminal proceedings. Clearly a jury cannot embark on a judicial investigation. So the material must be placed before the jury. It is sometimes said that the adversarial system leaves too much power in the hands of the police. But that criticism has been met, at least in part, by the creation of the Crown Prosecution Service. The great advantage of the adversarial system is that it enables the defendant to test the prosecution case in open court. Once there is sufficient evidence to commit a defendant for trial, the prosecution has to prove the case against him by calling witnesses to give oral testimony in the presence of the jury ...

(6) A disadvantage of the adversarial system may be that the parties are not evenly matched in resources ... But the inequality of resources is ameliorated by the obligation on the part of the prosecution to make available all material which may prove helpful to the defence ...

(7) No system is better than its human input. Like any other system of justice the adversarial system may be abused. The evidence adduced may be inadequate. Expert evidence may not have been properly researched or there may have been a deliberate attempt to undermine the system by giving false evidence. If there is a conflict of evidence there is no way of ensuring the jury will always get it right. This is particularly so where there is a conflict of expert evidence ... No human system can expect to be perfect.

(8) Just as the adversarial system prevails at the trial, so also it prevails in the Court of Appeal. It is for the appellants to raise the issues which they wish to lay before the court. Those issues are set out in the grounds of appeal ...' (See also *R v Blandford Justices, ex parte Pamment*.)

R v Maguire [1992] 2 WLR 767 (Court of Appeal)   **[129]**

The appellants were convicted of possessing explosives, contrary to s4(1) of the Explosive Substances Act 1883. On appeal against conviction they contended, inter alia, that the failure of the prosecution to inform the defence of relevant material known to the Crown's expert witnesses constituted a material irregularity in the course of the trial. *Held*, the appeals would be allowed and the convictions quashed. 'We are of the opinion that a forensic scientist who is an adviser to the prosecuting authority is under a duty to disclose material of which he knows and which may have "some bearing on the offence charged and the surrounding circumstances of the case" [Attorney General's guidelines *Practice Note* [1982] 1 All ER 734]. The disclosure will be to the authority which retains him and which must in turn (subject to sensitivity) disclose the information to the defence' (*per* STUART-SMITH LJ).

R v Manchester City Stipendiary Magistrate, ex parte Snelson **[130]**
[1977] 1 WLR 911

The prosecution, whose case was unprepared, applied for an adjournment of committal proceedings against the defendant who was charged with two offences under the Theft Act 1968. Their application was granted and a new date fixed but, when on the second appearance they were still unprepared, they applied for a further adjournment. The magistrate refused the application and, on the prosecution offering no evidence, discharged the defendant. The prosecution later, having fully prepared their case, instituted fresh committal proceedings. The defendant sought to prohibit the magistrate from inquiring further into the alleged offences. *Held*, the application would be dismissed. Where the defendant had been discharged on committal proceedings, if the prosecution wished to institute fresh proceedings relating to the same offence the magistrate was not barred from exercising his jurisdiction to entertain them.

R v Manchester Crown Court, ex parte Director of Public **[131]**
Prosecutions [1993] 1 WLR 1524 (House of Lords)

A former member of the European Parliament was committed for trial in the Crown Court, but the judge quashed the indictment on the ground that the Crown Court had no jurisdiction to entertain such proceedings. The Director of Public Prosecutions sought judicial review of this decision. *Held*, the application could not succeed as the judge's decision related to a trial on indictment within s29(3) of the Supreme Court Act 1981. However, judicial review could well not be excluded if the Crown Court's decision was truly collateral to the indictment and the trial would not be thereby delayed. 'If, in the future, the question arises whether jurisdiction to entertain a prosecution is excluded by the alleged "sovereignty" of the European Parliament, ... it may well prove to be appropriate for the judge to refer the point to the European Court of Justice for decision' (*per* LORD BROWNE-WILKINSON). (See also *R v Chelmsford Crown Court, ex parte Chief Constable of Essex.*)

R v Mason [1988] 1 WLR 139 (Court of Appeal)   **[132]**

The appellant was arrested and questioned regarding an offence of arson – setting fire to a car. At the time of the arrest, the police had no direct evidence to associate the appellant with the incident, but they told him and his solicitor that his fingerprints had been found on the bottle used to perpetrate the offence. This was a deliberate falsehood, but it was sufficient to cause the appellant to confess that he had been involved. At the trial, he maintained that the confession was inadmissible, but the judge, after considering s78(1) of the Police and Criminal Evidence Act 1984, concluded that it would not be unfair to allow the evidence to be adduced. On appeal against this decision, it was contended that s78 did not apply to confessions as they were expressly covered by s76. *Held*, this contention would be rejected as, in s78, 'evidence' included all evidence, including confessions. However, the conviction would be quashed because the judge had failed to consider the deceit practised on the appellant and his solicitor: had he done so, he would have excluded the confession. (See also *R* v *Samuel*.)

R v Maxwell [1990] 1 WLR 401 (House of Lords)   [133]

Appealing against conviction of robbery, the appellant contended that, in the light of s6(3) of the Criminal Law Act 1967, the judge (approving the prosecution's approach) should not have excluded the possibility of conviction of burglary, a lesser offence. *Held*, the appeal would be dismissed as, in the interests of justice, the judge had been entitled to conclude that the jury's attention should not be distracted from the essential issue of whether the appellant had intended violence to be used. 'What is required in any particular case where the judge fails to leave an alternative offence to the jury is that the court, before interfering with the verdict, must be satisfied that the jury may have convicted out of a reluctance to see the defendant get clean away with what, on any view, was disgraceful conduct. If they are so satisfied then the conviction cannot be safe or satisfactory' (*per* LORD ACKNER).

R v Metropolitan Stipendiary Magistrate, ex parte London   [134] Waste Regulation Authority [1993] 3 All ER 113

When considering an alleged offence in relation to the disposal of controlled waste, the Queen's Bench Divisional Court was referred to one of its own previous (1990) decisions on the same point. *Held*, this previous decision would not be followed as, in their Lordships' opinion, it had been wrongly decided. 'Strictly speaking, there is no rule of stare decisis as between decisions of the Divisional Court, because such a rule must mean that the later court has not the jurisdiction to depart from the previous decision, whatever it thinks of its correctness; but, of course, it is clear that this court must be firmly satisfied that one of its previous decisions is erroneous before it departs from it' (*per* WATKINS LJ). (See also *C* v *Director of Public Prosecutions*.)

R v Okinikan [1993] 1 WLR 173 (Court of Appeal)   [135]

On appeal against sentence, questions arose in relation to pre-sentence reports and the suspending of sentences in the light of s5(1) of the Criminal Justice Act 1991. *Held*, the appeal would be dismissed as, on the facts, the requirements of s3 of the Criminal Justice Act 1991 as to pre-sentence reports had been satisfied and the sentence of imprisonment had been appropriate. 'Without in any way minimising the importance courts should attach to the proper performance of the obligations imposed by the statutory provisions relating to pre-sentence reports, in our judgment it is for the trial judge to decide whether the report actually available to the court is adequate for sentencing purposes and constitutes proper compliance with the statute. Provided the report is in writing and is made or submitted by a probation officer or social worker and gives appropriate information about the offender in relation to the offences which bring him before the court, the judge is not obliged to ensure that every detail of information put before him by counsel is checked and confirmed in a further pre-sentence report or by way of addendum. If he considers that a further written report is required to confirm further information, he may of course adjourn the case, but he is not obliged to do so ... Parliament has given statutory force to the principle that a suspended sentence should not be regarded as a soft option, but should only be imposed in exceptional circumstances. This court cannot lay down a definition of "exceptional circumstances". They will inevitably depend on the facts of each individual case. However, taken on their own, or in combination, good character, youth and an early plea are not exceptional circumstances justifying a suspended sentence. They are common features of many cases. They may amount to mitigation sufficient to persuade the court that a custodial sentence should not be passed or to reduce its length. The statutory language is clear and unequivocal ... In the present case exceptional circumstances were not shown. It would therefore have been inappropriate for the sentence of imprisonment to have been suspended' (*per* LORD TAYLOR OF GOSFORTH CJ).

R v Parole Board, ex parte Wilson [1992] 2 WLR 707 [136]
(Court of Appeal)

Serving a discretionary life sentence for buggery of a boy aged under 16, a man contended that, before a review, he was entitled to see the reports which were to be put before the Parole Board. The Court of Appeal had previously decided (*Payne* v *Lord Harris of Greenwich* [1981] 1 WLR 754) that a prisoner was not so entitled when he was serving a manadatory life sentence. *Held*, the man could see the reports. The court was not bound by *Payne* as that decision related to mandatory as opposed to discretionary life sentences and was therefore distinguishable on that ground.

R v Pitman [1991] 1 All ER 468 (Court of Appeal) [137]

In the course of a trial for allegedly causing death by reckless driving, the judge asked counsel to see him in his private room. He said that he believed there was no defence to the charge and that the accused should plead guilty: if he did so, when it came to sentencing, he would receive substantial credit. Although the accused's counsel had previously advised him to plead not guilty, in the light of the discussion with the judge he changed his plea and on conviction he was sentenced to nine months' imprisonment and disqualified for four years. *Held*, there had been a material irregularity and a conviction would therefore be quashed. LORD LANE CJ said that there appeared to be a steady flow of appeals to the Court of Appeal arising from visits by counsel to the judge in his private room. No amount of criticism and no amount of warnings and no amount of exhortation seemed to be able to prevent this happening. Here, the discussion placed improper pressure, albeit indirectly, on the appellant to change his plea to one of guilty, in the fear that what the judge had said meant, first, that his chances were, to say the least, very slim, and that if he was convicted by the verdict of the jury he would most certainly go to prison. (See also *R v Turner.*)

R v Poplar Coroner, ex parte Thomas [1993] 2 WLR 547 [138]
(Court of Appeal)

A woman suffered a severe asthma attack at 1am. An ambulance arrived at 1.33am but she died shortly after that time. A post-mortem examination revealed that the death was due to natural causes. The coroner decided that an inquest was unnecessary, but the woman's mother applied for and was granted judicial review of this decision and the Divisional Court ordered the coroner to hold an inquest. The coroner appealed. *Held*, the appeal would be allowed as the death had indeed been from natural causes: it had not been turned into an 'unnatural' death because of the ambulance's delayed arrival. 'I agree that "unnatural" is an ordinary word of the English language and that there is nothing to suggest that in s8(1) of the Coroners Act 1988 it is being used in any unusual sense. That, however, is not to say that whether or not a particular death is properly to be regarded as unnatural is a pure question of fact. On the contrary, it seems to me that some guidance at least can and should be given as a matter of law by the courts to coroners so that they may focus their attention upon the real considerations material to the decision and, one hopes, thereby achieve an essential measure of consistency in their approach to the section ... I agree further that the question whether or not a death is natural or unnatural depends ultimately upon the view one takes as to the cause of death ... Congested traffic, or other transportation or communication difficulties causing delayed arrivals are not, I fear, rare, and certainly could not as a matter of common sense be thought directly causative of the death such as to make it in this context unnatural' (*per* SIMON BROWN LJ).

R v Powell (1994) 98 Cr App R 224 (Court of Appeal)   [139]

As a Crown Court jury (which included an attractive, smartly dressed young lady) was returning to deliver their verdict, there was a wolf whistle from the back of the court. The appellant acknowledged that he was responsible and he was convicted of contempt of court. *Held*, his appeal against conviction would be dismissed and their Lordships added that s12 of the Contempt of Court Act 1981 gave a good indication of the type of conduct that amounted to contempt in the face of the court at common law. (But see *Balogh* v *St Albans Crown Court*.)

R v Preston [1993] 3 WLR 891 (House of Lords)   [140]

The defendants were convicted of conspiracy to import prohibited drugs from Holland. At the trial, the judge had refused to exclude evidence that a large number of telephone calls had been made between the defendants and between the defendants and Holland and to order the prosecution to disclose details of the intercepted calls. The defendants appealed. *Held*, their appeals would be dismissed. 'I turn to the ... argument for the defendants, that if the physical intercept materials were rightly destroyed and their contents irretrievably lost the interests of fairness demanded that the evidence derived from the "metering" of the telephone calls should have been ruled out under s78(1) of the Police and Criminal Evidence Act 1984 ... It will be recalled that we are here concerned with the exercise of a discretion by the trial judge. This should not lightly be overruled, and still less so (as it seems to me) by this House when the Court of Appeal has declined to intervene. Nevertheless the discretion must of course be set aside if it is wrong in principle or manifestly ill-judged ... I would reject this ground of appeal' (*per* LORD MUSTILL). (See also *R* v *Jefferson*.)

R v Puddick See R v Banks.

R v R (Rape: Marital Exemption) [1991] 4 All ER 481   [141]
(House of Lords)

Although the Court of Appeal dismissed a man's appeal against conviction of, inter alia, attempted rape of his wife, it granted leave to appeal and certified as a point of law of general public importance the question: 'Is a husband criminally liable for raping his wife?' *Held*, the appeal would be dismissed and the question answered in the affirmative. While textbooks written by Sir Matthew Hale (1736), East (1803) and Archbold (1822) had accurately reflected the common law at those times when they asserted that a husband could not be guilty of a rape upon his wife, the common law is 'capable of evolving in the light of changing social, economic and cultural developments ... Since then the status of women, and particularly of married women, has changed out of all recognition ... one of the most important changes is that marriage is in modern times regarded as a partnership of equals, and no longer one in which the wife must be the subservient chattel of the husband. Hale's proposition involves that by marriage a wife gives her irrevocable consent to sexual intercourse with her husband under all circumstances and irrespective of the state of her health or how she happens to be feeling at the time. In modern times any reasonable person must regard that conception as quite unacceptable ... The position ... is that the part of Hale's proposition which asserts that a wife cannot retract the consent to sexual intercourse which she gives on marriage has been departed from in a series of decided cases. On grounds of principle there is no good reason why the whole proposition should not be held inapplicable in modern times' (*per* LORD KEITH OF KINKEL). (But see *Lim Poh Choo* v *Camden & Islington Area Health Authority*.)

R v Reading Crown Court, ex parte Bello (1991) 92   [142]
Cr App R 303 (Court of Appeal)

The applicant had stood as surety for the accused and he had been ordered to forfeit £5,000, half of his recognizance. He had contended that this order should be set aside because (a) he was not notified that the accused was required to attend Reading Crown Court on 3 February 1986, (b) the accused was already then in police custody in The Netherlands, and (c) he (the applicant) was blameless. *Held*, the appeal would be allowed as it had not been shown that the accused was ever required to attend on 3 February 1986 or on any other date. PARKER LJ added that the failure of the accused to surrender when required triggered the power to forfeit but the court before deciding what should be done had to enquire into the question of fault. If it was satisfied that the surety was blameless throughout it would then be proper to remit the whole of the amount of the recognizance and in exceptional circumstances that would be the only proper course. (See also *R* v *Wood Green Crown Court, ex parte Howe*.)

R v Redbridge Justices, ex parte Gurmit Ram [1992] 2 WLR 197   [143]

Two justices hearing an information charging theft were unable to agree on a verdict. *Held*, in order to discharge their obligation under s9(2) of the Magistrates' Courts Act 1980, it was their duty to adjourn the case for hearing by a bench of three justices.

R v Registrar General, ex parte Smith [1991] 2 WLR 782   [144]
(Court of Appeal)

Under s51 of the Adoption Act 1976, the Registrar General was required to give an adopted person a copy of his birth certificate. The appellant, an adopted person and a convicted murderer, applied for such a copy, but the Registrar General refused to supply it, believing that the appellant's natural mother might be at risk. *Held*, as there was ample evidence to justify the Registrar General's belief, her decision would not be overruled. 'If it be the law that Parliament, even when enacting statutory duties in apparently absolute terms, is presumed not to have intended that they should apply so as to reward serious crime in the past, it seems to me that Parliament must likewise be presumed not to have intended to promote serious crime in the future. that is consistent with the growing tendency, perhaps encouraged by Europe, towards a purposive construction of statutes, at all events if they do not deal with penal or revenue matters … It is and always has been public policy to prevent crime … For present purposes, it is sufficient to hold that a statutory duty is not to be enforced if there is a significant risk that to do so would facilitate crime resulting in danger to life. Parliament is presumed not to have intended that, unless it has said so in plain terms … this is not the exercise of the discretion either by officials with statutory duties to perform or by the court. It is in no way connected with the discretion of the court to refuse relief in judicial review cases. It is a rule of law to be applied in the interpretation of Acts of Parliament, on the facts of each case' (*per* STAUGHTON LJ). (See also *R v Highbury Magistrates' Court, ex parte Di Matteo*.)

R v Robinson [1993] 1 WLR 168 (Court of Appeal)   [145]

When aged 16, the appellant was convicted of the attempted rape of a frail woman aged 87. He was sentenced to eight years' detention under s53 of the Children and Young Persons Act 1933 and he appealed against that sentence. *Held*, his appeal would be dismissed. Attempted rape was both a 'sexual offence' and a 'violent offence' within s31(1) of the Criminal Justice Act 1991 and, for the purpose of sentencing, the defendant's age is his age at the date of conviction.

R v Samuel [1988] 2 WLR 920 (Court of Appeal)   [146]

Arrested on suspicion of robbery, that day and the next the appellant was interviewed by the police on four occasions about the robbery and two burglaries, in all of which the appellant denied any involvement. During the second interview he asked for access to a solicitor, but his request was refused on the ground of likelihood of other suspects involved in the robbery being inadvertently warned. At the fourth interview the appellant confessed to the two burglaries and he was charged with those offences at 4.30pm. At 4.45pm a solicitor was informed of the charges, but denied access. Shortly afterwards the appellant confessed to the robbery and the solicitor was allowed to see him one hour later. Under the Code of Practice for Detention issued under s66 of the Police and Criminal Evidence Act 1984, access could not be denied after a person had been charged with a 'serious arrestable offence' – and one of the burglaries was such an offence. At the trial, the appellant contended that evidence of the latter confession should be excluded under s78(1) of the 1984 Act, but it was admitted and he was convicted of robbery. *Held*, the appellant had been wrongly denied access to a solicitor before his last interview and the conviction of robbery would therefore be quashed. 'This appellant was denied improperly one of the most important and fundamental rights of a citizen. The trial judge fell into error is not so holding. If he had arrived at correct decisions on the … points argued before him he might well have concluded that the refusal of access and consequent unlawful interview compelled him to find that the admission of evidence as to the final interview would have "such an adverse effect on the fairness of the proceedings" that he ought not to admit it. Such a decision would, of course, have very significantly weakened the prosecution case' (*per* HODGSON J). (See also *R v Canale*.)

R v Sang [1980] AC 402 (House of Lords)   [147]

The appellant pleaded not guilty to a charge that he had conspired with others to utter forged United States banknotes. Requesting a trial within a trial, his counsel said that he hoped to establish that the appellant had been induced to commit the offence by an informer acting on the instructions of the police and that but for such persuasion the appellant would not have committed the offence. Counsel then hoped that the judge would rule, in the exercise of his discretion, that no evidence of the offence so incited should be admitted and that he would direct the entry of a not guilty verdict. The judge ruled that he had no discretion to exclude the evidence. *Held*, the judge's ruling had been correct. A judge always had a discretion to refuse to admit evidence if he thought its prejudicial effect outweighed its probative value and in the case of admissions, confessions and evidence obtained from the accused after the commission of the alleged offence. Here the evidence should not have been excluded, whether or not it had been obtained as a result of the activities of an agent provocateur. (See now ss76, 78 and 82(3) of the Police and Criminal Evidence Act 1984.) (See also *R* v *Fulling*.)

R v Secretary of State for Foreign and Commonwealth   [148]
Affairs, ex parte Rees-Mogg [1994] 2 WLR 115

Counsel invited the court to look at *Hansard* in order to resolve an alleged ambiguity in s1(2) of the European Communities (Amendment) Act 1993. *Held*, it would not do so. 'Parliament has enacted s1(2) of the 1993 Act in the light of clear statements made in both Houses as to its intended scope. If there had been any ambiguity, which there is not, we would have regarded this as an appropriate case in which to resort to *Hansard*, in accordance with the principles stated in *Pepper* v *Hart*' (*per* LLOYD LJ).

R v Secretary of State for the Home Department, ex parte   [149]
Leech [1993] 3 WLR 1125 (Court of Appeal)

Section 47(1) of the Prison Act 1952 empowered the Secretary of State to make by statutory instrument rules for the regulation and management of prisons. The applicant, a prisoner, sought judicial review by way of declaration that one rule (r33(3)) so made was ultra vires s47(1) of the 1952 Act on the ground that it permitted the reading and stopping of confidential letters between a prisoner and a solicitor on wider grounds than merely to ascertain whether they were in truth bona fide communications between a solicitor and client. *Held*, the declaration would be granted. 'We accept that s47(1) by necessary implication authorises some screening of correspondence passing between a prisoner and a solicitor. The authorised intrusion must, however, be the minimum necessary to ensure that the correspondence is in truth bona fide legal correspondence. ... But r33(3) is extravagantly wide ... In our view the Secretary of State strayed beyond the proper limits of s47(1) when he made r33(3)' (*per* SIMON BROWN LJ). (See also *Director of Public Prosecutions* v *Hutchinson*.)

R v Secretary of State for Transport, ex parte Factortame   [150]
Ltd (No 3) (Case C221/89) [1991] 3 All ER 769
(European Court of Justice)

The applicants, English companies with most of their directors and shareholders Spanish nationals, sought to challenge by way of judicial review the validity of United Kingdom legislation (the Merchant Shipping Act 1988 and regulations made under it) which excluded them from a new register of British fishing vessels. They contended that the legislation contravened the EEC Treaty by depriving them of their Community law rights under articles 7, 52 and 221. The Divisional Court requested a preliminary ruling from the Court of Justice under article 177 as to the interpretation of the relevant provisions of Community law. *Held*, the United Kingdom legislation was contrary to Community law and the registration system was therefore ineffective in relation to nationals of other member states.

R v Self [1992] 1 WLR 657 (Court of Appeal)   [151]

Believing that the appellant had stolen a bar of chocolate, outside the store an assistant attempted to effect a citizen's arrest. Another young man came to the assistant's aid: both were kicked by the appellant in his struggles to get away. After being acquitted on a count of theft but convicted of assault, the appellant appealed against this conviction. *Held*, the appeal would be allowed as s24(5) of the Police and Criminal Evidence Act 1984 made it abundantly clear that the powers of arrest without a warrant where an arrestable offence had been committed required, as a condition precedent, an offence committed. It followed that the two offences of assault, contrary to s38 of the Offences Against the Person Act 1861, could not have been committed because there had been no power to apprehend or detain the appellant. (See also *Walters* v *WH Smith & Son Ltd*.)

R v Shepherd [1994] 2 All ER 243 (Court of Appeal)   [152]

The defendant pleaded guilty at the Crown Court to two counts of causing death (that of his passenger and her baby) by careless driving after having consumed alcohol above the prescribed limit contrary to s3A of the Road Traffic Act 1988, as inserted by s3 of the Road Traffic Act 1991. He was fined £250 and disqualified from driving for two years. Pursuant to s36 of the Criminal Justice Act 1988 and with leave of the Court of Appeal the Attorney General referred the case to that court on the ground that the sentence was too lenient. *Held*, sentences of three months' imprisonment on each count concurrently would be imposed and the two-year disqualification would not be disturbed. 'To fine the offender was to do no more than would have been appropriate had he simply been found guilty of driving with excess alcohol. Parliament has clearly indicated that this offence is to be treated much more punitively than that ... we consider that the sentence passed by the learned judge was unduly lenient. A custodial sentence was required' (*per* LORD TAYLOR OF GOSFORTH CJ).

R v Southwark Crown Court, ex parte Tawfick,   [153]
Crown Prosecution Service intervening
(1994) The Times 1 December

Judicial review was sought of a Crown Court judge's decision that there was no power to allow a private prosecution to be conducted in person in the Crown Court. *Held*, as this was a matter relating to trial on indictment, in the light of s29(3) of the Supreme Court Act 1981 the application would be dismissed for want of jurisdiction. However, GLIDEWELL LJ thought that s27(2)(c) of the Courts and Legal Services Act 1990 gave the necessary power, although it was a discretion which would only be occasionally exercised.

R v Spencer [1985] QB 771 (Court of Appeal, Criminal Division);   [154]
affd [1987] AC 128 (House of Lords)

On appeal against conviction of ill-treating patients at a special hospital, the appellants sought to rely on a previous decision of the Court of Appeal (*R* v *Bagshaw* [1984] 1 WLR 477). In *Bagshaw*, the court's attention was not drawn to a contrary Court of Appeal decision in *R* v *Beck* [1982] 1 WLR 461. *Held*, the appeals would be dismissed as the decision in *Bagshaw* was per incuriam and it would not be followed. 'As a matter of principle we ... find it difficult to see why there should in general be any difference in the application of the principle of stare decisis between the Civil and Criminal Divisions of this court, save that we must remember that in the latter we may be dealing with the liberty of the subject and if a departure from authority is necessary in the interests of justice to an appellant, then this court should not shrink from so acting.' (*per* MAY LJ). 'The Court of Appeal was ... fully entitled to conclude that had the court in *Bagshaw* had the benefit of the full argument which it had had in these two appeals, and, in particular, had its attention drawn to *Beck*, a different conclusion might have been reached. It accordingly concluded that it was not bound by the decision in *Bagshaw*. I consider that it was entitled so to decide' (*per* LORD ACKNER). (See also *Rakhit* v *Carty*.)

R v Telford Justices, ex parte Badham [1991] 2 WLR 866   [155]
(Court of Appeal)

It was alleged that Badham had committed rape on a day unknown between 15 February 1973 and 14 February 1974. Complaint had been made in mid-September 1988. The justices took the view that the delay had been justifiable and that there had been no abuse of process. *Held*, further committal proceedings would be prohibited. 'Our conclusion is that justices sitting to inquire into an offence as examining justices do have, as part of their inherent jurisdiction, the power to refuse to undertake the inquiry on the ground that it would be an abuse of process to do so ... Leaving aside cases (of which this is not one) where the elapse of time is due to an accused having concealed his offence or his person, we are of the view that an elapse of time for which the prosecuting authorities are not to blame can be such that an accused can be heard to say that a fair trial is no longer possible and the committal proceedings would therefore be an abuse of process ... we think the onus will normally be on the accused to show that on the balance of probability a fair trial is now impossible ... A consideration of the committal papers, which tells us of the circumstances of the case, and of the period of between 15 and 16 years, leave us in no doubt that this is a case where we should infer prejudice and conclude that a fair trial would not now be possible. The justices were wrong in focusing upon the justifiability of delaying the complaint. They should have asked whether a fair trial would be possible' (*per* MANN LJ). (See also *R* v *Horseferry Road Magistrates' Court, ex parte Bennett*.)

R v Thompson [1962] 1 All ER 65 (Court of Appeal)   [156]

The appellant was convicted of offences by a jury quite late in the day and the sentence was to be pronounced the following day. Before this a member of the public was informed by a juror that all of the jurors were in favour of acquitting the appellant until the foreman produced to them a list of his previous convictions. They then agreed to convict him. The question was whether there was jurisdiction to enquire into what had occurred in the jury room. *Held*, there was no such jurisdiction. 'The court does not entertain or admit evidence by a juryman of what took place in the jury room either by way of explaining the grounds on which the jury arrived at their conclusion or by way of a statement as to what he believes its effect to be' (*per* ATKIN LJ). (Se also *Attorney General* v *Associated Newspapers Ltd*.)

R v Tower Bridge Metropolitan Stipendiary Magistrate,   [157]
ex parte Chaudhry [1993] 3 WLR 1154

The applicant's motor cyclist son having died as a result of injuries received in a collision with a van and the Crown Prosecution Service having laid information against the van driver alleging three relatively minor road traffic offences, the applicant had laid an information alleging that the death had been caused by reckless driving. The magistrate refused to issue such a summons and the applicant applied for judicial review of this decision. *Held*, the application would be dismissed. '*R* v *West London Magistrates, ex parte Klahn* [1979] 1 WLR 933 ... says in terms that [the magistrate] should consider "the whole of the relevant circumstances" and may need to consider information beyond that provided by the informant, in order to decide if it is a proper case in which to issue a summons, provided of course, that he does not go so far as to conduct a preliminary hearing. Underlying all of [counsel's] submissions is of course the individual's right to prosecute, and before us no one has questioned it. ... It is also allowed for by the wording of s6(1) of the Prosecution of Offences Act 1985, but I see no conflict between the existence of that right and of the discretion of a magistrate to decide whether or not to issue a summons. After all ... an individual prosecutor does not have the unfettered right to pursue his prosecution to trial. By virtue of s6(2) of the 1985 Act the Director of Public Prosecutions may, at any stage, take over in order to abort ... and he may even bring the magistrates' court proceedings to an end by notice pursuant to s23 of the 1985 Act. So, as it seems to me, in any given case, a private prosecutor will have two hurdles to surmount. He will have to persuade a magistrate to issue a summons, and thereafter, if he wishes to retain control of the case, he may have to persuade the Director of Public Prosecutions not to take it over. But in reality, the criteria applied by the magistrate and the Director will be different ... If a magistrate does decide to issue a summons, the Director in deciding whether or not to exercise her powers under s6(2) of the 1985 Act will no doubt look at the evidence in a way that the magistrate was not expecting to do when he decided to issue the summons ... In my judgment the magistrate in the present case ... was right to have regard to the action already taken by the Crown Prosecution Service and to the Director's powers under s6(2) of the 1985 Act, and accordingly this court cannot and should not interfere with his conclusion, arrived at in the exercise of his discretion, that in the interests of justice a summons should not be issued' (*per* KENNEDY LJ).

R v Turner [1970] 2 WLR 1093 (Court of Appeal)   [158]

After pleading not guilty to theft, the appellant was advised by his counsel to change his plea in the hope of avoiding a custodial sentence. After this discussion, counsel said he wished to discuss the matter with the trial judge. On his return, counsel said that a guilty plea would not result in imprisonment: he stressed that the choice was the appellant's but left the appellant with the impression that he was repeating the judge's view. The appellant pleaded guilty and was duly convicted. *Held*, the appeal would be allowed and a new trial ordered. Although counsel had not exceeded his duty, in all the circumstances the appellant could not be said to have been making a free choice when deciding to retract his original plea. 'The judge should, subject to the one exception ..., never indicate the sentence which he is minded to impose. The only exception to this rule is that it should be permissible for a judge to say, if it be the case, that, whatever happens, whether the accused pleads guilty or not guilty, the sentence will or will not take a particular form, eg a probation order or a fine, or a custodial sentence. Finally, where any such discussion on sentence has taken place between judge and counsel, counsel for the defence should disclose this to the accused and inform him of what took place' (*per* LORD PARKER CJ). (See also *R* v *Pitman*.)

R v Walsall Justices, ex parte W (A Minor) [1989] 3 WLR 1311   [159]

W, a juvenile, was charged with causing grievous bodily harm – it was alleged that he had shot and wounded a boy aged 12 with an airgun. At the trial on 11 October the prosecution applied for an adjournment: as the law then stood, independent corroboration of the victim's evidence could have been required; on the very next day a statutory provision abolishing this requirement would come into force. The magistrates granted the adjournment 'in the interests of justice'. *Held*, the magistrates' decision would be quashed as they had acted outside their powers. 'It is the function of courts to apply the law, and to allow a court to choose whether or not to do so depending on its view of the justice of the particular case would be to undermine if not destroy the rule of law on which democracy depends. If a particular law is thought to cause injustice, it is for Parliament to change it. Here Parliament has considered that in the interests of justice the law should be changed. It determined (through subordinate legislation) that 12 October 1988 should be the date on which that change should come into effect. Until that date, it was in our judgment the duty of the courts to apply the existing law' (*per* SAVILLE J).

R v West London Magistrates, ex parte Klahn See R v Tower Bridge Metropolitan Stipendiary Magistrate, ex parte Chaudhry.

R v Wood Green Crown Court, ex parte Howe   **[160]**
[1992] 1 WLR 702

On 14 November 1988 the applicant (for judicial review) stood surety for her brother in the sum of £35,000, knowing that (then) she would be unable to pay that amount if he failed to appear. The trial was rescheduled for 3 April 1989 and the brother kept in touch with the applicant until 7 March 1989. On the following day the applicant reported the brother's disappearance to the police and recorded a wish to withdraw her surety. The Crown Court judge refused to allow withdrawal of the recognisance and, the brother having failed to appear on 3 April, on 17 April he ordered forfeiture of its full amount. *Held*, the application would be granted and the case remitted for rehearing. 'In summary, the court is required to make such order as seems fair and just in the circumstances, having regard in particular to the culpability of the surety (in failing to procure the appearance of the defendant at the appointed place and time) and having regard also to his means ... It is accepted by the applicant that the burden of showing that the order for forfeiture should *not* be made rests upon her ... Questions arose in argument as to whether the surety can "seek to withdraw", as the applicant sought to do, when the defendant disappears or seems unlikely to appear for trial. A surety might wish to do the same if a change of circumstances means that they can no longer pay the amount which they have undertaken to pay. There is no power, it seems to us, for a surety to withdraw unless the defendant is before the court and appropriate application is made by the prosecution or by him under s3(8) of the Bail Act 1976. Apart from this, s7(3) of that Act gives a constable power to arrest the defendant without warrant where a surety has made complaint in writing at a police station that the defendant is unlikely to surrender to custody. This course is, therefore, open to the surety, and it may mean that in practice the police will be able to produce the defendant in court if they can find and arrest him before the hearing. But the surety remains bound to produce him, in our view, at the appointed time and place, and if the defendant does not appear the recognisance may be estreated ...' (*per* WATKINS LJ). (See also *R v Reading Crown Court, ex parte Bello*.)

Racz v Home Office [1994] 2 WLR 23 (House of Lords)   **[161]**

The plaintiff remand prisoner claimed damages for misfeasance in public office in respect of the period for which he had been held – allegedly without justification – in a strip cell. Was he entitled to trial by jury? *Held*, on the facts, the Court of Appeal had properly exercised its discretion to refuse a jury trial and his appeal against that decision would therefore be dismissed. '[Counsel for the plaintiff], while accepting that s69(3) [of the Supreme Court Act 1981] created a presumption against jury trial, argued that issues, including the question of exemplary damages which were likely to arise when this case went to trial, were so closely related to those which would arise in a case of false imprisonment, where a right to jury trial existed, that the above presumption should be rebutted and discretion exercised in favour of allowing a jury trial ... My Lords, if there were any discernible connection between all four types of tort enumerated in s69(1) there might be some force in the above argument as to close relationship. However, that is not the case ... One is left with a strong impression that Parliament has retained these four torts for historical rather than for any logical reason, from which it follows that the similarity to any of these of some other tort is not a factor which must be taken into account by the court in determining, in the exercise of its discretion, whether it is appropriate to rebut the presumption against jury trial created by s69(3)' (*per* LORD JAUNCEY OF TULLICHETTLE). (See also *M* v *Ministry of Defence*.)

Rakhit v Carty [1990] 2 All ER 202 (Court of Appeal)   [162]

On appeal against a decision granting, inter alia, possession of a flat, it appeared that a decision of the Court of Appeal (*Kent* v *Millmead Properties Ltd* (1982) 44 P & CR 353), by which the county court judge had felt he was bound, had been given per incuriam as the Court of Appeal had not there considered a relevant provision of the Rent Act 1977. *Kent's* case had been followed by the Court of Appeal in *Cheniston Investments Ltd* v *Waddock* [1988] 2 EGLR 136. *Held*, the court would not follow either of its previous decisions. 'The appeal involves the application of the principles of binding precedent as enunciated by LORD GREENE MR in *Young* v *Bristol Aeroplane Co Ltd* ... the decision in *Kent's* case was given per incuriam and this court is not bound to follow it. It falls within the third exception to the rule stated by LORD GREENE MR in *Young's* case ... In *Cheniston's* case this court only decided as it did because it considered that it was bound to follow *Kent's* case. But it was not then argued that the decision in *Kent's* case was given per incuriam, and this court in *Cheniston's* case was in error in thinking that it was bound to follow *Kent's* case. The error is now exposed. This court is entitled to refuse to follow either *Kent's* case or *Cheniston's* case and should so refuse' (*per* SIR ROUALEYN CUMMING-BRUCE).

Rantzen v Mirror Group Newspapers (1986) Ltd   [163]
[1993] 3 WLR 953 (Court of Appeal)

In an action for libel, the jury awarded the plaintiff television presenter £250,000 by way of damages. The defendant newspaper appealed, inter alia, pursuant to s8 of the Courts and Legal Services Act 1990 and RSC Ord 59, r11(4), contending that the damages were excessive. *Held*, the appeal would be allowed and an award of £110,000 substituted for the jury's award. 'How then should the Court of Appeal interpret its power to order a new trial on the ground that the damages awarded by the jury were excessive? How is the word "excessive" in s8(1) of the 1990 Act to be interpreted? After careful consideration we have come to the conclusion that we must interpret our power so as to give proper weight to the guidance given by the House of Lords and by the court in Strasbourg ... The question becomes: could a reasonable jury have thought that this award was necessary to compensate the plaintiff and to re-establish his reputation?' (*per* NEILL LJ).

Rastin v British Steel plc [1994] 2 All ER 641 (Court of Appeal)   **[164]**

On the hearing of six appeals from county courts, the basic question was: If an action is automatically struck out under CCR Ord 17, r11(9) on the plaintiff's failure to request the fixing of a hearing day, has a county court jurisdiction to extend the time for compliance retrospectively and so in effect to reinstate the action? *Held*, a county court does have such jurisdiction under CCR Ord 13, r4. 'A retrospective application to extend time should not succeed unless the plaintiff (in which expression we include his advisers) is able to show that he has, save in his failure to comply with r11(3)(d) and (4), prosecuted his case with at least reasonable diligence ... The plaintiff's failure to comply with the rule can never be justifiable, but he must in all the circumstances persuade the court that it is excusable ... If, but only if, the plaintiff can discharge these burdens should the court consider the interests of justice, the positions of the parties and the balance of hardship in a more general way. If it appears that the defendant might be expected to suffer significant prejudice if the action were reinstated which he would not have suffered if the plaintiff had complied with the rule, that will always be a powerful and usually a conclusive reason for not exercising discretion in the plaintiff's favour. The absence of such prejudice is not, however, a potent reason for exercising discretion in the plaintiff's favour. At this stage, but not before, it is relevant to consider matters such as the availability of an alternative remedy to the plaintiff if the action is not reinstated, the expiry of the limitation period and any admission of liability or payment into court that there may have been' (*per* SIR THOMAS BINGHAM MR).

Restick v Crickmore [1994] 1 WLR 420 (Court of Appeal)   **[165]**

Five personal injury claims were wrongly commenced in the High Court and, in each case, the judge struck them out under s40 of the County Courts Act 1984. The plaintiffs appealed. *Held*, the appeals would be allowed. 'Once the conditions set out in the opening words of s40(1) are fulfilled, the court is required to do one of two things, to transfer the proceedings to the county court or strike it out ... The court is required to make a choice between the two alternatives, but it can only strike out if the additional condition is satisfied, namely that the person bringing the proceedings knew, or ought to have known, of the requirement. But otherwise the choice or discretion is unfettered ... The construction I prefer accords with the well-established policy of the courts, which is this: provided proceedings are started within the time permitted by the statute of limitations, are not frivolous, vexatious or an abuse of the process of the court and disclose a cause of action, they will not as a rule be struck out because of some mistake in procedure on the part of the plaintiff or his advisers ... The ordinary sanction for failure to comply with the requirements will be in costs. Moreover, the Supreme Court Act 1981, s51, as amended by the 1990 Act, deals with costs in the High Court and county courts. Subsections (6) and (7) provide for wasted costs awards to be given against legal advisers in respect of costs incurred as a result of their improper, unreasonable or negligent acts or omissions ... Since none of the judges in these cases considered that they had any discretion to transfer, it is necessary for this court to exercise the discretion. In all the cases I am satisfied that the two conditions in s40(1) are satisfied' (*per* STUART-SMITH LJ).

Richards v R [1992] 3 WLR 928 (Privy Council)   [166]

Charged with murder, a man pleaded guilty to manslaughter and the Crown accepted this plea. However, after the trial had been adjourned to enable the defence to call character witnesses, the Director of Public Prosecutions intervened and the proceedings were terminated. On a fresh indictment, the man was convicted of murder. He appealed, relying on the doctrine autrefois convict. *Held*, the appeal would be dismissed. 'The underlying rationale of autrefois convict ... is to prevent duplication of punishment. But if the plea can be supported by a finding of guilt alone, a defendant might escape punishment altogether. Where a defendant is tried before a judge and jury, both have their roles to play and together they constitute the court of trial. If, in any case following trial and conviction by the jury, the judge were to die before passing sentence, there would be no court seised of the case by which sentence could be passed. The defendant, it seems to their Lordships, would in those circumstances have to be rearranged before another court and if he again pleaded not guilty would have to be retried. But it would be absurd that he should be able to plead the jury's verdict in the first trial as a bar to the second. In the case of autrefois acquit the position is, of course, different, because the jury's verdict of not guilty is a final adjudication and disposal of the case and the judge has no further function to perform. The need for finality of adjudication by the court whose decision is relied on to found a plea of autrefois convict is even more clearly apparent where a defendant has pleaded guilty. Not only may the defendant be permitted, in the discretion of the court, to change that plea at any time before sentence, but, when a plea of guilty to a lesser offence than that charged has initially been accepted by the prosecutor with the approval of the court, there can, it appears to their Lordships, be no finality in that "acceptance" until sentence is passed' (*per* LORD BRIDGE OF HARWICH). (See also *Connelly* v *Director of Public Prosecutions*.)

Rickards v Rickards [1989] 3 WLR 748 (Court of Appeal)   [167]

Following a divorce, the registrar made a 'clean break' financial order against the former husband. Under the relevant rules, he had five days within which to appeal; he failed to do so, but later applied to the county court judge for an extension of time. The judge refused this application and the former husband appealed to the Court of Appeal against this decision. There was a previous Court of Appeal decision that such an appeal could not be entertained, notwithstanding a statutory provision apparently to the contrary. *Held*, the appeal could be heard but, in all the circumstances, it would be dismissed. 'This court is justified in refusing to follow one of its own previous decisions not only where that decision is given in ignorance or forgetfulness of some inconsistent statutory provision or some authority binding on it, but also, in rare and exceptional cases, if it is satisfied that the decision involved a manifest slip or error' (*per* LORD DONALDSON OF LYMINGTON MR). (See also *Young* v *British Aeroplane Co Ltd*.)

Ridehalgh v Horsefield [1994] 3 WLR 462 (Court of Appeal)   [168]

In what circumstances should the court make a wasted costs order in favour of one party to litigation against the legal representative of the other? It was a question of growing significance and the court should give guidance. *Held*, inter alia, (1) in s51(7) of the Supreme Court Act 1981 '"improper" ... covers, but is not confined to, conduct which would ordinarily be held to justify disbarment, striking off, suspension from practice or other serious professional penalty ... Conduct which would be regarded as improper according to the consensus of professional (including judicial) opinion can be fairly stigmatised as such whether or not it violates the letter of a professional code. "Unreasonable" aptly describes conduct which is vexatious, designed to harass the other side rather than advance the resolution of the case, and it makes no difference that the conduct is the product of excessive zeal and not improper motive ... The acid test is whether the conduct permits of a reasonable explanation. If so, the course adopted may be regarded as optimistic and as reflecting on a practitioner's judgment, but it is not unreasonable ... "Negligent" should be understood in an untechnical way to denote failure to act with the competence reasonably to be expected of ordinary members of the profession ... we would however wish firmly to discountenance any suggestion that an applicant for a wasted costs order under this head need prove anything less than he would have to prove in an action for negligence ... (2) A legal representative is not to be held to have acted improperly, unreasonably or negligently simply because he acts for a party who pursues a claim or a defence which is plainly doomed to fail ... It is, however, one thing for a legal representative to present, on instructions, a case which he regards as bound to fail; it is quite another to lend his assistance to proceedings which are an abuse of the processes of the court ... in practice it is not hard to say which is which and if there is doubt the legal representative is entitled to the benefit of it ... (3) As emphasised in *Re a Barrister (wasted costs order) (No 1 of 1991)* [1992] 3 All ER 429, [1993] QB 293, the court has jurisdiction to make a wasted costs order only where the improper, unreasonable or negligent conduct complained of has caused a waste of costs and only to the extent of such wasted costs. Demonstration of a causal link is essential. Where the conduct is proved but no waste of costs is shown to have resulted, the case may be one to be referred to the appropriate disciplinary body or the legal aid authorities, but it is not one for exercise of the wasted costs jurisdiction ... (4) A solicitor does not abdicate his professional responsibility when he seeks the advice of counsel. He must apply his mind to the advice received. But the more specialist the nature of the advice, the more reasonable it is likely to be for a solicitor to accept it and act on it ... (5) Even if the court is satisfied that a legal representative has acted improperly, unreasonably or negligently and that such conduct has caused the other side to incur an identifiable sum of wasted costs, it is not bound to make an order, but in that situation it would of course have to give sustainable reasons for exercising its discretion against making an order ... (6) We ... hope that this judgment may give guidance which will be of value to criminal courts as to civil, but we fully appreciate that the conduct of criminal cases will often raise different questions and depend on different circumstances. The relevant discretions are vested in, and only in, the court conducting the relevant hearing' (*per* SIR THOMAS BINGHAM MR). (See also *Filmlab Systems International Ltd* v *Pennington*.)

Roberts Petroleum Ltd v Bernard Kenny Ltd [1983] 2 WLR 305   [169]
(House of Lords)

In the course of the hearing of an appeal, counsel referred to transcripts of judgments given in the Court of Appeal, Civil Division, which had not been included in any series of law reports. *Held*, in future the House would not allow such transcripts to be cited on the hearing of appeals unless leave were given to do so; such leave would only be granted on counsel's giving an assurance that the transcript contained a statement of some principle of law relevant to an issue in the appeal, that it was binding on the Court of Appeal and that the substance of it, as distinct from the mere choice of phraseology, was not to be found in any judgment of that court that had appeared in one of the generalised or specialised series of reports. 'If a civil judgment of the Court of Appeal ... has not found its way into the generalised series of law reports or even into one of the specialised series, it is most unlikely to be of any assistance to your Lordships on an appeal which is sufficiently important to reach this House' (*per* LORD DIPLOCK).

Roebuck v Mungovin [1994] 2 WLR 290 (House of Lords)   **[170]**

Having been injured in an road accident in August 1984, in April 1986 the plaintiff issued a writ and in July the defendant served a defence admitting liability but putting damages in issue. On the same day the defendant asked for further and better particulars: no reply was received. Correspondence passed between solicitors between April 1990 and 14 May 1991 when the plaintiff's solicitors said that a schedule of special damages (first promised on 18 October 1990) would be finalised at the end of the month. No such schedule having been received, the defendant's solicitors applied to strike out the action for want of prosecution. *Held*, the action would be struck out. 'In *Birkett v James* [1978] AC 197 this House held that a judge has a discretionary power to strike out an action for want of prosecution if two preconditions are satisfied, viz (1) that the plaintiff has been guilty of inordinate and inexcusable delay and (2) that such delay gives rise to a substantial risk that it is not possible to have a fair trial or is likely to cause or to have caused serious prejudice to the defendant ... [Here], although there has been very great delay by the plaintiff which has prejudiced the defendant, the defendant subsequently urged the plaintiff to take steps required to bring the case to trial. The plaintiff incurred minor expenditure in so doing ... Where a plaintiff has been guilty of inordinate and inexcusable delay which has prejudiced the defendant, subsequent conduct by the defendant which induces the plaintiff to incur further expense in pursuing the action does not, in law, constitute an absolute bar preventing the defendant from obtaining a striking out order. Such conduct of the defendant is, of course, a relevant factor to be taken into account by the judge in exercising his discretion whether or not to strike out the claim, the weight to be attached to such conduct depending upon all the circumstances of the particular case' (*per* LORD BROWNE-WILKINSON).

Rondel v Worsley [1967] 3 All ER 993 (House of Lords)   **[171]**

The plaintiff was convicted of causing grievous bodily arm with intent to X, and nearly six years later issued a writ for negligence against the defendant, a barrister who had appeared for him, arguing that he would have been acquitted if the defendant had conducted his case properly. He argued that since *Hedley Byrne & Co Ltd v Heller & Partners Ltd* [1963] 2 All ER 575 the position with regard to liability for professional negligence as between barrister and client had altered, so that there was liability. *Held*, no action lay at the suit of a client against a barrister, for negligence in the conduct of a cause. The immunity of counsel from being sued for professional negligence in the conduct of a cause, civil or criminal, is based on public policy, not on his contractual incapacity to sue for fees, and it is in the public interest that the immunity should be retained. (Se also s62 of the Courts and Legal Services Act 1990; but see *Saif Ali v Sidney Mitchell & Co*.)

Rookes v Barnard [1964] AC 1129 (House of Lords)   **[172]**

A good cause of action at common law for the tort of intimidation having been established, the question arose as to whether the plaintiff was entitled to exemplary damages. *Held*, he was not as exemplary damages should be awarded only in the case of oppressive, arbitrary or unconstitutional action by the servants of the government or where the defendant's conduct was calculated by him to make a profit for himself which could well exceed the compensation payable to the plaintiff. There was nothing to bring this case within either of those categories.

Ross v Caunters [1979] 3 All ER 580   **[173]**

A testator instructed the defendant solicitors to draw up his will which included a gift in favour of the plaintiff. The defendants sent the will to the testator with instructions as to its execution but they failed to warn him that attestation by a beneficiary's spouse would invalidate the gift to that beneficiary. The plaintiff's husband attested the will: when it was returned to the defendants they failed to notice that he had done so. After the testator's death, the defendants told the plaintiff that the gift to her was void and she sued them for damages in negligence. *Held*, her action would succeed as a solicitor who was instructed by his client to carry out a transaction to confer a benefit on an identified third party owed a duty to that third party to use proper care in carrying out the instructions and the defendants had been in breach of that duty. The fact that the plaintiff's claim in negligence was for purely financial loss did not preclude it. (But see *Rondel* v *Worsley*.)

Saif Ali v Sydney Mitchell & Co [1978] 3 All ER 1033 **[174]**
(House of Lords)

In an action by a client against his solicitor for negligence, the solicitor joined as third party the barrister who had advised in the matter. The barrister had settled proceedings in respect of a road accident against the husband of the driver of the car, on the basis that the wife was his agent. He did not join the wife as a defendant, and when it was sought to do so, any action against her was statute barred. *Held*, although public policy required that a barrister should be immune from suit for negligence in respect of his acts or omissions in the conduct and management of litigation which caused damage to his client, such immunity was an exception to the principle that a professional person who held himself out as qualified to practise that profession was under a duty to use reasonable care and skill and was not to be given any wider application than was absolutely necessary in the interests of the administration of justice. Accordingly, a barrister's immunity from suit extended only to those matters of pre-trial work which were so intimately connected with the conduct of the case in court that they could fairly be said to be preliminary decisions affecting the way that case was conducted when it came to a hearing. Inasmuch as the barrister's advice and settling of the pleadings in fact prevented the plaintiff's case from coming to court as it should have done, it could not be said to have been intimately connected with the conduct of the plaintiff's case in court, and was therefore not within the sphere of a barrister's immunity from suit for negligence. A solicitor acting as an advocate in court enjoys the same immunity as a barrister. (See also *Ross* v *Caunters*.)

St Bartholomew's, Aldbrough, Re [1990] 3 All ER 440 **[175]**
(York Consistory Court)

A parish church petitioned for a faculty to permit the sale of an ancient helmet which was associated with a tomb within the church of a person who died in 1377. The church faced serious financial difficulties. *Held*, in all the circumstances, a faculty would be granted, provided, inter alia, the purchaser kept the helmet on public display in England.

Seaconsar Far East Ltd v Bank Markazi Jomhouri Islami Iran **[176]**
[1993] 4 All ER 456 (House of Lords)

The question was whether an application under RSC Ord 11, r1(1)(d) or (e) for leave to serve proceedings outside the jurisdiction had been correctly refused.

Held, on the facts, it had not and leave would now be granted. 'A judge faced with a question of leave to serve proceedings out of the jurisdiction under Ord 11 will in practice have to consider both (1) whether jurisdiction has been sufficiently established, on the criterion of the good arguable case laid down in *Korner's* case, under one of the paragraphs of r1(1), and (2) whether there is a serious issue to be tried, so as to enable him to exercise his discretion to grant leave, before he goes on to consider the exercise of that discretion ...' (*per* LORD GOFF OF CHIEVELEY).

Shaw v Director of Public Prosecutions [1962] AC 220 [177]
(House of Lords)

The appellant published the *Ladies Directory* which gave information about prostitutes and their services. He was convicted of conspiring with others to corrupt public morals. *Held*, his appeal against conviction would be dismissed. 'Need I say ... that I am no advocate of the right of the judges to create new criminal offences? But I am at a loss to understand how it can be said either that the law does not recognise a conspiracy to corrupt public morals or that, though there may not be an exact precedent for such a conspiracy as this case reveals, it does not fall fairly within the general words by which it is described ... In the sphere of criminal law, I entertain no doubt that there remains in the courts of law a residual power to enforce the supreme and fundamental purpose of the law, to conserve not only the safety and order but also the moral welfare of the state, and that it is their duty to guard it against attacks which may be the more insidious because they are novel and unprepared for ... Such occasions will be rare, for Parliament has not been slow to legislate when attention has been sufficiently aroused. But gaps remain and will always remain since no one can foresee every way in which the wickedness of man may disrupt the order of society' (*per* VISCOUNT SIMONDS).

Sirros v Moore [1974] 3 WLR 459 (Court of Appeal) [178]

It having been established that a Crown Court judge was functus officio when ordering the plaintiff to be taken into custody, the plaintiff now sued the judge (and the police officers who had acted on the judge's order) for damages for assault and false imprisonment. *Held*, although the plaintiff's detention had been unlawful, his action could not succeed as the judge had acted judicially and in good faith. 'So long as [the judge] does his work in the honest belief that it is within his jurisdiction, then he is not liable to an action. He may be mistaken in fact. He may be ignorant in law. What he does may be outside his jurisdiction – in fact or in law – but so long as he honestly believes it to be within his jurisdiction, he should not be liable. Once he honestly entertains this belief, nothing else will make him liable. He is not to be plagued with allegations of malice or ill-will or bias or anything of the kind. Actions based on such allegations have been struck out and will continue to be struck out. Nothing will make him liable except it be shown that he was not acting judicially, knowing that he had no jurisdiction to do it' (*per* LORD DENNING MR). (But see ss44 and 45 of the Justices of the Peace Act 1979.)

Smith, Re [1988] 3 All ER 203 [179]

When considering whether a county court had power to stay committal proceedings in a magistrates' court for non-payment of rates, Warner J was confronted by conflicting decisions of the Court of Appeal. *Held*, he should and would follow the later decision. 'Where a judge at first instance is confronted with conflicting decisions of the Court of Appeal, in the later of which the earlier has been fully considered, he is bound to follow the later decision ... a High Court judge need never follow another if convinced that that other was wrong. A High Court judge is not, however, free not to follow a decision of the Court of Appeal on that ground' (*per* WARNER J).

Stoke-on-Trent City Council v B & Q plc [1993] 2 WLR 730   **[180]**
(European Court of Justice; House of Lords)

The council sought injunctions to restrain B & Q from opening their stores on Sundays in contravention of s47 of the Shops Act 1950. B & Q contended that this provision was unenforceable because, as it prevented the sale on Sundays of goods imported from other member states, it infringed article 30 of the EEC Treaty (prohibition of 'quantative restrictions' on imports). Under article 177 of the Treaty, the House of Lords sought the European court's clarification of the relevance of article 30 to the present dispute. *Held*, article 30's prohibition did not apply to s47 of the 1950 Act. In the light of this decision, the House of Lords dismissed B & Q's appeal.

Stubbings v Webb [1993] AC 498 (House of Lords)   **[181]**

A woman now aged 30 claimed damages for, inter alia, rape which she had allegedly suffered when she was aged 12. The question was whether this was an action 'for damages, for negligence, nuisance or breach of duty ... where the damages claimed ... consist of or include damages in respect of personal injuries' within s11(1) of the Limitation Act 1980 and was therefore subject to the special time limit for which provision was made by that section. *Held*, it was not, and the action was therefore time-barred by virtue of s2 of the 1980 Act. In reaching this conclusion, their Lordships considered the development of the law on limitation of liability since the passing of the Limitation Act 1939, the Tucker Committee's *Report on the Limitation of Actions* presented to Parliament in 1949 and Parliament's intentions as recorded in *Hansard*. 'Even without reference to *Hansard* I should not myself have construed "breach of duty" as including a deliberate assault. The phrase lying in juxtaposition with "negligence" and "nuisance" carries with it the implication of a breach of duty of care not to cause personal injury, rather than an obligation not to infringe any legal right of another person. If I invite a lady to my house one would naturally think of a duty to take care that the house is safe but would one really be thinking of a duty not to rape her? But, however this may be, the terms in which this Bill was introduced to my mind make it clear beyond peradventure that the intention was to give effect to the Tucker recommendation ...' (*per* LORD GRIFFITHS). (See also *Pepper* v *Hart* and *Chief Adjudication Officer* v *Foster.*)

Sweet v Parsley [1970] AC 132 (House of Lords)   **[182]**

The appellant was the sub-tenant of a farmhouse and let out rooms to tenants. She no longer lived there herself but retained a room and returned occasionally to collect rent and mail. Drugs were found on the property and she was charged with being 'concerned in the management' of premises used for drug taking contrary to s5 of the Dangerous Drugs Act 1965. The prosecutor conceded that she was unaware of the existence of the drugs. She was convicted of the offence. *Held*, the appeal against conviction would be allowed as, in the true meaning of s5 of the 1965 Act, the appellant could not be convicted of this offence without proof of mens rea. 'Our first duty is to consider the words of the Act; if they show a clear intention to create an absolute offence, that is an end of the matter. But such cases are very rare. Sometimes the words of the section which creates a particular offence make it clear that mens rea is required in one form or another. Such cases are quite frequent. But in a very large number of cases there is no clear indication either way. In such cases there has for centuries been a presumption that Parliament did not intend to make criminals of persons who were in no way blameworthy in what they did. That means that, whenever a section is silent as to mens rea, there is a presumption that, in order to give effect to the will of Parliament, we must read in words appropriate to require mens rea ... it is a universal principle that if a penal provision is reasonably capable of two interpretations, that interpretation which is most favourable to the accused must be adopted' (*per* LORD REID).

Symphony Group plc v Hodgson [1993] 3 WLR 830   [183]
(Court of Appeal)

The plaintiff manufacturers of kitchen units employed the defendant as an estimating supervisor. In breach of his contract of employment, he went to work for Halvanto Kitchens Ltd, one of the plaintiffs' competitors. After the plaintiffs had obtained an ex parte injunction, the defendant was granted legal aid. The plaintiffs had not joined Halvanto as a defendant nor initiated separate proceedings against them. At the trial, the judge granted the plaintiffs substantial injunctive relief and make an order for costs against the defendant. Before the hearing, the plaintiffs had not told Halvanto that they might seek an order for costs against them. The judge found that Halvanto had known that, by working for them, the defendant would be in breach of his contract with the plaintiffs. At the end of the judgment, counsel for the plaintiffs applied for an order for costs against Halvanto. *Held*, the application would fail as, to grant it, would, in all the circumstances, be a wrongful exercise of the court's discretion under s51(1) of the Supreme Court Act 1981. 'Until the decision of the House of Lords in *Aiden Shipping Co Ltd* v *Interbulk Ltd, The Vimeira* [1986] 2 WLR 1051, it had not been appreciated that the wording of s51 of the Supreme Court Act 1981, or of its statutory predecessors, empowered the court to order a non-party to proceedings to pay costs. It was thought that some limitation must be put upon the generality of the words ... – and that limitation was that the court could only order the costs to be paid by any of the parties. To that limitation there was one apparent exception, namely the ability to order a solicitor to a party to pay costs occasioned by his misconduct, but this was understood to be an exercise by the court of its inherent jurisdiction over solicitors as officers of the court, and was in any event regulated by the provisions of the Rules of the Supreme Court (now Ord 62, r11). In the *Aiden Shipping* case the House of Lords held that s51 should not be interpreted as being subject to the implied limitation, and that the *jurisdiction* to award costs was without limit. However in the course of his leading speech in that case Lord Goff made it clear that the *exercise* of the jurisdiction should be limited in accordance with the requirements of reason and justice ...' (*per* BALCOMBE LJ).

Tucker v Director of Public Prosecutions [1992] 4 All ER 901   [184]

A man appealed by way of case stated to the Queen's Bench Divisional Court in respect of disqualification by magistrates for a road traffic offence. *Held*, the appeal would be dismissed as the sentence was not wrong in law or in excess of jurisdiction in its harshness. 'If a person who is convicted by the magistrates wishes to challenge the sentence which is imposed, in all but the most exceptional case [ie, where it appears to be, by any acceptable standard, 'truly astonishing': per WATKINS LJ in *R* v *Crown Court at Croydon, ex parte Miller* (1986) 85 Cr App R 152], the appropriate course for him to adopt is to go before the Crown Court where there will be a rehearing' (*per* WOOLF LJ).

Universal Thermosensors Ltd v Hibben [1992] 1 WLR 840   **[185]**

When giving judgment in an action for misuse of confidential information in which an Anton Piller 'search and seize' order had been obtained and in the execution of which serious mistakes had been made, SIR DONALD NICHOLLS V-C made points as follows: '(1) Anton Piller orders normally contain a term that before complying with the order the defendant may obtain legal advice, provided this is done forthwith ... But such a term, if it is to be of use, requires that in general Anton Piller orders should be permitted to be executed only on working days in office hours, when a solicitor can be expected to be available ... (2) ... If the order is to be executed at a private house, and it is at all likely that a woman may be in the house alone, the solicitor serving the order must be, or must be accompanied by, a woman ... (3) ... in general Anton Piller orders should expressly provide that, unless this is seriously impracticable, a detailed list of the items being removed should be prepared at the premises before they are removed, and that the defendant should be given an opportunity to check this list at the time. (4) Anton Piller orders frequently contain an injunction restraining those on whom they are served from informing others of the existence of the order for a limited period. This is to prevent one defendant from alerting others to what is happening. There is an exception for communication with a lawyer for the purpose of seeking legal advice. In the present case that injunction was expressed to last for a whole week. That is far too long. ... (5) ... Orders should provide that, unless there is good reason for doing otherwise, the order should not be executed at business premises save in the presence of a responsible officer or representative of the company or trader in question. (6) [One of the plaintiffs' directors] carried out a thorough search of all the documents of a competitor company. This is most unsatisfactory ... consideration should be given to devising some means, appropriate to the facts of the case, by which this situation can be avoided. (7) Anton Piller orders invariably provide for service to be effected by a solicitor. The court relies heavily on the solicitor, as an officer of the court, to see that the order is properly executed ... judges should give serious consideration to the desirability of providing, by suitable undertakings and otherwise, (a) that the order should be served, and its execution should be supervised, by a solicitor other than a member of the firm of solicitors acting for the plaintiff in the action, (b) that he or she should be an experienced solicitor having some familiarity with the workings of Anton Piller orders, and with judicial observations on this subject ... (c) that the solicitor should prepare a written report on what occurred when the order was executed, (d) that a copy of the report should be served on the defendants and (e) that in any event and within the next few days the plaintiff must return to the court and present that report at an inter partes hearing, preferably to the judge who made the order ...' His Lordship added: 'It must be appreciated ... that *in suitable and strictly limited cases*, Anton Piller orders furnish courts with a valuable aid in their efforts to do justice between two parties. Especially is this so in blatant cases of fraud ... If plaintiffs wish to take advantage of this truly Draconian type of order, they must be prepared to pay for the safeguards which experience has shown are necessary if the interests of defendants are fairly to be protected.' (See also *Anton Piller KG* v *Manufacturing Processes Ltd* and *Practice Direction* [1994] 4 All ER 52 (guidelines in relation to Mareva injunctions and Anton Piller orders).

Van Duyn v Home Office [1974] 1 WLR 1107;   **[186]**
[1975] 2 WLR 760 (European Court of Justice)

The plaintiff, a Dutch national, sought to enter the United Kingdom to work at a Scientology establishment in Sussex. The Home Office regarded the entry of foreign nationals to work or study at the establishment as being contrary to public policy and she was refused leave to enter. She applied to the High Court for a reference to the European Court for a preliminary ruling under article 177 of the EEC Treaty on the question whether, inter alia, article 48 of the Treaty conferred on her a right of entry enforceable in United Kingdom courts. *Held*, the question would be so referred. The European Court held that the obligations imposed on member states by article 48 to abolish discrimination based on nationality as regards employment were directly applicable so as to confer an individuals rights enforceable by them in the courts of member states since those provisions imposed on member states a precise obligation which did not require the adoption of any further measures by the Community or member states. However, the voluntary act of an individual in associating with a particular organisation, which involved participation in its activities and identification with its aims, could properly be regarded as a matter of 'personal conduct' within article 3(I) of EEC Directive 64/221. A member state was therefore permitted, under article 48 and article 3(1), to prohibit entry on grounds of public policy.

Van Gend en Loos v Netherlands Fiscal Administration [187] (Case 26/62) [1963] ECR 1 (European Court of Justice)

The plaintiff objected to paying an import duty of 8 per cent when the tariff under article 12 was only 3 per cent. The question was whether an article of the EEC treaty conferred rights on individual citizens of the EEC which a national court must enforce. *Held*, the community constitutes in international law a new rule of law in favour of which the states have, in a limited measure, restricted their sovereignty and under which not only the member states but their subjects too have rights. In the same way as community law creates, independently of legislation of the member states, obligations for private parties, it is also able to create rights which private parties can make applicable on their own behalf.

Walker v Turpin [1994] 1 WLR 196 (Court of Appeal) [188]

Arising out of an alleged oral agreement for the sale of certain shares in a company, two plaintiffs sued four defendants. The defendants made payments into court, but the plaintiffs sought apportionment of the total sum as their claims were not identical. *Held*, in exercise of the court's overriding power under RSC Ord 22, r1(5), an apportionment should be made as each plaintiff should have been able to decide whether to accept the payment in and withdraw from the action. However, in the light of this direction, the defendants could revise or withdraw the payments in should they so wish.

Walters v W H Smith & Son Ltd [1914] 1 KB 595 [189]

The plaintiff was employed by the defendants at a bookstall in King's Cross Station; he also owned a newsagent's shop. Over a period of several months the bookstall suffered a series of thefts and, consequently, the defendants set a trap for the thief by secretly marking some of the stock, including a book entitled *Traffic*. They later sent an agent to the newsagent's shop to buy a copy of the book and it was found to bear the secret mark. On being interviewed by the defendants the plaintiff admitted taking the book but said that he had intended to pay for it. The plaintiff was arrested and he was subsequently prosecuted for theft. On being found not guilty the plaintiff sued the defendants for false imprisonment. *Held*, he had been falsely imprisoned since the plaintiffs were wrong in believing that he had committed a crime. 'When a person, instead of having recourse to legal proceedings by applying for a judicial warrant for arrest or laying an information or issuing other process well known to the law, gives another into custody, he takes a risk upon himself by which he must abide' (*per* ISAACS CJ). (See also *R* v *Self.*)

Ward v James See H v Ministry of Defence

Warwickshire County Council v Johnson [1993] 1 All ER 299   [190]
(House of Lords)

The question, inter alia, was whether, for the purpose of s20(2)(a) of the Consumer Protection Act 1987, an employed branch manager who fails to comply with a price indication so that the same is to be regarded as misleading does so 'in the course of any business of his'. *Held*, the answer was in the negative. Their Lordships acknowledged that the language used was obscure and they reached their conclusion after considering other provisions of the 1987 Act; views expressed by learned commentators and statements made by a minister when the Consumer Protection Bill was before Parliament. 'Your Lordships' House has now given judgment in *Pepper* v *Hart*. It has thus become proper in the strictly limited circumstances defined by LORD BROWNE-WILKINSON ... to have regard to what was said in Parliament in the course of the passage of the Bill ... the answers given by the minister are consistent with the construction I have felt obliged to put upon this legislation' (*per* LORD ROSKILL). (See also *Stubbings* v *Webb*; but see *R* v *Secretary of State for Foreign and Commonwealth Affairs, ex parte Rees-Mogg*.)

Willowgreen Ltd v Smithers [1994] 2 All ER 533   [191]
(Court of Appeal)

In the plaintiff landlords' action for forfeiture and possession of a flat, the address stated in the request for the summons was that of the flat, where the defendant tenant had never lived or worked – he had allowed his stepfather to stay there, rent-free, but step-father had since disappeared. The summons had not reached the defendant and the question was whether, in the light of CCR Ord 7, r10(1)(b), the summons had been properly served on him. *Held*, it had not and the plaintiffs' judgment would therefore be set aside. '"Address" ... does not include a place at which the defendant is never present and at which the process does not come to his notice, albeit that it is a place which ... may well have had a direct and immediate connection with him' (*per* NOURSE LJ).

Wilson v Dagnall [1972] 1 QB 509 (Court of Appeal)   [192]

The plaintiff's husband was killed in a motor accident in 1969. On 19 March 1970 she commenced proceedings claiming, inter alia, damages under the Fatal Accidents Acts. The hearing was on 27 July 1971: the defendant admitted liability and formal judgment was entered on 30 July. On 1 July 1971 the Law Reform (Miscellaneous Provisions) Act 1971 received the Royal Assent and the Act stipulated that it was to come into force on 1 August 1971. The Act provided (in s4) that, in assessing damages under the Fatal Accidents Acts, no longer was account to be taken of a widow's prospects of remarriage. As the 21 year old plaintiff enjoyed such prospects, the judge assessed her damages as though the 1971 Act were already in force. The defendant's appeal was heard in December 1971. *Held*, the judge had been wrong to apply the 1971 Act and the plaintiff's damages would therefore be reduced to take account of her prospects of remarriage. 'Parliament has unambiguously said that the Act is to come into operation on 1 August 1971. It means that Parliament has ordained that up to that date ... the law is to remain as before ... I should have thought it was ... beyond dispute, as an essential part of the unwritten constitutional law of England, by which courts of law are ineluctably bound, that those courts must loyally give effect to what Parliament has provided, and not seek to give effect to what they may think that Parliament ought to have provided' (*per* MEGAW LJ).

Winchester Cigarette Machinery Ltd v Payne (No 2)   [193]
(1993) The Times 15 December (Court of Appeal)

The defendants applied for a stay of execution of the money judgment made against them in an action brought by the defendants, pending their appeal against that judgment. *Held*, the application would be dismissed. In granting a stay a court exercises an unfettered discretion, but it begins with the assumption that a person should not be denied the benefit of the money judgment made in his favour, even if an appeal is pending. It is now a matter of commonsense and a balance of advantage, but in holding any such balance full and proper weight is given to the starting principle that there has to be a good reason – some special circumstances – for depriving a plaintiff from obtaining the fruits of a judgment.

Wolstanton Ltd and Duchy of Lancaster v   [194]
Newcastle-under-Lyme Borough Council
[1940] 3 All ER 101 (House of Lords)

The appellant owned some houses near to the respondents' coal and ironstone mine. The houses were damaged by subsidence due to the mine workings, but the respondents denied being liable to pay compensation, claiming, inter alia, that they had a customary right to work the mine without being liable to pay compensation for damage caused by subsidence. *Held*, any such custom would be unreasonable and therefore void. 'To give validity to a custom it must possess three characteristics. It must be certain, reasonable in itself, and of immemorial origin. As regards the last, it means that the custom must have been in existence from a time preceding the memory of man, which has been fixed as meaning 1189, the first year of the reign of Richard I: see, for the explanation of this date, the opinion of LORD BLACKBURN in *Dalton* v *Angus* (1881) 6 App Cas 740. The courts, however, have decided that, in the case of an alleged custom, it is sufficient to prove facts from which it may be presumed that the custom existed at that remote date, and that this presumption should in general be raised by evidence showing continuous user as of right going as far back as living testimony can go. The presumption is rebuttable, and, for instance, can be rebutted by proof that the custom alleged could not have existed in the time of Richard I. The presumption itself in most cases is little more than a fiction ... In the present case ... we are called upon to assume, in determining the point of law, that the custom is being attacked only on the point that it is unreasonable, and we must, therefore, assume that in other respects it either has been, or can be, proved to be valid ... I find it very difficult, if not impossible, to hold that a custom for the lord to get minerals beneath the surface of copyhold or customary freehold lands without making compensation for subsidence and damage to buildings is a reasonable custom' (*per* VISCOUNT MAUGHAM).

Woodley v Woodley (No 2) [1993] 4 All ER 1010   [195]
(Court of Appeal)

In divorce proceedings, a husband was ordered to pay his wife £60,000, but execution was stayed provided he appealed within 14 days, which he did. Before the appeal was heard (and dismissed) the husband was declared bankrupt. The wife issued a judgment summons under s5 of the Debtors Act 1869 to enforce payment of the £60,000. *Held*, while a bankrupt may be committed to prison under s5 of the 1869 Act for failing to pay a judgment debt, due before his bankruptcy, which before his bankruptcy he had the means to pay, here committal would not be appropriate. 'Although I entertain no doubt that the existence of the stay of execution did not affect the liability of the husband to pay a lump sum order ... he as a layman may very well have thought that it did ... it is this which has persuaded me that we should not now send the husband to prison' (per BALCOMBE LJ).

Woolwich Building Society v Inland Revenue Commissioners [196]
[1992] 3 WLR 366 (House of Lords)

The plaintiffs paid tax in accordance with a demand made under statutory regulations which, in subsequent proceedings by way of judicial review, were held to be ultra vires and void. The defendants repaid the capital but refused to pay interest on the money for the period between the date of payment and the judgment at judicial review. *Held*, by virtue of their rights at common law, the plaintiffs' claim to the interest would be successful.

Yonge v Toynbee [1910] 1 KB 215 Court of Appeal [197]

A firm of solicitors was instructed to act for the defendant in an action brought against him. Soon afterwards the defendant was certified as of unsound mind but the solicitors, ignorant of this fact, entered an appearance for him and prepared the defence. Subsequently, the trial not having yet begun, the plaintiff applied for the appearance and subsequent proceedings to be struck out and the solicitors ordered to pay all the plaintiff's costs, on the ground that they had acted without authority. *Held*, although the solicitors had acted throughout in good faith, they had taken on themselves to act for the defendant and had thereby impliedly warranted that they had the authority to do so: they were therefore liable to pay the plaintiff's costs. 'It is, in my opinion, essential to the proper conduct of legal business that a solicitor should be held to warrant the authority which he claims of representing the client; if it were not so, no one would be safe in assuming that his opponent's solicitor was duly authorised in what he said or did, and it would be impossible to conduct legal business upon the footing now existing' (*per* SWINFEN EADY J).

Young v Bristol Aeroplane Co Ltd [1944] KB 718 [198]
(Court of Appeal); affd [1946] AC 163

On an appeal by the plaintiff against a judgment that he was not entitled to damages for breach by the defendants of their statutory duty, it was contended, inter alia, that the Court of Appeal is not bound by its own earlier decisions. *Held*, subject to three exceptions, the court is so bound. 'What can be done by a full [Court of Appeal] can equally well be done by a division of the court. The corollary of this is, we think, clearly true, namely, that what cannot be done by a division of the court cannot be done by the full court ... so far as dicta are concerned, we are, of course, not bound to follow them ... On a careful examination of the whole matter we have come to the clear conclusion that this court is bound to follow previous decisions of its own as well as those of courts of coordinate jurisdiction. The only exceptions to this rule (two of them apparent only) ... we here summarise: (i) The court is entitled and bound to decide which of two conflicting decisions of its own it will follow. (ii) The court is bound to refuse to follow a decision of its own which, though not expressly overruled, cannot in its opinion stand with a decision of the House of Lords. (iii) The court is not bound to follow a decision of its own if it is satisfied that the decision was given per incuriam' (*per* LORD GREENE MR). (See also *Rakhit* v *Carty*, *Rickards* v *Rickards* and *Langley* v *North West Water Authority*).

Statutes

COURT OF CHANCERY ACT 1851
(14 & 15 Vict c 83)

16 Quorum of Judicial Committee [199]

No matter shall be heard, nor shall any order, report, or recommendation be made, by the Judicial Committee, in pursuance of any Act, unless in the presence of at least three members of the said committee, exclusive of the Lord President of Her Majesty's Privy Council for the time being.

[As amended by the Statute Law Revision Acts 1875 and 1892.]

DEBTORS ACT 1869
(32 & 33 Vict c 62)

5 Saving of power of committal for small debts [200]

Subject to the provisions herein-after mentioned, and to the prescribed rules, any court may commit to prison for a term not exceeding six weeks, or until payment of the sum due, any person who makes default in payment of any debt or instalment of any debt due from him in pursuance of any order or judgment of that or any other competent court: Provided –

(1) That the jurisdiction by this section given of committing a person to prison shall, in the case of any court other than the superior courts of law and equity, be exercised only subject to the following restrictions; that is to say,

(a) Be exercised only by a judge or his deputy, and by an order made in open court and showing on its face the ground on which it is issued:
(c) Be exercised only as respects a judgment of a county court by a county court judge or his deputy.

(2) That such jurisdiction shall only be exercised where it is proved to the satisfaction of the court that the person making the default either has or has had since the date of the order or judgment the means to pay the sum in respect of which he has made default, and has refused or neglected, or refuses or neglects, to pay the same.

Proof of the means of the person making default may be given in such manner as the court thinks just; and for the purposes of such proof the debtor and any witnesses may be summoned and examined on oath, according to the prescribed rules.

Any jurisdiction by this section given to the superior courts may be exercised by a judge sitting in chambers, or otherwise, in the prescribed manner.

For the purposes of this section any court may direct any debt due from any person in pursuance of any order or judgment of that or any other competent court to be paid by instalments, and may from time to time rescind or vary such order: ...

This section, so far as it relates to any county court, shall be deemed to be substituted for sections ninety-eight and ninety-nine of the County Court Act 1846 and that Act and the Acts amending the same shall be construed accordingly, and shall extend to orders made by the county court with respect to sums due in pursuance of any order or judgment of any court other than a county court.

No imprisonment under this section shall operate as a satisfaction or extinguishment of any debt or demand or cause of action, or deprive any person of any right to take out execution against the lands, goods, or chattels of the person imprisoned, in the same manner as if such imprisonment had not taken place ...

[As amended by the Bankruptcy Act 1883, s169(1), Schedule 5.]

APPELLATE JURISDICTION ACT 1876
(39 & 40 Vict c 59)

3 Cases in which appeal lies to House of Lords   [201]

Subject as in this Act mentioned an appeal shall lie to the House of Lords from any order or judgment of any of the courts following; that is to say,

(1) of Her Majesty's Court of Appeal in England; and
(2) of any Court in Scotland from which error or an appeal at or immediately before the commencement of this Act lay to the House of Lords by common law or by statute.

4 Form of appeal to House of Lords   [202]

Every appeal shall be brought by way of petition to the House of Lords, praying that the matter of the order or judgment appealed against may be reviewed before Her Majesty the Queen in her Court of Parliament, in order that the said Court may determine what of right, and according to the law and custom of this realm, ought to be done in the subject-matter of such appeal.

5 Attendance of certain number of Lords of Appeal required   [203]
at hearing and determination of appeals

An appeal shall not be heard and determined by the House of Lords unless there are present at such hearing and determination not less than three of the following persons, in this Act designated Lords of Appeal; that is to say,

(1) the Lord Chancellor of Great Britain for the time being; and
(2) the Lords of Appeal in Ordinary to be appointed as in this Act mentioned; and
(3) such Peers of Parliament as are for the time being holding or have held any of the offices in this Act described as high judicial offices.

6 Appointment of Lords of Appeal in Ordinary   [204]
by Her Majesty

For the purpose of aiding the House of Lords in the hearing and determination of appeals, Her Majesty may by letters patent appoint qualified persons to be Lords of Appeal in Ordinary.

A person shall not be qualified to be appointed by Her Majesty a Lord of Appeal in Ordinary unless he has been at or before the time of his appointment the holder for a period of not less than two years of some one or more of the offices in this Act described as high judicial offices, or has been at or before such time as aforesaid, for not less than 15 years,

> (a) a person who has a Supreme Court qualification, within the meaning of section 71 of the Courts and Legal Services Act 1990;
> (b) an advocate in Scotland, or a solicitor entitled to appear in the Court of Session and the High Court of Justiciary; or
> (c) a practising member of the Bar of Northern Ireland

Every Lord of Appeal in Ordinary shall hold his office during good behaviour, but he may be removed from such office on the address of both Houses of Parliament.

Every Lord of Appeal in Ordinary, unless he is otherwise entitled to sit as a member of the House of Lords, shall by virtue and according to the date of his appointment be entitled during his life to rank as a Baron by such style as Her Majesty may be pleased to appoint, and shall be entitled to a writ of summons to attend, and to sit and vote in the House of Lords; his dignity as a Lord of Parliament shall not descend to his heirs.

On any Lord of Appeal in Ordinary vacating his office, by death resignation or otherwise, Her Majesty may fill up the vacancy by the appointment of another qualified person.

A Lord of Appeal in Ordinary shall, if a Privy Councillor, be a member of the Judicial Committee of the Privy Council, and, subject to the due performance by a Lord of Appeal in Ordinary of his duties as to the hearing and determining of appeals in the House of Lords, it shall be his duty, being a Privy Councillor, to sit and act as a member of the Judicial Committee of the Privy Council.

25 Definitions: 'high judicial office': 'superior courts' [205]

In this Act, if not inconsistent with the context, the following expressions have the meaning herein-after respectively assigned to them; that is to say,

> 'High judicial office' means any of the following offices; that is to say,
> The office of Lord Chancellor of Great Britain or of Judge of one of Her Majesty's superior courts of Great Britain and Ireland:
> 'Superior courts of Great Britain and Ireland' means and includes –
> As to England, Her Majesty's High Court of Justice and Her Majesty's Court of Appeal; and
> As to Northern Ireland, Her Majesty's High Court of Justice in Northern Ireland and Her Majesty's Court of Appeal in Northern Ireland; and
> As to Scotland, the Court of Session.

[As amended by the Judicature (Northern Ireland) Act 1978, s122(1), Schedule 5, Pt II; Courts and Legal Services Act 1990, s71(2), Schedule 10, para 1.]

JUDICIAL COMMITTEE ACT 1881
(44 & 45 Vict c 3)

1 Lords Justices of Appeal to be members of Judicial Committee [206]

Every person holding or who has held in England the office of a Lord Justice of Appeal shall, if a member of Her Majesty's Privy Council in England, be a member of the Judicial Committee of the Privy Council.

APPELLATE JURISDICTION ACT 1887
(50 & 51 Vict c 70)

3 Amendment of 3 & 4 Will 4 c 41   [207]

The Judicial Committee of the Privy Council as formed under the provision of the first section of the Judicial Committee Act 1833 shall include such members of Her Majesty's Privy Council as are for the time being holding or have held any of the offices in the Appellate Jurisdiction Act 1876, and this Act, described as high judicial offices.

5 Amendment of 39 & 40 Vict c 59, s25   [208]

The expression 'high judicial office' as defined in the 25th section of the Appellate Jurisdiction Act 1876 shall be deemed to include the office of a Lord of Appeal in Ordinary and the office of a member of the Judicial Committee of the Privy Council.

JUDICIAL COMMITTEE AMENDMENT ACT 1895
(58 & 59 Vict c 44)

1 Provision as to persons being or having been   [209]
Colonial Chief Justices or Judges

(1) If any person being or having been Chief Justice or a Judge of the Supreme Court of any of the Australasian colonies mentioned in the schedule to this Act, or of any other Superior Court in Her Majesty's Dominions named in that behalf by Her Majesty in Council, is a member of Her Majesty's Privy Council, he shall be a member of the Judicial Committee of the Privy Council.

(3) The provisions of this Act shall be in addition to, and shall not affect, any other enactment for the appointment of or relating to members of the Judicial Committee.

SCHEDULE

New South Wales
New Zealand
Queensland
South Australia
Tasmania
Victoria
Western Australia

[As amended by the Appellate Jurisdiction Act 1913, s3; Statute Law (Repeals) Act 1986.]

APPELLATE JURISDICTION ACT 1908
(8 Edw 7 c 51)

3 Extension of 58 & 59 Vict c 44   [210]

(1) Section one of the Judicial Committee Amendment Act 1895 shall have effect

as if the persons named therein included any person being or having been chief justice or a justice of the High Court of Australia.

4 Resignation of members of the Judicial Committee [211]

Any member of the Judicial Committee of the Privy Council may resign his office as member of that Committee by giving notice of his resignation in writing to the Lord President of the Council.

JUDICIAL COMMITTEE ACT 1915
(5 & 6 Geo 5 c 92)

1 Power of Judicial Committee of the Privy Council [212]
to sit in more than one division at the same time

(1) The Judicial Committee of the Privy Council may, subject to the approval of the Lord Chancellor and the Lord President of the Council, sit in more than one division at the same time, and in such case anything which may be done to, by or before the Judicial Committee may be done to, by or before any such division of the Judicial Committee.

(2) The power of His Majesty in Council to make rules as to the practice and procedure before the Judicial Committee shall include the power to make orders for the constituting of divisions and the holding of divisional sittings of the Judicial Committee.

CHILDREN AND YOUNG PERSONS ACT 1933
(23 Geo 5 c 12)

34 Attendance at court of parent of child or [213]
young person charged with an offence, etc

(2) Where a child or young person is in police detention, such steps as are practicable shall be taken to ascertain the identity of a person responsible for his welfare.

(3) If it is practicable to ascertain the identity of a person responsible for the welfare of the child or young person, that person shall be informed, unless it is not practicable to do so –

    (a) that the child or young person has been arrested;

    (b) why he has been arrested; and

    (c) where he is being detained.

(4) Where information falls to be given under subsection (3) above, it shall be given as soon as it is practicable to do so.

(5) For the purposes of this section the persons who may be responsible for the welfare of a child or young person are –

    (a) his parent or guardian; or

    (b) any other person who has for the time being assumed responsibility for his welfare.

(6) If it is practicable to give a person responsible for the welfare of the child or young person the information required by subsection (3) above, that person shall be given it as soon as it is practicable to do so.

(7) If it appears that at the time of his arrest a supervision order, as defined in

section 11 of the Children and Young Persons Act 1969 or Part IV of the Children Act 1989, is in force in respect of him, the person responsible for his supervision shall also be informed as described in subsection (3) above as soon as it is reasonably practicable to do so.

(7A) If it appears that at the time of his arrest the child or young person is being provided with accommodation by or on behalf of a local authority under section 20 of the Children Act 1989, the local authority shall also be informed as described in subsection (3) above as soon as it is reasonably practicable to do so.

(8) The reference to a parent or guardian in subsection (5) above is in the case of a child or young person in the care of a local authority, a reference to that authority.

(9) The rights conferred on a child or young person by subsections (2) to (8) above are in addition to his rights under section 56 of the Police and Criminal Evidence Act 1984.

(10) The reference in subsection (2) above to a child or young person who is in police detention includes a reference to a child or young person who has been detained under the terrorism provisions; and in subsection (3) above 'arrest' includes such detention.

(11) In subsection (10) above 'the terrorism provisions' has the meaning assigned to it by section 65 of the Police and Criminal Evidence Act 1984.

53 Punishment of certain grave crimes [214]

(1) A person convicted of an offence who appears to the court to have been under the age of eighteen years at the time the offence was committed shall not, if he is convicted of murder, be sentenced to imprisonment for life, nor shall sentence of death be pronounced on or recorded against any such person; but in lieu thereof the court shall (notwithstanding anything in this or any other Act sentence him to be detained during Her Majesty's pleasure, and if so sentenced he shall be liable to be detained in such place and under such conditions as the Secretary of State may direct.

(2) Where –

(a) a young person is convicted on indictment of any offence punishable in the case of an adult with imprisonment for fourteen years or more, not being an offence the sentence for which is fixed by law; or

(aa) a young person is convicted of –

(i) an offence under section 1 of the Road Traffic Act 1988 (causing death by dangerous driving); or

(ii) an offence under section 3A of that Act (causing death by careless driving while under influence of drink or drugs); or

(b) a child is convicted of manslaughter,

and the court is of opinion that none of the other methods in which the case may legally be dealt with is suitable, the court may sentence the offender to be detained for such period [not exceeding the maximum term of imprisonment with which the offence is punishable in the case of an adult] as may be specified in the sentence; and where such a sentence has been passed the child or young person shall, during that period, ... be liable to be detained in such place and on such conditions as the Secretary of State may direct.

(3) A person detained pursuant to the directions of the Secretary of State under this section shall, while so detained, be deemed to be in legal custody.

[As substituted by the Children and Young Persons Act 1963, s25(1) and amended by the Police and Criminal Evidence Act 1984, s57, and the Children Act 1989, s108(5), (7), Schedule 13, paras 2, 6, Schedule 15; as amended by the Criminal Justice Act 1961, s41(1), (3), Schedule 4; Murder (Abolition of Death Penalty) Act 1965, ss1(5), 4; Criminal Justice Act 1988, s126; Criminal Justice Act 1993, s67(2).]

ADMINISTRATION OF JUSTICE (APPEALS) ACT 1934
(24 & 25 Geo 5 c 40)

1 Restrictions on appeals from Court of Appeal to House of Lords [215]

(1) No appeal shall lie to the House of Lords from any order or judgment made or given by the Court of Appeal after the first day of October nineteen hundred and thirty-four, except with the leave of that Court or of the House of Lords.

(2) The House of Lords may by order provide for the hearing and determination by a Committee of that House of petitions for leave to appeal from the Court of Appeal:

Provided that section 5 of the Appellate Jurisdiction Act 1876 shall apply to the hearing and determination of any such petition by a Committee of the House as it applies to the hearing and determination of an appeal by the House.

(3) Nothing in this section shall affect any restriction existing, apart from this section, on the bringing of appeals from the Court of Appeal to the House of Lords.

2 Appeals from county courts [216]

(1) Every appeal from a judgment, direction, decision, decree or order of a judge of a county court given or made after such date as the Lord Chancellor may by order appoint, being an appeal under any of the enactments set out in the first column of the Schedule to this Act, shall lie to the Court of Appeal instead of to the High Court; and accordingly those enactments shall have effect in relation to any such appeal subject to the modifications respectively specified in the second column of that Schedule.

[As amended by the County Courts Act 1934, s193, Schedule 5.]

APPELLATE JURISDICTION ACT 1947
(10 & 11 Geo 6 c 11)

1 Additional Lords of Appeal [217]

(1) Except in the event of the number of the Lords of Appeal in Ordinary being at any time less than seven, His Majesty shall not be advised to make an appointment to fill any vacancy among them unless the Lord Chancellor, with the concurrence of the Treasury, is satisfied that the state of business requires that the vacancy should be filled.

[As amended by the Administration of Justice Act 1968, s1(5), Schedule.]

CRIMINAL JUSTICE ACT 1948
(11 & 12 Geo 6 c 58)

27 Remand and committal or persons aged 17 to 20   [218]

(1) Where a court remands a person charged with or convicted of an offence or commits him for trial or sentence and he is not less than seventeen but under twenty-one years old and is not released on bail, then, if the court has been notified by the Secretary of State that a remand centre is available for the reception from the court of persons of his class or description, it shall commit him to a remand centre, and if it has not been so notified, it shall commit him to a prison.

(2) Where a person is committed to a remand centre in pursuance of this section, the centre shall be specified in the warrant and he shall be detained there for the period for which he is remanded or until he is delivered thence in due course of law.

(3) In this section 'court' includes a justice; and nothing in this section affects the provisions of section 128(7) of the Magistrates' Courts Act 1980 (which provides for remands to the custody of a constable).

37 Bail on appeal, case stated or application for certiorari   [219]

(1) Without prejudice to the powers vested before the commencement of this Act in any court to admit or direct the admission of a person to bail –

    (b) the High Court grant bail to a person –

        (i) who, after the decision of his case by the Crown Court, has applied to the Crown Court for the statement of a case for the High Court on that decision, or

        (ii) who has applied to the High Court for an order of certiorari to remove proceedings in the Crown Court in his case into the High Court, or has applied to the High Court for leave to make such an application;

    (d) the High Court may grant bail to a person who has been convicted or sentenced by a magistrates' court and has applied to the High Court for an order of certiorari to remove the proceedings into the High Court or has applied to the High Court for leave to make such an application.

(1A) Where the court grants bail to a person under paragraph (d) of subsection (1) above –

    (a) the time at which he is to appear in the event of the conviction or sentence not being quashed by the High Court shall be such time within ten days after the judgment of the High Court has been given as may be specified by the High Court; and

    (b) the place at which he is to appear in that event shall be a magistrates' court acting for the same petty sessions area as the court which convicted or sentenced him.

(4) Rules of court may be made under section 84 of the Supreme Court Act 1981 –

    (b) for authorising the recommittal, in such cases and by such courts or justices as may be prescribed by the rules, of persons released from custody under this section.

(6) The time during which a person is released on bail under paragraph (b) or (d) or subsection (1) of this section shall not count as part of any term of imprisonment under his sentence; and any sentence of imprisonment imposed by a court of summary jurisdiction, or, on appeal, by a Crown Court, after the

imposition of which a person is so released on bail, shall be deemed to begin to run or to be resumed as from the day on which he is received in prison under the sentence; and for the purposes of this subsection the expression 'prison' shall be deemed to include young offender institution and remand home and the expression 'imprisonment' shall be construed accordingly.

[As amended by the Criminal Justice Act 1967, s103(2), Schedule 7, Pt I; Children and Young Persons Act 1969, s72(3), Schedule 5, para 24; Courts Act 1971, s56(1), (4), Schedule 8, Pt II, paras 24(b), 28(1), Schedule 11, Pt IV; Bail Act 1976, s12, Schedule 2, para 11, Schedule 3; Magistrates' Courts Act 1980, s154, Schedule 7, para 7; Supreme Court Act 1981, s152(1), (4), Schedules 5, 7; Criminal Justice Act 1988, s123(6), Schedule 8, Pt I, para 1, Pt II.]

JUDICIAL PENSIONS ACT 1959
(8 & 9 Eliz 2 c 9)

2 Retiring age [220]

(1) A person who holds an office listed in the First Schedule to this Act shall vacate that office on the day on which he attains the age of 75 years.

FIRST SCHEDULE

Lord of Appeal in Ordinary ...

CRIMINAL JUSTICE ACT 1967
(1967 c 80)

17 Entry of verdict of not guilty by order of a judge [221]

Where a defendant arraigned on an indictment or inquisition pleads not guilty and the prosecutor proposes to offer no evidence against him, the court before which the defendant is arraigned may, if it thinks fit, order that a verdict of not guilty shall be recorded without the defendant being given in charge to a jury, and the verdict shall have the same effect as if the defendant had been tried and acquitted on the verdict of a jury.

22 Extensions of power of High Court to grant, or vary conditions of, bail [222]

(1) Where a magistrates' court withholds bail in criminal proceedings or imposes conditions in granting bail in criminal proceedings, the High Court may grant bail or vary the conditions.

(2) Where the High Court grants a person bail under this section it may direct him to appear at a time and place which the magistrates' court could have directed and the recognizance of any surety shall be conditioned accordingly.

(3) Subsections (4) and (6) of section 37 of the Criminal Justice Act 1948 (ancillary provisions as to persons granted bail by the High Court under that section and the currency of sentence in the case of persons so admitted) shall apply in relation to the powers conferred by this section and persons granted bail in pursuance of those powers as it applies in relation to the powers conferred by that section and persons admitted to bail in pursuance of those powers, except that the said

subsection (6) shall not apply in relation to a person granted bail pending an appeal from a magistrates' court to the Crown Court.

(4) In this section 'bail in criminal proceedings' and 'vary' have the same meanings as they have in the Bail Act 1976.

(5) The powers conferred on the High Court by this section shall be in substitution for the powers so conferred by paragraphs (a), (b) and (c) of section 37(1) of the Criminal Justice Act 1948, but except as aforesaid this section shall not prejudice any powers of the High Court to admit or direct the admission of persons to bail.

[As amended by the Courts Act 1971, s56(1), Schedule 8, para 48(b); Bail Act 1976, s12(1), (2), Schedule 2, para 37, Schedule 3; Criminal Law Act 1977, s65(4), Schedule 12.]

ADMINISTRATION OF JUSTICE ACT 1968
(1968 c 5)

1 Maximum number of Lords of Appeal in Ordinary and certain other judges [223]

(1) The maximum number –

(a) of Lords of Appeal in Ordinary shall be 11 ...

(2) Her Majesty may by Order in Council from time to time amend the foregoing subsection so as to increase or further increase the maximum number of appointments which may be made to any of the offices therein mentioned.

(3) No recommendation shall be made to Her Majesty in Council to make an Order under this section unless a draft of the Order has been laid before Parliament and approved by resolution of each House of Parliament ...

CRIMINAL APPEAL ACT 1968
(1968 c 19)

PART I

APPEAL TO COURT OF APPEAL IN CRIMINAL CASES

1 Right of appeal [224]

(1) Subject to subsection (3) below a person convicted of an offence on indictment may appeal to the Court of Appeal against his conviction.

(2) The appeal may be –

(a) on the ground which involves a question of law alone; and
(b) with the leave of the Court of Appeal, on any ground which involves a question of fact alone, or a question of mixed law and fact, or on any other ground which appears to the Court of Appeal to be a sufficient ground of appeal;

but if the judge of the court of trial grants a certificate that the case is fit for appeal on a ground which involves a question of fact, or a question of mixed law and fact, an appeal lies under this section without the leave of the Court of Appeal.

(3) Where a person is convicted before the Crown Court of a scheduled offence it shall not be open to him to appeal to the Court of Appeal against the conviction

on the ground that the decision of the court which committed him for trial as to the value involved was mistaken.

(4) In subsection (3) above 'scheduled offence' and 'the value involved' have the same meanings as they have in section 22 of the Magistrates' Courts Act 1980 (certain offences against property to be tried summarily if value of property or damage is small).

2 Grounds for allowing an appeal under s1 [225]

(1) Except as provided by this Act, the Court of Appeal shall allow an appeal against conviction if they think –

(a) that the conviction should be set aside on the ground that under all the circumstances of the case it is unsafe or unsatisfactory; or
(b) that the judgment of the court of trial should be set aside on the ground of a wrong decision of any question of law; or
(c) that there was a material irregularity in the course of the trial

and in any other case shall dismiss the appeal: Provided that the Court may, notwithstanding that they are of opinion that the point raised in the appeal might be decided in favour of the appellant, dismiss the appeal if they consider that no miscarriage of justice has actually occurred.

(2) In the case of an appeal against conviction the Court shall, if they allow the appeal, quash the conviction.

(3) An order of the Court of Appeal quashing a conviction shall, except when under section 7 below the appellant is ordered to be retried, operate as a direction to the court of trial to enter, instead of the record of conviction, a judgment and verdict of acquittal.

3 Power to substitute conviction of alternative offence [226]

(1) This section applies on an appeal against conviction, where the appellant has been convicted of an offence and the jury could on the indictment have found him guilty of some other offence, and on the finding of the jury it appears to the Court of Appeal that the jury must have been satisfied of facts which proved him guilty of the other offence.

(2) The Court may, instead of allowing or dismissing the appeal, substitute for the verdict found by the jury a verdict of guilty of the other offence, and pass such sentence in substitution for the sentence passed at the trial as may be authorised by law for the other offence, not being a sentence of greater severity.

4 Sentence when appeal allowed on part of an indictment [227]

(1) This section applies where, on an appeal against conviction on an indictment containing two or more counts, the Court of Appeal allow the appeal in respect of part of the indictment.

(2) Except as provided by subsection (3) below, the Court may in respect of any count on which the appellant remains convicted pass such sentence, in substitution for any sentence passed thereon at the trial, as they think proper and is authorised by law for the offence of which he remains convicted on that count.

(3) The Court shall not under this section pass any sentence such that the appellant's sentence on the indictment as a whole will, in consequence of the appeal, be of greater severity than the sentence (taken as a whole) which was passed at the trial for all offences of which he was convicted on the indictment.

7 Power to order retrial   [228]

(1) Where the Court of Appeal allow an appeal against conviction and it appears to the Court that the interests of justice so require, they may order the appellant to be retried.

(2) A person shall not under this section be ordered to be retried for any offence other than –

(a) the offence of which he was convicted at the original trial and in respect of which his appeal is allowed as mentioned in subsection (1) above;
(b) an offence of which he could have been convicted at the original trial on an indictment for the first-mentioned offence; or
(c) an offence charged in an alternative court of the indictment in respect of which the jury were discharged from giving a verdict in consequence of convicting him of the first-mentioned offence.

9 Appeal against sentence following conviction   [229]
on indictment

(1) A person who has been convicted of an offence on indictment may appeal to the Court of Appeal against any sentence (not being a sentence fixed by law) passed on him for the offence, whether passed on his conviction or in subsequent proceedings.

(2) A person who on conviction on indictment has also been convicted of a summary offence under section 41 of the Criminal Justice Act 1988 (power of Crown Court to deal with summary offence where person committed for either way offence) may appeal to the Court of Appeal against any sentence passed on him for the summary offence (whether on his conviction or in subsequent proceedings) under subsection (7) of that section.

10 Appeal against sentence in other cases dealt with   [230]
at the Crown Court

(1) This section has effect for providing rights of appeal against sentence when a person is dealt with by the Crown Court (otherwise than on appeal from a magistrates' court) for an offence of which he was not convicted on indictment.

(2) The proceedings from which an appeal against sentence lies under this section are those where an offender convicted of an offence by a magistrates' court –

(a) is committed by the court to be dealt with for his offence at the Crown Court; or
(b) having been made the subject of an order for conditional discharge or a community order within the meaning of Part I of the Criminal Justice Act 1991 (other than a supervision order within the meaning of that Part) or given a suspended sentence, appears or is brought before the Crown Court to be further dealt with for his offence.

(3) An offender dealt with for an offence at the Crown Court in a proceeding to which subsection (2) of this section applies may appeal to the Court of Appeal against sentence in any of the following cases:

(a) where either for that offence alone or for that offence and other offences for which sentence is passed in the same proceeding, he is sentenced to imprisonment or to detention in a young offender institution for a term of six months or more; or
(b) where the sentence is one which the court convicting him had not power to pass; or

(c) where the court in dealing with him for the offence makes in respect of him –

 (i) a recommendation for deportation; or
 (ii) an order disqualifying him for holding or obtaining a licence to drive a motor vehicle under Part II of the Road Traffic Act 1960;
 (iii) an order under section 23(1) of the Powers of Criminal Courts Act 1973 (orders as to existing suspended sentence when person subject to the sentence is again convicted); or
 (iv) a restriction order under section 15 of the Football Spectators Act 1989; or
 (v) a declaration of relevance under the Football Spectators Act 1989.

(4) For purposes of subsection (3)(a) of this section and section 11 of this Act, any two or more sentences are to be treated as passed in the same proceeding if –

 (a) they are passed on the same day; or
 (b) they are passed on different days but the court in passing any one of them states that it is treating that one together with the other or others as substantially one sentence;

and consecutive terms of imprisonment and terms which are wholly or partly concurrent are to be treated as a single term.

17 Reference by Home Secretary [231]

(1) Where a person has been convicted on indictment, or been tried on indictment and found not guilty by reason of insanity, or been found by a jury to be under disability and to have done the act or made the omission charged against him, the Secretary of State may, if he thinks fit, at any time either –

 (a) refer the whole case to the Court of Appeal and the case shall then be treated for all purposes as an appeal to the Court by that person; or
 (b) if he desires the assistance of the Court on any point arising in the case, refer that point to the Court for their opinion, thereon, and the Court shall consider the point so referred and furnish the Secretary of State with their opinion thereon accordingly.

(2) A reference by the Secretary of State under this section may be made by him either on an application by the person referred to in subsection (1), or without any such application.

19 Bail [232]

(1) The Court of Appeal may, if they think fit, –

 (a) grant an appellant bail pending the determination of his appeal; or
 (b) revoke bail granted to an appellant by the Crown Court under paragraph (f) of section 81(1) of the Supreme Court Act 1981 or paragraph (a) above; or
 (c) vary the conditions of bail granted to an appellant in the exercise of the power conferred by either of those paragraphs.

(2) The powers conferred by subsection (1) above may be exercised –

 (a) on the application of an appellant; or
 (b) if it appears to the registrar of criminal appeals of the Court of Appeal (hereafter referred to as 'the registrar') that any of them ought to be exercised, on a reference to the court by him.

20 Disposal of groundless appeal or application for leave to appeal   [233]

If it appears to the registrar that a notice of appeal or application for leave to appeal does not show any substantial ground of appeal, he may refer the appeal or application for leave to the Court for summary determination; and where the case is so referred the Court may, if they consider that the appeal or application for leave is frivolous or vexatious, and can be determined without adjourning it for a full hearing, dismiss the appeal or application for leave summarily, without calling on anyone to attend the hearing or to appear for the Crown thereon.

22 Right of appellant to be present   [234]

(1) Except as provided by this section, an appellant shall be entitled to be present, if he wishes it, on the hearing of his appeal, although he may be in custody.

(2) A person in custody shall not be entitled to be present –

(a) where his appeal is on some ground involving a question of law alone; or
(b) on an application by him for leave to appeal; or
(c) on any proceedings preliminary or incidental to an appeal; or
(d) where he is in custody in consequence of a verdict of not guilty by reason of insanity or of a finding of disability,

unless the Court of Appeal give him leave to be present.

(3) The power of the Court of Appeal to pass sentence on a person may be exercised although he is for any reason not present.

PART II

APPEAL TO THE HOUSE OF LORDS FROM COURT OF APPEAL (CRIMINAL DIVISION)

33 Right of appeal to House of Lords   [235]

(1) An appeal lies to the House of Lords, at the instance of the defendant or the prosecutor, from any decision of the Court of Appeal on an appeal to that court under Part I of this Act or section 9 (preparatory hearings) of the Criminal Justice Act 1987.

(2) The appeal lies only with the leave of the Court of Appeal or the House of Lords; and leave shall not be granted unless it is certified by the Court of Appeal that a point of law of general public importance is involved in the decision and it appears to the Court of Appeal or the House of Lords (as the case may be) that the point is one which ought to be considered by that House.

(3) Except as provided by this Part of the Act and section 13 of the Administration of Justice Act 1960 (appeal in cases of contempt of court), no appeal shall lie from any decision of the criminal division of the Court of Appeal.

35 Hearing and disposal of appeal   [236]

(1) An appeal under this Part of the Act shall not be heard and determined by the House of Lords unless there are present at least three of the persons designated Lords of Appeal by section 5 of the Appellate Jurisdiction Act 1876.

(2) Any order of the House of Lords which provides for the hearing of applications for leave to appeal by a committee constituted in accordance with section 5 of the said Act of 1876 may direct that the decision of that committee shall be taken on behalf of the House.

(3) For the purpose of disposing of an appeal, the House of Lords may exercise any powers of the Court of Appeal or may remit the case to the Court.

36 Bail on appeal by defendant [237]

The Court of Appeal may, if it seems fit, on the application of a person appealing or applying for leave to appeal to the House of Lords, other than a person appealing or applying for leave to appeal from a decision on an appeal under section 9(11) of the Criminal Justice Act 1987 (appeals against orders or rulings at preparatory hearings), grant him bail pending the determination of his appeal.

37 Detention of defendant on appeal by the Crown [238]

(1) The following provisions apply where, immediately after a decision of the Court of Appeal from which an appeal lies to the House of Lords, the prosecutor is granted or gives notice that he intends to apply for, leave to appeal.

(2) If, but for the decision of the Court of Appeal, the defendant would be liable to be detained, the Court of Appeal may make an order providing for his detention, or directing that he shall not be released except on bail (which may be granted by the Court as under section 36 above), so long as an appeal to the House of Lords is pending.

(3) An order under this section shall (unless the appeal has previously been disposed of) cease to have effect at the expiration of the period for which the defendant would have been liable to be detained but for the decision of the Court of Appeal ...

38 Presence of defendant at hearing [239]

A defendant who has been convicted of an offence and who is detained pending an appeal to the House of Lords shall not be entitled to be present on the hearing of the appeal or of any proceedings preliminary or incidental thereto, except where an order of the House of Lords authorises him to be present, or where the House or the Court of Appeal, as the case may be, give him leave to be present.

43 Effect of appeal on sentence [240]

(1) Where a person subject to a sentence is granted bail under section 36 or 37 of this Act, the time during which he is released on bail shall be disregarded in computing the term of his sentence.

(2) Subject to the foregoing subsection, any sentence passed on an appeal to the House of Lords in substitution for another sentence shall, unless that House or the Court of Appeal otherwise direct, begin to run from the time when the other sentence would have begun to run.

PART III

MISCELLANEOUS AND GENERAL

45 Construction of references in Parts I and II to Court of Appeal ... [241]

(1) References in Parts I and II of this Act to the Court of Appeal shall be construed as references to the criminal division of the Court ...

51 Interpretation [242]

(1) In this Act, except where the context otherwise requires –

'appeal', where used in Part I or II of this Act, means appeal under that Part, and 'appellant' has a corresponding meaning and in Part I includes a person who has given notice of application for leave to appeal;

'the court of trial', in relation to an appeal, means the court from which the appeal lies;

'the defendant', in Part II of this Act, means, in relation to an appeal, the person who was the appellant before the criminal division of the Court of Appeal, and references to the prosecutor shall be construed accordingly; ...

'the judge of the court of trial' means, where the Crown Court comprises justices of the peace, the judge presiding; ...

'under disability' has the meaning assigned to it by section 4 of the Criminal Procedure (Insanity) Act 1964 (unfitness to plead) ...

[As amended by the Courts Act 1971, s56(1), Schedule 8, Pt II, para 57(1); Powers of Criminal Courts Act 1973, ss56(1), 60(2), Schedule 5, para 28; Bail Act 1976, s12(1), Schedule 2, paras 43, 44; Criminal Law Act 1977, s44; Magistrates' Courts Act 1980, s154, Schedule 7, para 71; Supreme Court Act 1981, s152(1), Schedule 5; Criminal Justice Act 1982, ss29(2)(b), 77, Schedule 14, para 23; Criminal Justice Act 1987, s15, Schedule 2, paras 3, 4, 5; Criminal Justice Act 1988, ss43(1), (2), 123(6), 157, 170(1), (2), Schedule 8, Pt I, para 2, Schedule 15, paras 20, 21, 22, 26, Schedule 16; Football Spectators Act 1989, ss15(7), 23(3)(a); Criminal Justice Act 1991, s100, Schedule 11, para 3; Criminal Procedure (Insanity and Unfitness to Plead) Act 1991, ss7, 8(2), Schedule 3, para 4.]

ADMINISTRATION OF JUSTICE ACT 1969
(1969 c 58)

12 Grant of certificate by trial judge [243]

(1) Where on the application of any of the parties to any proceedings to which this section applies the judge is satisfied –

(a) that the relevant conditions are fulfilled in relation to his decision in those proceedings, and

(b) that a sufficient case for an appeal to the House of Lords under this Part of this Act has been made out to justify an application for leave to bring such an appeal, and

(c) that all the parties to the proceedings consent to the grant of a certificate under this section,

the judge, subject to the following provisions of this Part of this Act, may grant a certificate to that effect.

(2) This section applies to any civil proceedings in the High Court which are either –

(a) proceedings before a single judge of the High Court, or

(c) proceedings before a Divisional Court.

(3) Subject to any Order in Council made under the following provisions of this section, for the purposes of this section the relevant conditions, in relation to a decision of the judge in any proceedings, are that a point of law of general public importance is involved in that decision and that that point of law either –

(a) relates wholly or mainly to the construction of an enactment or of a statutory instrument, and has been fully argued in the proceedings and fully considered in the judgment of the judge in the proceedings, or

(b) is one in respect of which the judge is bound by a decision of the Court of Appeal or of the House of Lords in previous proceedings, and was fully considered in the judgments given by the Court of Appeal or the House of Lords (as the case may be) in those previous proceedings.

(4) Any application for a certificate under this section shall be made to the judge immediately after he gives judgment in the proceedings:

Provided that the judge may in any particular case entertain any such application made at any later time before the end of the period of 14 days beginning with the date on which that judgment is given or such other period as may be prescribed by rules of court.

(5) No appeal shall lie against the grant or refusal of a certificate under this section.

(6) Her Majesty may by Order in Council amend subsection (3) of this section by altering, deleting, or substituting one or more new paragraphs for, either or both of paragraphs (a) and (b) of that subsection, or by adding one or more further paragraphs.

(7) Any Order in Council made under this section shall be subject to annulment in pursuance of a resolution of either House of Parliament.

(8) In this Part of this Act 'civil proceedings' means any proceedings other than proceedings in a criminal cause or matter, and 'the judge', in relation to any proceedings to which this section applies, means the judge referred to in paragraph (a) of subsection (2) of this section, or the Divisional Court referred to in paragraph (c) of that subsection, as the case may be.

13 Leave to appeal to House of Lords [244]

(1) Where in any proceedings the judge grants a certificate under section 12 of this Act, then, at any time within one month from the date on which that certificate is granted or such extended time as in any particular case the House of Lords may allow, any of the parties to the proceedings may make an application to the House of Lords under this section.

(2) Subject to the following provisions of this section, if on such an application it appears to the House of Lords to be expedient to do so, the House may grant leave for an appeal to be brought directly to the House; and where leave is granted under this section –

(a) no appeal from the decision of the judge to which the certificate relates shall lie to the Court of Appeal, but
(b) an appeal shall lie from that decision to the House of Lords.

(3) Applications under this section shall be determined without a hearing.

(4) Any order of the House of Lords which provides for applications under this section to be determined by a committee of the House –

(a) shall direct that the committee shall consist of or include not less than three of the persons designated as Lords of Appeal in accordance with section 5 of the Appellate Jurisdiction Act 1876, and
(b) may direct that the decision of the committee on any such application shall be taken on behalf of the House.

(5) Without prejudice to subsection (2) of this section, no appeal shall lie to the Court of Appeal from a decision of the judges in respect of which a certificate is granted under section 12 of this Act until –

(a) the time within which an application can be made under this section has expired, and

87

(b) where such an application is made, that application has been determined in accordance with the preceding provisions of this section.

14 Appeal where leave granted   [245]

In relation to any appeal which lies to the House of Lords by virtue of subsection (2) of section 13 of this Act –

(a) section 4 of the Appellate Jurisdiction Act 1876 (which provides for the bringing of appeals to the House of Lords by way of petition),
(b) section 5 of that Act (which regulates the composition of the House for the hearing and determination of appeals), and
(c) except in so far as those orders otherwise provide, any orders of the House of Lords made with respect to the matters specified in section 11 of that Act (which relates to the procedure on appeals),

shall have effect as they have effect in relation to appeals under that Act.

15 Cases excluded from s12   [246]

(1) No certificate shall be granted under section 12 of this Act in respect of a decision of the judge in any proceedings where by virtue of any enactment, apart from the provisions of this Part of this Act, no appeal would lie from that decision to the Court of Appeal, with or without the leave of the judge or of the Court of Appeal.

(2) No certificate shall be granted under section 12 of this Act in respect of a decision of the judge where –

(b) by virtue of any enactment, apart from the provisions of this Part of this Act, no appeal would (with or without the leave of the Court of Appeal or of the House of Lords) lie from any decision of the Court of Appeal on an appeal from the decision of the judge.

(3) Where by virtue of any enactment, apart from the provisions of this Part of this Act, no appeal would lie to the Court of Appeal from the decision of the judge except with the leave of the judge or of the Court of Appeal, no certificate shall be granted under section 12 of this Act in respect of that decision unless it appears to the judge that apart from the provisions of this Part of this Act it would be a proper case for granting such leave.

(4) No certificate shall be granted under section 12 of this Act where the decision of the judge, or any order made by him in pursuance of that decision, is made in the exercise of jurisdiction to punish for contempt of court.

[As amended by the Supreme Court Act 1981, s152(4), Schedule 7.]

ADMINISTRATION OF JUSTICE ACT 1970
(1970 c 31)

11 Restriction on power of committal under   [247]
Debtors Act 1869

The jursidiction given by section 5 of the Debtors Act 1869 to commit to prison a person who makes default in payment of a debt, or instalment of a debt, due from him in pursuance of an order or judgment shall be exercisable only –

(a) by the High Court in respect of a High Court maintenance order; and

(b) by a county court in respect of –

(i) a High Court or a county court maintenance order; or

(ii) a judgment or order which is enforceable by a court in England and Wales and is for the payment of any of the taxes, contributions, or liabilities specified in Schedule 4 to this Act.

28 Other provisions for interpretation of Part II   **[248]**

(1) In this part of this Act, except where the context otherwise requires –

'High Court maintenance order', 'county court maintenance order' mean respectively a maintenance order enforceable by the High Court, a county court;

'maintenance order' means any order specified in Schedule 8 to this Act and includes such an order which has been discharged, if any arrears are recoverable thereunder.

SCHEDULE 4

TAXES, SOCIAL INSURANCE CONTRIBUTIONS, ETC SUBJECT TO SPECIAL ENFORCEMENT PROVISIONS IN PART II

1. Income tax or any other tax liability recoverable under section 65, 66 or 68 of the Taxes Management Act 1970.

3. State scheme premiums under Part III of the Pension Schemes Act 1993.

3A. Class 1, 2 and 4 contributions under Part I of the Social Security Contributions and Benefits Act 1992.

SCHEDULE 8

MAINTENANCE ORDERS FOR PURPOSES OF PART II OF THIS ACT

1. An order for alimony, maintenance or other payments made, or having effect as if made, under Part II of the Matrimonial Causes Act 1965 (ancillary relief in actions for divorce, etc).

2. An order for payments to or in respect of a child being an order made, or having effect as if made, under Part III of the said Act of 1965 (maintenance of children following divorce, etc).

2A. An order for periodical or other payments made, or having effect as if made, under Part II of the Matrimonial Causes Act 1973.

3. An order for maintenance or other payments to or in respect of a spouse or child being an order made under Part I of the Domestic Proceedings and Magistrates' Courts Act 1978.

4. An order for periodical or other payments made or having effect as if made under Schedule 1 to the Children Act 1989 …

[As amended by the Matrimonial Causes Act 1973, s54(1), Schedule 2, para 10(2); Courts and Legal Services Act 1990, s116, Schedule 16, para 37(1); Social Security (Consequential Provisions) Act 1992, s4 Schedule 2, para 6; Pension Schemes Act 1993, s190, Schedule 8, para 2.]

COURTS ACT 1971
(1971 c 23)

16 Appointment of Circuit judges   [249]

(1) Her Majesty may from time to time appoint as Circuit judges, to serve in the Crown Court and county courts and to carry out such other judicial functions as may be conferred on them under this or any other enactment, such qualified persons as may be recommended to Her by the Lord Chancellor.

(2) The maximum number of Circuit judges shall be such as may be determined from time to time by the Lord Chancellor with the concurrence of the Minister for the Civil Service.

(3) No person shall be qualified to be appointed a Circuit judge unless –

(a) he has a ten year Crown Court or ten year county court qualification within the meaning of section 71 of the Courts and Legal Services Act 1990;
(b) he is a Recorder; or
(c) he has held as a full-time appointment for at least three years one of the offices listed in Part 1A of Schedule 2.

(4) Before recommending any person to Her Majesty for appointment as a Circuit judge, the Lord Chancellor shall take steps to satisfy himself that that person's health is satisfactory ...

17 Retirement, removal and disqualification   [250]
of Circuit judges

(1) Subject to subsections (2) to (4) below, a Circuit judge shall vacate his office at the end of the completed year of service in which he attains the age of 72.

(2) Where the Lord Chancellor considers it desirable in the public interest to retain a Circuit judge in office after the time at which he would otherwise retire in accordance with subsection (1) above, he may from time to time authorise the continuance in office of that judge until such date, not being later than the date on which the judge attains the age of 75, as he thinks fit ...

(4) The Lord Chancellor may, if he thinks fit, remove a Circuit judge from office on the ground of incapacity or misbehaviour.

21 Appointment of Recorders   [251]

(1) Her Majesty may from time to time appoint qualified persons, to be known as Recorders, to act as part-time judges of the Crown Court and to carry out such other judicial functions as may be conferred on them under this or any other enactment.

(2) Every appointment of a person to be a Recorder shall be of a person recommended to Her Majesty by the Lord Chancellor, and no person shall be qualified to be appointed a Recorder unless he has a ten year Crown Court or ten year county court qualification, within the meaning of section 71 of the Courts and Legal Services Act 1990.

(3) The appointment of a person as a Recorder shall specify the term for which he is appointed and the frequency and duration of the occasions during that term on which he will be required to be available to undertake the duties of a Recorder.

(4) Subject to subsection (5) below the Lord Chancellor may, with the agreement of the Recorder concerned, from time to time extend for such period as he thinks appropriate the term for which a Recorder is appointed.

(5) Neither the initial term for which a Recorder is appointed nor any extension of that term under subsection (4) above shall be such as to continue his appointment as a Recorder after the end of the completed year of service in which he attains the age of 72.

(6) The Lord Chancellor may if he thinks fit terminate the appointment of a Recorder on the ground of incapacity or mis-behaviour or of a failure to comply with any requirement specified under subsection (3) above in the terms of his appointment ...

24 Deputy Circuit judges and assistant Recorders [252]

(1) If it appears to the Lord Chancellor it is expedient as a temporary measure to make an appointment under this section in order to facilitate the disposal of business in the Crown Court or a county court or official referees' business in the High Court, he may –

(a) appoint to be a deputy Circuit judge, during such period or on such occasions as he thinks fit, any person who has held office as a judge of the Court of Appeal or of the High Court or as a Circuit judge; or

(b) appoint to be an assistant Recorder, during such period or on such occasions as he thinks fit, any person who has a ten year Crown Court or ten year county court qualification, within the meaning of section 71 of the Courts and Legal Services Act 1990.

(2) Except as provided by subsection (3) below, during the period or on the occasions for which a deputy Circuit judge or assistant Recorder is appointed under this section he shall be treated for all purposes as, and accordingly may perform any of the functions of, a Circuit judge or a Recorder, as the case may be.

(3) A deputy Circuit judge appointed under this section shall not be treated as a Circuit judge for the purpose of any provision made by or under any enactment and relating to the appointment, retirement, removal or disqualification of Circuit judges, the tenure of office and oaths to be taken by such judges, or the remuneration, allowances or pensions of such judges; and section 21 of this Act shall not apply to an assistant Recorder appointed under this section.

(4) Notwithstanding the expiry of any period for which a person is appointed under this section a deputy Circuit judge or an assistant Recorder, he may attend at the Crown Court or a county court or, in the case of a deputy Circuit judge, as regards official referees' business, at the High Court for the purpose of continuing to deal with, giving judgment in, or dealing with any ancillary matter relating to, any case which may have been begun before him when sitting as a deputy Circuit judge or an assistant Recorder, and for that purpose and for the purpose of any proceedings subsequent thereon he shall be treated as a Circuit Judge or a Recorder, as the case may be ...

29 Accommodation in City of London [253]

(1) The courthouse and accommodation which up to the appointed day have been respectively known as the Central Criminal Court and the Mayor's and City of London Court shall continue to be known by those names, and it shall be the duty of the Common Council of the City of London (in this section referred to as 'the Common Council') to continue to make the said premises available for use for the sittings and business of those courts respectively ...

42 Local court for City of London ... [254]

(2) For the purpose of establishing a court to exercise so much of the jurisdiction

previously exercised by the Mayor's and City of London Court as is appropriate to a county court and for exercising any other jurisdiction which may hereafter be conferred on a county court, the City of London shall, by virtue of this section, become a county court district and accordingly the enactments relating to county courts shall apply in relation to the county court for the City of London as they apply in relation to a county court for any other county court district.

(3) Without prejudice to subsection (1) above, the county court for the district constituted by subsection (2) above shall be known as the Mayor's and City of London Court and the Circuit judge assigned to that district under section 20(1) of this Act shall be known as the judge of the Mayor's and City of London Court.

SCHEDULE 2

PART IA

Social Security Commissioner appointed under section 97 of the Social Security Act 1975.

President of Social Security Appeal Tribunals and Medical Appeal Tribunals or chairman of such a tribunal appointed under Schedule 10 to that Act ...

Coroner appointed under section 2 of the Coroners Act 1988.

Master of the Queen's Bench Division ...

Taxing Master of the Supreme Court ...

District judge.

Stipendiary magistrate.

[As amended by the Supreme Court Act 1981, s146; Courts and Legal Services Act 1990, s71(2), Schedule 10, para 31(1), (2), 32(2).]

ADMINISTRATION OF JUSTICE ACT 1973
(1973 c 15)

12 Retirement of higher judiciary in event of incapacity [255]

(1) Where the Lord Chancellor is satisfied by means of a medical certificate that a person holding office as Lord of Appeal in Ordinary ... is disabled by permanent infirmity from the performance of the duties of his office but is for the time being incapacitated from resigning it, then subject to subsection (2) ... below the Lord Chancellor may by instrument under his hand declare that person's office to have been vacated, and the instrument shall have the like effect for all purposes as if that person had on the date of the instrument resigned his office.

(2) A declaration under this section with respect to a Lord of Appeal in Ordinary shall be of no effect unless it is made with the concurrence of the senior of the Lords of Appeal or, if made with respect to him, with that of the next senior of them.

JURIES ACT 1974
(1974 c 23)

1 Qualification for jury service [256]

Subject to the provisions of this Act, every person shall be qualified to serve as a juror in the Crown Court, the High Court and county courts and be liable accordingly to attend for jury service when summoned under this Act, if –

(a) he is for the time being registered as a parliamentary or local government elector and is not less than 18 nor more than 70 years of age; and

(b) he has been ordinarily resident in the United Kingdom, the Channel Islands or the Isle of Man for any period of at least five years since attaining the age of thirteen,

but not if he is for the time being ineligible or disqualified for jury service; and the persons who are ineligible, and those who are disqualified, are those respectively listed in Parts I and II of Schedule 1 to this Act.

11 The ballot and swearing of jurors [257]

(1) The jury to try an issue before a court shall be selected by ballot in open court from the panel, or part of the panel, of jurors summoned to attend at the time and place in question.

(2) The power of summoning jurors under section 6 of this Act may be exercised after balloting has begun, as well as earlier, and if exercised after balloting has begun the court may dispense with balloting for persons summoned under that section.

(3) No two or more members of a jury to try an issue in a court shall be sworn together.

(4) Subject to subsection (5) below, the jury selected by any one ballot shall try only one issue (but any juror shall be liable to be selected on more than one ballot).

(5) Subsection (4) above shall not prevent –

(a) the trial of two or more issues by the same jury if the trial of the second or last issue begins within 24 hours from the time when the jury is constituted, or
(b) in a criminal case, the trial of fitness to plead by the same jury as that by whom the accused is being tried, if that is so directed by the court under section 4(4)(b) of the Criminal Procedure (Insanity) Act 1964, or
(c) in a criminal case beginning with a special plea, the trial of the accused on the general issue by the jury trying the special plea.

(6) In the cases within subsection (5)(a), (b) and (c) above the court may, on the trial of the second or any subsequent issue, instead of proceeding with the same jury in its entirety, order any juror to withdraw, if the court considers he could be justly challenged or excused, or if the parties to the proceedings consent, and the juror to replace him shall, subject to subsection (2) above, be selected by ballot in open court.

12 Challenge [258]

(1) In proceedings for the trial of any person for an offence on indictment –

(a) that person may challenge all or any of the jurors for cause, and
(b) any challenge for cause shall be tried by the judge before whom that person is to be tried.

(2) Any party to county court proceedings to be tried by a jury shall have the same right of challenge to all or any of the jurors as he would have in the High Court.

(3) A challenge to a juror in any court shall be made after his name has been drawn by ballot (unless the court, pursuant to section 11(2) of this Act, has dispensed with balloting for him) and before he is sworn.

(4) The fact that a person summoned to serve on a jury is not qualified to serve shall be a ground of challenge for cause; but subject to that, and to the foregoing provisions of this section, nothing in this Act affects the law relating to challenge of jurors.

(5) In section 29 of the Juries Act 1825 (challenges to jurors by the Crown) the words 'the Crown Court' shall continue to be substituted for the words 'any of the courts hereinbefore mentioned', notwithstanding the repeal by this Act of paragraph 3(2) of Schedule 4 to the Courts Act 1971 and of the entries relating to the said Act in Schedule 5 to the Criminal Justice Act 1972.

(6) Without prejudice to subsection (4) above, the right of challenge to the array, that is to say the right of challenge on the ground that the person responsible for summoning the jurors in question is biased or has acted improperly, shall continue to be unaffected by the fact that, since the coming into operation of section 31 of the Courts Act 1971 (which is replaced by this Act), the responsibility for summoning jurors for service in the Crown Court, the High Court and county courts has lain with the Lord Chancellor.

17 Majority verdicts   [259]

(1) Subject to subsections (3) and (4) below, the verdict of a jury in proceedings in the Crown Court or the High Court need not be unanimous if –

(a) in a case where there are not less than 11 jurors, ten of them agree on the verdict; and
(b) in a case where there are ten jurors, nine of them agree on the verdict.

(2) Subject to subsection (4) below, the verdict of a jury (that is to say a complete jury of eight) in proceedings in a county court need not be unanimous if seven of them agree on the verdict.

(3) The Crown Court shall not accept a verdict of guilty by virtue of subsection (1) above unless the foreman of the jury has stated in open court the number of jurors who respectively agreed to and dissented from the verdict.

(4) No court shall accept a verdict by virtue of subsection (1) or (2) above unless it appears to the court that the jury have had such period of time for deliberation as the court thinks reasonable having regard to the nature and complexity of the case; and the Crown Court shall in any event not accept such a verdict unless it appears to the court that the jury have had at least two hours for deliberation.

(5) This section is without prejudice to any practice in civil proceedings by which a court may accept a majority verdict with the consent of the parties, or by which the parties may agree to proceed in any case with an incomplete jury.

SCHEDULE 1

INELIGIBILITY AND DISQUALIFICATION FOR AND EXCUSAL FROM JURY SERVICE

PART I

PERSONS INELIGIBLE

GROUP A

The Judiciary

Holders of high judicial office within the meaning of the Appellate Jurisdiction Act 1876.

Circuit judges and Recorders.

Masters of the Supreme Court.

Registrars and assistant registrars of any court.

Metropolitan and other stipendiary magistrates.

Justices of the peace.

The Chairman or President, the Vice-Chairman or Vice-President, and the registrar and assistant registrar of any Tribunal.

A person who has at any time been a person falling within any description specified above in this Group.

GROUP B

Others concerned with administration of justice

Barristers and solicitors, whether or not in actual practice as such.

Solicitors' articled clerks.

Barristers' clerks and their assistants.

Any person who is not a barrister or solicitor but who is an authorised advocate or authorised litigator (as defined by section 119(1) of the Courts and Legal Services Act 1990) and –

(a) any legal executive or person corresponding to a legal executive; or
(b) any person corresponding to a barristers' clerk or assistant clerk,

who is employed by such an authorised advocate or authorised litigator.

Legal executives in the employment of solicitors.

Public notaries.

The Director of Public Prosecutions and members of his staff.

Officers employed under the Lord Chancellor and concerned wholly or mainly with the day-to-day administration of the legal system or any part of it.

Officers and staff of any court, if their work is wholly or mainly concerned with the day-to-day administration of the court.

Coroners, deputy coroners and assistant coroners.

Justices' clerks and their assistants.

Clerks and other officers appointed under section 15 of the Administration of Justice Act 1964 (Inner London magistrates courts administration).

Active Elder Brethren of the Corporation of Trinity House of Deptford Strond.

A shorthandwriter in any court.

Governors, chaplains, medical officers and other officers of penal establishments; members of boards of visitors for penal establishments.

('Penal establishment' for this purpose means any establishment regulated by the Prison Act 1952.)

The warden or a member of the staff of a probation hostel or bail hostel (within the meaning of the Probation Service Act 1993).

Probation officers and persons appointed to assist them.

Members of the Parole Board; members of local review committees established under the Criminal Justice Act 1967.

A member of any police force (including a person on central service under section 43 of the Police Act 1964); special constables; a member of any constabulary maintained under statute; a person employed in any capacity by virtue of which he has the powers and privileges of a constable.

A member of a police authority within the meaning of the Police Act 1964; a member of any body (corporate or other) with responsibility for appointing members of a constabulary maintained under statute.

Inspectors of Constabulary appointed by Her Majesty; assistant inspectors of constabulary appointed by the Secretary of State.

Civilians employed for police purposes under section 10 of the Police Act 1964, members of the metropolitan civil staffs within the meaning of section 15 of the Superannuation (Miscellaneous Provisions) Act 1967 (persons employed under the Commissioner of Police of the Metropolis, Inner London justices' clerks, etc.)

A person in charge of, or employed in, any forensic science laboratory.

Court security officers.

Prisoner custody officers

A person who at any time within the last ten years has been a person falling within any description specified above in this Group.

GROUP C

The clergy, etc

A man in holy orders; a regular minister of any religious denomination.

A vowed member of any religious order living in a monastery, convent or other religious community.

GROUP D

Mentally disordered persons

A person who suffers or has suffered from mental illness, psychopathic disorder, mental handicap or severe mental handicap and on account of that condition either –

(a) is resident in a hospital or other similar institution; or

(b) regularly attends for treatment by a medical practitioner.

A person for the time being in guardianship under section 7 of the Mental Health Act 1983.

A person who, under Part VII of that Act, has been determined by a judge to be incapable, by reason of mental disorder, of managing and administering his property and affairs.

(In this Group –

(a) 'mental handicap' means a state of arrested or incomplete development of mind (not amounting to severe mental handicap) which includes significant impairment of intelligence and social functioning;

(b) 'severe mental handicap' means a state of arrested or incomplete development of mind which includes severe impairment of intelligence and social functioning;

(c) other expressions are to be construed in accordance with the said Act of 1983.)

PART II

PERSONS DISQUALIFIED

A person who has at any time been sentenced in the United Kingdom. the Channel Islands or the Isle of Man –

(a) to imprisonment for life, custody for life or to a term of imprisonment or youth custody of five years or more, or

(b) to be detained during Her Majesty's pleasure, during the pleasure of the Secretary of State or during the pleasure of the Governor of Northern Ireland.

A person who at any time in the last ten years has, in the United Kingdom or the Channel Islands or the Isle of Man –

(a) served any part of a sentence of imprisonment, youth custody or detention; or

(b) been detained in a Borstal institution; or

(c) had passed on him or (as the case may be) made in respect of him a suspended sentence of imprisonment or order for detention; or

(d) had made in respect of him a community service order.

A person who at any time in the last five years has, in the United Kingdom or the Channel Islands or the Isle of Man, been placed on probation.

PART III

PERSONS EXCUSABLE AS OF RIGHT

General

Persons more than 65 years of age.

Parliament

Peers and peeress entitled to receive writs of summons to attend the House of Lords.

Members of the House of Commons.

Officers of the House of Lords.

Officers of the House of Commons.

European Parliament

Representatives to the Parliament of the European Communities.

The Forces

Full-time serving members of any of Her Majesty's naval, military or air forces.

(A person excusable under this head shall be under no obligation to attend in pursuance of a summons for jury service if his commanding officer certifies to the officer issuing the summons that it would be prejudicial to the efficiency of the service if the person were required to be absent from duty.)

Medical and other similar professions

The following, if actually practising their profession and registered (including provisionally or temporarily registered), enrolled or certified under the enactments relating to that profession –

medical practitioners,

dentists,

nurses,

midwives,

veterinary surgeons and veterinary practitioners,

pharmaceutical chemists.

[As amended by the Criminal Law Act 1977, s65, Schedule 12; European Assembly Elections Act 1978, s5(1); Criminal Justice Act 1982, s77, Schedule 14, para 35(b)(i); Mental Health (Amendment) Act 1982, s65(1), Schedule 3, Pt I; Mental Health Act 1983, s148, Schedule 4, para 37; Juries (Disqualification) Act 1984, s1(1); Criminal Justice Act 1988, ss119(1), (2), 170(2), Schedule 16, s123(6), Schedule 8, Pt I, para 8; Courts and Legal Services Act 1990, s125(2), (3), Schedule 17, para 7, Schedule 18, para 5; Criminal Justice Act 1991, s100, Schedule 11, para 18; Probation Service Act 1993, s32(2), (3), Schedule 3, para 5, Schedule 4.]

SOLICITORS ACT 1974
(1974 c 47)

1 Qualifications for practising as solicitor [260]

No person shall be qualified to act as a solicitor unless –

(a) he has been admitted as a solicitor, and

(b) his name is on the roll, and

(c) he has in force a certificate issued by the Society in accordance with the provisions of this Part authorising him to practise as a solicitor (in this Act referred to as a 'practising certificate').

1A Practising certificates: employed solicitors [261]

A person who has been admitted as a solicitor and whose name is on the roll shall, if he would not otherwise be taken to be acting as a solicitor, be taken for the purposes of this Act to be so acting if he is employed in connection with the provision of any legal services –

(a) by any person who is qualified to act as a solicitor;

(b) by any partnership at least one member of which is so qualified; or

(c) by a body recognised by the Council of the Law Society under section 9 of the Administration of Justice Act 1985 (incorporated practices).

2 Training regulations [262]

(1) The Society, with the concurrence of the Lord Chancellor, the Lord Chief Justice and the Master of the Rolls, may make regulations (in this Act referred to as 'training regulations') about education and training for persons seeking to be admitted or to practise as solicitors

(3) Training regulations –

(a) may prescribe –

(i) the education and training, whether by service under articles or otherwise, to be undergone by persons seeking admission as solicitors;

(ii) any education or training to be undergone by persons who have been admitted as solicitors;

(iii) the examinations or other tests to be undergone by persons seeking admission as solicitors or who have been admitted;

(iv) the qualifications and reciprocal duties and responsibilities of persons undertaking to give education or training for the purposes of the regulations or undergoing such education or training; and

(v) the circumstances in which articles may be discharged or education or training under the regulations may be terminated;

(b) may require persons who have been admitted as solicitors to hold practising certificates while they are undergoing education or training under the regulations;

(c) may include provision for the charging of fees by the Society and the application of fees which the Society receives;

(d) may make different provision for different classes of persons and different circumstances.

(4) Where, under Schedule 4 to the Courts and Legal Services Act 1990 (approval of certain regulations in connection with the grant of rights of audience or rights to conduct litigation), the Lord Chancellor, the Lord Chief Justice or the Master of the Rolls approves any regulation made under this section he shall be taken, for the purposes of this section, to have concurred in the making of that regulation.

(5) Subsection (4) shall have effect whether or not the regulation required to be approved under Schedule 4 to the Act of 1990.

3 Admission as solicitor [263]

(1) Subject to section 4 and to section 20(3) of the Justices of the Peace Act 1949 (which relates to the admission as solicitors of certain persons who have served as assistant to a justices' clerk), no person shall be admitted as a solicitor unless he has obtained a certificate from the Society that the Society –

(a) is satisfied that he has complied with training regulations, and

(b) is satisfied as to his character and his suitability to be a solicitor.

(2) Any person who has obtained a certificate that the Society is satisfied as mentioned in subsection (1) may apply to the Master of the Rolls to be admitted as a solicitor; and if any such person so applies, the Master of the Rolls shall, unless cause to the contrary is shown to his satisfaction, in writing, and in such manner and form as the Master of the Rolls may from time to time think fit, admit that person to be a solicitor.

6 Keeping of the roll   [264]

(1) The Society shall continue to keep a list of all solicitors of the Supreme Court, called 'the roll'.

(2) The roll may be kept by means of a computer.

(3) If the roll is kept by means of a computer, the Society shall make any entry available for inspection in legible form during office hours, without payment, by any person who applies to inspect it.

(4) If the roll is not kept by means of a computer, any person may inspect it during office hours without payment.

10 Issue of practising certificates   [265]

(1) Subject to sections 11 and 12, the Society shall issue a practising certificate to a person who applies for one, if it is satisfied, within 21 days of receipt of his application, –

    (a) that his name is on the roll; and
    (b) that he is not suspended from practice; and
    (c) that his application complies with any regulations under section 28; and
    (d) that he is complying with such training regulations (if any) as apply to him; and
    (e) that he is complying with any indemnity rules or is exempt from them.

(2) At any time when regulations under section 28 specify a training condition or training conditions, any practising certificate issued to an applicant by the Society shall be issued subject to that condition or one of those conditions if it appears to the Society that training regulations will apply to him at the end of 21 days from the Society's receipt of his application.

(3) At any time when regulations under section 28 specify an indemnity condition or indemnity conditions, any practising certificate issued to an applicant by the Society shall be issued subject to that condition or one of those conditions if it appears to the Society that he will be exempt from indemnity rules at the end of 21 days from the Society's receipt of his application.

19 Rights of practising and rights of audience   [266]

(1) Subject to subsection (2), every person qualified in accordance with section 1 may practise as a solicitor –

    (a) in the Supreme Court;
    (b) in any county court;
    (c) in all courts and before all persons having jurisdiction in ecclesiastical matters; and
    (d) in all matters relating to applications to obtain notarial faculties,

and shall be entitled to all the rights and privileges, and may exercise and perform all the powers and duties, formerly appertaining to the office or profession of a proctor in the provincial, diocesan or other jurisdictions in England and Wales.

(2) Nothing in subsection (1) shall affect the provisions of section 94 of the Supreme Court Act 1981, section 13 or 60 of the County Courts Act 1984 or any other enactment in force at the commencement of this Act which restricts the right of any solicitor to practise as such in any court.

(3) Nothing in subsection (1) or (2) shall prejudice or affect any right of practising or being heard in, before or by any court, tribunal or other body which immediately before the commencement of this Act was enjoyed by virtue of any enactment, rule, order or regulation or by custom or otherwise by persons qualified to act as solicitors.

31 Rules as to professional practice, conduct [267] and discipline

(1) Without prejudice to any other provision of this Part the Council may, if they think fit, make rules, with the concurrence of the Master of the Rolls, for regulating in respect of any matter the professional practice, conduct and discipline of solicitors.

(2) If any solicitor fails to comply with rules made under this section, any person may make a complaint in respect of that failure to the Tribunal.

(3) Where, under Schedule 4 to the Courts and Legal Services Act 1990 (approval of certain rules in connection with the grant of rights of audience or rights to conduct litigation), the Master of the Rolls approves any rule made under this section he shall be taken, for the purposes of this section, to have concurred in the making of that rule.

(4) Subsection (3) shall have effect whether or not the rule required to be approved under Schedule 4 to the Act of 1990.

46 Solicitors Disciplinary Tribunal [268]

(1) Applications and complaints made by virtue of any provision of this Act shall be made, except so far as other provision is made by this Act or by any regulations under it, to the tribunal known as the 'Solicitors Disciplinary Tribunal'.

(2) The Master of the Rolls shall appoint the members of the Tribunal.

(3) The Tribunal shall consist –

(a) of practising solicitors of not less than ten years' standing (in this section referred to as 'solicitor members'); and
(b) of persons who are neither solicitors nor barristers (in this section referred to as 'lay members').

(4) A member of the Tribunal shall hold and vacate his office in accordance with the terms of his appointment and shall, on ceasing to hold office, be eligible for re-appointment.

(5) There shall be paid to the lay members out of money provided by Parliament such fees and allowances as the Lord Chancellor may, with the approval of the Minister for the Civil Service, determine.

(6) Subject to subsections (7) and (8), the Tribunal shall be deemed to be properly constituted if –

(a) at least three members are present; and
(b) at least one lay member is present; and
(c) the number of solicitor members present exceeds the number of lay members present.

(7) For the purpose of hearing and determining applications and complaints the Tribunal shall consist of not more than three members.

(8) A decision of the Tribunal on an application or complaint may be announced by a single member ...

47 Jurisdiction and powers of Tribunal [269]

(1) Any application –

(a) to strike the name of a solicitor off the roll;

(b) to require a solicitor to answer allegations contained in an affidavit;

(c) to require a former solicitor whose name has been removed from or struck off the roll to answer allegations contained in an affidavit relating to a time when he was a solicitor;

(d) by a solicitor who has been suspended from practice for an unspecified period, by order of the Tribunal, for the termination of that suspension;

(e) by a former solicitor whose name has been struck off the roll to have his name restored to the roll;

(f) by a former solicitor in respect of whom a direction has been given under subsection (2)(g) to have his name restored to the roll,

shall be made to the Tribunal; but nothing in this subsection shall affect any jurisdiction over solicitors exercisable by the Master of the Rolls, or by any judge of the High Court, by virtue of section 50.

(2) Subject to subsection (3) and to section 54, on the hearing of any application or complaint made to the Tribunal under this Act, other than an application under section 43, the Tribunal shall have power to make such order as it may think fit, and any such order may in particular include provision for any of the following matters –

(a) the striking off the roll of the name of the solicitor to whom the application or complaint relates;

(b) the suspension of that solicitor from practice indefinitely or for a specified period;

(c) the payment by that solicitor or former solicitor of a penalty not exceeding £5,000, which shall be forfeit to Her Majesty;

(d) in the circumstances referred to in subsection (2A), the exclusion of that solicitor from legal aid work (either permanently or for a specified period);

(e) the termination of that solicitor's unspecified period of suspension from practice;

(f) the restoration to the roll of the name of a former solicitor whose name has been struck off the roll and to whom the application relates;

(g) in the case of a former solicitor whose name has been removed from the roll, a direction prohibiting the restoration of his name to the roll except by order of the Tribunal;

(h) in the case of an application under subsection (1)(f), the restoration of the applicant's name to the roll;

(i) the payment by any party of costs or a contribution towards costs of such amount as the Tribunal may consider reasonable.

(2A) An order of the Tribunal may make provision for the exclusion of a solicitor from legal aid work as mentioned in subsection (2)(d) where the Tribunal determines that there is good reason for doing so arising out of –

(a) his conduct in connection with the giving of advice or assistance under Part I of the Legal Aid Act 1974;

(b) his conduct in connection with the provision of services for any persons receiving legal aid under that Part of that Act;

(c) his conduct in connection with the provision of services for any legally assisted person in pursuance of Part II of that Act; or

(d) his conduct in connection with the provision of advice and representation pursuant to section 1 of the Legal Aid Act 1982 (duty solicitors); or

(e) his professional conduct generally;

and the reference in each of paragraphs (b) and (c) to the provision of services for any such person as is there mentioned includes the provision of services for any such person in the capacity of agent for that person's solicitor.

(2B) Where the Tribunal makes any such order as is re-referred to in subsection (2A) in the case of a solicitor who is a member of a firm of solicitors, the Tribunal may, if it thinks fit, order that any other person who is for the time being a member of the firm shall be excluded (either permanently or for a specified period) from legal aid work.

(2C) The Tribunal shall not make an order under subsection (2B) excluding any person from legal aid work unless an opportunity is given to him to show cause why the order should not be made.

(2D) Any person excluded from legal aid work by an order under this section may make an application to the Tribunal for an order terminating his exclusion from such work.

(3) On proof of the commission of an offence with respect to which express provision is made by any section of this Act, the Tribunal shall, without prejudice to its power of making an order as to costs, impose the punishment, or one of the punishments, specified in that section.

(3A) Where, on the hearing of any application or complaint under this Act, the Tribunal is satisfied that more than one allegation is proved against the person to whom the application or complaint relates it may impose a separate penalty (by virtue of subsection (2)(c)) with respect to each such allegation ...

[As amended by the Supreme Court Act 1981, s152(1), Schedule 5; County Courts Act 1984, s148(1), Schedule 2, Pt V, para 49; Administration of Justice Act 1985, s44; Courts and Legal Services Act 1990, ss85, 92(1)-(4), 125(2), (7), Schedule 17, paras 8, 10, Schedule 20.]

SEX DISCRIMINATION ACT 1975
(1975 c 65)

35A Discrimination by, or in relation to, barristers   [270]

(1) It is unlawful for a barrister or barrister's clerk, in relation to any offer of a pupillage or tenancy, to discriminate against a woman –

(a) in the arrangements which are made for the purpose of determining to whom it should be offered;

(b) in respect of any terms on which it is offered; or

(c) by refusing, or deliberately omitting, to offer it to her.

(2) It is unlawful for a barrister or barrister's clerk, in relation to a woman who is a pupil or tenant in the chambers in question, to discriminate against her –

(a) in respect of any terms applicable to her as a pupil or tenant;

(b) in the opportunities for training, or gaining experience, which are afforded or denied to her;

(c) in the benefits, facilities or services which are afforded or denied to her; or

(d) by terminating her pupillage or by subjecting her to any pressure to leave the chambers or other detriment.

(3) It is unlawful for any person, in relation to the giving, withholding or acceptance of instructions to a barrister, to discriminate against a woman.

(4) In this section –

'barrister's clerk' includes any person carrying out any of the functions of a barrister's clerk; and

'pupil', 'pupillage', 'tenancy' and 'tenant' have the meanings commonly associated with their use in the context of a set of barristers' chambers.

(5) Section 3 applies for the purposes of this section as it applies for the purposes of any provision of Part II …

As inserted by the Courts and Legal Services Act 1990, s64(1).

BAIL ACT 1976
(1976 c 63)

1 Meaning of 'bail in criminal proceedings' [271]

(1) In this Act 'bail in criminal proceedings' means –

(a) bail grantable in or in connection with proceedings for an offence to a person who is accused or convicted of the offence, or

(b) bail grantable in connection with an offence to a person who is under arrest for the offence or for whose arrest for the offence a warrant (endorsed for bail) is being issued.

(2) In this Act 'bail' means bail grantable under the law (including common law) for the time being in force.

(3) Except as provided by section 13(3) of this Act, this section does not apply to bail in or in connection with proceedings outside England and Wales.

(4) This section does not apply to bail granted before the coming into force of this Act.

(5) This section applies –

(a) whether the offence was committed in England or Wales or elsewhere, and

(b) whether it is an offence under the law of England and Wales, or of any other country or territory.

(6) Bail in criminal proceedings shall be granted (and in particular shall be granted unconditionally or conditionally) in accordance with this Act.

2 Other definitions [272]

(1) In this Act, unless the context otherwise requires, 'conviction' includes –

(a) a finding of guilt,

(b) a finding that a person is not guilty by reason of insanity,

(c) a finding under section 30(1) of the Magistrates' Courts Act 1980 (remand for medical examination) that the person in question did the act or made the omission charged, and

(d) a conviction of an offence for which an order is made placing the offender on probation or discharging him absolutely or conditionally,

and 'convicted' shall be construed accordingly.

(2) In this Act, unless the context otherwise requires –

'bail hostel' and 'probation hostel' have the same meanings as in the Powers of Criminal Courts Act 1973,

'child' means a person under the age of 14,

'court' includes a judge of a court or a justice of the peace and, in the case of a specified court, includes a judge or (as the case may be) justice having powers

to act in connection with proceedings before that court,
'Courts-Martial Appeal rules' means rules made under section 49 of the Courts-Martial (Appeals) Act 1968,
'Crown Court rules' means rules made under section 15 of the Courts Act 1971,
'magistrates' courts rules' means rules made under section 15 of the Justices of the Peace Act 1949,
'offence' includes an alleged offence,
'proceedings against a fugitive offender' means proceeding under the Extradition Act 1989 or section 2(1) or 4(3) of the Backing of Warrants (Republic of Ireland) Act 1965,
'Supreme Court rules' means rules made under section 99 of the Supreme Court of Judicature (Consolidation) Act 1925,
'surrender to custody' means, in relation to a person released on bail, surrendering himself into the custody of the court or of the constable (according to the requirements of the grant of bail) at the time and place for the time being appointed for him to do so,
'vary', in relation to bail, means imposing further conditions after bail is granted, or varying or rescinding conditions,
'young person' means a person who has attained the age of 14 and is under the age of 17.

(3) Where an enactment (whenever passed) which relates to bail in criminal proceedings refers to the person bailed appearing before a court it is to be construed unless the context otherwise requires as referring to his surrendering himself into the custody of the court.

(4) Any reference in this Act to any other enactment is a reference thereto as amended, and includes a reference thereto as extended or applied, by or under any other enactment, including this Act.

3 General provisions [273]

(1) A person granted bail in criminal proceedings shall be under a duty to surrender to custody, and that duty is enforceable in accordance with section 6 of this Act.

(2) No recognizance for his surrender to custody shall be taken from him.

(3) Except as provided by this section –

(a) no security for his surrender to custody shall be taken from him,
(b) he shall not be required to provide a surety or sureties for his surrender to custody, and
(c) no other requirement shall be imposed on him as a condition of bail.

(4) He may be required, before release on bail, to provide a surety or sureties to secure his surrender to custody.

(5) If it appears that he is unlikely to remain in Great Britain until the time appointed for him to surrender to custody, he may be required, before release on bail, to give security for his surrender to custody.

The security may be given by him or on his behalf.

(6) He may be required (but only by a court) to comply, before release on bail or later, with such requirements as appear to the court to be necessary to secure that –

(a) he surrenders to custody,
(b) he does not commit an offence while on bail,
(c) he does not interfere with witnesses or otherwise obstruct the course of justice whether in relation to himself or any other person,

(d) he makes himself available for the purpose of enabling inquiries or a report to be made to assist the court in dealing with him for the offence.

(6ZA) Where he is required under subsection (6) above to reside in a bail hostel or probation hostel, he may also be required to comply with the rules of the hostel.

(6A) In the case of a person accused of murder the court granting bail shall, unless it considers that satisfactory reports on his mental condition have already been obtained, impose as conditions of bail –

(a) a requirement that the accused shall undergo examination by two medical practitioners for the purpose of enabling such reports to be prepared; and
(b) a requirement that he shall for that purpose attend such an institution or place as the court directs and comply with any other directions which may be given to him for that purpose by either of those practitioners.

(6B) Of the medical practitioners referred to in subsection (6A) above at least one shall be a practitioner approved for the purposes of section 12 of the Mental Health Act 1983.

(7) If a parent or guardian of a child or young person consents to be surety for the child or young person for the purposes of this subsection, the parent or guardian may be required to secure that the child or young person complies with any requirement imposed on him by virtue of subsection (6) or (6A) above but –

(a) no requirement shall be imposed on the parent or the guardian of a young person by virtue of this subsection where it appears that the young person will attain the age of 17 before the time to be appointed for him to surrender to custody; and
(b) the parent or guardian shall not be required to secure compliance with any requirement to which his consent does not extend and shall not, in respect of those requirements to which his consent does extend, be bound in a sum greater than £50.

(8) Where a court has granted bail in criminal proceedings that court or, where that court has committed a person on bail to the Crown Court for trial or to be sentenced or otherwise dealt with, that court or the Crown Court may on application

(a) by or on behalf of the person to whom bail was granted, or
(b) by the prosecutor or a constable,

vary the conditions of bail or impose conditions in respect of bail which has been granted unconditionally.

(8A) Where a notice of transfer is given under section 4 of the Criminal Justice Act 1987, subsection (8) above shall have effect in relation to a person in relation to whose case the notice is given as if he had been committed on bail to the Crown Court for trial.

(9) This section is subject to subsection (2) of section 30 of the Magistrates' Courts Act 1980 (conditions of bail on remand for medical examination).

(10) Where a custody time limit has expired this section shall have effect as if –

(a) subsections (4) and (5) (sureties and security for his surrender to custody) were omitted;
(b) in subsection (6) (conditions of bail) for the words 'before release on bail or later' there were substituted the words 'after release on bail'.

4 General right to bail of accused persons and others   [274]

(1) A person to whom this section applies shall be granted bail except as provided in Schedule 1 to this Act.

(2) This section applies to a person who is accused of an offence when –

(a) he appears or is brought before a magistrates' court or the Crown Court in the course of or in connection with proceedings for the offence, or

(b) he applies to a court for bail in connection with the proceedings.

This subsection does not apply as respects proceedings on or after a person's conviction of the offence or proceedings against a fugitive offender for the offence.

(3) This section also applies to a person who, having been convicted of an offence, appears or is brought before a magistrates' court to be dealt with under Part II of Schedule 2 to the Criminal Justice Act 1991 (breach of requirement of probation, community service, combination or curfew order).

(4) This section also applies to a person who has been convicted of an offence and whose case is adjourned by the court for the purpose of enabling inquiries or a report to be made to assist the court in dealing-with him for the offence.

(5) Schedule 1 to this Act also has effect as respects conditions of bail for a person to whom this section applies.

(6) In Schedule 1 to this Act 'the defendant' means a person to whom this section applies and any reference to a defendant whose case is adjourned for inquiries or a report is a reference to a person to whom this section applies by virtue of subsection (4) above.

(7) This section is subject to section 41 of the Magistrates' Courts Act 1980 (restriction of bail by magistrates' court in cases of treason).

(8) Where a custody time limit has expired this section shall have effect as if, in subsection (1), the words 'except as provided in Schedule 1 to this Act' were omitted.

5 Supplementary provisions about decisions on bail [275]

(3) Where a magistrates' court or the Crown Court –

(a) withholds bail in criminal proceedings, or

(b) imposes conditions in granting bail in criminal proceedings, or

(c) varies any conditions of bail or imposes conditions in respect of bail in criminal proceedings,

and does so in relation to a person to whom section 4 of this Act applies, then the court shall, with a view to enabling him to consider making an application in the matter to another court, give reasons for withholding bail or for imposing or varying the conditions.

(4) A court which is by virtue of subsection (3) above required to give reasons for its decision shall include a note of those reasons in the record of its decision and shall (except in a case where, by virtue of subsection (5) below, this need not be done) give a copy of that note to the person in relation to whom the decision was taken.

(5) The Crown Court need not give a copy of the note of the reasons for its decision to the person in relation to whom the decision was taken where that person is represented by counsel or a solicitor unless his counsel or solicitor requests the court to do so.

(6) Where a magistrates' court withholds bail in criminal proceedings from a person who is not represented by counsel or a solicitor, the court shall –

(a) if it is committing him for trial to the Crown Court, or if it issues a certificate under subsection (6A) below, inform him that he may apply to the High Court or to the Crown Court to be granted bail;

(b) in any other case, inform him that he may apply to the High Court for that purpose.

(6A) Where in criminal proceedings –

(a) a magistrates' court remands a person in custody under any of the following provisions of the Magistrates' Courts Act 1980 –

(i) section 5 (adjournment of inquiry into offence);
(ii) section 10 (adjournment of trial);
(iii) section 18 (initial procedure on information against adult for offence triable either way); or
(iv) section 30 (remand for medical examination),

after hearing full argument on an application for bail from him; and
(b) either –

(i) it has not previously heard such argument on an application for bail from him in those proceedings; or
(ii) it has previously heard full argument from him on such an application but it is satisfied that there has been a change in his circumstances or that new considerations have been placed before it,

it shall be the duty of the court to issue a certificate in the prescribed form that they heard full argument on his application for bail before they refused the application.

(6B) Where the court issues a certificate under subsection (6A) above in a case to which paragraph (b)(ii) of that subsection applies, it shall state in the certificate the nature of the change of circumstances or the new considerations which caused it to hear a further fully argued bail application.

(6C) Where a court issues a certificate under subsection (6A) above it shall cause the person to whom it refuses bail to be given a copy of the certificate.

(7) Where a person has given security in pursuance of section 3(5) above and a court is satisfied that he failed to surrender to custody then, unless it appears that he had reasonable cause for his failure, the court may order the forfeiture of the security.

(8) If a court orders the forfeiture of a security under subsection (7) above, the court may declare that the forfeiture extends to such amount less than the full value of the security as it thinks fit to order.

(8A) An order under subsection (7) above shall, unless previously revoked, take effect at the end of 21 days beginning with the day on which it is made.

(8B) A court which has ordered the forfeiture of a security under subsection (7) above may, if satisfied on an application made by or on behalf of the person who gave it that he did after all have reasonable cause for his failure to surrender to custody, by order remit the forfeiture or declare that it extends to such amount less than the full value of the security as it thinks fit to order.

(8C) An application under subsection (8B) above may be made before or after the order for forfeiture has taken effect, but shall not be entertained unless the court is satisfied that the prosecution was given reasonable notice of the applicant's intention to make it.

(9) A security which has been ordered to be forfeited by a court under subsection (7) above shall, to the extent of the forfeiture –

(a) if it consists of money, be accounted for and paid in the same manner as a fine imposed by that court would be;
(b) if it does not consist of money, be enforced by such magistrates' court as may be specified in the order.

(9A) Where an order is made under subsection (8B) above after the order for forfeiture of the security in question has taken effect, any money which would have fallen to be repaid or paid over to the person who gave the security if the order under subsection (8B) had been made before the order for forfeiture took effect shall be repaid or paid over to him.

(10) In this section 'prescribed' means, in relation to the decision of a court or an officer of a court, prescribed by Supreme Court rules, Courts-Martial Appeal rules, Crown Court rules or magistrates' courts rules, as the case requires or, in relation to a decision of a constable, prescribed by direction of the Secretary of State.

6 Offence of absconding by person released on bail   [276]

(1) If a person who has been released on bail in criminal proceedings fails without reasonable cause to surrender to custody he shall be guilty of an offence.

(2) If a person who –

(a) has been released on bail in criminal proceedings, and
(b) having reasonable cause therefor, has failed to surrender to custody,

fails to surrender to custody at the appointed place as soon after the appointed time as is reasonably practicable he shall be guilty of an offence.

(3) It shall be for the accused to prove that he had reasonable cause for his failure to surrender to custody.

(4) A failure to give to a person granted bail in criminal proceedings a copy of the record of the decision shall not constitute a reasonable cause for that person's failure to surrender to custody.

(5) An offence under subsection (1) or (2) above shall be punishable either on summary conviction or as if it were a criminal contempt of court.

(6) Where a magistrates' court convicts a person of an offence under subsection (1) or (2) above the court may, if it thinks –

(a) that the circumstances of the offence are such that greater punishment should be inflicted for that offence than the court has power to inflict, or
(b) in a case where it commits that person for trial to the Crown Court for another offence, that it would be appropriate for him to be dealt with for the offence under subsection (1) or (2) above by the court before which he is tried for the other offence,

commit him in custody or on bail to the Crown Court for sentence.

(7) A person who is convicted summarily of an offence under subsection (1) or (2) above and is not committed to the Crown Court for sentence shall be liable to imprisonment for a term not exceeding three months or to a fine not exceeding level 5 on the standard scale or to both and a person who is so committed for sentence or is dealt with as for such a contempt shall be liable to imprisonment for a term not exceeding 12 months or to a fine or to both ...

7 Liability to arrest for absconding or breaking conditions of bail   [277]

(1) If a person who has been released on bail in criminal proceedings and is under a duty to surrender into the custody of a court fails to surrender to custody at the time appointed for him to do so the court may issue a warrant for his arrest.

(2) If a person who has been released on bail in criminal proceedings absents himself from the court at any time after he has surrendered into the custody of the court and before the court is ready to begin or to resume the hearing of the proceedings, the court may issue a warrant for his arrest; but no warrant shall be

issued under this subsection where that person is absent in accordance with leave given to him by or on behalf of the court.

(3) A person who has been released on bail in criminal proceedings and is under a duty to surrender into the custody of a court may be arrested without warrant by a constable –

(a) if the constable has reasonable grounds for believing that that person is not likely to surrender to custody;

(b) if the constable has reasonable grounds for believing that that person is likely to break any of the conditions of his bail or has reasonable grounds for suspecting that that person has broken any of those conditions; or

(c) in a case where that person was released on bail with one or more surety or sureties, if a surety notifies a constable in writing that that person is unlikely to surrender to custody and that for that reason the surety wishes to be relieved of his obligations as a surety.

(4) A person arrested in pursuance of subsection (3) above –

(a) shall, except where he was arrested within 24 hours of the time appointed for him to surrender to custody, be brought as soon as practicable and in any event within 24 hours after his arrest before a justice of the peace for the petty sessions area in which he was arrested; and

(b) in the said excepted case shall be brought before the court at which he was to have surrendered to custody.

In reckoning for the purposes of this subsection any period of 24 hours, no account shall be taken of Christmas Day, Good Friday or any Sunday.

(5) A justice of the peace before whom a person is brought under subsection (4) above may, subject to subsection (6) below, if of the opinion that that person –

(a) is not likely to surrender to custody, or

(b) has broken or is likely to break any condition of his bail,

remand him in custody or commit him to custody, as the case may require, or alternatively, grant him bail subject to the same or to different conditions, but if not of that opinion shall grant him bail subject to the same conditions (if any) as were originally imposed.

(6) Where the person so brought before the justice is a child or young person and the justice does not grant him bail, subsection (5) above shall have effect subject to the provisions of section 23 of the Children and Young Persons Act 1969 (remands to the care of local authorities).

(7) Where a custody time limit has expired this section shall have effect as if, in subsection (3), paragraphs (a) and (c) were omitted.

8 Bail with sureties [278]

(1) This section applies where a person is granted bail in criminal proceedings on condition that he provides one or more surety or sureties for the purpose of securing that he surrenders to custody.

(2) In considering the suitability for that purpose of a proposed surety, regard may be had (amongst other things) to –

(a) the surety's financial resources;

(b) his character and any previous convictions of his; and

(c) his proximity (whether in point of kinship, place of residence or otherwise) to the person for whom he is to be surety.

(3) Where a court grants a person bail in criminal proceedings on such a condition but is unable to release him because no surety or no suitable surety is

available, the court shall fix the amount in which the surety is to be bound and subsection (4) and (5) below, or in a case where the proposed surety resides in Scotland subsection (6) below, shall apply for the purpose of enabling the recognizance of the surety to be entered into subsequently.

(4) Where this subsection applies the recognizance of the surety may be entered into before such of the following persons or descriptions of persons as the court may by order specify or, if it makes no such order, before any of the following persons, that is to say –

(a) where the decision is taken by a magistrates' court, before a justice of the peace, a justices' clerk or a police officer who either is of the rank of inspector or above or is in charge of a police station or, if magistrates' courts rules so provide, by a person of such other description as is specified in the rules;

(b) where the decision is taken by the Crown Court, before any of the persons specified in paragraph (a) above or, if Crown Court rules so provide, by a person of such other description as is specified in the rules;

(c) where the decision is taken by the High Court or the Court of Appeal, before any of the persons specified in paragraph (a) above or, if Supreme Court rules so provide, by a person of such other description as is specified in the rules;

(d) where the decision is taken by the Courts-Martial Appeal Court, before any of the persons specified in paragraph (a) above or, if Courts-Martial Appeal rules so provide, by a person of such other description as is specified in the rules;

and Supreme Court rules, Crown Court rules, Courts-Martial Appeal rules or magistrates' courts rules may also prescribe the manner in which a recognizance which is to be entered into before such a person is to be entered into and the persons by whom and the manner in which the recognizance may be enforced.

(5) Where a surety seeks to enter into his recognizance before any person in accordance with subsection (4) above but that person declines to take his recognizance because he is not satisfied of the surety's suitability, the surety may apply to –

(a) the court which fixed the amount of the recognizance in which the surety was to be bound, or

(b) a magistrates' court for the petty sessions area in which he resides,

for that court to take his recognizance and that court shall, if satisfied of his suitability, take his recognizance.

(6) Where this subsection applies, the court, if satisfied of the suitability of the proposed surety, may direct that arrangements be made for the recognizance of the surety to be entered into in Scotland before any constable, within the meaning of the Police (Scotland) Act 1967, having charge at any police office or station in like manner as the recognizance would be entered into in England or Wales.

(7) Where, in pursuance of subsection (4) or (6) above, a recognizance is entered into otherwise than before the court that fixed the amount of the recognizance, the same consequences shall follow as if it had been entered into before that court.

9 Offence of agreeing to indemnify sureties in criminal proceedings [279]

(1) If a person agrees with another to indemnify that other against any liability which that other may incur as a surety to secure the surrender to custody of a person accused or convicted of or under arrest for an offence, he and that other person shall be guilty of an offence.

(2) An offence under subsection (1) above is committed whether the agreement is made before or after the person to be indemnified becomes a surety and whether or not he becomes a surety and whether the agreement contemplates compensation in money or in money's worth.

(3) Where a magistrates' court convicts a person of an offence under subsection (1) above the court may, if it thinks –

   (a) that the circumstances of the offence are such that greater punishment should be inflicted for that offence than the court has power to inflict, or
   (b) in a case where it commits that person for trial to the Crown Court for another offence, that it would be appropriate for him to be dealt with for the offence under subsection (1) above by the court before which he is tried for the other offence,

commit him in custody or on bail to the Crown Court for sentence.

(4) A person guilty of an offence under subsection (1) above shall be liable –

   (a) on summary conviction, to imprisonment for a term not exceeding 3 months or to a fine not exceeding the prescribed sum or to both; or
   (b) on conviction on indictment or if sentenced by the Crown Court on committal for sentence under subsection (3) above, to imprisonment for a term not exceeding 12 months or to a fine or to both.

(5) No proceedings for an offence under subsection (1) above shall be instituted except by or with the consent of the Director of Public Prosecutions.

SCHEDULE 1

PERSONS ENTITLED TO BAIL: SUPPLEMENTARY PROVISIONS

PART I

DEFENDANTS ACCUSED OR CONVICTED
OF IMPRISONABLE OFFENCES

1. Where the offence or one of the offences of which the defendant is accused or convicted in the proceedings is punishable with imprisonment the following provisions of this Part of this Schedule apply.

2. The defendant need not be granted bail if the court is satisfied that there are substantial grounds for believing that the defendant, if released on bail (whether subject to conditions or not), would –

   (a) fail to surrender to custody, or
   (b) commit an offence while on bail, or
   (c) interfere with witnesses or otherwise obstruct the course of justice, whether in relation to himself or any other person.

3. The defendant need not be granted bail if the court is satisfied that the defendant should be kept in custody for his own protection or, if he is a child or young person, for his own welfare.

4. The defendant need not be granted bail if he is in custody in pursuance of the sentence of a court or of any authority acting under any of the Services Acts.

5. The defendant need not be granted bail where the court is satisfied that it has not been practicable to obtain sufficient information for the purpose of taking the decisions required by this Part of this Schedule for want of time since the institution of the proceedings against him.

6. The defendant need not be granted bail if, having been released on bail in or in connection with the proceedings for the offence, he has been arrested in pursuance of section 7 of this Act.

7. Where his case is adjourned for inquiries or a report, the defendant need not be granted bail if it appears to the court that it would be impracticable to complete the inquiries or make the report without keeping the defendant in custody.

8. (1) Subject to sub-paragraph (3) below, where the defendant is granted bail, no conditions shall be imposed under subsections (4) to (7) (except subsection (6)(d)) of section 3 of this Act unless it appears to the court that it is necessary to do so for the purpose of preventing the occurrence of any of the events mentioned in paragraph 2 of this Part of this Schedule.

(1A) No condition shall be imposed under section 3(6)(d) of this Act unless it appears to be necessary to do so for the purpose of enabling inquiries or a report to be made.

(2) Sub-paragraphs (1) and (1A) above also apply on any application to the court to vary the conditions of bail or to impose conditions in respect of bail which has been granted unconditionally.

(3) The restriction imposed by sub-paragraph (1A) above shall not apply to the conditions required to be imposed under section 3(6A) of this Act or operate to override the direction in section 30(2) of the Magistrates' Courts Act 1980 to a magistrates' court to impose conditions of bail under section 3(6)(d) of this Act of the description specified in the said section 30(2) in the circumstances so specified.

9. In taking the decisions required by paragraph 2 of this Part of this Schedule, the court shall have regard to such of the following considerations as appear to it to be relevant, that is to say –

(a) the nature and seriousness of the offence or default (and the probable method of dealing with the defendant for it),

(b) the character, antecedents, associations and community ties of the defendant,

(c) the defendant's record as respects the fulfilment of his obligations under previous grants of bail in criminal proceedings,

(d) except in the case of a defendant whose case is adjourned for inquiries or a report, the strength of the evidence of his having committed the offence or having defaulted,

as well as to any others which appear to be relevant.

9A. (1) If –

(a) the defendant is charged with an offence to which this paragraph applies; and

(b) representations are made as to any of the matters mentioned in paragraph 2 of this Part of this Schedule; and

(c) the court decides to grant him bail,

the court shall state the reasons for its decision and shall cause those reasons to be included in the record of the proceedings.

(2) The offences to which this paragraph applies are –

(a) murder;

(b) manslaughter;

(c) rape;

(d) attempted murder; and

(e) attempted rape.

9B. Where the court is considering exercising the power conferred by section 128A of the Magistrates' Courts Act 1980 (power to remand in custody for more than eight clear days), it shall have regard to the total length of time which the accused would spend in custody if it were to exercise the power.

PART II

DEFENDANTS ACCUSED OR CONVICTED OF NON-IMPRISONABLE OFFENCES

1. Where the offence or every offence of which the defendant is accused or convicted in the proceedings is one which is not punishable with imprisonment the following provisions of this Part of this Schedule apply.

2. The defendant need not be granted bail if –

(a) it appears to the court that, having been previously granted bail in criminal proceedings, he has failed to surrender to custody in accordance with his obligations under the grant of bail; and

(b) the court believes, in view of that failure, that the defendant, if released on bail (whether subject to conditions or not) would fail to surrender to custody.

3. The defendant need not be granted bail if the court is satisfied that the defendant should be kept in custody for his own protection or, if he is a child or young person, for his own welfare.

4. The defendant need not be granted bail if he is in custody in pursuance of the sentence of a court or of any authority acting under any of the Services Acts.

5. The defendant need not be granted bail if, having been released on bail in or in connection with the proceedings for the offence, he has been arrested in pursuance of section 7 of this Act.

PART IIA

DECISIONS WHERE BAIL REFUSED ON PREVIOUS HEARING

1. If the court decides not to grant the defendant bail, it is the court's duty to consider, at each subsequent hearing while the defendant is a person to whom section 4 above applies and remains in custody, whether he ought to be granted bail.

2. At the first hearing after that at which the court decided not to grant the defendant bail he may support an application for bail with any argument as to fact or law that he desires (whether or not he has advanced that argument previously).

3. At subsequent hearings the court need not hear arguments as to fact or law which it has heard previously.

PART III

INTERPRETATION

1. For the purposes of this Schedule the question whether an offence is one which is punishable with imprisonment shall be determined without regard to any enactment prohibiting or restricting the imprisonment of young offenders or first offenders.

2. References in this Schedule to previous grants of bail in criminal proceedings include references to bail granted before the coming into force of this Act.

3. References in this Schedule to a defendant's being kept in custody or being in custody include (where the defendant is a child or young person) references to his being kept or being in the care of a local authority in pursuance of a warrant of commitment under section 23(1) of the Children and Young Persons Act 1969.

4. In this Schedule –

'court', in the expression 'sentence of a court', includes a service court as defined in section 12(1) of the Visiting Forces Act 1952 and 'sentence', in that expression, shall be construed in accordance with that definition;
'default', in relation to the defendant, means the default for which he is to be dealt with under section 6 or section 16 of the Powers of Criminal Courts Act 1973;
'the Services Acts' means the Army Act 1955, the Air Force Act 1955 and the Naval Discipline Act 1957.

Note. Sections 3(10), 4(8) and 7(7) apply to certain proceedings covered by the Prosecution of Offences (Custody Time Limits) Regulations 1987, as amended.

[As amended by the Criminal Law Act 1977, s65(4), Schedule 12; Magistrates' Courts Act 1980, ss32(2), 154(1), Schedule 7, paras 143, 144, 145, 146; Criminal Justice Act 1982, ss38, 46, 60(2), (3); Mental Health (Amendment) Act 1982, s34(2), (3), (4); Mental Health Act 1983, s148, Schedule 4, para 46; Criminal Justice Act 1987, s15, Schedule 2, para 9; Criminal Justice Act 1988, ss131(1), (2), 153, 154, 155(2), 170(1), Schedule 15, para 52; Extradition Act 1989, s36(3); Criminal Justice Act 1991, ss100, 101(2), Schedule 11, paras 21, 22, Schedule 13.]

RACE RELATIONS ACT 1976
(1976 c 74)

26A Discrimination by, or in relation to, barristers [280]

(1) It is unlawful for a barrister or barrister's clerk, in relation to any offer of a pupillage or tenancy, to discriminate against a person –

(a) in the arrangements which are made for the purpose of determining to whom it should be offered;
(b) in respect of any terms on which it is offered; or
(c) by refusing, or deliberately omitting, to offer it to him.

(2) It is unlawful for a barrister or barrister's clerk, in relation to a pupil or tenant in the chambers in question, to discriminate against him –

(a) in respect of any terms applicable to him as a pupil or tenant;
(b) in the opportunities for training, or gaining experience which are afforded or denied to him;
(c) in the benefits, facilities or services which are afforded or denied to him; or
(d) by terminating his pupillage or by subjecting him to any pressure to leave the chambers or other detriment.

(3) It is unlawful for any person, in relation to the giving, withholding or acceptance of instructions to a barrister, to discriminate against any person.

(4) In this section –

'barrister's clerk' includes any person carrying out any of the functions of a barrister's clerk; and
'pupil', 'pupillage', 'tenancy' and 'tenant' have the meanings commonly associated with their use in the context of a set of barristers' chambers.

[As inserted by the Courts and Legal Services Act 1990, s64(2).]

JUSTICES OF THE PEACE ACT 1979
(1979 c 55)

6 Appointment and removal of justices of the peace   [281]

(1) Subject to the following provisions of this Act, justices of the peace for any commission area shall be appointed by the Lord Chancellor by instrument on behalf and in the name of Her Majesty, and a justice so appointed may be removed from office in like manner.

(2) The preceding subsection does not apply to stipendiary magistrates and shall be without prejudice to the position of the Lord Mayor and aldermen as justices for the City of London by virtue of the charters of the City.

7 Residence qualification   [282]

(1) Subject to the provisions of this section, a person shall not be appointed as a justice of the peace for a commission area in accordance with section 6 of this Act, nor act as a justice of the peace by virtue of any such appointment, unless he resides in or within 15 miles of that area.

(2) If the Lord Chancellor is of opinion that it is in the public interest for a person to act as a justice of the peace for a particular area though not qualified to do so under subsection (1) above, he may direct that, so long as any conditions specified in the direction are satisfied, that subsection shall not apply in relation to that person's appointment as a justice of the peace for the area so specified.

(3) Where a person appointed as a justice of the peace for a commission area in accordance with section 6 of this Act is not qualified under the preceding provisions of this section to act by virtue of the appointment, he shall be removed from office as a justice of the peace in accordance with section 6 of this Act if the Lord Chancellor is of opinion that the appointment ought not to continue having regard to the probable duration and other circumstances of the want of qualification.

(4) No act or appointment shall be invalidated by reason only of the disqualification or want of qualification under this section of the person acting or appointed.

8 Supplemental list for England and Wales   [283]

(1) There shall be kept in the office of the Clerk of the Crown in Chancery a supplemental list for England and Wales as provided for by this Act (in this Act referred to as 'the supplemental list').

(2) Subject to the following provisions of this section, there shall be entered in the supplemental list –

    (a) the name of any justice of the peace who is of the age of 70 years or over and neither holds nor has held high judicial office within the meaning of the Appellate Jurisdiction Act 1876, and

    (b) the name of any justice of the peace who holds or has held such office and is of the age of 75 years or over.

(3) A person who on the date when his name falls to be entered in the supplemental list in accordance with subsection (2) above holds office as chairman of the justices in a petty sessions area (whether by an election made, or having effect as if made, under section 17 of this Act, or, in the City of London, as Chief Magistrate or acting Chief Magistrate) shall have his name so entered on the expiry or sooner determination of the term for which he holds office on that date.

(4) The Lord Chancellor may direct that the name of a justice of the peace for any area shall be entered in the supplemental list if the Lord Chancellor is satisfied either –

(a) that by reason of the justice's age or infirmity or other like cause it is expedient that he should cease to exercise judicial functions as a justice for that area, or

(b) that the justice declines or neglects to take a proper part in the exercise of those functions.

(5) On a person's appointment as a justice of the peace for any area the Lord Chancellor may direct that his name shall be entered in the supplemental list, if that person is appointed a justice for that area on ceasing to be a justice for some other area.

(6) The name of a justice of the peace shall be entered in the supplemental list if he applies for it to be so entered and the application is approved by the Lord Chancellor.

(7) Nothing in this section shall apply to a person holding office as stipendiary magistrate.

9 Removal of name from supplemental list   [284]

(1) A person's name shall be removed from the supplemental list if he ceases to be a justice of the peace.

(2) The name of any person, if not required to be entered in the supplemental list by subsection (2) or subsection (3) of section 8 of this Act, shall be removed from the list if so directed by the Lord Chancellor.

10 Effect of entry of name in supplemental list   [285]

(1) Subject to the following subsections, a justice of the peace for any area, while his name is entered in the supplemental list, shall not by reason of being a justice for that area be qualified as a justice to do any act or to be a member of any committee or other body.

(2) Subsection (1) above shall not preclude a justice from doing all or any of the following acts as a justice, that is to say –

(a) signing any document for the purpose of authenticating another person's signature;

(b) taking and authenticating by his signature any written declaration not made on oath; and

(c) giving a certificate of facts within his knowledge or of his opinion as to any matter.

(3) The entry of a person's name in the supplemental list shall also not preclude him, if so authorised by the Lord Chancellor, from acting as a judge of the Crown Court so long as he has not attained the age of 72 years.

(4) No act or appointment shall be invalidated by reason of the disqualification under this section of the person acting or appointed.

13 Appointment and removal of stipendiary magistrates   [286]

(1) It shall be lawful for Her Majesty to appoint a person who has a seven year general qualification within the meaning of section 71 of the Courts and Legal Services Act 1990 to be, during Her Majesty's pleasure, a whole-time stipendiary magistrate in any commission area or areas outside the inner London area and the

City of London, and to appoint more than one such magistrate in the same area or areas.

(2) A person so appointed to be a magistrate in any commission area shall by virtue of his office be a justice of the peace for that area.

(3) Any appointment of a stipendiary magistrate under this section shall be of a person recommended to Her Majesty by the Lord Chancellor, and a stipendiary magistrate appointed under this section shall not be removed from office except on the Lord Chancellor's recommendation.

(4) The number of stipendiary magistrates appointed under this section shall not at any time exceed forty or such larger number as Her Majesty may from time to time by Order in Council specify.

(5) Her Majesty shall not be recommended to make an Order in Council under subsection (4) above unless a draft of the Order has been laid before Parliament and approved by resolution of each House.

14 Retirement of stipendiary magistrates   [287]

(1) A stipendiary magistrate appointed on or after 25 October 1968 shall vacate his office at the end of the completed year of service in the course of which he attains the age of 70:

Provided that where the Lord Chancellor considers it desirable in the public interest to retain him in office after that time, the Lord Chancellor may from time to time authorise him to continue in office up to such age not exceeding 72 as the Lord Chancellor thinks fit.

(2) A stipendiary magistrate appointed before 25 October 1968 shall vacate his office at the end of the completed year of service in the course of which he attains the age of 72:

Provided that where the Lord Chancellor considers it desirable in the public interest to retain him in office after that time, the Lord Chancellor may from time to time authorise him to continue in office up to such age not exceeding 75 as the Lord Chancellor thinks fit.

25 Appointment and removal of justices' clerks   [288]

(1) Justices' clerks shall be appointed by the magistrates' courts committee and shall hold office during the pleasure of the committee; and a magistrates' courts committee may appoint more than one justices' clerk for any area.

(2) The approval of the Secretary of State shall be required –

(a) for any decision to increase the number of justices' clerks in a petty sessions area or to have more than one justices' clerk in a new petty sessions area;
(b) for any appointment of justices' clerk;
(c) for the removal of the justices' clerk for a petty sessional division where the magistrates for the division do not consent to the removal.

(3) A magistrates' courts committee shall consult the magistrates for any petty sessional division on the appointment or removal of a justices' clerk for the division; and the Secretary of State, before approving the appointment or removal of a justices' clerk for such a division, shall consider any representations made to him by the magistrates for the division, and before approving the removal of any such clerk shall consider any representations made to him by the clerk.

(4) The magistrates' courts committee shall inform the Secretary of State of the age, qualifications and experience of any person proposed to be appointed a

justices' clerk and, if the Secretary of State so requires, of any other person offering himself for the appointment.

(5) Subsections (1) to (4) above shall not apply to the inner London area.

26 Qualifications for appointment as justices' clerk   **[289]**

(1) Except as provided by this section, no person shall be appointed as justices' clerk of any class or description unless either –

(a) at the time of appointment he has a five year magistrates' court qualification, within the meaning of section 71 of the Courts and Legal Services Act 1990, and is within any limit of age prescribed for appointment to a clerkship of that class or description, or
(b) he then is or has previously been a justices' clerk.

(2) A lower as well as an upper limit of age may be prescribed under subsection (1) above for appointments to any class or description of clerkship.

(3) A person not having the qualification as barrister or solicitor which is required by subsection (1)(a) above may be appointed a justices' clerk –

(a) if at the time of appointment he is a barrister or solicitor and has served for not less than five years in service to which this subsection applies, or
(b) if before 1 January 1960 he had served for not less than ten years in service to which this subsection applies and, in the opinion of the magistrates' courts committee and of the Secretary of State, there are special circumstances making the appointment a proper one.

(4) Subsection (3) above applies to service in any one or more of the following capacities, that is to say, service as assistant to a justices' clerk and service before 1 February 1969 –

(a) as clerk to a stipendiary magistrate;
(b) as clerk to a magistrates' court for the inner London area or as clerk to a metropolitan stipendiary court;
(c) as clerk at one of the justice rooms of the City of London; or
(d) as assistant to any such clerk as is mentioned in paragraphs (a) to (c) above.

(5) A person may be appointed a justices' clerk notwithstanding that he is over the upper limit of age mentioned in subsection (1) of this section if he has served continuously in service to which subsection (3) above applies from a time when he was below that limit to the time of appointment.

28 General powers and duties of justices' clerks   **[290]**

(1) Rules made in accordance with section 144 of the Magistrates' Courts Act 1980 may (except in so far as any enactment passed after 25 October 1968 otherwise directs) make provision enabling things authorised to be done by, to or before a single justice of the peace to be done instead by, to or before a justices' clerk.

(1A) Such rules may also make provision enabling things authorised to be done by, to or before a justices' clerk (whether by virtue of subsection (1) above or otherwise) to be done instead by, to or before –

(a) a person appointed by a magistrates' courts committee to assist him;
(b) where he is a part-time justices' clerk, any member of his staff who has been appointed by the magistrates' courts committee to assist him in his duties as such;
(c) any officer appointed by the committee of magistrates to be his deputy or to assist him.

(2) Any enactment (including any enactment contained in this Act) or any rule of law regulating the exercise of any jurisdiction or powers of justices of the peace, or relating to things done in the exercise or purported exercise of any such jurisdiction or powers, shall apply in relation to the exercise or purported exercise thereof by virtue of subsection (1) above by the clerk to any justices as if he were one of those justices.

(3) It is hereby declared that the functions of a justices' clerk include the giving to the justices to whom he is clerk or any of them, at the request of the justices or justice, of advice about law, practice or procedure on questions arising in connection with the discharge of their or his functions, including questions arising when the clerk is not personally attending on the justices or justice, and that the clerk may, at any time when he thinks he should do so, bring to the attention of the justices or justice any point of law, practice or procedure that is or may be involved in any question so arising.

In this subsection the reference to the functions of justices or a justice is a reference to any of their or his functions as justices or a justice of the peace, other than functions as a judge of the Crown Court.

(4) The enactment of subsection (3) above shall not be taken as defining or in any respect limiting the powers and duties belonging to a justices' clerk or the matters on which justices may obtain assistance from their clerk.

31 Appointment, removal and retirement of metropolitan [291] stipendiary magistrates

(1) Metropolitan stipendiary magistrates shall be appointed by Her Majesty, and Her Majesty shall from time to time appoint such number of persons as is necessary; but the number of metropolitan stipendiary magistrates shall not at any time exceed 60 or such larger number as Her Majesty may from time to time by Order in Council specify.

(2) A person shall not be qualified to be appointed a metropolitan stipendiary magistrate unless he has a seven year general qualification within the meaning of section 71 of the Courts and Legal Services Act 1990.

(3) The Lord Chancellor shall designate one of the metropolitan stipendiary magistrates to be the chief metropolitan stipendiary magistrate.

(4) The following provisions shall apply to each metropolitan stipendiary magistrate, that is to say –

   (a) he shall by virtue of his office be a justice of the peace for each of the London commission areas and for the counties of Essex, Hertfordshire, Kent and Surrey;
   (c) he may be removed from office by the Lord Chancellor for inability or misbehaviour.

(5) A metropolitan stipendiary magistrate who is by virtue of his office a justice of the peace for any area mentioned in subsection (4) above shall not, by reason only of his being a justice of the peace for that area by virtue of that office, be qualified to be chosen under section 17(1) of this Act as chairman or deputy chairman of the justices for a petty sessional division of that area or to vote under that subsection at the election of any such chairman or deputy chairman.

(6) Section 14 of this Act shall apply to metropolitan stipendiary magistrates as well as to other stipendiary magistrates in England or Wales.

(7) Her Majesty shall not be recommended to make an Order in Council under subsection (1) above unless a draft of the Order has been laid before Parliament and approved by resolution of each House.

39 Ex officio and appointed justices [292]

(1) The Lord Mayor and aldermen of the City shall by virtue of the charter granted by His late Majesty King George II dated 25 August 1741 continue to be justices of the peace for the City:

Provided that any of them may be excluded by the Lord Chancellor from the exercise of his functions as a justice.

(2) The persons holding office as justices of the peace for the City shall constitute a single body of justices, without distinction between those holding office by virtue of the charter and those appointed; and the jurisdiction and powers of the Lord Mayor and aldermen as justices by virtue of the charter shall be the same in all respects as those of appointed justices.

(3) The establishment of the City as a separate commission area shall not be taken to have constituted new courts for the City; and the jurisdiction and powers of the justices of the peace for the City are in continuation of those formerly belonging exclusively to the justices holding office by virtue of the charter.

(4) In this Part of this Act 'the City' means the City of London.

40 Chairman and deputy chairmen of justices [293]

(1) The Lord Mayor for the time being, if not disqualified, shall be chairman of the justices, with the style of Chief Magistrate, instead of a chairman being elected under section 17(1) of this Act; and, subject to subsection (3) below, the aldermen who have been Lord Mayor and are not disqualified (or, if there are more than eight such aldermen, the eight who were last Lord Mayor) shall be deputy chairmen in addition to any deputy chairmen elected under section 17(1) above.

(2) For the purposes of this section a Lord Mayor or alderman is disqualified at any time while his name is entered in the supplemental list.

(3) In the event of a Lord Mayor being disqualified, then during his mayoralty the senior of the aldermen designated as deputy chairmen in subsection (1) above shall, instead of being a deputy chairman, be chairman of the justices as acting Chief Magistrate ...

44 Immunity for acts within jurisdiction [294]

No action shall lie against any justice of the peace or justices' clerk in respect of any act or omission of his –

    (a) in the execution of his duty –

        (i) as such a justice; or
        (ii) as such a clerk exercising, by virtue of any statutory provision, any of the functions of a single justice; and

    (b) with respect to any matter within his jurisdiction.

45 Immunity for certain acts beyond jurisdiction [295]

An action shall lie against any justice of the peace or justices' clerk in respect of any act or omission of his –

    (a) in the purported execution of his duty –

        (i) as such a justice; or
        (ii) as such a clerk exercising, by virtue of any statutory provision, any of the functions of a single justice; but

    (b) with respect to a matter which is not within his jurisdiction,

if, but only if, it is proved that he acted in bad faith.

50 Where action prohibited, proceedings may be set aside   [296]

If any action is brought in circumstances in which this Part of this Act provides that no action is to be brought, a judge of the court in which the action is brought may, on the application of the defendant and upon an affidavit as to the facts, set aside the proceedings in the action, with or without costs, as the judge thinks fit.

63 Courses of instruction   [297]

(1) It shall be the duty of every magistrates' courts committee, in accordance with arrangements approved by the Lord Chancellor, to make and administer schemes providing for courses of instruction for justices of the peace of their area.

(2) It shall be the duty of the committee of magistrates, in accordance with arrangements approved by the Lord Chancellor, to make and administer schemes providing for courses of instruction for justices of the peace of the inner London area.

(3) There may be paid out of moneys provided by Parliament any expenses incurred by the Lord Chancellor in providing courses of instruction for justices of the peace.

(4) If courses of instruction are not provided for justices of the peace of any area as required by subsection (1) or subsection (2) above, then any expenses incurred by the Lord Chancellor in providing courses of instruction to make good the default shall be recoverable by him from the magistrates' courts committee or committee of magistrates in default; and any sums recovered by the Lord Chancellor under this subsection shall be paid into the Consolidated Fund.

(5) The Secretary of State may provide courses of instruction for justices' clerks and their staffs.

(6) In this section 'justices' clerk' includes a clerk of special sessions.

[As amended by the Magistrates' Courts Act 1980, s154, Schedule 7, para 194; Administration of Justice Act 1982, s65; Courts and Legal Services Act 1990, ss71(2), 108(1), (2), (3), 117, Schedule 10, paras 44(1), (2), 45, Schedule 20.]

MAGISTRATES' COURTS ACT 1980
(1980 c 43)

PART I

CRIMINAL JURISDICTION AND PROCEDURE

1 Issue of summons to accused or warrant for his arrest   [298]

(1) Upon an information being laid before a justice of the peace for an area to which this section applies that any person has, or is suspected of having, committed an offence, the justice may, in any of the events mentioned in subsection (2) below, but subject to subsections (3) to (5) below, –

    (a) issue a summons directed to that person requiring him to appear before a magistrates' court for the area to answer to the information, or
    (b) issue a warrant to arrest that person and bring him before a magistrates' court for the area or such magistrates' court as is provided in subsection (5) below.

(2) A justice of the peace for an area to which this section applies may issue a summons or warrant under this section –

(a) if the offence was committed or is suspected to have been committed within the area, or

(b) if it appears to the justice necessary or expedient, with a view to the better administration of justice, that the person charged should be tried jointly with, or in the same place as, some other person who is charged with an offence, and who is in custody, or is being or is to be proceeded against, within the area, or

(c) if the person charged resides or is, or is believed to reside or be, within the area, or

(d) if under any enactment a magistrates' court for the area has jurisdiction to try the offence, or

(e) if the offence was committed outside England and Wales and, where it is an offence exclusively punishable on summary conviction, if a magistrates' court for the area would have jurisdiction to try the offence if the offender were before it.

(3) No warrant shall be issued under this section unless the information is in writing and substantiated on oath.

(4) No warrant shall be issued under this section for the arrest of any person who has attained the age of 18 years unless –

(a) the offence to which the warrant relates is an indictable offence or is punishable with imprisonment, or

(b) the person's address is not sufficiently established for a summons to be served on him.

(5) Where the offence charged is not an indictable offence –

(a) no summons shall be issued by virtue only of paragraph (c) of subsection (2) above, and

(b) any warrant issued by virtue only of that paragraph shall require the person charged to be brought before a magistrates' court having jurisdiction to try the offence.

(6) Where the offence charged is an indictable offence, a warrant under this section may be issued at any time notwithstanding that a summons has previously been issued.

(7) A justice of the peace may issue a summons or warrant under this section upon an information being laid before him notwithstanding any enactment requiring the information to be laid before two or more justices.

(8) The areas to which this section applies are any county, any London commission area and the City of London.

2 Jurisdiction to deal with charges [299]

(1) A magistrates' court for a county, a London commission area or the City of London shall have jurisdiction to try all summary offences committed within the county, the London commission area or the City (as the case may be).

(2) Where a person charged with a summary offence appears or is brought before a magistrates' court in answer to a summons issued under paragraph (b) of section 1(2) above, or under a warrant issued under that paragraph, the court shall have jurisdiction to try the offence.

(3) A magistrates' court for a county, a London commission area or the City of London shall have jurisdiction as examining justices over any offence committed by a person who appears or is brought before the court, whether or not the offence was committed within the county, the London commission area or the City (as the case may be).

(4) Subject to sections 18 to 22 below and any other enactment (wherever contained) relating to the mode of trial of offences triable either way, a magistrates' court shall have jurisdiction to try summarily an offence triable either way in any case in which under subsection (3) above it would have jurisdiction as examining justices.

(5) A magistrates' court shall, in the exercise of its powers under section 24 below, have jurisdiction to try summarily an indictable offence in any case in which under subsection (3) above it would have jurisdiction as examining justices.

(6) A magistrates' court for any area by which a person is tried for an offence shall have jurisdiction to try him for any summary offence for which he could be tried by a magistrates' court for any other area.

(7) Nothing in this section shall affect any jurisdiction over offences conferred on a magistrates' court by an enactment not contained in this Act.

4 General nature of committal proceedings [300]

(1) The functions of examining justices may be discharged by a single justice.

(2) Examining justices shall sit in open court except where any enactment contains an express provision to the contrary and except where it appears to them as respects the whole or any part of committal proceedings that the ends of justice would not be served by their sitting in open court.

(3) Subject to subsection (4) below and section 102 below, evidence given before examining justices shall be given in the presence of the accused, and the defence shall be at liberty to put questions to any witness at the inquiry.

(4) Examining justices may allow evidence to be given before them in the absence of the accused if –

(a) they consider that by reason of his disorderly conduct before them it is not practicable for the evidence to be given in his presence, or
(b) he cannot be present for reasons of health but is represented by a legal representative and has consented to the evidence being given in his absence.

6 Discharge or committal for trial [301]

(1) Subject to the provisions of this and any other Act relating to the summary trial of indictable offences, if a magistrates' court inquiring into an offence as examining justices is of opinion, on consideration of the evidence and of any statement of the accused, that there is sufficient evidence to put the accused on trial by jury for any indictable offence, the court shall commit him for trial; and, if it is not of that opinion, it shall, if he is in custody for no other cause than the offence under inquiry, discharge him.

(2) A magistrates' court inquiring into an offence as examining justices may, if satisfied that all the evidence before the court (whether for the prosecution or the defence) consists of written statements tendered to the court under section 102 below, with or without exhibits, commit the accused for trial for the offence without consideration of the contents of those statements, unless –

(a) the accused or one of the accused has no legal representative acting for him in the case (whether present in court or not);
(b) a legal representative for the accused or one of the accused, as the case may be, has requested the court to consider a submission that the statements disclose insufficient evidence to put that accused on trial by jury for the offence;

and subsection (1) above shall not apply to a committal for trial under this subsection.

(3) Subject to section 4 of the Bail Act 1976 and section 41 below, the court may commit a person for trial –

(a) in custody, that is to say, by committing him to custody there to be safely kept until delivered in due course of law, or

(b) on bail in accordance with the Bail Act 1976, that is to say, by directing him to appear before the Crown Court for trial;

and where his release on bail is conditional on his providing one or more surety or sureties and, in accordance with section 8(3) of the Bail Act 1976, the court fixes the amount in which the surety is to be bound with a view to his entering into his recognizance subsequently in accordance with subsections (4) and (5) or (6) of that section the court shall in the meantime commit the accused to custody in accordance with paragraph (a) of this subsection.

(4) Where the court has committed a person to custody in accordance with paragraph (a) of subsection (3) above, then, if that person is in custody for no other cause, the court may, at any time before his first appearance before the Crown Court, grant him bail in accordance with the Bail Act 1976 subject to a duty to appear before the Crown Court for trial.

(5) Where a magistrates' court acting as examining justices commits any person for trial or determines to discharge him, the clerk of the court shall, on the day on which the committal proceedings are concluded or the next day, cause to be displayed in a part of the court house to which the public have access a notice –

(a) in either case giving that person's name, address, and age (if known);

(b) in a case where the court so commits him, stating the charge or charges on which he is committed and the court to which he is committed;

(c) in a case where the court determines to discharge him, describing the offence charged and stating that it has so determined;

but this subsection shall have effect subject to section 4 of the Sexual Offences (Amendment) Act 1976 (anonymity of complainant in rape, etc cases).

(6) A notice displayed in pursuance of subsection (5) above shall not contain the name or address of any person under the age of 18 years unless the justices in question have stated that in their opinion he would be mentioned in the notice apart from the preceding provisions of this subsection and should be mentioned in it for the purpose of avoiding injustice to him.

9 Procedure on trial [302]

(1) On the summary trial of an information, the court shall, if the accused appears, state to him the substance of the information and ask him whether he pleads guilty or not guilty.

(2) The court, after hearing the evidence and the parties, shall convict the accused or dismiss the information.

(3) If the accused pleads guilty, the court may convict him without hearing evidence.

17 Certain offences triable either way [303]

(1) The offences listed in Schedule 1 to this Act shall be triable either way.

(2) Subsection (1) above is without prejudice to any other enactment by virtue of which any offence is triable either way.

18 Initial procedure on information against adult   [304]
for offence triable either way

(1) Sections 19 to 23 below shall have effect where a person who has attained the age of 18 years appears or is brought before a magistrates' court on an information charging him with an offence triable either way.

(2) Without prejudice to section 11(1) above, everything that the court is required to do under sections 19 to 22 below must be done before any evidence is called and, subject to subsection (3) below and section 23 below, with the accused present in court.

(3) The court may proceed in the absence of the accused in accordance with such of the provisions of sections 19 to 22 below as are applicable in the circumstances if the court considers that by reason of his disorderly conduct before the court it is not practicable for the proceedings to be conducted in his presence; and subsections (3) to (5) of section 23 below, so far as applicable, shall have effect in relation to proceedings conducted in the absence of the accused by virtue of this subsection (references in those subsections to the person representing the accused being for this purpose read as references to the person, if any, representing him).

(4) A magistrates' court proceeding under sections 19 to 23 below may adjourn the proceedings at any time, and on doing so on any occasion when the accused is present may remand the accused, and shall remand him if –

(a) on the occasion on which he first appeared, or was brought, before the court to answer to the information he was in custody or, having been released on bail, surrendered to the custody of the court; or
(b) he has been remanded at any time in the course of proceedings on the information;

and where the court remands the accused, the time fixed for the resumption of the proceedings shall be that at which he is required to appear or be brought before the court in pursuance of the remand or would be required to be brought before the court but for section 128(3A) below.

(5) The functions of a magistrates' court under sections 19 to 23 below may be discharged by a single justice, but the foregoing provision shall not be taken to authorise the summary trial of an information by a magistrates' court composed of less than two justices.

19 Court to begin by considering which mode of trial   [305]
appears more suitable

(1) The court shall consider whether, having regard to the matters mentioned in subsection (3) below and any representations made by the prosecutor or the accused, the offence appears to the court more suitable for summary trial or for trial on indictment.

(2) Before so considering, the court –

(a) shall cause the charge to be written down, if this has not already been done, and read to the accused; and
(b) shall afford first the prosecutor and then the accused an opportunity to make representations as to which mode of trial would be more suitable.

(3) The matters to which the court is to have regard under subsection (1) above are the nature of the case; whether the circumstances make the offence one of serious character; whether the punishment which a magistrates' court would have power to inflict for it would be adequate; and any other circumstances which appear to the court to make it more suitable for the offence to be tried in one way rather than the other.

(4) If the prosecution is being carried on by the Attorney General, the Solicitor General or the Director of Public Prosecutions and he applies for the offence to be tried on indictment, the preceding provisions of this section and sections 20 and 21 below shall not apply, and the court shall proceed to inquire into the information as examining justices.

(5) The power of the Director of Public Prosecutions under subsection (4) above to apply for an offence to be tried on indictment shall not be exercised except with the consent of the Attorney General.

20 Procedure where summary trial appears more suitable [306]

(1) If, where the court has considered as required by section 19(1) above, it appears to the court that the offence is more suitable for summary trial, the following provisions of this section shall apply (unless excluded by section 23 below).

(2) The court shall explain to the accused in ordinary language –

(a) that it appears to the court more suitable for him to be tried summarily for the offence, and that he can either consent to be so tried or, if he wishes, be tried by a jury; and
(b) that if he is tried summarily and is convicted by the court, he may be committed for sentence to the Crown Court under section 38 below if the convicting court is of such opinion as is mentioned in subsection (2) of that section.

(3) After explaining to the accused as provided by subsection (2) above the court shall ask him whether he consents to be tried summarily or wishes to be tried by a jury, and –

(a) if he consents to be tried summarily, shall proceed to the summary trial of the information;
(b) if he does not so consent, shall proceed to inquire into the information as examining justices.

21 Procedure where trial on indictment appears more suitable [307]

If, where the court has considered as required by section 19(1) above, it appears to the court that the offence is more suitable for trial on indictment, the court shall tell the accused that the court has decided that it is more suitable for him to be tried for the offence by a jury, and shall proceed to inquire into the information as examining justices.

22 Certain offences triable either way to be tried summarily [308] if value involved is small

(1) If the offence charged by the information is one of those mentioned in the first column of Schedule 2 to this Act (in this section referred to as 'scheduled offences') then, subject to subsection (7) below, the court shall, before proceeding in accordance with section 19 above, consider whether, having regard to any representations made by the prosecutor or the accused, the value involved (as defined in subsection (10) below) appears to the court to exceed the relevant sum.

For the purposes of this section the relevant sum is £2,000.

(2) If, where subsection (1) above applies, it appears to the court clear that, for the offence charged, the value involved does not exceed the relevant sum, the

court shall proceed as if the offence were triable only summarily, and sections 19 to 21 above shall not apply.

(3) If, where subsection (1) above applies, it appears to the court clear that, for the offence charged, the value involved exceeds the relevant sum, the court shall thereupon proceed in accordance with section 19 above in the ordinary way without further regard to the provisions of this section.

(4) If, where subsection (1) above applies, it appears to the court for any reason not clear whether, for the offence charged, the value involved does or does not exceed the relevant sum, the provisions of subsections (5) and (6) below shall apply.

(5) The court shall cause the charge to be written down, if this has not already been done, and read to the accused, and shall explain to him in ordinary language –

(a) that he can, if he wishes, consent to be tried summarily for the offence and that if he consents to be so tried, he will definitely be tried in that way; and
(b) that if he is tried summarily and is convicted by the court, his liability to imprisonment or a fine will be limited as provided in section 33 below.

(6) After explaining to the accused as provided by subsection (5) above the court shall ask him whether he consents to be tried summarily and –

(a) if he so consents, shall proceed in accordance with subsection (2) above as if that subsection applied;
(b) if he does not so consent, shall proceed in accordance with subsection (3) above as if that subsection applied.

(8) Where a person is convicted by a magistrates' court of a scheduled offence, it shall not be open to him to appeal to the Crown Court against the conviction on the ground that the convicting court's decision as to the value involved was mistaken.

(9) If, where subsection (1) above applies, the offence charged is one with which the accused is charged jointly with a person who has not attained the age of 18 years, the reference in that subsection to any representations made by the accused shall be read as including any representations made by the person under 18.

(10) In this section 'the value involved', in relation to any scheduled offence, means the value indicated in the second column of Schedule 2 to this Act, measured as indicated in the third column of that Schedule; and in that Schedule 'the material time' means the time of the alleged offence.

(11) Where –

(a) the accused is charged on the same occasion with two or more scheduled offences and it appears to the court that they constitute or form part of a series of two or more offences of the same or a similar character; or
(b) the offence charged consists in incitement to commit two or more scheduled offences,

this section shall have effect as if any reference in it to the value involved were a reference to the aggregate of the values involved.

(12) Subsection (8) of section 12A of the Theft Act 1968 (which determines when a vehicle is recovered) shall apply for the purposes of paragraph 3 of Schedule 2 to this Act as it applies for the purposes of that section.

24 Summary trial of information against child or   **[309]** young person for indictable offence

(1) Where a person under the age of 18 years appears or is brought before a

magistrates' court on an information charging him with an indictable offence other than homicide, he shall be tried summarily unless –

(a) he has attained the age of 14 and the offence is such as is mentioned in subsection (2) of section 53 of the Children and Young Persons Act 1933 (under which young persons convicted on indictment of certain grave crimes may be sentenced to be detained for long periods) and the court considers that if he is found guilty of the offence it ought to be possible to sentence him in pursuance of that subsection; or

(b) he is charged jointly with a person who has attained the age of 18 years and the court considers it necessary in the interest of justice to commit them both for trial;

and accordingly in a case falling within paragraph (a) or (b) of this subsection the court shall commit the accused for trial if either it is of opinion that there is sufficient evidence to put him on trial or it has power under section 6(2) above so to commit him without consideration of the evidence.

(2) Where, in a case falling within subsection (1)(b) above, a magistrates' court commits a person under the age of 18 years for trial for an offence with which he is charged jointly with a person who has attained that age, the court may also commit him for trial for any other indictable offence with which he is charged at the same time (whether jointly with the person who has attained that age or not) if that other offence arises out of circumstances which are the same as or connected with those giving rise to the first-mentioned offence.

(3) If on trying a person summarily in pursuance of subsection (1) above the court finds him guilty, it may impose a fine of an amount not exceeding £1,000 or may exercise the same powers as it could have exercised if he had been found guilty of an offence for which, but for section 1(1) of the Criminal Justice Act 1982, it could have sentenced him to imprisonment for a term not exceeding –

(a) the maximum term of imprisonment for the offence on conviction on indictment; or

(b) six months,

whichever is the less.

(4) In relation to a person under the age of 14 subsection (3) above shall have effect as if for the words £1,000 there were substituted the words £250.

27 Effect of dismissal of information for offence triable either way [310]

Where on the summary trial of an information for an offence triable either way the court dismisses the information, the dismissal shall have the same effect as an acquittal on indictment.

29 Power of magistrates' court to remit a person under 17 for trial to a youth court in certain circumstances [311]

(1) Where –

(a) a person under the age of 18 years ('the juvenile') appears or is brought before a magistrates' court other than a youth court on an information jointly charging him and one or more other persons with an offence; and

(b) that other person, or any of those other persons, has attained that age,

subsection (2) below shall have effect notwithstanding proviso (a) in section 46(1) of the Children and Young Persons Act 1933 (which would otherwise require the charge against the juvenile to be heard by a magistrates' court other than a youth court).

In the following provisions of this section 'the older accused' means such one or more of the accused as have attained the age of 18 years.

(2) If –

(a) the court proceeds to the summary trial of the information in the case of both or all of the accused, and the older accused or each of the older accused pleads guilty; or

(b) the court –

(i) in the case of the older accused or each of the older accused, proceeds to inquire into the information as examining justices and either commits him for trial or discharges him; and

(ii) in the case of the juvenile, proceeds to the summary trial of the information,

then, if in either situation the juvenile pleads not guilty, the court may before any evidence is called in his case remit him for trial to a youth court acting for the same place as the remitting court or for the place where he habitually resides.

(3) A person remitted to a youth court under subsection (2) above shall be brought before and tried by a youth court accordingly.

(4) Where a person is so remitted to a youth court –

(a) he shall have no right of appeal against the order of remission; and

(b) the remitting court may give such directions as appear to be necessary with respect to his custody or for his release on bail until he can be brought before the youth court.

(5) The preceding provisions of this section shall apply in relation to a corporation as if it were an individual who has attained the age of 18 years.

31 General limit on power of magistrates' court [312]
to impose imprisonment

(1) Without prejudice to section 133 below, a magistrates' court shall not have power to impose imprisonment or a sentence of detention in a young offender institution for more than 6 months in respect of any one offence.

(2) Unless expressly excluded, subsection (1) above shall apply even if the offence in question is one for which a person would otherwise be liable on summary conviction to imprisonment or a sentence of detention in a young offender institution for more than 6 months.

(3) Any power of a magistrates' court to impose a term of imprisonment for non-payment of a fine, or for want of sufficient distress to satisfy a fine, shall not be limited by virtue of subsection (1) above.

(4) In subsection (3) above 'fine' includes a pecuniary penalty but does not include a pecuniary forfeiture or pecuniary compensation.

32 Penalties on summary conviction for offences [313]
triable either way

(1) On summary conviction of any of the offences triable either way listed in Schedule 1 to this Act a person shall be liable to imprisonment for a term not exceeding 6 months or to a fine not exceeding the prescribed sum or both, except that –

(a) a magistrates' court shall not have power to impose imprisonment for an offence so listed if the Crown Court would not have that power in the case of an adult convicted of it on indictment;

(b) on summary conviction of an offence consisting in the incitement to commit an offence triable either way a person shall not be liable to any greater penalty than he would be liable to on summary conviction of the last-mentioned offence.

(2) For any offence triable either way which is not listed in Schedule 1 to this Act, being an offence under a relevant enactment, the maximum fine which may be imposed on summary conviction shall by virtue of this subsection be the prescribed sum unless the offence is one for which by virtue of an enactment other than this subsection a larger fine may be imposed on summary conviction.

(3) Where, by virtue of any relevant enactment, a person summarily convicted of an offence triable either way would, apart from this section, be liable to a maximum fine of one amount in the case of a first conviction and of a different amount in the case of a second or subsequent conviction, subsection (2) above shall apply irrespective of whether the conviction is a first, second or subsequent one.

(4) Subsection (2) above shall not affect so much of any enactment as (in whatever words) makes a person liable on summary conviction to a fine not exceeding a specified amount for each day on which a continuing offence is continued after conviction or the occurrence of any other specified event.

(5) Subsection (2) above shall not apply on summary conviction of any of the following offences –

(a) offences under section 5(2) of the Misuse of Drugs Act 1971 (having possession of a controlled drug) where the controlled drug in relation to which the offence was committed was a Class B or Class C drug;

(b) offences under the following provisions of that Act, where the controlled drug in relation to which the offence was committed was a Class C drug, namely –

(i) section 4(2) (production, or being concerned in the production, of a controlled drug);

(ii) section 4(3) (supplying or offering a controlled drug or being concerned in the doing of either activity by another);

(iii) section 5(3) (having possession of a controlled drug with intent to supply it to another);

(iv) section 8 (being the occupier, or concerned in the management, of premises and permitting or suffering certain activities to take place there);

(v) section 12(6) (contravention of direction prohibiting practitioner, etc from possessing, supplying, etc controlled drugs); or

(vi) section 13(3) (contravention of direction prohibiting practitioner, etc from prescribing, supplying, etc controlled drugs).

(6) Where, as regards any offence triable either way, there is under any enactment (however framed or worded) a power by subordinate instrument to restrict the amount of the fine which on summary conviction can be imposed in respect of that offence –

(a) subsection (2) above shall not affect that power or override any restriction imposed in the exercise of that power; and

(b) the amount to which that fine may be restricted in the exercise of that power shall be any amount less than the maximum fine which could be imposed on summary conviction in respect of the offence apart from any restriction so imposed.

(8) In subsection (5) above 'controlled drug', 'Class B drug' and 'Class C drug' have the same meaning as in the Misuse of Drugs Act 1971.

(9) In this section –

'fine' includes a pecuniary penalty but does not include a pecuniary forfeiture or pecuniary compensation;

'the prescribed sum' means £5,000 or such sum as is for the time being substituted in this definition by an order in force under section 143(1) below; 'relevant enactment' means an enactment contained in the Criminal Law Act 1977 or in any Act passed before, or in the same Session as, that Act.

33 Maximum penalties on summary conviction in pursuance of section 22 [314]

(1) Where in pursuance of subsection (2) of section 22 above a magistrates' court proceeds to the summary trial of an information, then, if the accused is summarily convicted of the offence –

(a) subject to subsection (3) below the court shall not have power to impose on him in respect of that offence imprisonment for more than 3 months or a fine greater than level 4 on the standard scale; and

(b) section 38 below shall not apply as regards that offence.

(2) In subsection (1) above 'fine' includes a pecuniary penalty but does not include a pecuniary forfeiture or pecuniary compensation.

(3) Paragraph (a) of subsection (1) above does not apply to an offence under section 12A of the Theft Act 1968 (aggravated vehicle-taking).

36 Restriction on fines in respect of young persons [315]

(1) Where a person under 18 years of age is found guilty by a magistrates' court of an offence for which, apart from this section, the court would have power to impose a fine of an amount exceeding £1,000, the amount of any fine imposed by the court shall not exceed £1,000.

(2) In relation to a person under the age of 14 subsection (1) above shall have effect as if for the words '£1,000', in both the places where they occur, there were substituted the words '£250'.

37 Committal to Crown Court with a view to sentence of detention in a young offender institution [316]

(1) Where a person who is not less than 15 but under 18 years old is convicted by a magistrates' court of an offence punishable on conviction on indictment with a term of imprisonment exceeding six months, then, if the court is of opinion that he should be sentenced to a greater term of detention in a young offender institution than it has power to impose, the court may commit him in custody or on bail to the Crown Court for sentence.

(2) A person committed in custody under subsection (1) above shall be committed –

(a) if the court has been notified by the Secretary of State that a remand centre is available for the reception, from that court, of persons of the class or description of the person committed, to a remand centre;

(b) if the court has not been so notified, to a prison.

38 Committal for sentence on summary trial of offence triable either way [317]

(1) This section applies where on the summary trial of an offence triable either way (not being an offence as regards which this section is excluded by section 33 above) a person who is not less than 18 years old is convicted of the offence.

(2) If the court is of opinion –

(a) that the offence or the combination of the offence and one or more offences associated with it was so serious that greater punishment should be inflicted for the offence than the court has power to impose; or

(b) in the case of a violent or sexual offence committed by a person who is not less than 21 years old, that a sentence of imprisonment for a term longer than the court has power to impose is necessary to protect the public from serious harm from him,

the court may, in accordance with section 56 of the Criminal Justice Act 1967, commit the offender in custody or on bail to the Crown Court for sentence in accordance with the provisions of section 42 of the Powers of Criminal Courts Act 1973.

(3) Paragraphs (a) and (b) of subsection (2) above shall be construed as if they were contained in Part I of the Criminal Justice Act 1991.

(4) The preceding provisions of this section shall apply in relation to a corporation as if –

(a) the corporation were an individual who is not less than 18 years old; and

(b) in subsection (2) above, paragraph (b) and the words 'in custody or on bail' were omitted.

40 Restriction on amount payable under compensation   [318] order of magistrates' court

(1) The compensation to be paid under a compensation order made by a magistrates' court in respect of any offence of which the court has convicted the offender shall not exceed £5,000; and the compensation or total compensation to be paid under a compensation order or compensation orders made by a magistrates' court in respect of any offence or offences taken into consideration in determining sentence shall not exceed the difference (if any) between the amount or total amount which under the preceding provisions of this subsection is the maximum for the offence or offences of which the offender has been convicted and the amount or total amounts (if any) which are in fact ordered to be paid in respect of that offence or those offences.

(2) In subsection (1) above 'compensation order' has the meaning assigned to it by section 35(1) of the Powers of Criminal Courts Act 1973.

41 Restriction on grant of bail in treason   [319]

A person charged with treason shall not be granted bail except by order of a judge of the High Court or the Secretary of State.

42 Restriction on justices sitting after dealing with bail   [320]

(1) A justice of the peace shall not take part in trying the issue of an accused's guilt on the summary trial of an information if in the course of the same proceedings the justice has been informed, for the purpose of determining whether the accused shall be granted bail, that he has one or more previous convictions.

(2) For the purposes of this section any committal proceedings from which the proceedings on the summary trial arose shall be treated as part of the trial.

43 Bail on arrest   [321]

(1) Where a person has been granted bail under the Police and Criminal Evidence

Act 1984 subject to a duty to appear before a magistrates' court, the court before which he is to appear may appoint a later time as the time at which he is to appear and may enlarge the recognizances of any sureties for him at that time.

(2) The recognizance of any surety for any person granted bail subject to a duty to attend at a police station may be enforced as if it were conditioned for his appearance before a magistrates' court for the petty sessions area in which the police station named in the recognizance is situated.

PART II

CIVIL JURISDICTION AND PROCEDURE

51 Issue of summons on complaint [322]

Subject to the provisions of this Act, where a complaint is made to a justice of the peace acting for any petty sessions area upon which a magistrates' court acting for that area has power to make an order against any person, the justice may issue a summons directed to that person requiring him to appear before a magistrates' court acting for that area to answer to the complaint.

52 Jurisdiction to deal with complaints [323]

Where no express provision is made by any Act or the rules specifying what magistrates' courts shall have jurisdiction to hear a complaint, a magistrates' court shall have such jurisdiction if the complaint relates to anything done within the commission area for which the court is appointed or anything left undone that ought to have been done there, or ought to have been done either there or elsewhere, or relates to any other matter arising within that area.

In this section 'commission area' has the same meaning as in the Justices of the Peace Act 1979.

53 Procedure on hearing [324]

(1) On the hearing of a complaint, the court shall, if the defendant appears, state to him the substance of the complaint.

(2) The court, after hearing the evidence and the parties, shall make the order for which the complaint is made or dismiss the complaint.

(3) Where a complaint is for an order for the payment of a sum recoverable summarily as a civil debt, or for the variation of the rate of any periodical payments ordered by a magistrates' court to be made, or for such other matter as may be prescribed, the court may make the order with the consent of the defendant without hearing evidence.

58 Money recoverable summarily as civil debt [325]

(1) A magistrates' court shall have power to make an order on complaint for the payment of any money recoverable summarily as a civil debt.

(2) Any sum payment of which may be ordered by a magistrates' court shall be recoverable summarily as a civil debt except –

(a) a sum recoverable on complaint for a magistrates' court maintenance order; or

(b) a sum that may be adjudged to be paid by a summary conviction or by an order enforceable as if it were a summary conviction.

66 Composition of magistrates' courts for family proceedings: general [326]

(1) Subject to the provisions of this section, a magistrates' court when hearing family proceedings shall be composed of not more than three justices of the peace, including, so far as practicable, both a man and a woman.

(2) Subsection (1) above shall not apply to a magistrates' court for an inner London petty sessions area, and, notwithstanding anything in section 67 below, for the purpose of exercising jurisdiction to hear family proceedings such a court shall be composed of –

(a) a metropolitan stipendiary magistrate as chairman and one or two lay justices who are members of the family panel for that area; or
(b) two or three lay justices who are members of that panel;

or, if it is not practicable for such a court to be so composed, the court shall for that purpose be composed of a metropolitan stipendiary magistrate sitting alone.

(3) Where in pursuance of subsection (2) above a magistrates' court includes lay justices it shall, so far as practicable, include both a man and woman.

(4) In the preceding provisions of this section 'lay justices' means justices of the peace for the inner London area who are not metropolitan stipendiary magistrates.

(5) In this section 'inner London petty sessions area' means the City of London or any petty sessional division of the inner London area.

67 Family proceedings courts and family panels [327]

(1) Magistrates' courts constituted in accordance with the provisions of this section and sitting for the purpose of hearing family proceedings shall be known as family proceedings courts.

(2) A justice shall not be qualified to sit as a member of a family proceedings court unless he is a member of a family panel, that is to say a panel of justices specially appointed to deal with family proceedings ...

(7) A stipendiary magistrate who is a member of a family panel may, notwithstanding anything in section 66(1) above, hear and determine family proceedings when sitting alone.

(8) Nothing in this section shall require the formation of a family panel for the City of London.

69 Sittings of magistrates' courts for family proceedings [328]

(1) The business of magistrates' courts shall, so far as is consistent with the due dispatch of business, be arranged in such manner as may be requisite for separating the hearing and determination of family proceedings from other business.

(2) In the case of family proceedings in a magistrates' court other than proceedings under the Adoption Act 1976, no person shall be present during the hearing and determination by the court of the proceedings except –

(a) officers of the court;
(b) parties to the case before the court, their legal representatives, witnesses and other persons directly concerned in the case;
(c) representatives of newspapers or news agencies;
(d) any other person whom the court may in its discretion permit to be present, so, however, that permission shall not be withheld from a person who appears to the court to have adequate grounds for attendance.

(3) In relation to any family proceedings under the Adoption Act 1976, subsection (2) above shall apply with the omission of paragraphs (c) and (d).

(4) When hearing family proceedings, a magistrates' court may, if it thinks it necessary in the interest of the administration of justice or of public decency, direct that any persons, not being officers of the court or parties to the case, the parties' legal representatives, or other persons directly concerned in the case, be excluded during the taking of any indecent evidence.

(5) The powers conferred on a magistrates' court by this section shall be in addition and without prejudice to any other powers of the court to hear proceedings in camera.

(6) Nothing in this section shall affect the exercise by a magistrates' court of the power to direct that witnesses shall be excluded until they are called for examination.

PART III

SATISFACTION AND ENFORCEMENT

81 Enforcement of fines imposed on young offenders   [329]

(1) Where a magistrates' court would, but for section 1 of the Criminal Justice Act 1982, have power to commit to prison a person under the age of 18 for a default consisting in failure to pay, or want of sufficient distress to satisfy, a sum adjudged to be paid by a conviction, the court may, subject to the following provisions of this section, make –

    (a) an order requiring the defaulter's parent or guardian to enter into a recognizance to ensure that the defaulter pays so much of that sum as remains unpaid; or
    (b) an order directing so much of that sum as remains unpaid to be paid by the defaulter's parent or guardian instead of by the defaulter.

(2) An order under subsection (1) above shall not be made in respect of a defaulter –

    (a) in pursuance of paragraph (a) of that subsection, unless the parent or guardian in question consents;
    (b) in pursuance of paragraph (b) of that subsection, unless the court is satisfied in all the circumstances that it is reasonable to make the order.

(3) None of the following orders, namely –

    (a) an order under section 17(1) of the Criminal Justice Act 1982 for attendance at an attendance centre; or
    (b) any order under subsection (1) above,

shall be made by a magistrates' court in consequence of a default of a person under the age of 18 years consisting in failure to pay, or want of sufficient distress to satisfy, a sum adjudged to be paid by a conviction unless the court has since the conviction inquired into the defaulter's means in his presence on at least one occasion.

(4) An order under subsection (1) above shall not be made by a magistrates' court unless the court is satisfied that the defaulter has, or has had since the date on which the sum in question was adjudged to be paid, the means to pay the sum or any instalment of it on which he has defaulted, and refuses or neglects or, as the case may be, has refused or neglected, to pay it.

(5) An order under subsection (1) above may be made in pursuance of paragraph

(b) of that subsection against a parent or guardian who, having been required to attend, has failed to do so; but, save as aforesaid, an order under that subsection shall not be made in pursuance of that paragraph without giving the parent or guardian an opportunity of being heard.

(6) A parent or guardian may appeal to the Crown Court against an order under subsection (1) above made in pursuance of paragraph (b) of that subsection.

(7) Any sum ordered under subsection (1)(b) above to be paid by a parent or guardian may be recovered from him in like manner as if the order had been made on the conviction of the parent or guardian of an offence.

(8) In this section –

'guardian', in relation to a person under the age of 18, means a person appointed, according to law, to be his guardian, or by order of a court of competent jurisdiction;

'sum adjudged to be paid by a conviction' means any fine, costs, compensation or other sum adjudged to be paid by an order made on a finding of guilt, including an order made under section 35 of the Powers of Criminal Courts Act 1973 (compensation orders).

PART V

APPEAL AND CASE STATED

108 Right of appeal to the Crown Court [330]

(1) A person convicted by a magistrates' court may appeal to the Crown Court –

(a) if he pleaded guilty, against his sentence;

(b) if he did not, against the conviction or sentence.

(1A) Section 13 of the Powers of Criminal Courts Act 1973 (under which a conviction of an offence for which an order for conditional or absolute discharge is made is deemed not to be a conviction except for certain purposes) shall not prevent an appeal under this section, whether against conviction or otherwise.

(2) A person sentenced by a magistrates' court for an offence in respect of which a probation order or an order for conditional discharge has been previously made may appeal to the Crown Court against the sentence.

(3) In this section 'sentence' includes any order made on conviction by a magistrates' court, not being –

(b) an order for the payment of costs;

(c) an order under section 2 of the Protection of Animals Act 1911 (which enables a court to order the destruction of an animal); or

(d) an order made in pursuance of any enactment under which the court has no discretion as to the making of the order or its terms;

and also includes a declaration of relevance under the Football Spectators Act 1989.

111 Statement of case by magistrates' court [331]

(1) Any person who was a party to any proceeding before a magistrates' court or is aggrieved by the conviction, order, determination or other proceeding of the court may question the proceeding on the ground that it is wrong in law or is in excess of jurisdiction by applying to the justices composing the court to state a case for the opinion of the High Court on the question of law or jurisdiction involved; but a person shall not make an application under this section in respect

of a decision against which he has a right of appeal to the High Court or which by virtue of any enactment passed after 31 December 1879 is final.

(2) An application under subsection (1) above shall be made within 21 days after the day on which the decision of the magistrates' court was given.

(3) For the purpose of subsection (2) above, the day on which the decision of the magistrates' court is given shall, where the court has adjourned the trial of an information after conviction, be the day on which the court sentences or otherwise deals with the offender.

(4) On the making of an application under this section in respect of a decision any right of the applicant to appeal against the decision to the Crown Court shall cease.

(5) If the justices are of opinion that an application under this section is frivolous, they may refuse to state a case, and, if the applicant so requires, shall give him a certificate stating that the application has been refused; but the justices shall not refuse to state a case if the application is made by or under the direction of the Attorney General.

(6) Where justices refuse to state a case, the High Court may, on the application of the person who applied for the case to be stated, make an order of mandamus requiring the justices to state a case.

113 Bail on appeal or case stated [332]

(1) Where a person has given notice of appeal to the Crown Court against the decision of a magistrates' court or has applied to a magistrates' court to state a case for the opinion of the High Court, then, if he is in custody, the magistrates' court may grant him bail.

(2) If a person is granted bail under subsection (1) above, the time and place at which he is to appear (except in the event of the determination in respect of which the case is stated being reversed by the High Court) shall be –

(a) if he has given notice of appeal, the Crown Court at the time appointed for the hearing of the appeal;
(b) if he has applied for the statement of a case, the magistrates' court at such time within 10 days after the judgment of the High Court has been given as may be specified by the magistrates' court;

and any recognizance that may be taken from him or from any surety for him shall be conditioned accordingly.

(3) Subsection (1) above shall not apply where the accused has been committed to the Crown Court for sentence under section 37 or 38 above.

(4) Section 37(6) of the Criminal Justice Act 1948 (which relates to the currency of a sentence while a person is released on bail by the High Court) shall apply to a person released on bail by a magistrates' court under this section pending the hearing of a case stated as it applies to a person released on bail by the High Court under section 22 of the Criminal Justice Act 1967.

PART VI

RECOGNIZANCES

115 Binding over to keep the peace or be of good behaviour [333]

(1) The power of a magistrates' court on the complaint of any person to adjudge any other person to enter into a recognizance, with or without sureties, to keep

the peace or to be of good behaviour towards the complainant shall be exercised by order on complaint.

(2) Where a complaint is made under this section, the power of the court to remand the defendant under subsection (5) of section 55 above shall not be subject to the restrictions imposed by subsection (6) of that section.

(3) If any person ordered by a magistrates' court under subsection (1) above to enter into a recognizance, with or without sureties, to keep the peace or to be of good behaviour fails to comply with the order, the court may commit him to custody for a period not exceeding six months or until he sooner complies with the order.

120 Forfeiture of recognizance   [334]

(1) Where a recognizance to keep the peace or to be of good behaviour has been entered into before a magistrates' court or any recognizance is conditioned for the appearance of a person before a magistrates' court or for his doing any other thing connected with a proceeding before a magistrates' court, and the recognizance appears to the court to be forfeited, the court may, subject to subsection (2) below, declare the recognizance to be forfeited and adjudge the persons bound thereby, whether as principal or sureties, or any of them, to pay the sum in which they are respectively bound.

(2) Where a recognizance is conditioned to keep the peace or to be of good behaviour, the court shall not declare it forfeited except by order made on complaint.

(3) The court which declares the recognizance to be forfeited may, instead of adjudging any person to pay the whole sum in which he is bound, adjudge him to pay part only of the sum or remit the sum.

(4) Payment of any sum adjudged to be paid under this section, including any costs awarded against the defendant, may be enforced, and any such sum shall be applied, as if it were a fine and as if the adjudication were a summary conviction of an offence not punishable with imprisonment and so much of section 85(1) above as empowers a court to remit fines shall not apply to the sum but so much thereof as relates to remission after a term of imprisonment has been imposed shall so apply; but at any time before the issue of a warrant of commitment to enforce payment of the sum, or before the sale of goods under a warrant of distress to satisfy the sum, the court may remit the whole or any part of the sum either absolutely or on such conditions as the court thinks just.

(5) A recognizance such as is mentioned in this section shall not be enforced otherwise than in accordance with this section, and accordingly shall not be transmitted to the Crown Court nor shall its forfeiture be certified to that Court.

PART VII

MISCELLANEOUS AND SUPPLEMENTARY

121 Constitution and place of sitting of court   [335]

(1) A magistrates' court shall not try an information summarily or hear a complaint except when composed of at least two justices unless the trial or hearing is one that by virtue of any enactment may take place before a single justice.

(2) A magistrates' court shall not hold an inquiry into the means of an offender for the purposes of section 82 above or determine under that section at a hearing at

which the offender is not present whether to issue a warrant of commitment except when composed of at least two justices.

(3) A magistrates' court shall not –

(a) try summarily an information for an indictable offence or hear a complaint except when sitting in a petty-sessional court-house;

(b) try an information for a summary offence or hold an inquiry into the means of an offender for the purposes of section 82 above, or impose imprisonment, except when sitting in a petty-sessional court-house or an occasional court-house.

(4) Subject to the provisions of any enactment to the contrary, where a magistrates' court is required by this section to sit in a petty-sessional or occasional court-house, it shall sit in open court.

(5) A magistrates' court composed of a single justice, or sitting in an occasional court-house, shall not impose imprisonment for a period exceeding 14 days or order a person to pay more than £1.

(6) Subject to the provisions of subsection (7) below, the justices composing the court before which any proceedings take place shall be present during the whole of the proceedings; but, if during the course of the proceedings any justice absents himself, he shall cease to act further therein and, if the remaining justices are enough to satisfy the requirements of the preceding provisions of this section, the proceedings may continue before a court composed of those justices.

(7) Where the trial of an information is adjourned after the accused has been convicted and before he is sentenced or otherwise dealt with, the court which sentences or deals with him need not be composed of the same justices as that which convicted him; but, where among the justices composing the court which sentences or deals with an offender there are any who were not sitting when he was convicted, the court which sentences or deals with the offender shall before doing so make such inquiry into the facts and circumstances of the case as will enable the justices who were not sitting when the offender was convicted to be fully acquainted with those facts and circumstances.

(8) This section shall have effect subject to the provisions of this Act relating to family proceedings.

122 Appearance by legal representative   [336]

(1) A party to any proceedings before a magistrates' court may be represented by a legal representative.

(2) Subject to subsection (3) below, an absent party so represented shall be deemed not to be absent.

(3) Appearance of a party by a legal representative shall not satisfy any provision of any enactment or any condition of a recognizance expressly requiring his presence.

127 Limitation of time   [337]

(1) Except as otherwise expressly provided by any enactment and subject to subsection (2) below, a magistrates' court shall not try an information or hear a complaint unless the information was laid, or the complaint made, within 6 months from the time when the offence was committed, or the matter of complaint arose.

(2) Nothing in –

(a) subsection (1) above; or

(b) subject to subsection (4) below, any other enactment (however framed or worded) which, as regards any offence to which it applies, would but for this section impose a time-limit on the power of a magistrates' court to try an information summarily or impose a limitation on the time for taking summary proceedings,

shall apply in relation to any indictable offence.

(3) Without prejudice to the generality of paragraph (b) of subsection (2) above, that paragraph includes enactments which impose a time-limit that applies only in certain circumstances (for example, where the proceedings are not instituted by or with the consent of the Director of Public Prosecutions or some other specified authority).

(4) Where, as regards any indictable offence, there is imposed by any enactment (however framed or worded, and whether falling within subsection (2)(b) above or not) a limitation on the time for taking proceedings on indictment for that offence no summary proceedings for that offence shall be taken after the latest time for taking proceedings on indictment.

142 Power of magistrates' court to re-open cases to rectify mistakes etc   [338]

(1) Subject to subsection (4) below, a magistrates' court may vary or rescind a sentence or other order imposed or made by it when dealing with an offender; and it is hereby declared that this power extends to replacing a sentence or order which for any reason appears to be invalid by another which the court has power to impose or make.

(2) Where a person is found guilty by a magistrates' court in a case in which he has pleaded not guilty or the court has proceeded in his absence under section 11(1) above, and it subsequently appears to the court that it would be in the interests of justice that the case should be heard again by different justices, the court may, subject to subsection (4) below, so direct.

(3) Where a court gives a direction under subsection (2) above –

(a) the finding of guilty and any sentence or other order imposed or made in consequence thereof shall be of no effect; and
(b) section 10(4) above shall apply as if the trial of the person in question had been adjourned.

(4) The powers conferred by subsections (1) and (2) above shall be exercisable only within the period of 28 days beginning with the day on which the sentence or order was imposed or made or the person was found guilty, as the case may be, and only –

(a) by a court constituted in the same manner as the court by which the sentence or order was imposed or made or, as the case may be, by which the person in question was found guilty, or
(b) where that court comprised 3 or more justices of the peace, by a court which consists of or comprises a majority of those justices.

(5) Where a sentence or order is varied under subsection (1) above, the sentence or other order, as so varied, shall take effect from the beginning of the day on which it was originally imposed or made, unless the court otherwise directs.

144 Rule committee and rules of procedure   [339]

(1) The Lord Chancellor may appoint a rule committee for magistrates' courts, and may on the advice of or after consultation with the rule committee make rules for

regulating and prescribing the procedure and practice to be followed in magistrates' courts and by justices' clerks.

(2) The rule committee shall consist of the Lord Chief Justice, the President of the Family Division of the High Court, the chief metropolitan stipendiary magistrate and such number of other persons appointed by the Lord Chancellor as he may determine.

(3) Among the members of the committee appointed by the Lord Chancellor there shall be at least

(a) one justices' clerk;
(b) one person who has a Supreme Court qualification (within the meaning of section 71 of the Courts and Legal Services Act 1990); and
(c) one person who has been granted by an authorised body, under Part II of that Act, the right to conduct litigation in relation to all proceedings in the Supreme Court.

(4) The power to make rules conferred by this section shall be exercisable by statutory instrument which shall be subject to annulment by resolution of either House of Parliament.

(5) In this section the expression 'justices' clerk' means a clerk to the justices for a petty sessions area.

148 'Magistrates' court'   [340]

(1) In this Act the expression 'magistrates' court' means any justice or justices of the peace acting under any enactment or by virtue of his or their commission or under the common law.

(2) Except where the contrary is expressed, anything authorised or required by this Act to be done by, to or before the magistrates' court by, to or before which any other thing was done, or is to be done, may be done by, to or before any magistrates' court acting for the same petty sessions area as that court.

150 Interpretation of other terms   [341]

(1) In this Act, unless the context otherwise requires, the following expressions have the meaning hereby assigned to them, that is to say –

'bail in criminal proceedings' has the same meaning as in the Bail Act 1976;
'commit to custody' means commit to prison or, where any enactment authorises or requires committal to some other place of detention instead of committal to prison, to that other place;
'committal proceedings' means proceedings before a magistrates' court acting as examining justices; ...
'fine', except for the purposes of any enactment imposing a limit on the amount of any fine, includes any pecuniary penalty or pecuniary forfeiture or pecuniary compensation payable under a conviction;
'impose imprisonment' means pass a sentence of imprisonment or fix a term of imprisonment for failure to pay any sum of money, or for want of sufficient distress to satisfy any sum of money, or for failure to do or abstain from doing anything required to be done or left undone;
'legal representative' means an authorised advocate or authorised litigator, as defined by section 119(1) of the Courts and Legal Services Act 1990; ...
'petty-sessional court-house' means any of the following, that is to say –

(a) a court-house or place at which justices are accustomed to assemble for holding special or petty sessions or for the time being appointed as a substitute for such a court-house or place (including, where justices are accustomed to assemble for either special or petty sessions at more than one court-house or place in a petty sessional division, any such court-house or place);

(b) a court-house or place at which a stipendiary magistrate is authorised by law to do alone any act authorised to be done by more than one justice of the peace;

'petty sessions area' has the same meaning as in the Justices of the Peace Act 1979;

'prescribed' means prescribed by the rules;

'the register' means the register of proceedings before a magistrates' court required by the rules to be kept by the clerk of the court;

'the rules' means rules made under section 144 above;

'sentence' does not include a committal in default of payment of any sum of money, or for want of sufficient distress to satisfy any sum of money, or for failure to do or abstain from doing anything required to be done or left undone;

'sum enforceable as a civil debt' means –

(a) any sum recoverable summarily as a civil debt which is adjudged to be paid by the order of a magistrates' court;

(b) any other sum expressed by this or any other Act to be so enforceable;

...

(2) Except where the contrary is expressed or implied, anything required or authorised by this Act to be done by justices may, where two or more justices are present, be done by one of them on behalf of the others.

(3) Any reference in this Act to a sum adjudged to be paid by a conviction or order of a magistrates' court shall be construed as including a reference to any costs, damages or compensation adjudged to be paid by the conviction or order of which the amount is ascertained by the conviction or order; but this subsection does not prejudice the definition of 'sum adjudged to be paid by a conviction' contained in subsection (8) of section 81 above for the purposes of that section.

(4) Where the age of any person at any time is material for the purposes of any provision of this Act regulating the powers of a magistrates' court, his age at the material time shall be deemed to be or to have been that which appears to the court after considering any available evidence to be or to have been his age at that time ...

SCHEDULE 1

OFFENCES TRIABLE EITHER WAY BY VIRTUE OF SECTION 17

1. Offences at common law of public nuisance.

2. Offences under section 8 of the Disorderly Houses Act 1751 (appearing to be keeper of bawdy houses, etc) ...

5. Offences under the following provisions of the Offences against the Person Act 1861 –

(a) section 16 (threats to kill);

(b) section 20 (inflicting bodily injury, with or without a weapon);

(c) section 26 (not providing apprentices or servants with food, etc);

(d) section 27 (abandoning or exposing child);

(e) section 34 (doing or omitting to do anything so as to endanger railway passengers);

(f) section 36 (assaulting a clergyman at a place of worship, etc);

(g) section 38 (assault with intent to resist apprehension);

(h) section 47 (assault occasioning bodily harm);

(i) section 57 (bigamy);

(j) section 60 (concealing the birth of a child) ...

23. Offences under the following provisions of the Sexual Offences Act 1956 –

(a) section 6 (unlawful sexual intercourse with a girl under 16);

(b) section 13 (indecency between men) ;

(c) section 26 (permitting a girl under 16 to use premises for sexual intercourse) ...

26. The following offences under the Criminal Law Act 1967 –

(a) offences under section 4(1) (assisting offenders); and

(b) offences under section 5(1) (concealing arrestable offences and giving false information),

where the offence to which they relate is triable either way ...

28. All indictable offences under the Theft Act 1968 except: –

(a) robbery, aggravated burglary, blackmail and assault with intent to rob;

(b) burglary comprising the commission of, or an intention to commit, an offence which is triable only on indictment;

(c) burglary in a dwelling if any person in the dwelling was subjected to violence or the threat of violence ...

32. Committing an indecent assault upon a person whether male or female.

33. Aiding, abetting, counselling or procuring the commission of any offence listed in the preceding paragraphs of this Schedule except paragraph 26.

35. Any offence consisting in the incitement to commit an offence triable either way except an offence mentioned in paragraph 33.

SCHEDULE 2

OFFENCES FOR WHICH THE VALUE INVOLVED IS RELEVANT TO THE MODE OF TRIAL

Offence	*Value involved*	*How measured*
1. Offences under section 1 of the Criminal Damage Act 1971 (destroying or damaging property), excluding any offence committed by destroying or damaging property by fire.	As regards property alleged to have been destroyed, its value. As regards property alleged to have been damaged, the value of the alleged damaged.	[For property destroyed] What the property would probably have cost to buy in the open market at the material time. (a) If immediately after the material time the damage was capable of repair – (i) what would probably then have been the market price for the repair of the damage, or (ii) what the property alleged to have been damaged would probably have cost to buy in the open market at the material time, whichever is the less; or

Offence	Value involved	How measured
		(b) if immediately after the material time the damage was beyond repair, what the said property would probably have cost to buy in the open market at the material time.
2. The following offences, namely – (a) aiding, abetting, counselling or procuring the commission of any offence mentioned in paragraph 1 above; (b) attempting to commit any offence so mentioned; and (c) inciting another to commit any offence so mentioned.	The value indicated in paragraph 1 above for the offence alleged to have been aided, abetted, counselled or procured, or attempted or incited.	As for the corresponding entry in paragraph 1 above.
3. Offences under section 12A of the Theft Act 1968 (aggravated vehicle-taking) where no allegation is made under subsection (1)(b) other than of damage, whether to the vehicle or other property or both.	The total value of the damage alleged to have been caused.	(1) In the case of damage to any property other than the vehicle involved in the offence, as for the corresponding entry in paragraph 1 above, substituting a reference to the time of the accident concerned for any reference to the material time. (2) In the case of damage to the vehicle involved in the offence – (a) if immediately after the vehicle was recovered the damage was capable of repair – (i) what would probably then have been the market price for the repair of the damage, or (ii) what the vehicle would probably have cost to buy in the open market immediately before it was unlawfully taken, which is the less; or (b) if immediately after the vehicle was recovered the damage was beyond repair, what the vehicle would probably have cost to buy in the open market immediately before it was unlawfully taken.

[As amended by the Criminal Justice Act 1982, ss59, 61, 66(2), 77, 78, 79, Schedule 9, para 1(c), Schedule 14, paras 47, 48, 49, 51, Schedule 16, Schedule 17, para 1; Police and Criminal Evidence Act 1984, s47(8)(a); Local Government Act 1985, s12(11); Prosecution of Offences Act 1985, s31(5), Schedule 1, Pt I, para 2; Family Law Reform Act 1987, s33(1), Schedule 2, para 80; Criminal Justice Act 1988, ss38, 61(1), (6), 123(6), 170(1), (2), Schedule 8, Pt I, para 2, Schedule 15, paras 65, 66, 67, Schedule 16; Children Act 1989, ss92(11), 108(7), Schedule 11, Pt II, para 8(c)-(g), Schedule 15; Football Spectators Act 1989, s23(3)(c); Courts and Legal Services Act 1990, s125(3), Schedule 18, para 25(1), (2), (3)(a), (b), 4 (a), (6), (7); Criminal Justice Act 1991, ss17(2)(a), (b), (c), (3)(a), (b), 68, 100, 101(2), Schedule 4, Pts I, II, Schedule 8, para 6(1)(a), (b), (c), 6(2), Schedule 11, paras 25, 26, Schedule 13; Aggravated Vehicle-Taking Act 1992, s2(1), (2), (3); Criminal Justice Act 1993, s66(8).]

SUPREME COURT ACT 1981
(1981 c 54)

PART I

CONSTITUTION OF SUPREME COURT

1 The Supreme Court   [342]

(1) The Supreme Court of England and Wales shall consist of the Court of Appeal, the High Court of Justice and the Crown Court, each having such jurisdiction as is conferred on it by or under this or any other Act.

(2) The Lord Chancellor shall be president of the Supreme Court.

2 The Court of Appeal   [343]

(1) The Court of Appeal shall consist of ex-officio judges and not more than 29 ordinary judges.

(2) The following shall be ex-officio judges of the Court of Appeal –

(a) the Lord Chancellor;
(b) any person who has been Lord Chancellor;
(c) any Lord of Appeal in Ordinary who at the date of his appointment was, or was qualified for appointment as, an ordinary judge of the Court of Appeal or held an office within paragraphs (d) to (g);
(d) the Lord Chief Justice;
(e) the Master of the Rolls;
(f) the President of the Family Division; and
(g) the Vice-Chancellor;

but a person within paragraph (b) or (c) shall not be required to sit and act as a judge of the Court of Appeal unless at the Lord Chancellor's request he consents to do so.

(3) The ordinary judges of the Court of Appeal (including the vice-president, if any, of either division) shall be styled 'Lords Justices of Appeal'.

(4) Her Majesty may by Order in Council from time to time amend subsection (1) so as to increase or further increase the maximum number of ordinary judges of the Court of Appeal.

(5) No recommendation shall be made to Her Majesty in Council to make an Order under subsection (4) unless a draft of the Order has been laid before Parliament and approved by resolution of each House of Parliament.

(6) The Court of Appeal shall be taken to be duly constituted notwithstanding any vacancy in the office of Lord Chancellor, Lord Chief Justice, Master of the Rolls, President of the Family Division or Vice-Chancellor.

3 Divisions of Court of Appeal [344]

(1) There shall be two divisions of the Court of Appeal, namely the criminal division and the civil division.

(2) The Lord Chief Justice shall be president of the criminal division of the Court of Appeal, and the Master of the Rolls shall be president of the civil division of that court.

(3) The Lord Chancellor may appoint one of the ordinary judges of the Court of Appeal as vice-president of both divisions of that court, or one of those judges as vice-president of the criminal division and another of them as vice-president of the civil division.

(4) When sitting in a court of either division of the Court of Appeal in which no ex-officio judge of the Court of Appeal is sitting, the vice-president (if any) of that division shall preside.

(5) Any number of courts of either division of the Court of Appeal may sit at the same time.

4 The High Court [345]

(1) The High Court shall consist of –

    (a) the Lord Chancellor;
    (b) the Lord Chief Justice;
    (c) the President of the Family Division;
    (d) the Vice-Chancellor;
    (dd) the Senior Presiding Judge; and
    (e) not more than 98 puisne judges of the court.

(2) The puisne judges of the High Court shall be styled 'Justices of the High Court'.

(3) All the judges of the High Court shall, except where this Act expressly provides otherwise, have in all respects equal power, authority and jurisdiction.

(4) Her Majesty may by Order in Council from time to time amend subsection (1) so as to increase or further increase the maximum number of puisne judges of the High Court.

(5) No recommendation shall be made to Her Majesty in Council to make an Order under subsection (4) unless a draft of the Order has been laid before Parliament and approved by resolution of each House of Parliament.

(6) The High Court shall be taken to be duly constituted notwithstanding any vacancy in the office of Lord Chancellor, Lord Chief Justice, President of the Family Division, Vice-Chancellor or Senior Presiding Judge.

5 Divisions of High Court [346]

(1) There shall be three divisions of the High Court, namely –

    (a) the Chancery Division, consisting of the Lord Chancellor, who shall be president thereof, the Vice-Chancellor, who shall be vice-president thereof, and such of the puisne judges as are for the time being attached thereto in accordance with this section;
    (b) the Queen's Bench Division, consisting of the Lord Chief Justice, who shall

be president thereof, and such of the puisne judges as are for the time being so attached thereto; and

(c) the Family Division, consisting of the President of the Family Division and such of the puisne judges as are for the time being so attached thereto.

(2) The puisne judges of the High Court shall be attached to the various Divisions by direction of the Lord Chancellor; and any such judge may with his consent be transferred from one Division to another by direction of the Lord Chancellor, but shall be so transferred only with the concurrence of the senior judge of the Division from which it is proposed to transfer him.

(3) Any judge attached to any Division may act as an additional judge of any other Division at the request of the Lord Chief Justice made with the concurrence of the President of the Family Division or the Vice-Chancellor, or both, as appropriate.

(4) Nothing in this section shall be taken to prevent a judge of any Division (whether nominated under section 6(2) or not) from sitting, whenever required, in a divisional court of another Division or for any judge of another Division.

(5) Without prejudice to the provisions of this Act relating to the distribution of business in the High Court, all jurisdiction vested in the High Court under this Act shall belong to all the Divisions alike.

6 The Patents, Admiralty and Commercial Courts [347]

(1) There shall be –

(a) as part of the Chancery Division, a Patents Court; and
(b) as parts of the Queen's Bench Division, an Admiralty Court and a Commercial Court.

(2) The judges of the Patents Court, of the Admiralty Court and of the Commercial Court shall be such of the puisne judges of the High Court as the Lord Chancellor may from time to time nominate to be judges of the Patents Court, Admiralty Judges and Commercial Judges respectively.

7 Power to alter Divisions or transfer certain courts [348]
to different Divisions

(1) Her Majesty may from time to time, on a recommendation of the judges mentioned in subsection (2), by Order in Council direct that –

(a) any increase or reduction in the number of Divisions of the High Court; or
(b) the transfer of any of the courts mentioned in section 6(1) to a different Division,

be carried into effect in pursuance of the recommendation.

(2) Those judges are the Lord Chancellor, the Lord Chief Justice, the Master of the Rolls, the President of the Family Division and the Vice-Chancellor.

(3) An Order in Council under this section may include such incidental, supplementary or consequential provisions as appear to Her Majesty necessary or expedient, including amendments of provisions referring to particular Divisions contained in this Act or any other statutory provision.

(4) Any Order in Council under this section shall be subject to annulment in pursuance of a resolution of either House of Parliament.

8 The Crown Court [349]

(1) The jurisdiction of the Crown Court shall be exercisable by –

(a) any judge of the High Court; or

(b) any Circuit judge or Recorder; or

(c) subject to and in accordance with the provisions of sections 74 and 75(2), a judge of the High Court, Circuit judge or Recorder sitting with not more than four justices of the peace,

and any such persons when exercising the jurisdiction of the Crown Court shall be judges of the Crown Court.

(2) A justice of the peace shall not be disqualified from acting as a judge of the Crown Court for the reason that the proceedings are not at a place within the area for which he was appointed as a justice, or because the proceedings are not related to that area in any other way.

(3) When the Crown Court sits in the City of London it shall be known as the Central Criminal Court; and the Lord Mayor of the City and any Alderman of the City shall be entitled to sit as judges of the Central Criminal Court with any judge of the High Court or any Circuit judge or Recorder.

9 Assistance for transaction of judicial business [350] of Supreme Court

(1) A person within any entry in column 1 of the following Table may at any time, at the request of the appropriate authority, act –

(a) as a judge of a relevant court specified in the request; or

(b) if the request relates to a particular division of a relevant court so specified, as a judge of that court in that division.

	TABLE
1 *Judge or ex-judge*	**2** *Where competent to act on request*
1. A judge of the Court of Appeal.	The High Court and the Crown Court.
2. A person who has been a judge of the Court of Appeal.	The Court of Appeal, the High Court and the Crown Court.
3. A puisne judge of the High Court.	The Court of Appeal.
4. A person who has been a puisne judge of the High Court.	The Court of Appeal, the High Court and the Crown Court.
5. A Circuit judge.	The High Court.
6. A Recorder.	The High Court.

(2) In subsection (1) –

'the appropriate authority' –

(a) in the case of a request to a judge of the High Court to act in the criminal division of the Court of Appeal as a judge of that court, means the Lord Chief Justice or, at any time when the Lord Chief Justice is unable to make such a request himself or there is a vacancy in the office of Lord Chief Justice, the Master of the Rolls;

(b) in any other case means the Lord Chancellor;

'relevant court', in the case of a person within any entry in column 1 of the Table, means a court specified in relation to that entry in column 2 of the Table.

(3) In the case of –

(a) a request under subsection (1) to a Lord Justice of Appeal to act in the High Court; or

(b) any request under that subsection to a puisne judge of the High Court or a Circuit judge,

it shall be the duty of the person to whom the request is made to comply with it.

(4) Without prejudice to section 24 of the Courts Acts 1971 (temporary appointment of deputy Circuit judges and assistant Recorders), if it appears to the Lord Chancellor that it is expedient as a temporary measure to make an appointment under this subsection in order to facilitate the disposal of business in the High Court or the Crown Court, he may appoint a person qualified for appointment as a puisne judge of the High Court to be a deputy judge of the High Court during such period or on such occasions as the Lord Chancellor thinks fit; and during the period or on the occasions for which a person is appointed as a deputy judge under this subsection, he may act as a puisne judge of the High Court.

(5) Every person while acting under this section shall, subject to subsection (6), be treated for all purposes as, and accordingly may perform any of the functions of, a judge of the court in which he is acting.

(6) A person shall not by virtue of subsection (5) –

(a) be treated as a judge of the court in which he is acting for the purposes of section 98(2) or of any statutory provision relating to –

(i) the appointment, retirement, removal or disqualification of judges of that court;

(ii) the tenure of office and oaths to be taken by such judges; or

(iii) the remuneration, allowances or pensions of such judges; or

(b) subject to subsection (7), be treated as having been a judge of a court in which he has acted only under this section.

(7) Notwithstanding the expiry of any period for which a person is authorised by virtue of subsection (1) or (4) to act as a judge of a particular court –

(a) he may attend at that court for the purpose of continuing to deal with, giving judgment in, or dealing with any ancillary matter relating to, any case begun before him while acting as a judge of that court; and

(b) for that purpose, and for the purpose of any proceedings arising out of any such case or matter, he shall be treated as being or, as the case may be, having been a judge of that court.

(8) Such remuneration and allowances as the Lord Chancellor may, with the concurrence of the Minister for the Civil Service, determine may be paid out of money provided by Parliament –

(a) to any person who has been –

(i) a Lord of Appeal in Ordinary; or

(ii) a judge of the Court of Appeal; or

(iii) a judge of the High Court,

and is by virtue of subsection (1) acting as mentioned in that subsection;

(b) to any deputy judge of the High Court appointed under subsection (4).

10 Appointment of judges of Supreme Court   **[351]**

(1) Whenever the office of Lord Chief Justice, Master of the Rolls, President of the Family Division or Vice-Chancellor is vacant, Her Majesty may by letters patent appoint a qualified person to that office.

(2) Subject to the limits on numbers for the time being imposed by sections 2(1) and 4(1), Her Majesty may from time to time by letters patent appoint qualified persons as Lord Justices of Appeal or as puisne judges of the High Court.

(3) No person shall be qualified for appointment –

(a) as Lord Chief Justice, Master of the Rolls, President of the Family Division or Vice-Chancellor, unless he is qualified for appointment as a Lord Justice of Appeal or is a judge of the Court of Appeal;

(b) as a Lord Justice of Appeal, unless –

(i) he has a ten year High Court qualification within the meaning of section 71 of the Courts and Legal Services Act 1990; or

(ii) he is a judge of the High Court; or

(c) as a puisne judge of the High Court, unless –

(i) he has a ten year High Court qualification within the meaning of section 71 of the Courts and Legal Services Act 1990; or

(ii) he is a Circuit judge who has held that office for at least two years.

(4) Every person appointed to an office mentioned in subsection (1) or as a Lord Justice of Appeal or puisne judge of the High Court shall, as soon as may be after his acceptance of office, take the oath of allegiance and the judicial oath, as set out in the Promissory Oaths Act 1868, in the presence of the Lord Chancellor.

11 Tenure of office of judges of Supreme Court   **[352]**

(1) This section applies to the office of any judge of the Supreme Court except the Lord Chancellor.

(2) A person appointed to an office to which this section applies shall vacate it on the day on which he attains the age of 75 years unless by virtue of this section he has ceased to hold it before then.

(3) A person appointed to an office to which this section applies shall hold that office during good behaviour, subject to a power of removal by Her Majesty on an address presented to Her by both Houses of Parliament.

(4) A person holding an office within section 2(2)(d) to (g) shall vacate that office on becoming Lord Chancellor or a Lord of Appeal in Ordinary.

(5) A Lord Justice of Appeal shall vacate that office on becoming an ex-officio judge of the Court of Appeal.

(6) A puisne judge of the High Court shall vacate that office on becoming a judge of the Court of Appeal.

(7) A person who holds an office to which this section applies may at any time resign it by giving the Lord Chancellor notice in writing to that effect.

(8) The Lord Chancellor, if satisfied by means of a medical certificate that a person holding an office to which this section applies –

(a) is disabled by permanent infirmity from the performance of the duties of his office; and

(b) is for the time being incapacitated from resigning his office,

may, subject to subsection (9), by instrument under his hand declare that person's office to have been vacated; and the instrument shall have the like effect for all purposes as if that person had on the date of the instrument resigned his office.

(9) A declaration under subsection (8) with respect to a person shall be of no effect unless it is made –

(a) in the case of any of the Lord Chief Justice, the Master of the Rolls, the President of the Family Division and the Vice-Chancellor, with the concurrence of two others of them;

(b) in the case of a Lord Justice of Appeal, with the concurrence of the Master of the Rolls;

(c) in the case of a puisne judge of any Division of the High Court, with the concurrence of the senior judge of that Division.

13 Precedence of judges of Supreme Court   [353]

(1) When sitting in the Court of Appeal –

(a) the Lord Chief Justice and the Master of the Rolls shall rank in that order; and

(b) Lords of Appeal in Ordinary and persons who have been Lord Chancellor shall rank next after the Master of the Rolls and, among themselves, according to the priority of the dates on which they respectively became Lords of Appeal in Ordinary or Lord Chancellor, as the case may be.

(2) Subject to subjection (1)(b), the President of the Family Division shall rank next after the Master of the Rolls.

(3) The Vice-Chancellor shall rank next after the President of the Family Division.

(4) The vice-president or vice-presidents of the divisions of the Court of Appeal shall rank next after the Vice-Chancellor; and if there are two vice-presidents of those divisions, they shall rank, among themselves, according to the priority of the dates on which they respectively became vice-presidents.

(5) The Lord Justices of Appeal (other than the vice-president or vice-presidents of the divisions of the Court of Appeal) shall rank after the ex-officio judges of the Court of Appeal and, among themselves, according to the priority of the dates on which they respectively became judges of that court.

(6) The puisne judges of the High Court shall rank next after the judges of the Court of Appeal and, among themselves, according to the priority of the dates on which they respectively became judges of the High Court.

14 Power of judges of Supreme or Crown Court to act   [354]
in cases relating to rates and taxes

(1) A judge of the Supreme Court or of the Crown Court shall not be incapable of acting as such in any proceedings by reason of being, as one of a class of ratepayers, taxpayers, or persons of any other description, liable in common with others to pay, or contribute to, or benefit from, any rate or tax which may be increased, reduced or in any way affected by those proceedings.

(2) In this section 'rate or tax' means any rate, tax, duty or liability, whether public, general or local, and includes –

(a) any fund formed from the proceeds of any such rate, tax, duty or liability; and

(b) any fund applicable for purposes the same as, or similar to, those for which the proceeds of any such rate, tax, duty or liability are or might be applied.

PART II

JURISDICTION

THE COURT OF APPEAL

15 General jurisdiction of Court of Appeal [355]

(1) The Court of Appeal shall be a superior court of record.

(2) Subject to the provisions of this Act, there shall be exercisable by the Court of Appeal –

(a) all such jurisdiction (whether civil or criminal) as is conferred on it by this or any other Act; and
(b) all such other jurisdiction (whether civil or criminal) as was exercisable by it immediately before the commencement of this Act.

(3) For all purposes of or incidental to –

(a) the hearing and determination of any appeal to the civil division of the Court of Appeal; and
(b) the amendment, execution and enforcement of any judgment or order made on such an appeal,

the Court of Appeal shall have all the authority and jurisdiction of the court or tribunal from which the appeal was brought.

(4) It is hereby declared that any provision in this or any other Act which authorises or requires the taking of any steps for the execution or enforcement of a judgment or order of the High Court applies in relation to a judgment or order of the civil division of the Court of Appeal as it applies in relation to a judgment or order of the High Court.

16 Appeals from High Court [356]

(1) Subject as otherwise provided by this or any other Act (and in particular to the provision in section 13(2)(a) of the Administration of Justice Act 1969 excluding appeals to the Court of Appeal in cases where leave to appeal from the High Court directly to the House of Lords is granted under Part II of that Act), the Court of Appeal shall have jurisdiction to hear and determine appeals from any judgment or order of the High Court.

(2) An appeal from a judgment or order of the High Court when acting as a prize court shall not be to the Court of Appeal, but shall be to Her Majesty in Council in accordance with the Prize Acts 1864 to 1944.

17 Applications for new trial [357]

(1) Where any cause or matter, or any issue in any cause or matter, has been tried in the High Court, any application for a new trial thereof, or to set aside a verdict, finding or judgment therein, shall be heard and determined by the Court of Appeal except where rules of court made in pursuance of subsection (2) provide otherwise.

(2) As regards cases where the trial was by a judge alone and no error of the court at the trial is alleged, or any prescribed class of such cases, rules of court may provide that any such application as is mentioned in subsection (1) shall be heard and determined by the High Court.

(3) Nothing in this section shall alter the practice in bankruptcy.

18 Restrictions on appeals to Court of Appeal   [358]

(1) No appeal shall lie to the Court of Appeal –

(a) except as provided by the Administration of Justice Act 1960, from any judgment of the High Court in any criminal cause or matter;

(b) from any order of the High Court or any other court or tribunal allowing an extension of time for appealing from a judgment or order;

(c) from any order, judgment or decision of the High Court or any other court or tribunal which, by virtue of any provision (however expressed) of this or any other Act, is final;

(d) from a decree absolute of divorce or nullity of marriage, by a party who, having had time and opportunity to appeal from the decree nisi on which that decree was founded, has not appealed from the decree nisi;

(g) except as provided by the Arbitration Act 1979, from any decision of the High Court –

(i) on an appeal under section 1 of that Act on a question of law arising out of an arbitration award; or

(ii) under section 2 of that Act on a question of law arising in the course of a reference.

(1A) In any such class of case as may be prescribed by Rules of the Supreme Court, an appeal shall lie to the Court of Appeal only with the leave of the Court of Appeal or such court or tribunal as may be specified by the rules in relation to that class.

(1B) Any enactment which authorises leave to appeal to the Court of Appeal being given by a single judge, or by a court consisting of two judges, shall have effect subject to any provision which –

(a) is made by Rules of the Supreme Court; and

(b) in such classes of case as may be prescribed by the rules, requires leave to be given by such greater number of judges (not exceeding three) as may be so specified.

THE HIGH COURT

19 General jurisdiction   [359]

(1) The High Court shall be a superior court of record.

(2) Subject to the provisions of this Act, there shall be exercisable by the High Court –

(a) all such jurisdiction (whether civil or criminal) as is conferred on it by this or any other Act; and

(b) all such other jurisdiction (whether civil or criminal) as was exercisable by it immediately before the commencement of this Act (including jurisdiction conferred on a judge of the High Court by any statutory provision).

(3) Any jurisdiction of the High Court shall be exercised only by a single judge of that court, except in so far as it is –

(a) by or by virtue of rules of court or any other statutory provision required to be exercised by a divisional court; or

(b) by rules of court made exercisable by a master, registrar or other officer of the court, or by any other person.

(4) The specific mention elsewhere in this Act of any jurisdiction covered by subsection (2) shall not derogate from the generality of that subsection.

20 Admiralty jurisdiction of High Court [360]

(1) The Admiralty jurisdiction of the High Court shall be as follows, that is to say –

(a) jurisdiction to hear and determine any of the questions and claims mentioned in subsection (2);

(b) jurisdiction in relation to any of the proceedings mentioned in subsection (3);

(c) any other Admiralty jurisdiction which it had immediately before the commencement of this Act; and

(d) any jurisdiction connected with ships or aircraft which is vested in the High Court apart from this section and is for the time being by rules of court made or coming into force after the commencement of this Act assigned to the Queen's Bench Division and directed by the rules to be exercised by the Admiralty Court.

(2) The questions and claims referred to in subsection (1)(a) are –

(a) any claim to the possession or ownership of a ship or to the ownership of any share therein;

(b) any question arising between the co-owners of a ship as to possession, employment or earnings of that ship;

(c) any claim in respect of a mortgage of or charge on a ship or any share therein;

(d) any claim for damage received by a ship;

(e) any claim for damage done by a ship;

(f) any claim for loss of life or personal injury sustained in consequence of any defect in a ship or in her apparel or equipment, or in consequence of the wrongful act, neglect or default of –

(i) the owners, charterers or persons in possession or control of a ship; or

(ii) the master or crew of a ship, or any other person for whose wrongful acts, neglects or defaults the owners, charterers or persons in possession or control of a ship are responsible,

being an act, neglect or default in the navigation or management of the ship, in the loading, carriage or discharge of goods on, in or from the ship, or in the embarkation, carriage or disembarkation of persons on, in or from the ship; ...

(3) The proceedings referred to in subsection (1)(b) are –

(a) any application to the High Court under the Merchant Shipping Acts 1894 to 1979 other than an application under section 55 of the Merchant Shipping Act 1894 for the appointment of a person to act as a substitute for a person incapable of acting;

(b) any action to enforce a claim for damage, loss of life or personal injury arising out of –

(i) a collision between ships; or

(ii) the carrying out of or omission to carry out a manoeuvre in the case of one or more of two or more ships; or

(iii) non-compliance, on the part of one or more of two or more ships, with the collision regulations;

(c) any action by shipowners or other persons under the Merchant Shipping Acts 1894 to 1979 for the limitation of the amount of their liability in connection with a ship or other property.

(4) The jurisdiction of the High Court under subsection (2)(b) includes power to settle any account outstanding and unsettled between the parties in relation to the ship, and to direct that the ship, or any share thereof, shall be sold, and to make such other order as the court thinks fit.

(5) Subsection (2)(e) extends to –

(a) any claim in respect of a liability incurred under the Merchant Shipping (Oil Pollution) Act 1971; and

(b) any claim in respect of a liability falling on the International Oil Pollution Compensation Fund, or on the International Oil Pollution Compensation Fund 1984, under Part I of the Merchant Shipping Act 1974 ...

25 Probate jurisdiction of High Court [361]

(1) Subject to the provisions of Part V, the High Court shall, in accordance with section 19(2), have the following probate jurisdiction, that is to say all such jurisdiction in relation to probates and letters of administration as it had immediately before the commencement of this Act, and in particular all such contentious and non-contentious jurisdiction as it then had in relation to –

(a) testamentary causes or matters;

(b) the grant, amendment or revocation of probates and letters of administration; and

(c) the real and personal estate of deceased persons.

(2) Subject to the provisions of Part V, the High Court shall, in the exercise of its probate jurisdiction, perform all such duties with respect to the estates of deceased persons as fell to be performed by it immediately before the commencement of this Act.

26 Matrimonial jurisdiction of High Court [362]

The High Court shall, in accordance with section 19(2), have all such jurisdiction in relation to matrimonial causes and matters as was immediately before the commencement of the Matrimonial Causes Act 1857 vested in or exercisable by any ecclesiastical court or person in England or Wales in respect of –

(a) divorce a mensa et thoro (renamed judicial separation by that Act);

(b) nullity of marriage; and

(c) any matrimonial cause or matter except marriage licences.

27 Prize jurisdiction of High Court [363]

The High Court shall, in accordance with section 19(2), have as a prize court –

(a) all such jurisdiction as is conferred on it by the Prize Acts 1864 to 1944 (in which references to the High Court of Admiralty are by virtue of paragraph 1 of Schedule 4 to this Act to be construed as references to the High Court); and

(b) all such other jurisdiction on the high seas and elsewhere as it had as a prize court immediately before the commencement of this Act.

28 Appeals from Crown Court and inferior courts [364]

(1) Subject to subsection (2), any order, judgment or other decision of the Crown Court may be questioned by any party to the proceedings, on the ground that it is wrong in law or is in excess of jurisdiction, by applying to the Crown Court to have a case stated by that court for the opinion of the High Court.

(2) Subsection (1) shall not apply to –

(a) a judgment or other decision of the Crown Court relating to trial on indictment; or

(b) any decision of that court under the Betting, Gaming and Lotteries Act 1963, the Licensing Act 1964, the Gaming Act 1968 or the Local Government

(Miscellaneous Provisions) Act 1982 which, by any provision of any of those Acts, is to be final.

(3) Subject to the provisions of this Act and to rules of court, the High Court shall, in accordance with section 19(2), have jurisdiction to hear and determine –

(a) any application, or any appeal (whether by way of case stated or otherwise), which it has power to hear and determine under or by virtue of this or any other Act; and

(b) all such other appeals as it had jurisdiction to hear and determine immediately before the commencement of this Act.

28A Proceedings on case stated by magistrates' court [365]

(1) The following provisions apply where a case is stated for the opinion of the High Court under section 111 of the Magistrates' Courts Act 1980 (case stated on question of law or jurisdiction).

(2) The High Court may, if it thinks fit, cause the case to be sent back for amendment, whereupon it shall be amended accordingly.

(3) The High Court shall hear and determine the question arising on the case (or the case as amended) and shall –

(a) reverse, affirm or amend the determination in respect of which the case has been stated, or

(b) remit the matter to the justice or justices with the opinion of the court,

and may make such other order in relation to the matter (including as to costs) as it thinks fit.

(4) Except as provided by the Administration of Justice Act 1960 (right of appeal to House of Lords in criminal cases), a decision of the High Court under this section is final and conclusive on all parties.

29 Orders of mandamus, prohibition and certiorari [366]

(1) The High Court shall have jurisdiction to make orders of mandamus, prohibition and certiorari in those classes of cases in which it had power to do so immediately before the commencement of this Act.

(2) Every such order shall be final, subject to any right of appeal therefrom.

(3) In relation to the jurisdiction of the Crown Court, other than its jurisdiction in matters relating to trial on indictment, the High Court shall have all such jurisdiction to make orders of mandamus, prohibition or certiorari as the High Court possesses in relation to the jurisdiction of an inferior court.

(4) The power of the High Court under any enactment to require justices of the peace or a judge or officer of a county court to do any act relating to the duties of their respective offices, or to require a magistrates' court to state a case for the opinion of the High Court, in any case where the High Court formerly had by virtue of any enactment jurisdiction to make a rule absolute, or an order, for any of those purposes, shall be exercisable by order of mandamus
...

30 Injunctions to restrain persons from acting in offices in which they are not entitled to act [367]

(1) Where a person not entitled to do so acts in an office to which this section applies, the High Court may –

(a) grant an injunction restraining him from so acting; and

(b) if the case so requires, declare the office to be vacant.

(2) This section applies to any substantive office of a public nature and permanent character which is held under the Crown or which has been created by any statutory provision or royal charter.

31 Application for judicial review [368]

(1) An application to the High Court for one or more of the following forms of relief, namely –

(a) an order of mandamus, prohibition or certiorari;
(b) a declaration or injunction under subsection (2); or
(c) an injunction under section 30 restraining a person not entitled to do so from acting in an office to which that section applies,

shall be made in accordance with rules of court by a procedure to be known as an application for judicial review.

(2) A declaration may be made or an injunction granted under this subsection in any case where an application for judicial review, seeking that relief, has been made and the High Court considers that, having regard to –

(a) the nature of the matters in respect of which relief may be granted by orders of mandamus, prohibition or certiorari;
(b) the nature of the persons and bodies against whom relief may be granted by such orders; and
(c) all the circumstances of the case,

it would be just and convenient for the declaration to be made or the injunction to be granted, as the case may be.

(3) No application for judicial review shall be made unless the leave of the High Court has been obtained in accordance with rules of court; and the court shall not grant leave to make such an application unless it considers that the applicant has a sufficient interest in the matter to which the application relates.

(4) On an application for judicial review the High Court may award damages to the applicant if –

(a) he has joined with his application a claim for damages arising from any matter to which the application relates; and
(b) the court is satisfied that, if the claim had been made in an action begun by the applicant at the time of making his application, he would have been awarded damages.

(5) If, on an application for judicial review seeking an order of certiorari, the High Court quashes the decision to which the application relates, the High Court may remit the matter to the court, tribunal or authority concerned, with a direction to reconsider it and reach a decision in accordance with the findings of the High Court.

(6) Where the High Court considers that there has been undue delay in making an application for judicial review, the court may refuse to grant –

(a) leave for the making of the application; or
(b) any relief sought on the application,

if it considers that the granting of the relief sought would be likely to cause substantial hardship to, or substantially prejudice the rights of, any person or would be detrimental to good administration.

(7) Subsection (6) is without prejudice to any enactment or rule of court which has the effect of limiting the time within which an application for judicial review may be made.

32 Orders for interim payment   **[369]**

(1) As regards proceedings pending in the High Court, provision may be made by rules of court for enabling the court, in such circumstances as may be prescribed, to make an order requiring a party to the proceedings to make an interim payment of such amount as may be specified in the order, with provision for the payment to be made to such other party to the proceedings as may be so specified or, if the order so provides, by paying it into court.

(2) Any rules of court which make provision in accordance with subsection (1) may include provision for enabling a party to any proceedings who, in pursuance of such an order, has made an interim payment to recover the whole or part of the amount of the payment in such circumstances, and from such other party to the proceedings, as may be determined in accordance with the rules ...

(5) In this section 'interim payment', in relation to a party to any proceedings, means a payment on account of any damages, debt or other sum (excluding any costs) which that party may be held liable to pay to or for the benefit of another party to the proceedings if a final judgment or order of the court in the proceedings is given or made in favour of that other party.

32A Orders for provisional damages for personal injuries   **[370]**

(1) This section applies to an action for damages for personal injuries in which there is proved or admitted to be a chance that at some definite or indefinite time in the future the injured person will, as a result of the act or omission which gave rise to the cause of action, develop some serious disease or suffer serious deterioration in his physical or mental condition.

(2) Subject to subsection (4) below, as regards any action for damages to which this section applies in which a judgment is given in the High Court, provision may be made by rules of court for enabling the court, in such circumstances as may be prescribed, to award the injured person –

(a) damages assessed on the assumption that the injured person will not develop the disease or suffer the deterioration in his condition; and
(b) further damages at a future date if he develops the disease or suffers the deterioration.

(3) Any rules made by virtue of this section may include such incidental, supplementary and consequential provisions as the rule-making authority may consider necessary or expedient.

(4) Nothing in this section shall be construed –

(a) as affecting the exercise of any power relating to costs, including any power to make rules of court relating to costs; or
(b) as prejudicing any duty of the court under any enactment or rule of law to reduce or limit the total damages which would have been recoverable apart from any such duty.

35A Power of High Court to award interest on debts   **[371]**
and damages

(1) Subject to rules of court, in proceedings (whenever instituted) before the High Court for the recovery of a debt or damages there may be included in any sum for which judgment is given simple interest, at such rate as the court thinks fit or as rules of court may provide, on all or any part of the debt or damages in respect of which judgment is given, or payment is made before judgment, for all or any part of the period between the date when the cause of action arose and –

(a) in the case of any sum paid before judgment, the date of the payment; and

(b) in the case of the sum for which judgment is given, the date of the judgment.

(2) In relation to a judgment given for damages for personal injuries or death which exceed £200 subsection (1) shall have effect –

(a) with the substitution of 'shall be included' for 'may be included'; and

(b) with the addition of 'unless the court is satisfied that there are special reasons to the contrary' after 'given', where first occurring.

(3) Subject to rules of court, where –

(a) there are proceedings (whenever instituted) before the High Court for the recovery of a debt; and

(b) the defendant pays the whole debt to the plaintiff (otherwise than in pursuance of a judgment in the proceedings),

the defendant shall be liable to pay the plaintiff simple interest at such rate as the court thinks fit or as rules of court may provide on all or any part of the debt for all or any part of the period between the date when the cause of action arose and the date of the payment.

(4) Interest in respect of a debt shall not be awarded under this section for a period during which, for whatever reason, interest on the debt already runs.

(5) Without prejudice to the generality of section 84, rules of court may provide for a rate of interest by reference to the rate specified in section 17 of the Judgments Act 1838 as that section has effect from time to time or by reference to a rate for which any other enactment provides.

(6) Interest under this section may be calculated at different rates in respect of different periods.

(7) In this section 'plaintiff' means the person seeking the debt or damages and 'defendant' means the person from whom the plaintiff seeks the debt or damages and 'personal injuries' includes any disease and any impairment of a person's physical or mental condition.

(8) Nothing in this section affects the damages recoverable for the dishonour of a bill of exchange.

37 Powers of High Court with respect to injunctions and receivers [372]

(1) The High Court may by order (whether interlocutory or final) grant an injunction or appoint a receiver in all cases in which it appears to the court to be just and convenient to do so.

(2) Any such order may be made either unconditionally or on such terms and conditions as the court thinks just.

(3) The power of the High Court under subsection (1) to grant an interlocutory injunction restraining a party to any proceedings from removing from the jurisdiction of the High Court, or otherwise dealing with, assets located within that jurisdiction shall be exercisable in cases where that party is, as well as in cases where he is not, domiciled, resident or present within that jurisdiction.

(4) The power of the High Court to appoint a receiver by way of equitable execution shall operate in relation to all legal estates and interests in land; and that power –

(a) may be exercised in relation to an estate or interest in land whether or not a charge has been imposed on that land under section 1 of the Charging Orders Act 1979 for the purpose of enforcing the judgment, order or award in question; and

(b) shall be in addition to, and not in derogation of, any power of any court to appoint a receiver in proceedings for enforcing such a charge.

(5) Where an order under the said section 1 imposing a charge for the purpose of enforcing a judgment, order or award has been, or has effect as if, registered under section 6 of the Land Charges Act 1972, subsection (4) of the said section 6 (effect of non-registration of writs and orders registrable under that section) shall not apply to an order appointing a receiver made either –

(a) in proceedings for enforcing the charge; or

(b) by way of equitable execution of the judgment, order or award or, as the case may be, of so much of it as requires payment of moneys secured by the charge.

42 Restriction of vexatious legal proceedings [373]

(1) If, on an application made by the Attorney General under this section, the High Court is satisfied that any person has habitually and persistently and without any reasonable ground –

(a) instituted vexatious civil proceedings, whether in the High Court or any inferior court, and whether against the same person or against different persons; or

(b) made vexatious applications in any civil proceedings, whether in the High Court or any inferior court, and whether instituted by him or another; or

(c) instituted vexatious prosecutions (whether against the same person or different persons),

the court may, after hearing that person or giving him an opportunity of being heard, make a civil proceedings order, a criminal proceedings order or an all proceedings order.

(1A) In this section –

'civil proceedings order' means an order that –

(a) no civil proceedings shall without the leave of the High Court be instituted in any court by the person against whom the order is made;

(b) any civil proceedings instituted by him in any court before the making of the order shall not be continued by him without the leave of the High Court; and

(c) no application (other than one for leave under this section) shall be made by him, in any civil proceedings instituted in any court by any person, without the leave of the High Court;

'criminal proceedings order' means that an order that –

(a) no information shall be laid before a justice of the peace by the person against whom the order is made without the leave of the High Court; and

(b) no application for leave to prefer a bill of indictment shall be made by him without the leave of the High Court; and

'all proceedings order' means an order which has the combined effect of the two other orders.

(2) An order under subsection (1) may provide that it is to cease to have effect at the end of a specified period, but shall otherwise remain in force indefinitely.

(3) Leave for the institution or continuance of, or for the making of an application in, any civil proceedings by a person who is the subject of an order for the time being in force under subsection (1) shall not be given unless the High Court is satisfied that the proceedings or application are not an abuse of the process of the court in question and that there are reasonable grounds for the proceedings o application.

(3A) Leave for the laying of an information or for an application for leave to prefer a bill of indictment by a person who is the subject of an order for the time being in force under subsection (1) shall not be given unless the High Court is satisfied that the institution of the prosecution is not an abuse of the criminal process and that there are reasonable grounds for the institution of the prosecution by the applicant.

(4) No appeal shall lie from a decision of the High Court refusing leave required by virtue of this section.

(5) A copy of any order made under subsection (1) shall be published in the London Gazette.

THE CROWN COURT

45 General jurisdiction of Crown Court [374]

(1) The Crown Court shall be a superior court of record.

(2) Subject to the provisions of this Act, there shall be exercisable by the Crown Court –

> (a) all such appellate and other jurisdiction as is conferred on it by or under this or any other Act; and
> (b) all such other jurisdiction as was exercisable by it immediately before the commencement of this Act.

(3) Without prejudice to subsection (2), the jurisdiction of the Crown Court shall include all such powers and duties as were exercisable or fell to be performed by it immediately before the commencement of this Act.

(4) Subject to section 8 of the Criminal Procedure (Attendance of Witnesses) Act 1965 (substitution in criminal cases of procedure in that Act for procedure by way of subpoena) and to any provision contained in or having effect under this Act, the Crown Court shall, in relation to the attendance and examination of witnesses, any contempt of court, the enforcement of its orders and all other matters incidental to its jurisdiction, have the like powers, rights, privileges and authority as the High Court.

(5) The specific mention elsewhere in this Act of any jurisdiction covered by subsections (2) and (3) shall not derogate from the generality of those subsections.

46 Exclusive jurisdiction of Crown Court in trial [375]
on indictment

(1) All proceedings on indictment shall be brought before the Crown Court.

(2) The jurisdiction of the Crown Court with respect to proceedings on indictment shall include jurisdiction in proceedings on indictment for offences wherever committed, and in particular proceedings on indictment for offences within the jurisdiction of the Admiralty of England.

48 Appeals to Crown Court [376]

(1) The Crown Court may, in the course of hearing any appeal, correct any error or mistake in the order or judgment incorporating the decision which is the subject of the appeal.

(2) On the termination of the hearing of an appeal the Crown Court –

(a) may confirm, reverse or vary any part of the decision appealed against, including a determination not to impose a separate penalty in respect of an offence; or

(b) may remit the matter with its opinion thereon to the authority whose decision is appealed against; or

(c) may make such other order in the matter as the court thinks just, and by such order exercise any power which the said authority might have exercised.

(3) Subsection (2) has effect subject to any enactment relating to any such appeal which expressly limits or restricts the powers of the court on the appeal.

(4) If the appeal is against a conviction or a sentence, the preceding provisions of this section shall be construed as including power to award any punishment, whether more or less severe than that awarded by the magistrates' court whose decision is appealed against, if that is a punishment which that magistrates' court might have awarded.

(5) This section applies whether or not the appeal is against the whole of the decision.

(6) In this section 'sentence' includes any order made by a court when dealing with an offender, including –

(a) a hospital order under Part III of the Mental Health Act 1983, with or without a restriction order, and an interim hospital order under that Act; and

(b) a recommendation for deportation made when dealing with an offender ...

GENERAL PROVISIONS

49 Concurrent administration of law and equity [377]

(1) Subject to the provisions of this or any other Act, every court exercising jurisdiction in England or Wales in any civil cause or matter shall continue to administer law and equity on the basis that, wherever there is any conflict or variance between the rules of equity and the rules of common law with reference to the same matter, the rules of equity shall prevail.

(2) Every such court shall give the same effect as hitherto –

(a) to all equitable estates, titles, rights, reliefs, defences and counterclaims, and to all equitable duties and liabilities; and

(b) subject thereto, to all legal claims and demands and all estates, titles, rights, duties, obligations and liabilities existing by the common law or by any custom or created by any statute,

and, subject to the provisions of this or any other Act, shall so exercise its jurisdiction in every cause or matter before it as to secure that, as far as possible, all matters in dispute between the parties are completely and finally determined, and all multiplicity of legal proceedings with respect to any of those matters is avoided.

(3) Nothing in this Act shall affect the power of the Court of Appeal or the High Court to stay any proceedings before it, where it thinks fit to do so, either of its own motion or on the application of any person, whether or not a party to the proceedings.

50 Power to award damages as well as, or in substitution [378] for, injunction or specific performance

Where the Court of Appeal or the High Court has jurisdiction to entertain an application for an injunction or specific performance, it may award damages in addition to, or in substitution for, an injunction or specific performance.

51 Costs in civil division of Court of Appeal, High Court [379]
and county courts

(1) Subject to the provisions of this or any other enactment and to rules of court, the costs of and incidental to all proceedings in –

(a) the civil division of the Court of Appeal;
(b) the High Court; and
(c) any county court,

shall be in the discretion of the court.

(2) Without prejudice to any general power to make rules of court, such rules may make provision for regulating matters relating to the costs of those proceedings including, in particular, prescribing scales of costs to be paid to legal or other representatives.

(3) The court shall have full power to determine by whom and to what extent the costs are to be paid.

(4) In subsections (1) and (2) 'proceedings' includes the admin-istration of estates and trusts.

(5) Nothing in subsection (1) shall alter the practice in any criminal cause, or in bankruptcy.

(6) In any proceedings mentioned in subsection (1), the court may disallow, or (as the case may be) order the legal or other representative concerned to meet, the whole of any wasted costs or such part of them as may be determined in accordance with rules of court.

(7) In subsection (6), 'wasted costs' means any costs incurred by a party –

(a) as a result of any improper, unreasonable or negligent act or omission on the part of any legal or other representative or any employee of such a representative; or
(b) which, in the light of any such act or omission occurring after they were incurred, the court considers it is unreasonable to expect that party to pay.

(8) Where –

(a) a person has commenced proceedings in the High Court; but
(b) those proceedings should, in the opinion of the court, have been commenced in a county court in accordance with any provision made under section 1 of the Courts and Legal Services Act 1990 or by or under any other enactment,

the person responsible for determining the amount which is to be awarded to that person by way of costs shall have regard to those circumstances.

(9) Where, in complying with subsection (8), the responsible person reduces the amount which would otherwise be awarded to the person in question –

(a) the amount of that reduction shall not exceed 25 per cent; and
(b) on any taxation of the costs payable by that person to his legal representative, regard shall be had to the amount of the reduction.

(10) The Lord Chancellor may by order amend subsection (9)(a) by substituting, for the percentage for the time being mentioned there, a different percentage.

(11) Any such order shall be made by statutory instrument and may make such transitional or incidental provision as the Lord Chancellor considers expedient.

(12) No such statutory instrument shall be made unless a draft of the instrument has been approved by both Houses of Parliament.

(13) In this section 'legal or other representative', in relation to a party to proceedings, means any person exercising a right of audience or right to conduct litigation on his behalf.

PART III

PRACTICE AND PROCEDURE

THE COURT OF APPEAL

53 Distribution of business between civil   [380]
and criminal divisions

(1) Rules of court may provide for the distribution of business in the Court of Appeal between the civil and criminal divisions, but subject to any such rules business shall be distributed in accordance with the following provisions of this section.

(2) The criminal division of the Court of Appeal shall exercise –

(a) all jurisdiction of the Court of Appeal under Parts I and II of the Criminal Appeal Act 1968;
(b) the jurisdiction of the Court of Appeal under section 13 of the Administration of Justice Act 1960 (appeals in cases of contempt of court) in relation to appeals from orders and decisions of the Crown Court;
(c) all other jurisdiction expressly conferred on that division by this or any other Act; and
(d) the jurisdiction to order the issue of writs of venire de novo.

(3) The civil division of the Court of Appeal shall exercise the whole of the jurisdiction of that court not exercisable by the criminal division.

(4) Where any class of proceedings in the Court of Appeal is by any statutory provision assigned to the criminal division of that court, rules of court may provide for any enactment relating to –

(a) appeals to the Court of Appeal under Part I of the Criminal Appeal Act 1968; or
(b) any matter connected with or arising out of such appeals,

to apply in relation to proceedings of that class or, as the case may be, to any corresponding matter connected with or arising out of such proceedings, as it applies in relation to such appeals or, as the case may be, to the relevant matter within paragraph (b), with or without prescribed modifications in either case.

54 Court of civil division   [381]

(1) This section relates to the civil division of the Court of Appeal; and in this section 'court', except where the context otherwise requires, means a court of that division.

(2) A court shall be duly constituted for the purpose of exercising any of its jurisdiction if it consists of an uneven number of judges not less than three.

(3) Where –

(a) part of any proceedings before a court has been heard by an uneven number of judges greater than three; and
(b) one or more members of the court are unable to continue,

the court shall remain duly constituted for the purpose of those proceedings so long as the number of members (whether even or uneven) is not reduced to less than three.

(4) A court shall, if it consists of two judges, be duly constituted for the purpose of –

(a) hearing and determining any appeal against an interlocutory order or interlocutory judgment;

(aa) hearing and determining any application for leave to appeal;

(b) hearing and determining any appeal against a decision of a single judge acting by virtue of section 58(1);

(c) hearing and determining any appeal where all the parties have before the hearing filed a consent to the appeal being heard and determined by two judges;

(d) hearing the remainder of, and determining, any appeal where part of it has been heard by three or more judges of whom one or more are unable to continue and all the parties have consented to the remainder of the appeal being heard, and the appeal being determined, by two remaining judges; or

(e) hearing and determining an appeal of any such description or in any such circumstances not covered by paragraphs (a) to (d) as may be prescribed for the purposes of this subsection by an order made by the Lord Chancellor with the concurrence of the Master of the Rolls.

(5) Where –

(a) an appeal has been heard by a court consisting of an even number of judges; and

(b) the members of the court are equally divided,

the case shall, on the application of any party to the appeal, be re-argued before and determined by an uneven number of judges not less than three, before any appeal to the House of Lords.

(6) An application to the civil division of the Court of Appeal for leave to appeal to that court may be determined by a single judge of that court, and no appeal shall lie from a decision of a single judge acting under this subsection.

(7) In any cause or matter pending before the civil division of the Court of Appeal a single judge of that court may at any time during vacation make an interim order to prevent prejudice to the claims of any parties pending an appeal ...

55 Court of criminal division   [382]

(1) This section relates to the criminal division of the Court of Appeal; and in this section 'court' means a court of that division.

(2) A court shall be duly constituted for the purpose of exercising any of its jurisdiction if it consists of an uneven number of judges not less than three.

(3) Where –

(a) part of any proceedings before a court has been heard by an uneven number of judges greater than three; and

(b) one or more members of the court are unable to continue,

the court shall remain duly constituted for the purpose of those proceedings so long as the number of members (whether even or uneven) is not reduced to less than three.

(4) A court shall, if it consists of two judges, be duly constituted for every purpose except –

(a) determining an appeal against –

(i) conviction; or

(ii) a verdict of not guilty by reason of insanity; or

(iii) a finding of a jury under section 4 of the Criminal Procedure (Insanity) Act 1964 (unfitness to plead) that a person is under a disability;

(aa) reviewing sentencing under Part IV of the Criminal Justice Act 1988;

(b) determining an application for leave to appeal to the House of Lords; and

(c) refusing an application for leave to appeal to the criminal division against conviction or any such verdict or finding as is mentioned in paragraph (a)(ii) or (iii), other than an application which has been refused by a single judge.

(5) Where an appeal has been heard by a court consisting of an even number of judges and the members of the court are equally divided, the case shall be re-argued before and determined by an uneven number of judges not less than three.

56 Judges not to sit on appeal from their own judgments, etc   **[383]**

(1) No judge shall sit as a member of the civil division of the Court of Appeal on the hearing of, or shall determine any application in proceedings incidental or preliminary to, an appeal from a judgment or order made in any case by himself or by any court of which he was a member.

(2) No judge shall sit as a member of the criminal division of the Court of Appeal on the hearing of, or shall determine any application in proceedings incidental or preliminary to, an appeal against –

(a) a conviction before himself or a court of which he was a member; or

(b) a sentence passed by himself or such a court.

THE HIGH COURT

61 Distribution of business among Divisions   **[384]**

(1) Subject to any provision made by or under this or any other Act (and in particular to any rules of court made in pursuance of subsection (2) and any order under subsection (3)), business in the High Court of any description mentioned in Schedule 1, as for the time being in force, shall be distributed among the Divisions in accordance with that Schedule.

(2) Rules of court may provide for the distribution of business in the High Court among the Divisions; but any rules made in pursuance of this subsection shall have effect subject to any orders for the time being in force under subsection (3).

(3) Subject to subsection (5), the Lord Chancellor may by order –

(a) direct that any business in the High Court which is not for the time being assigned by or under this or any other Act to any Division be assigned to such Division as may be specified in the order;

(b) if at any time it appears to him desirable to do so with a view to the more convenient administration of justice, direct that any business for the time being assigned by or under this or any other Act to any Division be assigned to such other Division as may be specified in the order; and

(c) amend Schedule 1 so far as may be necessary in consequence of provision made by order under paragraph (a) or (b).

(4) The powers conferred by subsection (2) and subsection (3) include power to assign business of any description to two or more Divisions concurrently.

(5) No order under subsection (3)(b) relating to any business shall be made without the concurrence of the senior judge of –

(a) the Division or each of the Divisions to which the business is for the time being assigned; and

(b) the Division or each of the Divisions to which the business is to be assigned by the order.

(6) Subject to rules of court, the fact that a cause or matter commenced in the High Court falls within a class of business assigned by or under this Act to a particular Division does not make it obligatory for it to be allocated or transferred to that Division.

(7) Without prejudice to subsections (1) to (5) and section 63, rules of court may provide for the distribution of the business (other than business required to be heard by a divisional court) in any Division of the High Court among the judges of that Division.

(8) Any order under subsection (3) shall be made by statutory instrument, which shall be laid before Parliament after being made.

62 Business of Patents, Admiralty and Commercial Courts   [385]

(1) The Patents Court shall take such proceedings relating to patents as are within the jurisdiction conferred on it by the Patents Act 1977, and such other proceedings relating to patents or other matters as may be prescribed.

(2) The Admiralty Court shall take Admiralty business, that is to say causes and matters assigned to the Queen's Bench Division and involving the exercise of the High Court's Admiralty jurisdiction or its jurisdiction as a prize court.

(3) The Commercial Court shall take such causes and matters as may in accordance with rules of court be entered in the commercial list.

64 Choice of Division by plaintiff   [386]

(1) Without prejudice to the power of transfer under section 65, the person by whom any cause or matter is commenced in the High Court shall in the prescribed manner allocate it to whichever Division he thinks fit.

(2) Where a cause or matter is commenced in the High Court, all subsequent interlocutory or other steps or proceedings in the High Court in that cause or matter shall be taken in the Division to which the cause or matter is for the time being allocated (whether under subsection (1) or in consequence of its transfer under section 65).

65 Power of transfer   [387]

(1) Any cause or matter may at any time and at any stage thereof, and either with or without application from any of the parties, be transferred, by such authority and in such manner as rules of court may direct, from one Division or judge of the High Court to another Division or judge thereof.

(2) The transfer of a cause or matter under subsection (1) to a different Division or judge of the High Court shall not affect the validity of any steps or proceedings taken or order made in that cause or matter before the transfer.

66 Divisional courts of High Court   [388]

(1) Divisional courts may be held for the transaction of any business in the High Court which is, by or by virtue of rules of court or any other statutory provision, required to be heard by a divisional court.

(2) Any number of divisional courts may sit at the same time.

(3) A divisional court shall be constituted of not less than two judges.

(4) Every judge of the High Court shall be qualified to sit in any divisional court.

(5) The judge who is, according to the order of precedence under this Act, the

senior of the judges constituting a divisional court shall be the president of the court.

69 Trial by jury   [389]

(1) Where, on the application of any party to an action to be tried in the Queen's Bench Division, the court is satisfied that there is in issue –

(a) a charge of fraud against that party; or
(b) a claim in respect of libel, slander, malicious prosecution or false imprisonment; or
(c) any question or issue of a kind prescribed for the purposes of this paragraph,

the action shall be tried with a jury, unless the court is of opinion that the trial requires any prolonged examination of documents or accounts or any scientific or local investigation which cannot conveniently be made with a jury.

(2) An application under subsection (1) must be made not later than such time before the trial as may be prescribed.

(3) An action to be tried in the Queen's Bench Division which does not by virtue of subsection (1) fall to be tried with a jury shall be tried without a jury unless the court in its discretion orders it to be tried with a jury.

(4) Nothing in subsections (1) to (3) shall affect the power of the court to order, in accordance with rules of court, that different questions of fact arising in any action be tried by different modes of trial; and where any such order is made, subsection (1) shall have effect only as respects questions relating to any such charge, claim, question or issue as is mentioned in that subsection.

(5) Where for the purpose of disposing of any action or other matter which is being tried in the High Court by a judge with a jury it is necessary to ascertain the law of any other country which is applicable to the facts of the case, any question as to the effect of the evidence given with respect to that law shall, instead of being submitted to the jury, be decided by the judge alone.

THE CROWN COURT

73 General provisions   [390]

(1) Subject to the provisions of section 8(1)(c), 74 and 75(2) as respects courts comprising justices of the peace, all proceedings in the Crown Court shall be heard and disposed of before a single judge of that court.

(2) Crown Court Rules may authorise or require a judge of the High Court, Circuit judge or Recorder, in such circumstances as are specified by the rules, at any stage to continue with any proceedings with a court from which any one or more of the justices initially constituting the court has withdrawn, or is absent for any reason.

(3) Where a judge of the High Court, Circuit judge or Recorder sits with justices of the peace he shall preside, and –

(a) the decision of the Crown Court may be a majority decision; and
(b) if the members of the court are equally divided, the judge of the High Court, Circuit judge or Recorder shall have a second and casting vote.

74 Appeals and committals for sentence   [391]

(1) On any hearing by the Crown Court –

(a) of any appeal; or

(b) of proceedings on committal to the Crown Court for sentence,

the Crown Court shall consist of a judge of the High Court or a Circuit judge or a Recorder who, subject to the following provisions of this section, shall sit with not less than two nor more than four justices of the peace.

(2) Crown Court Rules may, with respect to hearings falling within subsection (1) –

(a) prescribe the number of justices of the peace constituting the court (within the limits mentioned in that subsection); and

(b) prescribe the qualifications to be possessed by any such justices of the peace;

and the rules may make different provision for different descriptions of cases, different places of sitting or other different circumstances.

(3) Crown Court Rules may authorise or require a judge of the High Court, Circuit judge or Recorder, in such circumstances as are specified by the rules, to enter on, or at any stage to continue with, any proceedings with a court not comprising the justices required by subsections (1) and (2).

(4) The Lord Chancellor may from time to time, having regard to the number of justices, or the number of justices with any prescribed qualifications, available for service in the Crown Court, give directions providing that, in such descriptions of proceedings as may be specified by the Lord Chancellor, the provisions of subsections (1) and (2) shall not apply.

(5) Directions under subsection (4) may frame descriptions of proceedings by reference to the place of trial, or by reference to the time of trial, or in any other way.

(6) No decision of the Crown Court shall be questioned on the ground that the court was not constituted as required by or under subsections (1) and (2) unless objection was taken by or on behalf of a party to the proceedings not later than the time when the proceedings were entered on, or when the alleged irregularity began ...

75 Allocation of cases according to composition of court, etc   [392]

(1) The cases or classes of cases in the Crown Court suitable for allocation respectively to a judge of the High Court and to a Circuit judge or Recorder, and all other matters relating to the distribution of Crown Court business, shall be determined in accordance with directions given by or on behalf of the Lord Chief Justice with the concurrence of the Lord Chancellor.

(2) Subject to section 74(1), the cases or classes of cases in the Crown Court suitable for allocation to a court comprising justices of the peace (including those by way of trial on indictment which are suitable for allocation to such a court) shall be determined in accordance with directions given by or on behalf of the Lord Chief Justice with the concurrence of the Lord Chancellor.

81 Bail   [393]

(1) The Crown Court may grant bail to any person –

(a) who has been committed in custody for appearance before the Crown Court or in relation to whose case a notice of transfer has been given under section 4 of the Criminal Justice Act 1987; or

(b) who is in custody pursuant to a sentence imposed by a magistrates' court, and who has appealed to the Crown Court against his conviction or sentence; or

(c) who is in the custody of the Crown Court pending the disposal of his case by that court; or

(d) who, after the decision of his case by the Crown Court, has applied to that court for the statement of a case for the High Court on that decision; or

(e) who has applied to the High Court for an order of certiorari to remove proceedings in the Crown Court in his case into the High Court, or has applied to the High Court for leave to make such an application; or

(f) to whom the Crown Court has granted a certificate under section 1(2) or 11(1A) of the Criminal Appeal Act 1968 or under subsection (1B) below; or

(g) who has been remanded in custody by a magistrates' court on adjourning a case under –

    (i) section 5 (adjournment of inquiry into offence);
    (ii) section 10 (adjournment of trial);
    (iii) section 18 (initial procedure on information against adult for offence triable either way); or
    (iv) section 30 (remand for medical examination),

  of the Magistrates' Courts Act 1980;

and the time during which a person is released on bail under any provision of this subsection shall not count as part of any term of imprisonment or detention under his sentence.

(1A) The power of conferred by subsection (1)(f) does not extend to a case to which section 12 or 15 of the Criminal Appeal Act 1968 (appeal against verdict of not guilty by reason of insanity or against findings that the accused is under a disability and that he did the act or made the omission charged against him) applies.

(1B) A certificate under this subsection is a certificate that a case is fit for appeal on a ground which involves a question of law alone.

(1C) The power conferred by subsection (1)(f) is to be exercised –

(a) where the appeal is under section 1 or 9 of the Criminal Appeal Act 1968, by the judge who tried the case; and

(b) where it is under section 10 of that Act, by the judge who passed the sentence.

(1D) The power may only be exercised within 28 days from the date of the conviction appealed against, or in the case of appeal against sentence, from the date on which sentence was passed or, in the case of an order made or treated as made on conviction, from the date of the making of the order.

(1E) The power may not be exercised if the appellant has made an application to the Court of Appeal for bail in respect of the offence or offences to which the appeal relates.

(1F) It shall be a condition of bail granted in the exercise of the power that, unless a notice of appeal has previously been lodged in accordance with subsection (1) of section 18 of the Criminal Appeal Act 1968 –

(a) such a notice shall be so lodged within the period specified in subsection (2) of that section; and

(b) not later than 14 days from the end of that period, the appellant shall lodge with the Crown Court a certificate from the registrar of criminal appeals that a notice of appeal was given within that period.

(1G) If the Crown Court grants bail to a person in the exercise of the power, it may direct him to appear –

(a) if a notice of appeal is lodged within the period specified in section 18(2) of the Criminal Appeal Act 1968, at such time and place as the Court of Appeal may require, and

(b) if no such notice is lodged within that period, at such time and place as the Crown Court may require.

(1H) Where the Crown Court grants a person bail under subsection (1)(g) it may direct him to appear at a time and place which the magistrates' court could have directed and the recognizance of any surety shall be conditioned accordingly.

(1J) The Crown Court may only grant bail to a person under subsection (1)(g) if the magistrates' court which remanded him in custody has certified under section 5(6A) of the Bail Act 1976 that it heard full argument on his application for bail before it refused the application.

(2) Provision may be made by Crown Court Rules as respects the powers of the Crown Court relating to bail, including any provision –

(a) except in the case of bail in criminal proceedings (within the meaning of the Bail Act 1976), allowing the court instead of requiring a person to enter into a recognizance, to consent to his giving other security;

(b) allowing the court to direct that a recognizance shall be entered into or other security given before a magistrates' court or a justice of the peace, or, if the rules so provide, a person of such other description as is specified in the rules;

(c) prescribing the manner in which a recognizance is to be entered into or other security given, and the persons by whom and the manner in which the recognizance or security may be enforced;

(d) authorising the recommittal, in such cases and by such courts or justices as may be prescribed by the rules, of persons released from custody in pursuance of the powers;

(e) making provision corresponding to sections 118 and 119 of the Magistrates' Courts Act 1980 (varying or dispensing with requirements as to sureties, and postponement of taking recognizances).

(3) Any reference in any enactment to a recognizance shall include, unless the context otherwise requires, a reference to any other description of security given instead of a recognizance, whether in pursuance of subsection (2)(a) or otherwise.

(4) The Crown Court, on issuing a warrant for the arrest of any person, may endorse the warrant for bail, and in any such case –

(a) the person arrested under the warrant shall, unless the Crown Court otherwise directs, be taken to a police station; and

(b) the officer in charge of the station shall release him from custody if he, and any sureties required by the endorsement and approved by the officer, enter into recognizances of such amount as may be fixed by the endorsement:

Provided that in the case of bail in criminal proceedings (within the meaning of the Bail Act 1976) the person arrested shall not be required to enter into a recognizance.

(5) A person in custody in pursuance of a warrant issued by the Crown Court with a view to his appearance before that court shall be brought forthwith before either the Crown Court or a magistrates' court.

(6) A magistrates' court shall have jurisdiction, and a justice of the peace may act, under or in pursuance of rules under subsection (2) whether or not the offence was committed, or the arrest was made, within the court's area, or the area for which he was appointed.

83 Right of audience for solicitors in certain Crown Court centres [394]

(1) The Lord Chancellor may at any time direct, as respects one or more specified places where the Crown Court sits, that solicitors, or such category of solicitors as may be specified in the direction, may have rights of audience in the Crown Court.

(2) Any such direction may be limited to apply only in relation to proceedings of a description specified in the direction.

(3) In considering whether to exercise his powers under this section the Lord Chancellor shall have regard, in particular, to the need to secure the availability of persons with rights of audience in the court or proceedings in question.

(4) Any direction under this section may be revoked by direction of the Lord Chancellor.

(5) Any direction under this section may be subject to such conditions and restrictions as appear to the Lord Chancellor to be necessary or expedient.

(6) Any exercise by the Lord Chancellor of his power to give a direction under this section shall be with the concurrence of the Lord Chief Justice, the Master of the Rolls, the President of the Family Division and the Vice-Chancellor.

84 Power to make rules of court [395]

(1) Rules of court may be made for the purpose of regulating and prescribing the practice and procedure to be followed in the Supreme Court ...

85 The Supreme Court Rule Committee [396]

(1) The power to make rules of court under section 84 in relation to the High Court and the civil division of the Court of Appeal shall be exercisable by the Lord Chancellor together with any four or more of the following persons, namely –

(a) the Lord Chief Justice,
(b) the Master of the Rolls,
(c) the President of the Family Division,
(d) the Vice-Chancellor,
(e) three other judges of the Supreme Court,
(f) two persons who have a Supreme Court qualification (within the meaning of section 71 of the Courts and Legal Services Act 1990); and
(g) two persons who have been granted by an authorised body, under Part II of that Act, the right to conduct litigation in relation to all proceedings in the Supreme Court.

(2) The persons mentioned in subsection (1), acting in pursuance of that subsection, shall be known as 'the Supreme Court Rule Committee'.

(3) The persons to act in pursuance of subsection (1) with the Lord Chancellor, other than those eligible to act by virtue of their office, shall be appointed by the Lord Chancellor for such time as he may think fit.

(4) Before appointing a person under paragraph (f) or (g) of subsection (1), the Lord Chancellor shall consult any authorised body with members who are eligible for appointment under that paragraph.

86 The Crown Court Rule Committee [397]

(1) The power to make rules of court under section 84 in relation to the Crown

Court and the criminal division of the Court of Appeal shall be exercisable by the Lord Chancellor together with any four or more of the following persons, namely –

>(a) the Lord Chief Justice,
>(b) two other judges of the Supreme Court,
>(c) two Circuit judges,
>(d) the registrar of criminal appeals,
>(e) a justice of the peace,
>(f) two persons who have a Supreme Court qualification (within the meaning of section 71 of the Courts and Legal Services Act 1990); and
>(g) two persons who have been granted by an authorised body, under Part II of that Act, the right to conduct litigation in relation to all proceedings in the Supreme Court.

(2) The persons mentioned in subsection (1), acting in pursuance of that subsection, shall be known as 'the Crown Court Rule Committee'.

(3) The persons to act in pursuance of subsection (1) with the Lord Chancellor, other than those eligible to act by virtue of their office, shall be appointed by the Lord Chancellor for such time as he may think fit.

(4) Before appointing a person under paragraph (f) or (g) of subsection (1), the Lord Chancellor shall consult any authorised body with members who are eligible for appointment under that paragraph.

PART V

PROBATE CAUSES AND MATTERS

127 Probate rules [398]

(1) The President of the Family Division may, with the concurrence of the Lord Chancellor, make rules of court (in this Part referred to as 'probate rules') for regulating and prescribing the practice and procedure of the High Court with respect to non-contentious or common form probate business.

(2) Without prejudice to the generality of subsection (1), probate rules may make provision for regulating the classes of persons entitled to grants of probate or administration in particular circumstances and the relative priorities of their claims thereto.

(3) Probate rules shall be made by statutory instrument subject to annulment in pursuance of a resolution of either House of Parliament; and the Statutory Instruments Act 1946 shall apply to a statutory instrument containing probate rules in like manner as if they had been made by a Minister of the Crown.

128 Interpretation of Part V and other probate provisions [399]

In this Part, and in the other provisions of this Act relating to probate causes and matters, unless the context otherwise requires –

>'administration' includes all letters of administration of the effects of deceased persons, whether with or without a will annexed, and whether granted for general, special or limited purposes;
>'estate' means real and personal estate, and 'real estate' includes –

>>(a) chattels real and land in possession, remainder or reversion and every interest in or over land to which the deceased person was entitled at the time of his death, and

(b) real estate held on trust or by way of mortgage or security, but not money to arise under a trust for sale of land, nor money secured or charged on land;

'grant' means a grant of probate or administration;

'non-contentious or common form probate business' means the business of obtaining probate and administration where there is no contention as to the right thereto, including –

(a) the passing of probates and administrations through the High Court in contentious cases where the contest has been terminated,

(b) all business of a non-contentious nature in matters of testacy and intestacy not being proceedings in any action, and

(c) the business of lodging caveats against the grant of probate or administration;

'Principal Registry' means the Principal Registry of the Family Division;

'probate rules' means rules of court made under section 127;

'trust corporation' means the Public Trustee or a corporation either appointed by the court in any particular case to be a trustee or authorised by rules made under section 4(3) of the Public Trustee Act 1906 to act as a custodian trustee;

'will' includes a nuncupative will and any testamentary document of which probate may be granted.

PART VI

MISCELLANEOUS AND SUPPLEMENTARY

138 Effect of writs of execution against goods [400]

(1) Subject to subsection (2), a writ of fieri facias or other writ of execution against goods issued from the High Court shall bind the property in the goods of the execution debtor as from the time when the writ is delivered to the sheriff to be executed.

(2) Such a writ shall not prejudice the title to any goods of the execution debtor acquired by a person in good faith and for valuable consideration unless he had, at the time when he acquired his title –

(a) notice that that writ or any other such writ by virtue of which the goods of the execution debtor might be seized or attached had been delivered to and remained unexecuted in the hands of the sheriff; or

(b) notice that an application for the issue of a warrant of execution against the goods of the execution debtor had been made to the registrar of a county court and that the warrant issued on the application either –

(i) remained unexecuted in the hands of the registrar of the court from which it was issued; or

(ii) had been sent for execution to, and received by, the registrar of another county court, and remained unexecuted in the hands of the registrar of that court.

(3) For the better manifestation of the time mentioned in subsection (1), it shall be the duty of the sheriff (without fee) on receipt of any such writ as is there mentioned to endorse on its back the hour, day, month and year when he received it.

(3A) Every sheriff or officer executing any writ of execution issued from the High Court against the goods of any person may by virtue of it seize –

(a) any of that person's goods except –

(i) such tools, books, vehicles and other items of equipment as are necessary to that person for use personally by him in his employment, business or vocation;

(ii) such clothing, bedding, furniture, household equipment and provisions as are necessary for satisfying the basic domestic needs of that person and his family; and

(b) any money, banknotes, bills of exchange, promissory notes, bonds, specialties or securities for money belonging to that person.

(4) For the purposes of this section –

(a) 'property' means the general property in goods, and not merely a special property;

(b) 'sheriff' includes any officer charged with the enforcement of a writ of execution;

(c) any reference to the goods of the execution debtor includes a reference to anything else of his that may lawfully be seized in execution; and

(d) a thing shall be treated as done in good faith if it is in fact done honestly, whether it is done negligently or not.

138A Sales under executions   [401]

(1) Where any goods seized under a writ of execution issued from the High Court are to be sold for a sum exceeding £20 (including legal incidental expenses), the sale shall, unless the court otherwise orders, be made by public auction, and not by bill of sale or private contract, and shall be publicly advertised by the sheriff on, and during three days preceding, the day of sale.

(2) Where any goods are seized under a writ of execution issued from the High Court and the sheriff has notice of another execution or other executions, the court shall not consider an application for leave to sell privately until the prescribed notice has been given to the other execution creditor or creditors, who may appear before the court and be heard on the application.

138B Protection of officer selling goods under execution   [402]

(1) Where any goods in the possession of an execution debtor at the time of seizure by a sheriff or other officer charged with the enforcement of a writ of execution issued from the High Court are sold by the sheriff or other officer without any claims having been made to them –

(a) the purchaser of the goods so sold shall acquire a good title to those goods; and

(b) no person shall be entitled to recover against the sheriff or other officer, or anyone lawfully acting under his authority, for any sale of the goods or for paying over the proceeds prior to the receipt of a claim to the goods,

unless it is proved that the person from whom recovery is sought had notice, or might by making reasonable enquiry have ascertained, that the goods were not the property of the execution debtor.

(2) Nothing in this section shall affect the right of any lawful claimant (that it to say, any person who proves that at the time of sale he had a title to any goods so seized and sold) to any remedy to which he may be entitled against any person other than the sheriff or other officer.

(3) The provisions of this section have effect subject to those of sections 183, 184 and 346 of the Insolvency Act 1986.

151 Interpretation of this Act, and rules of construction [403]
for other Acts and documents

(1) In this Act, unless the context otherwise requires –

'action' means any civil proceedings commenced by writ or in any other manner prescribed by rules of court;

'appeal', in the context of appeals to the civil division of the Court of Appeal, includes –

(a) an application for a new trial, and

(b) an application to set aside a verdict, finding or judgment in any cause or matter in the High Court which has been tried, or in which any issue has been tried, by a jury;

'arbitration agreement' has the same meaning as it has in the Arbitration Act 1950 by virtue of section 32 of that Act;

'cause' means any action or any criminal proceedings;

'Division', where it appears with a capital letter, means a division of the High Court;

'judgment' includes a decree;

'jurisdiction' includes powers;

'matter' means any proceedings in court not in a cause;

'party', in relation to any proceedings, includes any person who pursuant to or by virtue of rules of court or any other statutory provision has been served with notice of, or has intervened in, those proceedings;

'prescribed' means –

(a) except in relation to fees, prescribed by rules of court; and

(b) in relation to fees, prescribed by an order under section 130;

'senior judge', where the reference is to the senior judge of a Division, means –

(a) in the case of the Chancery Division, the Vice-Chancellor;

(b) in the other case, the president of the Division in question;

'solicitor' means a solicitor of the Supreme Court;

'statutory provision' means any enactment, whenever passed, or any provision contained in subordinate legislation (as defined in section 21(1) of the Interpretation Act 1978), whenever made;

'this or any other Act' includes an Act passed after this Act.

(2) Section 128 contains definitions of expressions used in Part V and in the other provisions of this Act relating to probate causes and matters.

(3) Any reference in this Act to rules of court under section 84 includes a reference to rules of court under any provision of this or any other Act which confers on the Supreme Court Rule Committee or the Crown Court Rule Committee power to make rules of court.

(4) Except where the context otherwise requires, in this or any other Act –

'Criminal Appeal Rules' means rules of court made by the Crown Court Rule Committee in relation to the criminal division of the Court of Appeal;

'Crown Court Rules' means rules of court made by the Crown Court Rule Committee in relation to the Crown Court;

'divisional court' (with or without capital letters) means a divisional court constituted under section 66;

'judge of the Supreme Court' means –

(a) a judge of the Court of Appeal other than an ex-officio judge within paragraph (b) or (c) of section 2(2), or

(b) a judge of the High Court,

and accordingly does not include, as such, a judge of the Crown Court;
'official referees' business' has the meaning given by section 68(6);
'Rules of the Supreme Court' means rules of court made by the Supreme Court
Rule Committee.

(5) The provisions of Schedule 4 (construction of references to superseded courts
and officers) shall have effect.

SCHEDULE 1

DISTRIBUTION OF BUSINESS IN HIGH COURT

1. To the Chancery Division are assigned all causes and matters relating to –

(a) the sale, exchange or partition of land, or the raising of charges on land;
(b) the redemption or foreclosure of mortgages;
(c) the execution of trusts;
(d) the administration of the estates of deceased persons;
(e) bankruptcy;
(f) the dissolution of partnerships or the taking of partnership or other accounts;
(g) the rectification, setting aside or cancellation of deeds or other instruments in writing;
(h) probate business, other than non-contentious or common form business;
(i) patents, trade marks, registered designs, copyright or design right;
(j) the appointment of a guardian of a minor's estate,

and all causes and matters involving the exercise of the High Court's jurisdiction under the enactments relating to companies.

2. To the Queen's Bench Division are assigned –

(a) applications for writs of habeas corpus, except applications made by a parent or guardian of a minor for such a writ concerning the custody of the minor;
(b) applications for judicial review;
(c) all causes and matters involving the exercise of the High Court's Admiralty jurisdiction or its jurisdiction as a prize court; and
(d) all causes and matters entered in the commercial list.

3. To the Family Division are assigned –

(a) all matrimonial causes and matters (whether at first instance or on appeal);
(b) all causes and matters (whether at first instance or on appeal) relating to –

(i) legitimacy;
(ii) the exercise of the inherent jurisdiction of the High Court with respect to minors, the maintenance of minors and any proceedings under the Children Act 1989, except proceedings solely for the appointment of a guardian of a minor's estate;
(iii) adoption;
(iv) non-contentious or common form probate business;

(c) applications for consent to the marriage of a minor or for a declaration under section 27B(5) of the Marriage Act 1949;
(d) proceedings on appeal under section 13 of the Administration of Justice Act 1960 from an order or decision made under section 63(3) of the Magistrates' Courts Act 1980 to enforce an order of a magistrates' court made in matrimonial proceedings or with respect to the guardianship of a minor;
(e) applications under Part III of the Family Law Act 1986;

(e) proceedings under the Children Act 1989;

(f) all proceedings under –

(i) the Domestic Violence and Matrimonial Proceedings Act 1976;

(ii) the Child Abduction and Custody Act 1985;

(iii) the Family Law Act 1986;

(iv) section 30 of the Human Fertilisation and Embryology Act 1990; and

(g) all proceedings for the purpose of enforcing an order made in any proceedings of a type described in this paragraph;

(h) all proceedings under the Child Support Act 1991.

[As amended by the Local Government (Miscellaneous Provisions) Act 1982, s2, Schedule 3, para 27(6); Administration of Justice Act 1982, ss6(1), 15(1), 29(1), 58, 60(1); Mental Health (Amendment) Act 1982, s65(1); Mental Health Act 1983, s148, Schedule 4, para 58; Prosecution of Offences Act 1985, s24(1)-(6); Family Law Act 1986, s68(1), (2), Schedule 1, paras 25, 26, Schedule 2; Maximum Number of Judges Order 1987; Merchant Shipping Act 1988, s57(4), Schedule 6; Criminal Justice Act 1988, ss15, 156, Schedule 2, para 12; Children Act 1989, s108(5), Schedule 13, para 45(1), (3); Statute Law (Repeals) Act 1989, s1(2), Schedule 2, Pt I, para 4; Courts and Legal Services Act 1990, ss4(1), 7, 15(1), 67, 71(1), 72(6), s125(2), (3), (7), Schedule 17, para 12, Schedule 18, paras 36, 41, Schedule 20; Criminal Procedure (Insanity and Unfitness to Plead) Act 1991, s7, Schedule 3, para 6; High Court (Distribution of Business) Order 1991; Maximum Number of Judges Order 1993; High Court (Distribution of Business) Order 1993; Maximum Number of Judges (No 2) Order 1993; Statute Law (Repeals) Act 1993, s1(2), Schedule 2, Pt I, para 9.]

CRIMINAL JUSTICE ACT 1982
(1982 c 48)

37 The standard scale of fines for summary offences [404]

(1) There shall be a standard scale of fines for summary offences, which shall be known as 'the standard scale'.

(2) The standard scale is shown below –

Level on the scale	Amount of fine
1	£200
2	£500
3	£1,000
4	£2,500
5	£5,000

(3) Where any enactment (whether contained in an Act passed before or after this Act) provides –

(a) that a person convicted of a summary offence shall be liable on conviction to a fine or a maximum fine by reference to a specified level on the standard scale; or

(b) confers power by subordinate instrument to make a person liable on conviction of a summary offence (whether or not created by the instrument) to a fine or maximum fine by reference to a specified level on the standard scale,

it is to be construed as referring to the standard scale for which this section provides as that standard scale has effect from time to time by virtue either of this section or of an order under section 143 of the Magistrates' Courts Act 1980.

[As amended by the Criminal Justice Act 1991, ss17(1), 101(1), Schedule 12, para 6.]

COUNTY COURTS ACT 1984
(1984 c 28)

PART I

CONSTITUTION AND ADMINISTRATION

1 County courts to be held for districts   [405]

(1) For the purposes of this Act, England and Wales shall be divided into districts, and a court shall be held under this Act for each district at one or more places in it; and throughout the whole of each district the court so held for the district shall have such jurisdiction and powers as are conferred by this Act and any other enactment for the time being in force.

(2) Every court so held shall be called a county court and shall be a court of record and shall have a seal.

(3) Nothing in this section affects the operation of section 42 of the Courts Act 1971 (City of London).

5 Judges of county courts   [406]

(1) Every Circuit judge shall, by virtue of his office, be capable of sitting as a judge for any county court district in England and Wales, and the Lord Chancellor shall assign one or more Circuit judges to each district and may from time to time vary the assignment of Circuit judges among the districts.

(2) Subject to any directions given by or on behalf of the Lord Chancellor, in any case where more than one Circuit judge is assigned to a district under subsection (1), any function conferred by or under this Act on the judge for a district may be exercised by any of the Circuit judges for the time being assigned to that district.

(3) The following, that is –

every judge of the Court of Appeal,
every judge of the High Court,
every Recorder,

shall, by virtue of his office, be capable of sitting as a judge for any county court district in England and Wales and, if he consents to do so, shall sit as such a judge at such times and on such occasions as the Lord Chancellor considers desirable.

(4) Notwithstanding that he is not for the time being assigned to a particular district, a Circuit judge –

(a) shall sit as a judge of that district at such times and on such occasions as the Lord Chancellor may direct; and
(b) may sit as a judge of that district in any case where it appears to him that the judge of that district is not, or none of the judges of that district is, available to deal with the case.

6 District judges   [407]

(1) Subject to the provisions of this section, there shall be a district judge for each district, who shall be appointed by the Lord Chancellor and paid such salary as the Lord Chancellor may, with the concurrence of the Treasury, direct.

(2) The Lord Chancellor may, if he thinks fit, appoint a person to be district judge for two or more districts.

(3) The Lord Chancellor may, if he thinks fit, appoint two or more persons to execute jointly the office of district judge for a district and may, in any case where joint district judges are appointed, give directions with respect to the division between them of the duties of the office.

(4) The Lord Chancellor may, as he thinks fit, on the death, resignation or removal of a joint district judge, either appoint another person to be joint district judge in his place or give directions that the continuing district judge shall act as sole district judge or, as the case may be, that the continuing district judges shall execute jointly the office of district judge.

(5) The district judge for any district shall be capable of acting in any other district for the district judge of that other district.

7 Assistant district judges [408]

(1) The Lord Chancellor may, with the concurrence of the Treasury as to numbers and salaries, appoint in connection with any court such assistant district judges as he considers necessary for carrying out the work of the court.

(2) An assistant district judge shall be capable of discharging any of the functions of the district judge, and in so doing shall have the same powers and be subject to the same liabilities as if he were the district judge.

8 Deputy district judges [409]

(1) If it appears to the Lord Chancellor that it is expedient as a temporary measure to make an appointment under this subsection in order to facilitate the disposal of business in county courts, he may appoint a person to be deputy district judge for any county court district during such period or on such occasions as the Lord Chancellor thinks fit; and a deputy district judge, while acting under his appointment, shall have the same powers and be subject to the same liabilities as if he were the district judge.

(2) Notwithstanding the expiry of any period for which a person is appointed under this section to be deputy district judge, he may act as such for the purpose of continuing to deal with, giving judgment in, or dealing with any ancillary matters relating to, any case with which he may have been concerned during the period of his appointment, and for that purpose shall be treated as acting under that appointment.

(3) The Lord Chancellor may pay to any person appointed under this section as deputy district judge such remuneration and allowances as he may, with the approval of the Treasury, determine.

9 Qualifications [410]

No person shall be appointed a district judge, assistant district judge or deputy district judge unless he has a seven year general qualification, within the meaning of section 71 of the Courts and Legal Services Act 1990.

11 Tenure of office [411]

(1) This subsection applies –

(a) to the office of district judge or assistant district judge; and
(b) to the office of part-time district judge or part-time assistant district judge.

(2) Subject to the following provisions of this section, a person who holds an office to which subsection (1) applies shall vacate his office at the end of the completed year of service in which he attains the age of 72 years.

(3) Where the Lord Chancellor considers it desirable in the public interest to retain in office a person who holds an office to which subsection (1) applies after the time when he would otherwise retire in accordance with subsection (2), the Lord Chancellor may from time to time authorise the continuance in office of that person until such date, not being later than the date on which that person attains the age of 75 years, as he thinks fit.

(4) A person appointed to an office to which subsection (1) applies shall hold that office during good behaviour.

(5) The power to remove such a person from his office on account of misbehaviour shall be exercisable by the Lord Chancellor.

(6) The Lord Chancellor may also remove such a person from his office on account of inability to perform the duties of his office.

PART II

JURISDICTION AND TRANSFER OF PROCEEDINGS

15 General jurisdiction in actions of contract and tort   [412]

(1) Subject to subsection (2), a county court shall have jurisdiction to hear and determine any action founded on contract or tort.

(2) A county court shall not, except as in this Act provided, have jurisdiction to hear and determine –

(b) any action in which the title to any toll, fair, market or franchise is in question; or
(c) any action for libel or slander.

16 Money recoverable by statute   [413]

A county court shall have jurisdiction to hear and determine an action for the recovery of a sum recoverable by virtue of any enactment for the time being in force, if –

(a) it is not provided by that or any other enactment that such sums shall only be recoverable in the High Court or shall only be recoverable summarily.

17 Abandonment of part of claim to give court jurisdiction   [414]

(1) Where a plaintiff has a cause of action for more than the county court limit in which, if it were not for more than the county court limit a county court would have jurisdiction, the plaintiff may abandon the excess, and thereupon a county court shall have jurisdiction to hear and determine the action, but the plaintiff shall not recover in the action an amount exceeding the county court limit.

(2) Where the court has jurisdiction to hear and determine an action by virtue of this section, the judgment of the court in the action shall be in full discharge of all demands in respect of the cause of action, and entry of the judgment shall be made accordingly.

18 Jurisdiction by agreement in certain actions   [415]

If the parties to any action, other than an action which, if commenced in the High Court, would have been assigned to the Chancery Division or to the Family Division or have involved the exercise of the High Court's Admiralty jurisdiction, agree, by a memorandum signed by them or by their respective legal representatives, that a county court specified in the memorandum shall have jurisdiction in the action, that court shall have jurisdiction to hear and determine the action accordingly.

21 Actions for recovery of land and actions where title is in question [416]

(1) A county court shall have jurisdiction to hear and determine any action for the recovery of land.

(2) A county court shall have jurisdiction to hear and determine any action in which the title to any hereditament comes in question.

(3) Where a mortgage of land consists of or includes a dwelling-house and no part of the land is situated in Greater London then, subject to subsection (4), if a county court has jurisdiction by virtue of this section to hear and determine an action in which the mortgagee under that mortgage claims possession of the mortgaged property, no court other than a county court shall have jurisdiction to hear and determine that action.

(4) Subsection (3) shall not apply to an action for foreclosure or sale in which a claim for possession of the mortgaged property is also made.

(7) In this section –

'dwelling-house' includes any building or part of a building which is used as a dwelling;
'mortgage' includes a charge and 'mortgagor' and 'mortgagee' shall be construed accordingly;
'mortgagor' and 'mortgagee' include any person deriving title under the original mortgagor or mortgagee.

(8) The fact that part of the premises comprised in a dwelling-house is used as a shop or office or for business, trade or professional purposes shall not prevent the dwelling-house from being a dwelling-house for the purposes of this section.

(9) This section does not apply to a mortgage securing an agreement which is a regulated agreement within the meaning of the Consumer Credit Act 1974.

23 Equity jurisdiction [417]

A county court shall have all the jurisdiction of the High Court to hear and determine –

(a) proceedings for the administration of the estate of a deceased person, where the estate does not exceed in amount or value the county court limit;
(b) proceedings –

(i) for the execution of any trust, or
(ii) for a declaration that a trust subsists, or
(iii) under section 1 of the Variation of Trusts Act 1958,

where the estate or fund subject, or alleged to be subject, to the trust does not exceed in amount or value the county court limit;
(c) proceedings for foreclosure or redemption of any mortgage or for enforcing any charge or lien, where the amount owing in respect of the mortgage, charge or lien does not exceed the county court limit;
(d) proceedings for the specific performance, or for the rectification, delivery up or cancellation, of any agreement for the sale, purchase or lease of any property, where, in the case of a sale or purchase, the purchase money, or in the case of a lease, the value of the property, does not exceed the county court limit;

(e) proceedings relating to the maintenance or advancement of a minor, where the property of the minor does not exceed in amount or value the county court limit;

(f) proceedings for the dissolution or winding-up of any partnership (whether or not the existence of the partnership is in dispute), where the whole assets of the partnership do not exceed in amount or value the county court limit;

(g) proceedings for relief against fraud or mistake, where the damage sustained or the estate or fund in respect of which relief is sought does not exceed in amount or value the county court limit.

24 Jurisdiction by agreement in certain equity proceedings [418]

(1) If, as respects any proceedings to which this section applies, the parties agree, by a memorandum signed by them or by their respective legal representatives or agents, that a county court specified in the memorandum shall have jurisdiction in the proceedings, that court shall, notwithstanding anything in any enactment, have jurisdiction to hear and determine the proceedings accordingly.

(2) Subject to subsection (3), this section applies to any proceedings in which a county court would have jurisdiction by virtue of –

(a) section 113(3) of the Settled Land Act 1925,

(b) section 63A of the Trustee Act 1925,

(c) sections 3(7), 49(4), 66(4), 89(7), 90(3), 91(8), 92(2), 136(3), 181(2), 188(2) of, and paragraph 3A of Part III and paragraph 1(3A) and (4A) of Part IV of Schedule 1 to, the Law of Property Act 1925,

(d) sections 17(2), 38(4), 41(1A) and 43(4) of the Administration of Estates Act 1925,

(e) section 6(1) of the Leasehold Property (Repairs) Act 1938,

(f) sections 1(6A) and 5(11) of the Land Charges Act 1972, and

(g) sections 23 and 25 of this Act,

but for the limits of the jurisdiction of the court provided by those enactments.

(3) This section does not apply to proceedings under section 1 of the Variation of Trusts Act 1958.

25 Jurisdiction under Inheritance (Provision for Family and Dependants) Act 1975 [419]

A county court shall have jurisdiction to hear and determine any application for an order under section 2 of the Inheritance (Provision for Family and Dependants) Act 1975 (including any application for permission to apply for such an order and any application made, in the proceedings on an application for such an order, for an order under any other provision of that Act).

26 Districts for Admiralty purposes [420]

(1) If at any time it appears expedient to the Lord Chancellor that any county court should have Admiralty jurisdiction, it shall be lawful for him, by order –

(a) to appoint that court to have, as from such date as may be specified in the order, such Admiralty jurisdiction as is provided in this Act; and

(b) to assign to that court as its district for Admiralty purposes any part or parts of any county court district or of two or more county court districts.

(2) Where a district has been so assigned to a court as its district for Admiralty purposes, the parts of the sea (if any) adjacent to that district to a distance of three miles from the shore thereof shall be deemed to be included in that district,

and the judge and all officers of the court shall have jurisdiction and authority for those purposes throughout that district as if it were the district for the court for all purposes.

(3) Where an order is made under this section for the discontinuance of the Admiralty jurisdiction of any county court, whether wholly or within a part of the district assigned to it for Admiralty purposes, provision may be made in the order with respect to any Admiralty proceedings commenced in that court before the order comes into operation.

(4) The power to make orders under this section shall be exercisable by statutory instrument.

27 Admiralty jurisdiction [421]

(1) Subject to the limitations of amount specified in subsection (2), an Admiralty county court shall have the following Admiralty jurisdiction, that is to say, jurisdiction to hear and determine –

(a) any claim for damage received by a ship;
(b) any claim for damage done by a ship;
(c) any claim for loss of life or personal injury sustained in consequence of any defect in a ship or in her apparel or equipment, or in consequence of the wrongful act, neglect or default of –

(i) the owners, charterers or persons in possession or control of a ship; or
(ii) the master or crew of a ship, or any other person for whose wrongful acts, neglects or defaults the owners, charterers or persons in possession or control of a ship are responsible,

being an act, neglect or default in the navigation or management of the ship, in the loading, carriage or discharge of goods on, in or from the ship, or in the embarkation, carriage or disembarkation of persons on, in or from the ship; ...

(2) The limitations of amount referred to in subsection (1) are that the court shall not have jurisdiction to hear and determine –

(a) a claim in the nature of salvage where the value of the property salved exceeds £15,000; or
(b) any other claim mentioned in that subsection for an amount exceeding £5,000 ...

(6) If, as regards any proceedings as to any such claim as is mentioned in subsection (1), the parties agree, by a memorandum signed by them or by their respective legal representatives or agents, that a particular county court specified in the memorandum shall have jurisdiction in the proceedings, that court shall, notwithstanding anything in subsection (2) or in county court rules for prescribing the courts in which proceedings shall be brought, have jurisdiction to hear and determine the proceedings accordingly.

(7) Nothing in this section shall be taken to affect the jurisdiction of any county court to hear and determine any proceedings in which it has jurisdiction by virtue of section 15 or 17.

(8) Nothing in this section, or in section 26 or in any order made under that section, shall be taken to confer on a county court the jurisdiction of a prize court within the meaning of the Naval Prize Acts 1864 to 1916 ...

32 Contentious probate jurisdiction [422]

(1) Where –

(a) an application for the grant or revocation of probate or administration has been made through the principal registry of the Family Division or district probate registry under section 105 of the Supreme Court Act 1981; and

(b) it is shown to the satisfaction of a county court that the value at the date of the death of the deceased of his net estate does not exceed the county court limit,

the county court shall have the jurisdiction of the High Court in respect of any contentious matter arising with the grant or revocation.

(2) In subsection (1) 'net estate', in relation to a deceased person, means the estate of that person exclusive of any property he was possessed of or entitled to as a trustee and not beneficially, and after making allowances for funeral expenses and for debts and liabilities.

35 Division of causes of action   [423]

It shall not be lawful for any plaintiff to divide any cause of action for the purpose of bringing two or more actions in one or more of the county courts.

36 No action on judgment of High Court   [424]

No action shall be brought in a county court on any judgment of the High Court.

37 Persons who may exercise jurisdiction of court   [425]

(1) Any jurisdiction and powers conferred by this or any other Act –

(a) on a county court; or
(b) on the judge of a county court,

may be exercised by any judge of the court.

(2) Subsection (1) applies to jurisdiction and power conferred on all county courts or judges of county courts or on any particular county court or the judge of any particular county court.

38 Remedies available in county courts   [426]

(1) Subject to what follows, in any proceedings in a county court the court may make any order which could be made by the High Court if the proceedings were in the High Court.

(2) Any order made by a county court may be –

(a) absolute or conditional;
(b) final or interlocutory.

(3) A county court shall not have power –

(a) to order mandamus, certiorari or prohibition; or
(b) to make any order of a prescribed kind.

(4) Regulations under subsection (3) –

(a) may provide for any of their provisions not to apply in such circumstances or descriptions of case as may be specified in the regulations;
(b) may provide for the transfer of the proceedings to the High Court for the purpose of enabling an order of a kind prescribed under subsection (3) to be made;
(c) may make such provision with respect to matters of procedure as the Lord Chancellor considers expedient; and
(d) may make provision amending or repealing any provision made by or under any enactment, so far as may be necessary or expedient in consequence of the regulations.

(5) In this section 'prescribed' means prescribed by regulations made by the Lord Chancellor under this section.

(6) The power to make regulations under this section shall be exercised by statutory instrument.

(7) No such statutory instrument shall be made unless a draft of the instrument has been approved by both Houses of Parliament.

40 Transfer of proceedings to county court [427]

(1) Where the High Court is satisfied that any proceedings before it are required by any provision of a kind mentioned in subsection (8) to be in a county court it shall –

(a) order the transfer of the proceedings to a county court; or
(b) if the court is satisfied that the person bringing the proceedings knew, or ought to have known, of that requirement, order that they be struck out.

(2) Subject to any such provision, the High Court may order the transfer of any proceedings before it to a county court.

(3) An order under this section may be made either on the motion of the High Court itself or on the application of any party to the proceedings.

(4) Proceedings transferred under this section shall be transferred to such county court as the High Court considers appropriate, having taken into account the convenience of the parties and that of any other persons likely to be affected and the state of business in the courts concerned.

(5) The transfer of any proceedings under this section shall not affect any right of appeal from the order directing the transfer.

(6) Where proceedings for the enforcement of any judgment or order of the High Court are transferred under this section –

(a) the judgment or order may be enforced as if it were a judgment or order of a county court; and
(b) subject to subsection (7), it shall be treated as a judgment or order of that court for all purposes.

(7) Where proceedings for the enforcement of any judgment or order of the High Court are transferred under this section –

(a) the powers of any court to set aside, correct, vary or quash a judgment or order of the High Court, and the enactments relating to appeals from such a judgment or order, shall continue to apply; and
(b) the powers of any court to set aside, correct, vary or quash a judgment or order of a county court, and the enactments relating to appeals from such a judgment or order, shall not apply.

(8) The provisions referred to in subsection (1) are any made –

(a) under section 1 of the Courts and Legal Services Act 1990; or
(b) by or under any other enactment.

(9) This section does not apply to family proceedings within the meaning of Part V of the Matrimonial and Family Proceedings Act 1984.

41 Transfer to High Court by order of High Court [428]

(1) If at any stage in proceedings commenced in a county court or transferred to a county court under section 40, the High Court thinks it desirable that the proceedings, or any part of them, should be heard and determined in the High Court, it may order the transfer to the High Court of the proceedings or, as the case may be, of that part of them.

(2) The power conferred by subsection (1) is without prejudice to section 29 of the Supreme Court Act 1981 (power of High Court to issue prerogative orders) but shall be exercised in relation to family proceedings (within the meaning of Part V of the Matrimonial and Family Proceedings Act 1984) in accordance with any directions given under section 37 of that Act (directions as to distribution and transfer of family business and proceedings).

(3) The power conferred by subsection (1) shall be exercised subject to any provision made –

(a) under section 1 of the Courts and Legal Services Act 1990; or
(b) by or under any other enactment.

42 Transfer to High Court by order of a county court   [429]

(1) Where a county court is satisfied that any proceedings before it are required by any provision of a kind mentioned in subsection (7) to be in the High Court, it shall –

(a) order the transfer of the proceedings to the High Court; or
(b) if the court is satisfied that the person bringing the proceedings knew, or ought to have known, of that requirement, order that they be struck out.

(2) Subject to any such provision, a county court may order the transfer of any proceedings before it to the High Court.

(3) An order under this section may be made either on the motion of the court itself or on the application of any party to the proceedings.

(4) The transfer of any proceedings under this section shall not affect any right of appeal from the order directing the transfer.

(5) Where proceedings for the enforcement of any judgment or order of a county court are transferred under this section –

(a) the judgment or order may be enforced as if it were a judgment or order of the High Court; and
(b) subject to subsection (6), it shall be treated as a judgment or order of that court for all purposes.

(6) Where proceedings for the enforcement of any judgment or order of a county court are transferred under this section –

(a) the powers of any court to set aside, correct, vary or quash a judgment or order of a county court, and the enactments relating to appeals from such a judgment or order, shall continue to apply; and
(b) the powers of any court to set aside, correct, vary or quash a judgment or order of the High Court, and the enactments relating to appeals from such a judgment or order, shall not apply.

(7) The provisions referred to in subsection (1) are any made –

(a) under section 1 of the Courts and Legal Services Act 1990; or
(b) by or under any other enactment.

(8) This section does not apply to family proceedings within the meaning of Part V of the Matrimonial and Family Proceedings Act 1984.

PART III

PROCEDURE

47 Minors [430]

A minor may prosecute any action in a county court for any sum of money not exceeding the county court limit which may be due to him for wages or piece work, or for work as a servant, in the same manner as if he were of full age.

58 Persons who may take affidavits for use in county courts

(1) An affidavit to be used in a county court may be sworn before –

(a) the judge or registrar of any court; or
(b) any justice of the peace; or
(c) an officer of any court appointed by the judge of that court for the purpose,

as well as before a commissioner for oaths or any other person authorised to take affidavits under the Commissioner for Oaths Acts 1889 and 1891.

(2) An affidavit sworn before a judge or registrar or before any such officer may be sworn without the payment of any fee.

60 Right of audience [431]

(2) Where an action is brought in a county court by a local authority for either or both of the following –

(a) the recovery of possession of a house belonging to the authority;
(b) the recovery of any rent, mesne profits, damages or other sum claimed by the authority in respect of the occupation by any person of such a house,

then, in so far as the proceedings in the action are heard by the district judge, any officer of the authority authorised by the authority in that behalf, may address the district judge.

(3) In this section –

'local authority' means a county council, a district council, the Broads Authority, a London borough council, a police authority established under section 3 of the Police Act 1964, a joint authority established by Part IV of the Local Government Act 1985 or the Common Council of the City of London; and
'house' includes a part of a house, a flat or any other dwelling and also includes any yard, garden, outhouse or appurtenance occupied with a house or part of a house or with a flat or other dwelling,
and any reference to the occupation of a house by a person includes a reference to anything done by that person, or caused or permitted by him to be done, in relation to the house as occupier of the house, whether under a tenancy or licence or otherwise.

61 Right of audience by direction of Lord Chancellor [432]

(1) The Lord Chancellor may at any time direct that such categories of persons in relevant legal employment as may be specified in the direction may address the court in any proceedings in a county court, or in proceedings in a county court of such description as may be so specified.

(2) In subsection (1), 'relevant legal employment' means employment which consists of or includes giving assistance in the conduct of litigation to a legal representative whether in private practice or not.

(3) A direction under this section may be given subject to such conditions and restrictions as appear to the Lord Chancellor to be necessary or expedient, and may be expressed to have effect as respects every county court or as respects a specified county court or as respects one or more specified places where a county court sits.

(4) The power to give directions conferred by this section includes a power to vary or rescind any direction given under this section.

64 Reference to arbitration   [433]

(1) County court rules –

(a) may prescribe cases in which proceedings are (without any order of the court) to be referred to arbitration, and
(b) may prescribe the manner in which and the terms on which cases are to be so referred, and
(c) may, where cases are so referred, require other matters within the jurisdiction of the court in dispute between the parties also to be referred to arbitration.

(2) County court rules –

(a) may prescribe cases in which proceedings may be referred to arbitration by order of the court, and
(b) may authorise the court also to order other matters in dispute between the parties and within the jurisdiction of the court to be so referred.

(2A) County court rules may prescribe the procedures and rules of evidence to be followed on any reference under subsection (1) or (2).

(2B) Rules made under subsection (2A) may, in particular, make provision with respect to the manner of taking and questioning evidence.

(3) On a reference under subsection (1) or (2) the award of the arbitrator, arbitrators or umpire shall be entered as the judgment in the proceedings and shall be as binding and effectual to all intents, subject to subsection (4), as if it had been given by the judge.

(4) The judge may, if he thinks fit, on application made to him within such time as may be prescribed, set aside the award, or may, with the consent of the parties, revoke the reference or order another reference to be made in the manner specified in this section.

(5) In this section 'award' includes an interim award.

66 Trial by jury   [434]

(1) In the following proceedings in a county court the trial shall be without a jury –

(a) Admiralty proceedings;
(b) proceedings arising –

(i) under Part I, II or III of the Rent (Agriculture) Act 1976; or
(ii) under any provision of the Rent Act 1977 other than a provision contained in Part V, sections 103 to 106 or Part IX; or
(iii) under Part I of the Protection from Eviction Act 1977; or
(iv) under Part I of the Housing Act 1988;

(c) any appeal to the county court under the Housing Act 1985.

(2) In all other proceedings in a county court the trial shall be without a jury unless the court otherwise orders on an application made in that behalf by any party to the proceedings in such manner and within such time before the trial as may be prescribed.

(3) Where, on any such application, the court is satisfied that there is in issue –

(a) a charge of fraud against the party making the application; or
(b) a claim in respect of libel, slander, malicious prosecution or false imprisonment; or
(c) any question or issue of a kind prescribed for the purposes of this paragraph,

the action shall be tried with a jury, unless the court is of opinion that the trial requires any prolonged examination of documents or accounts or any scientific or local investigation which cannot conveniently be made with a jury.

(4) There shall be payable, in respect of the trial with a jury of proceedings in a county court, such fees as may be prescribed by the fees order.

67 Impanelling and swearing of jury [435]

At any county court where proceedings are to be tried with a jury, eight jurymen shall be impanelled and sworn as occasion requires to give their verdicts in the proceedings brought before them, and being once sworn need not be re-sworn in each trial.

69 Power to award interest on debts and damages [436]

(1) Subject to county court rules, in proceedings (whenever instituted) before a county court for the recovery of a debt or damages there may be included in any sum for which judgment is given simple interest, at such rate as the court thinks fit or as may be prescribed, on all or any part of the debt or damages in respect of which judgment is given, or payment is made before judgment, for all or any part of the period between the date when the cause of action arose and –

(a) in the case of any sum paid before judgment, the date of the payment; and
(b) in the case of the sum for which judgment is given, the date of the judgment.

(2) In relation to a judgment given for damages for personal injuries or death which exceed £200 subsection (1) shall have effect –

(a) with the substitution of 'shall be included' for 'may be included'; and
(b) with the addition of 'unless the court is satisfied that there are special reasons to the contrary' after 'given', where first occurring.

(3) Subject to county court rules, where –

(a) there are proceedings (whenever instituted) before a county court for the recovery of a debt; and
(b) the defendant pays the whole debt to the plaintiff (otherwise than in pursuance of a judgment in the proceedings),

the defendant shall be liable to pay the plaintiff simple interest, at such rate as the court thinks fit or as may be prescribed, on all or any part of the debt for all or any part of the period between the date when the cause of action arose and the date of the payment.

(4) Interest in respect of a debt shall not be awarded under this section for a period during which, for whatever reason, interest on the debt already runs.

(5) Interest under this section may be calculated at different rates in respect of different periods.

(6) In this section 'plaintiff' means the person seeking the debt or damages and 'defendant' means the person from whom the plaintiff seeks the debt or damages and 'personal injuries' includes any disease and any impairment of a person's physical or mental condition.

(7) Nothing in this section affects the damages recoverable for the dishonour of a bill of exchange.

(8) In determining whether the amount of any debt or damages exceeds that prescribed by or under any enactment, no account shall be taken of any interest payable by virtue of this section except where express provision to the contrary is made by or under that or any other enactment.

75 County court rules [437]

(1) The rule committee may make county court rules regulating the practice of the courts and forms of proceedings in them and prescribing scales of costs to be paid to counsel and solicitors.

(2) The power to make county court rules shall extend to all matters of procedure or practice, or matters relating to or concerning the effect or operation in law of any procedure or practice, in any case within the cognisance of county courts as to which rules of the Supreme Court have been or might lawfully be made for cases within the cognisance of the High Court ...

(7) The rule committee shall consist of the following persons appointed by the Lord Chancellor –

(a) five judges of county courts;
(b) two district judges;
(c) two persons who have a Supreme Court qualification (within the meaning of section 71 of the Courts and Legal Services Act 1990); and
(d) two persons who have been granted by an authorised body, under Part II of that Act, the right to conduct litigation in relation to all proceedings in the Supreme Court ...

(9) Any rules made by the rule committee shall be certified under the hands of the members of the committee, or any three or more of them, and submitted to the Lord Chancellor, who may allow or disallow or alter them.

(10) Any rules so made, as allowed or altered by the Lord Chancellor, shall –

(a) come into operation on such day as the Lord Chancellor may direct;
(b) be embodied in a statutory instrument to which the Statutory Instruments Act 1946 shall apply as if it embodied rules made by a Minister of the Crown.

76 Application of practice of High Court [438]

In any case not expressly provided for by or in pursuance of this Act, the general principles of practice in the High Court may be adopted and applied to proceedings in a county court.

PART IV

APPEALS, ETC

77 Appeals: general provisions [439]

(1) Subject to the provisions of this section and the following provisions of this Part of this Act, if any party to any proceedings in a county court is dissatisfied with the determination of the judge or jury, he may appeal from it to the Court of Appeal in such manner and subject to such conditions as may be provided by the rules of the Supreme Court.

(1A) Without prejudice to the generality of the power to make county court rules under section 75, such rules may make provision for any appeal from the exercise by a district judge, assistant district judge or deputy district judge of any power given to him by virtue of any enactment to be to a judge of a county court.

(2) The Lord Chancellor may by order prescribe classes of proceedings in which there is to be no right of appeal under this section without the leave either of the judge of the county court or of the Court of Appeal ...

(6) In proceedings in which either the plaintiff or the defendant is claiming possession of any premises this section shall not confer any right of appeal on any question of fact if by virtue of –

(a) section 13(4) of the Landlord and Tenant Act 1954; or
(b) Cases III to IX in Schedule 4 to the Rent (Agriculture) Act 1976; or
(c) section 98 of the Rent Act 1977, as it applies to Cases 1 to 6 and 8 and 9 in Schedule 15 to that Act, or that section as extended or applied by any other enactment; or
(d) section 99 of the Rent Act 1977, as it applies to Cases 1 to 6 and 9 in Schedule 15 to that Act; or
(e) section 84(2)(a) of the Housing Act 1985; or
(ee) section 7 of the Housing Act 1988, as it applies to the grounds in Part II of Schedule 2 to that Act; or
(f) any other enactment,

the court can only grant possession on being satisfied that it is reasonable to do so ...

79 Agreement not to appeal [440]

(1) No appeal shall lie from any judgment, direction, decision or order of a judge of county courts if, before the judgment, direction, decision or order is given or made, the parties agree, in writing signed by themselves or their legal representatives or agents, that it shall be final.

80 Judge's note on appeal [441]

(1) At the hearing of any proceedings in a county court in which there is a right of appeal or from which an appeal may be brought with leave, the judge shall, at the request of any party, make a note –

(a) of any question of law raised at the hearing; and
(b) of the facts in evidence in relation to any such question; and
(c) of his decision on any such question and of his determination of the proceedings.

(2) Where such a note has been taken, the judge shall (whether notice of appeal has been served or not), on the application of any party to the proceedings, and

on payment by that party of such fee as may be prescribed by the fees orders, furnish him with a copy of the note, and shall sign the copy, and the copy so signed shall be used at the hearing of the appeal.

81 Powers of Court of Appeal on appeal   [442]
from county court

(1) On the hearing of an appeal, the Court of Appeal may draw any inference of fact and either –

(a) order a new trial on such terms as the court thinks just; or

(b) order judgment to be entered for any party; or

(c) make a final or other order on such terms as the court thinks proper to ensure the determination on the merits of the real question in controversy between the parties.

(2) Subject to any rules of the Supreme Court, on any appeal from a county court the Court of Appeal may reverse or vary, in favour of a party seeking to support the judgment or order of the county court in whole or in part, any determination made in the county court on questions of fact, notwithstanding that the appeal is an appeal on a point of law only, or any such determinations on points of law, notwithstanding that the appeal is an appeal on a question of fact only.

(3) Subsection (2) shall not enable the Court of Appeal to reverse or vary any determination, unless the party dissatisfied with the determination would have been entitled to appeal in respect of it if aggrieved by the judgment or order.

82 Decision of Court of Appeal on probate appeals   [443]
to be final

No appeal shall lie from the decision of the Court of Appeal on any appeal from a county court in any probate proceedings.

PART V

ENFORCEMENT OF JUDGMENTS AND ORDERS

85 Execution of judgments or orders for payment of money   [444]

(1) Subject to article 8 of the High Court and County Courts Jurisdiction Order 1991, any sum of money payable under a judgment or order of a county court may be recovered, in case of default or failure of payment, forthwith or at the time or times and in the manner thereby directed, by execution against the goods of the party against whom the judgment or order was obtained.

(2) The district judge, on the application of the party prosecuting any such judgment or order, shall issue a warrant of execution in the nature of a writ of fieri facias whereby the district judge shall be empowered to levy or cause to be levied by distress and sale of the goods, wherever they may be found within the district of the court, the money payable under the judgment or order and the costs of the execution.

(3) The precise time of the making of the application to the district judge to issue such a warrant shall be entered by him in the record prescribed for the purpose under section 12 and on the warrant.

(4) It shall be the duty of every constable within his jurisdiction to assist in the execution of every such warrant.

89 Goods which may be seized [445]

(1) Every bailiff or officer executing any warrant of execution issued from a county court against the goods of any person may by virtue of it seize –

(a) any of that person's goods except –

(i) such tools, books, vehicles and other items of equipment as are necessary to that person for use personally by him in his employment, business or vocation;

(ii) such clothing, bedding, furniture, household equipment and provisions as are necessary for satisfying the basic domestic needs of that person and his family;

(b) any money, banknotes, bills of exchange, promissory notes, bonds, specialties or securities for money belonging to that person.

(2) Any reference to the goods of an execution debtor in this Part of this Act includes a reference to anything else of his that may lawfully be seized in execution.

93 Period to elapse before sale [446]

No goods seized in execution under process of a county court shall be sold for the purpose of satisfying the warrant of execution until the expiration of a period of at least five days next following the day on which the goods have been so seized unless –

(a) the goods are of a perishable nature; or

(b) the person whose goods have been seized so requests in writing.

94 Goods not to be sold except by brokers or appraisers [447]

No goods seized in execution under process of a county court shall be sold for the purpose of satisfying the warrant of execution except by one of the brokers or appraisers appointed under this Part of this Act.

95 Appointment of brokers, appraisers, etc [448]

(1) The district judge may from time to time as he thinks fit appoint such number of persons for keeping possession, and such number of brokers and appraisers for the purpose of selling or valuing any goods seized in execution under process of the court, as appears to him to be necessary.

(2) The district judge may direct security to be taken from any broker, appraiser or other person so appointed for such sum and in such manner as he thinks fit for the faithful performance of his duties without injury or oppression.

(3) The judge or district judge may dismiss any broker, appraiser or other person so appointed.

(4) There shall be payable to brokers and appraisers so appointed in respect of their duties, out of the produce of goods distrained or sold, such fees as may be prescribed by the fees orders.

97 Sales under executions to be published unless otherwise ordered [449]

(1) Where any goods are to be sold under execution for a sum exceeding £20 (including legal incidental expenses), the sale shall, unless the court from which the warrant of execution issued otherwise orders, be made by public auction and

not by bill of sale or private contract, and shall be publicly advertised by the district judge on, and during three days next preceding, the day of sale.

(2) Where any goods are seized in execution and the district judge has notice of another execution or other executions, the court shall not consider an application for leave to sell privately until the prescribed notice has been given to the other execution creditor or creditors, who may appear before the court and be heard upon the application.

107 Receivers   [450]

(1) The power of the county court to appoint a receiver by way of equitable execution shall operate in relation to all legal estates and interests in land.

(2) The said power may be exercised in relation to an estate or interest in land whether or not a charge has been imposed on that land under section 1 of the Charging Orders Act 1979 for the purpose of enforcing the judgment, decree, order or award in question, and the said power shall be in addition to and not in derogation of any power of any court to appoint a receiver in proceedings for enforcing such a charge.

(3) Where an order under section 1 of the Charging Orders Act 1979 imposing a charge for the purpose of enforcing a judgment, decree, order or award has been registered under section 6 of the Land Charges Act 1972, subsection (4) of that section (which provides that, amongst other things, an order appointing a receiver and any proceedings pursuant to the order or in obedience to it, shall be void against a purchaser unless the order is for the time being registered under that section) shall not apply to an order appointing a receiver made either in proceedings for enforcing the charge or by way of equitable execution of the judgment, decree, order or award or, as the case may be, of so much·of it as requires payment of moneys secured by the charge.

108 Attachment of debts   [451]

(1) Subject to any order for the time being in force under subsection (4), this section applies to the following accounts, namely –

(a) any deposit account with a bank or other deposit-taking institution; and
(b) any withdrawable share account with any deposit-taking institution.

(2) In determining whether, for the purposes of the jurisdiction of the county court to attach debts for the purpose of satisfying judgments or orders for the payment of money, a sum standing to the credit of a person in an account to which this section applies is a sum due or accruing to that person and, as such, attachable in accordance with county court rules, any condition mentioned in subsection (3) which applies to the account shall be disregarded.

(3) Those conditions are –

(a) any condition that notice is required before any money or share is withdrawn;
(b) any condition that a personal application must be made before any money or share is withdrawn;
(c) any condition that a deposit book or share-account book must be produced before any money or share is withdrawn; or
(d) any other prescribed condition.

(4) The Lord Chancellor may by order make such provision as he thinks fit, by way of amendment of this section or otherwise, for all or any of the following purposes, namely –

(a) including in, or excluding from, the accounts to which this section applies accounts of any description specified in the order;

(b) excluding from the accounts to which this section applies all accounts with any particular deposit-taking institution so specified or with any deposit-taking institution of a description so specified.

(5) An order under subsection (4) shall be made by statutory instrument subject to annulment in pursuance of a resolution of either House of Parliament.

PART VI

ADMINISTRATION ORDERS

112 Power to make administration order   **[452]**

(1) Where a debtor –

(a) is unable to pay forthwith the amount of a judgment obtained against him; and

(b) alleges that his whole indebtedness amounts to a sum not exceeding the county court limit, inclusive of the debt for which the judgment was obtained;

a county court may make an order providing for the administration of his estate.

(2) In this Part of this Act –

'administration order' means an order under this section; and

'the appropriate court', in relation to an administration order, means the court which has the power to make the order.

(3) Before an administration order is made, the appropriate court shall, in accordance with county court rules, send to every person whose name the debtor has notified to the appropriate court as being a creditor of him, a notice that that person's name has been so notified.

(4) So long as an administration order is in force, a creditor whose name is included in the schedule to the order shall not, without the leave of the appropriate court, be entitled to present, or join in, a bankruptcy petition against the debtor unless –

(a) his name was so notified; and

(b) the debt by virtue of which he presents, or joins in, the petition, exceeds £1,500; and

(c) the notice given under subsection (3) was received by the creditor within 28 days immediately preceding the day on which the petition is presented.

(5) An administration order shall not be invalid by reason only that the total amount of the debts is found at any time to exceed the county court limit, but in that case the court may, if it thinks fit, set aside the order.

(6) An administration order may provide for the payment of the debts of the debtor by instalments or otherwise, and either in full or to such extent as appears practicable to the court under the circumstances of the case, and subject to any conditions as to his future earnings or income which the court may think just.

(7) The Secretary of State may by regulations increase or reduce the sum for the time being specified in subsection (4)(b); but no such increase in the sum so specified shall affect any case in which the bankruptcy petition was presented before the coming into force of the increase.

(8) The power to make regulations under subsection (7) shall be exercisable by statutory instrument; and no such regulations shall be made unless a draft of them has been approved by resolution of each House of Parliament.

114 Effect of administration order   [453]

(1) Subject to sections 115 and 116, when an administration order is made, no creditor shall have any remedy against the person or property of the debtor in respect of any debt –

(a) of which the debtor notified the appropriate court before the administration order was made; or

(b) which has been scheduled to the order,

except with the leave of the appropriate court, and on such terms as that court may impose.

(2) Subject to subsection (3), any county court in which proceedings are pending against the debtor in respect of any debt so notified or scheduled shall, on receiving notice of the administration order, stay the proceedings, but may allow costs already incurred by the creditor, and such costs may, on application, be added to the debt.

(3) The requirement to stay proceedings shall not operate as a requirement that a county court in which proceedings in bankruptcy against the debtor are pending shall stay those proceedings.

PART VII

COMMITTALS

118 Power to commit for contempt   [454]

(1) If any person –

(a) wilfully insults the judge of a county court, or any juror or witness, or any officer of the court during his sitting or attendance in court, or in going to or returning from the court; or

(b) wilfully interrupts the proceedings of a county court or otherwise misbehaves in court;

any officer of the court, with or without the assistance of any other person, may, by order of the judge, take the offender into custody and detain him until the rising of the court, and the judge may, if he thinks fit –

(i) make an order committing the offender for a specified period not exceeding one month to prison; or

(ii) impose upon the offender, for every offence, a fine of an amount not exceeding £2,500, or may both make such an order and impose such a fine.

(2) The judge may at any time revoke an order committing a person to prison under this section and, if he is already in custody, order his discharge.

(3) A district judge, assistant district judge or deputy district judge shall have the same powers under this section in relation to proceedings before him as a judge.

147 Interpretation   [455]

(1) In this Act, unless the context otherwise requires –

'action' means any proceedings in a county court which may be commenced as prescribed by plaint;

'Admiralty county court' means a county court appointed to have Admiralty jurisdiction by order under this Act;

'Admiralty proceedings' means proceedings in which the claim would not be within the jurisdiction of a county court but for sections 26 and 27;

'bailiff' includes a district judge;

'the county court limit' means –

(a) in relation to any enactment contained in this Act for which a limit is for the time being specified by an Order under section 145, that limit,

(c) in relation to any enactment contained in this Act and not within paragraph (a), the county court limit for the time being specified by any other Order in Council or order defining the limit of county court jurisdiction for the purposes of that enactment;

'county court rules' means rules made under section 75;

'court' and 'county court' mean a court held for a district under this Act; ...

'district' and 'county district' mean a district for which a court is to be held under section 2; ...

'hearing' includes trial, and 'hear' and 'heard' shall be construed accordingly;

...

'judge', in relation to a county court, means a judge assigned to the district of that court under subsection (1) of section 5 and any person sitting as a judge for that district under subsection (3) or (4) of that section;

'judgment summons' means a summons issued on the application of a person entitled to enforce a judgment or order under section 5 of the Debtors Act 1869 requiring a person, or, where two or more persons are liable under the judgment or order, requiring any one or more of them, to appear and be examined on oath as to his or their means; ...

'legal representative' means an authorised advocate or authorised litigator, as defined by section 119(1) of the Courts and Legal Services Act 1990;

'matter' means every proceeding in a county court which may be commenced as prescribed otherwise than by plaint;

'officer', in relation to a court, means any district judge, deputy district judge or assistant district judge of that court, and any clerk, bailiff, usher or messenger in the service of that court; ...

'party' includes every person served with notice of, or attending, any proceeding, whether named as a party to that proceeding or not;

'prescribed' means prescribed by county court rules;

'probate proceedings' means proceedings brought in a county court by virtue of section 32 or transferred to that court under section 40;

'proceedings' includes both actions and matters; ...

'return day' means the day appointed in any summons or proceeding for the appearance of the defendant or any other day fixed for the hearing of any proceedings;

'the rule committee' means the committee constituted under section 75;

'ship' includes any description of vessel used in navigation;

'solicitor' means solicitor of the Supreme Court.

Note. For an addition to s58(1) above in the case of family proceedings, see the Family Proceedings Rules 1991, r10.13.

[As amended by the Matrimonial and Family Proceedings Act 1984, s46(1), Schedule 1, para 30; Insolvency Act 1985, s220(2); Housing (Consequential Provisions) Act 1985, s4, Schedule 2, para 57(2), (3); Administration of Justice Act 1985, s67(1), (2), Schedule 7, para 8, Schedule 8, Pt II; Statute Law (Repeals) Act 1986; Housing Act 1988, s140(1), Schedule 17, Pt I, para 35(1), (2); Courts and Legal Services Act 1990, ss2(1), (2), 3, 6, 16, 71(2), 74(6), 125(2), (3), (7), Schedule 10, para 57, Schedule 17, para 15, Schedule 18, paras 42, 46, 47, 49(2), (3), Schedule 20; High Court and County Courts Jurisdiction Order 1991; Criminal Justice Act 1991, s17(3)(a), Schedule 4, Pt I; Police and Magistrates' Courts Act 1994, s43, Schedule 4, Pt II, para 57.]

POLICE AND CRIMINAL EVIDENCE ACT 1984
(1984 c 60)

PART I

POWERS TO STOP AND SEARCH

1 Power of constable to stop and search persons, vehicles, etc   [456]

(1) A constable may exercise any power conferred by this section –

(a) in any place to which at the time when he proposes to exercise the power the public or any section of the public has access, on payment or otherwise, as of right or by virtue of express or implied permission; or
(b) in any other place to which people have ready access at the time when he proposes to exercise the power but which is not a dwelling.

(2) Subject to subsections (3) to (5) below, a constable –

(a) may search –

(i) any person or vehicle;
(ii) anything which is in or on a vehicle,

for stolen or prohibited articles or any article to which subsection (8A) below applies; and
(b) may detain a person or vehicle for the purpose of such a search.

(3) This section does not give a constable power to search a person or vehicle or anything in or on a vehicle unless he has reasonable grounds for suspecting that he will find stolen or prohibited articles or any article to which subsection (8A) below applies.

(4) If a person is in a garden or yard occupied with and used for the purposes of a dwelling or on other land so occupied and used, a constable may not search him in the exercise of the power conferred by this section unless the constable has reasonable grounds for believing –

(a) that he does not reside in the dwelling; and
(b) that he is not in the place in question with the express or implied permission of a person who resides in the dwelling.

(5) If a vehicle is in a garden or yard occupied with and used for the purposes of a dwelling or on other land so occupied and used, a constable may not search the vehicle or anything in or on it in the exercise of the power conferred by this section unless he has reasonable grounds for believing –

(a) that the person in charge of the vehicle does not reside in the dwelling; and
(b) that the vehicle is not in the place in question with the express or implied permission of a person who resides in the dwelling.

(6) If in the course of such a search a constable discovers an article which he has reasonable grounds for suspecting to be a stolen or prohibited article or an article to which subsection (8A) below applies, he may seize it.

(7) An article is prohibited for the purposes of this Part of this Act if it is –

(a) an offensive weapon; or
(b) an article –

(i) made or adapted for use in the course of or in connection with an offence to which this sub-paragraph applies; or

(ii) intended by the person having it with him for such use by him or by some other person.

(8) The offences to which subsection (7)(b)(i) above applies are –

(a) burglary;
(b) theft;
(c) offences under section 12 of the Theft Act 1968 (taking motor vehicle or other conveyance without authority); and
(d) offences under section 15 of that Act (obtaining property by deception).

(8A) This subsection applies to any article in relation to which a person has committed, or is committing or is going to commit an offence under section 139 of the Criminal Justice Act 1988.

(9) In this Part of this Act 'offensive weapon' means any article –

(a) made or adapted for use for causing injury to persons; or
(b) intended by the person having it with him for such use by him or by some other person.

2 Provisions relating to search under section 1 and other powers

[457]

(1) A constable who detains a person or vehicle in the exercise –

(a) of the power conferred by section 1 above; or
(b) of any other power –

(i) to search a person without first arresting him; or
(ii) to search a vehicle without making an arrest,

need not conduct a search if it appears to him subsequently –

(i) that no search is required; or
(ii) that a search is impracticable.

(2) If a constable contemplates a search, other than a search of an unattended vehicle, in the exercise –

(a) of the power conferred by section 1 above; or
(b) of any other power, except the power conferred by section 6 below and the power conferred by section 27(2) of the Aviation Security Act 1982 –

(i) to search a person without first arresting him; or
(ii) to search a vehicle without making an arrest,

it shall be his duty, subject to subsection (4) below, to take reasonable steps before he commences the search to bring to the attention of the appropriate person –

(i) if the constable is not in uniform, documentary evidence that he is a constable; and
(ii) whether he is in uniform or not, the matters specified in subsection (3) below;

and the constable shall not commence the search until he has performed that duty.

(3) The matters referred to in subsection (2)(ii) above are –

(a) the constable's name and the name of the police station to which he is attached;
(b) the object of the proposed search;
(c) the constable's grounds for proposing to make it; and
(d) the effect of section 3(7) or (8) below, as may be appropriate.

(4) A constable need not bring the effect of section 3(7) or (8) below to the

attention of the appropriate person if it appears to the constable that it will not be practicable to make the record in section 3(1) below.

(5) In this section 'the appropriate person' means –

(a) if the constable proposes to search a person, that person; and

(b) if he proposes to search a vehicle, or anything in or on a vehicle, the person in charge of the vehicle.

(6) On completing a search of an unattended vehicle or anything in or on such a vehicle in the exercise of any such power as is mentioned in subsection (2) above a constable shall leave a notice –

(a) stating that he has searched it;

(b) giving the name of the police station to which he is attached;

(c) stating that an application for compensation for any damage caused by the search may be made to that police station; and

(d) stating the effect of section 3(8) below.

(7) The constable shall leave the notice inside the vehicle unless it is not reasonably practicable to do so without damaging the vehicle.

(8) The time for which a person or vehicle may be detained for the purposes of such a search is such time as is reasonably required to permit a search to be carried out either at the place where the person or vehicle was first detained or nearby.

(9) Neither the power conferred by section 1 above nor any other power to detain and search a person without first arresting him or to detain and search a vehicle without making an arrest is to be construed –

(a) as authorising a constable to require a person to remove any of his clothing in public other than an outer coat, jacket or gloves; or

(b) as authorising a constable not in uniform to stop a vehicle.

(10) This section and section 1 above apply to vessels, aircraft and hovercraft as they apply to vehicles.

3 Duty to make records concerning searches [458]

(1) Where a constable has carried out a search in the exercise of any such power as is mentioned in section 2(1) above, other than a search –

(a) under section 6 below; or

(b) under section 27(2) of the Aviation Security Act 1982,

he shall make a record of it in writing unless it is not practicable to do so.

(2) If –

(a) a constable is required by subsection (1) above to make a record of a search; but

(b) it is not practicable to make the record on the spot,

he shall make it as soon as practicable after the completion of the search.

(3) The record of a search of a person shall include a note of his name, if the constable knows it, but a constable may not detain a person to find out his name.

(4) If a constable does not know the name of a person whom he has searched, the record of the search shall include a note otherwise describing that person.

(5) The record of a search of a vehicle shall include a note describing the vehicle.

(6) The record of a search of a person or a vehicle –

(a) shall state –

(i) the object of the search;

(ii) the grounds for making it;

(iii) the date and time when it was made;

(iv) the place where it was made;

(v) whether anything, and if so what, was found;

(vi) whether any, and if so what, injury to a person or damage to property appears to the constable to have resulted from the search; and

(b) shall identify the constable making it.

(7) If a constable who conducted a search of a person made a record of it, the person who was searched shall be entitled to a copy of the record if he asks for one before the end of the period specified in subsection (9) below.

(8) If –

(a) the owner of a vehicle which has been searched or the person who was in charge of the vehicle at the time when it was searched asks for a copy of the record of the search before the end of the period specified in sub-section (9) below; and

(b) the constable who conducted the search made a record of it,

the person who made the request shall be entitled to a copy.

(9) The period mentioned in subsections (7) and (8) above is the period of 12 months beginning with the date on which the search was made.

(10) The requirements imposed by this section with regard to records of searches of vehicles shall apply also to records of searches of vessels, aircraft and hovercraft.

4 Road checks [459]

(1) This section shall have effect in relation to the conduct of road checks by police officers for the purpose of ascertaining whether a vehicle is carrying –

(a) a person who has committed an offence other than a road traffic offence or a vehicles excise offence;

(b) a person who is a witness to such an offence;

(c) a person intending to commit such an offence; or

(d) a person who is unlawfully at large.

(2) For the purposes of this section a road check consists of the exercise in a locality of the power conferred by section 163 of the Road Traffic Act 1988 in such a way as to stop during the period for which its exercise in that way in that locality continues all vehicles or vehicles selected by any criterion.

(3) Subject to subsection (5) below, there may only be such a road check if a police officer of the rank of superintendent or above authorises it in writing.

(4) An officer may only authorise a road check under subsection (3) above –

(a) for the purpose specified in subsection (1)(a) above, if he has reasonable grounds –

(i) for believing that the offence is a serious arrestable offence; and

(ii) for suspecting that the person is, or is about to be, in the locality in which vehicles would be stopped if the road check were authorised;

(b) for the purpose specified in subsection (1)(b) above, if he has reasonable grounds for believing that the offence is a serious arrestable offence;

(c) for the purpose specified in subsection (1)(c) above, if he has reasonable grounds –

(i) for believing that the offence would be a serious arrestable offence; and

(ii) for suspecting that the person is, or is about to be, in the locality in which vehicles would be stopped if the road check were authorised;

(d) for the purpose specified in subsection (1)(d) above, if he has reasonable grounds for suspecting that the person is, or is about to be, in that locality.

(5) An officer below the rank of superintendent may authorise such a road check if it appears to him that it is required as a matter of urgency for one of the purposes specified in subsection (1) above.

(6) If an authorisation is given under subsection (5) above, it shall be the duty of the officer who gives it –

(a) to make a written record of the time at which he gives it; and
(b) to cause an officer of the rank of superintendent or above to be informed that it has been given.

(7) The duties imposed by subsection (6) above shall be performed as soon as it is practicable to do so.

(8) An officer to whom a report is made under subsection (6) above may, in writing, authorise the road check to continue.

(9) If such an officer considers that the road check should not continue, he shall record in writing –

(a) the fact that it took place; and
(b) the purpose for which it took place.

(10) An officer giving an authorisation under this section shall specify the locality in which vehicles are to be stopped.

(11) An officer giving an authorisation under this section, other than an authorisation under subsection (5) above –

(a) shall specify a period, not exceeding seven days, during which the road check may continue; and
(b) may direct that the road check –

(i) shall be continuous; or
(ii) shall be conducted at specified times,

during that period.

(12) If it appears to an officer of the rank of superintendent or above that a road check ought to continue beyond the period for which it has been authorised he may, from time to time, in writing specify a further period, not exceeding seven days, during which it may continue.

(13) Every written authorisation shall specify –

(a) the name of the officer giving it;
(b) the purpose of the road check; and
(c) the locality in which vehicles are to be stopped.

(14) The duties to specify the purposes of a road check imposed by subsections (9) and (13) above include duties to specify any relevant serious arrestable offence.

(15) Where a vehicle is stopped in a road check, the person in charge of the vehicle at the time when it is stopped shall be entitled to obtain a written statement of the purpose of the road check if he applies for such a statement not later than the end of the period of 12 months from the day on which the vehicle was stopped.

(16) Nothing in this section affects the exercise by police officers of any power to stop vehicles for purposes other than those specified in subsection (1) above.

6 Statutory undertakers, etc [460]

(1) A constable employed by statutory undertakers may stop, detain and search

any vehicle before it leaves a goods area included in the premises of the statutory undertakers.

(2) In this section 'goods area' means any area used wholly or mainly for the storage or handling of goods.

(3) For the purposes of section 6 of the Public Stores Act 1875, any person appointed under the Special Constables Act 1923 to be a special constable within any premises which are in the possession or under the control of British Nuclear Fuels Limited shall be deemed to be a constable deputed by a public department and any goods and chattels belonging to or in the possession of British Nuclear Fuels Limited shall be deemed to be Her Majesty's Stores ...

7 Part I – supplementary [461]

(3) In this Part of this Act 'statutory undertakers' means persons authorised by any enactment to carry on any railway, light railway, road transport, water transport, canal, inland navigation, dock or harbour undertaking.

PART II

POWERS OF ENTRY, SEARCH AND SEIZURE

8 Power of justice of the peace to authorise entry and [462] search of premises

(1) If on an application made by a constable a justice of the peace is satisfied that there are reasonable grounds for believing –

(a) that a serious arrestable offence has been committed; and
(b) that there is material on premises specified in the application which is likely to be of substantial value (whether by itself or together with other material) to the investigation of the offence; and
(c) that the material is likely to be relevant evidence; and
(d) that it does not consist of or include items subject to legal privilege, excluded material or special procedure material; and
(e) that any of the conditions specified in subsection (3) below applies,

he may issue a warrant authorising a constable to enter and search the premises.

(2) A constable may seize and retain anything for which a search has been authorised under subsection (1) above.

(3) The conditions mentioned in subsection (1)(e) above are –

(a) that it is not practicable to communicate with any person entitled to grant entry to the premises;
(b) that it is practicable to communicate with a person entitled to grant entry to the premises but it is not practicable to communicate with any person entitled to grant access to the evidence;
(c) that entry to the premises will not be granted unless a warrant is produced;
(d) that the purpose of a search may be frustrated or seriously prejudiced unless a constable arriving at the premises can secure immediate entry to them.

(4) In this Act 'relevant evidence', in relation to an offence, means anything that would be admissible in evidence at a trial for the offence.

(5) The power to issue a warrant conferred by this section is in addition to any such power otherwise conferred.

9 Special provisions as to access   [463]

(1) A constable may obtain access to excluded material or special procedure material for the purposes of a criminal investigation by making an application under Schedule 1 below and in accordance with that Schedule.

(2) Any Act (including a local Act) passed before this Act under which a search of premises for the purposes of a criminal investigation could be authorised by the issue of a warrant to a constable shall cease to have effect so far as it relates to the authorisation of searches –

(a) for items subject to legal privilege; or
(b) for excluded material; or
(c) for special procedure material consisting of documents or records other than documents.

10 Meaning of 'items subject to legal privilege'   [464]

(1) Subject to subsection (2) below, in this Act 'items subject to legal privilege' means –

(a) communications between a professional legal adviser and his client or any person representing his client made in connection with the giving of legal advice to the client;
(b) communications between a professional legal adviser and his client or any person representing his client or between such an adviser or his client or any such representative and any other person made in connection with or in contemplation of legal proceedings and for the purposes of such proceedings; and
(c) items enclosed with or referred to in such communications and made –

(i) in connection with the giving of legal advice; or
(ii) in connection with or in contemplation of legal proceedings and for the purposes of such proceedings,

when they are in the possession of a person who is entitled to possession of them.

(2) Items held with the intention of furthering a criminal purpose are not items subject to legal privilege.

11 Meaning of 'excluded material'   [465]

(1) Subject to the following provisions of this section, in this Act 'excluded material' means –

(a) personal records which a person has acquired or created in the course of any trade, business, profession or other occupation or for the purposes of any paid or unpaid office and which he holds in confidence;
(b) human tissue or tissue fluid which has been taken for the purposes of diagnosis or medical treatment and which a person holds in confidence;
(c) journalistic material which a person holds in confidence and which consists –

(i) of documents; or
(ii) of records other than documents.

(2) A person holds material other than journalistic material in confidence for the purposes of this section if he holds it subject –

(a) to an express or implied undertaking to hold it in confidence; or
(b) to a restriction on disclosure or an obligation of secrecy contained in any enactment, including an enactment contained in an Act passed after this Act.

(3) A person holds journalistic material in confidence for the purposes of this section if –

(a) he holds it subject to such an undertaking, restriction or obligation; and

(b) it has been continuously held (by one or more persons) subject to such an undertaking, restriction or obligation since it was first acquired or created for the purposes of journalism.

12 Meaning of 'personal records' [466]

In this Part of this Act 'personal records' means documentary and other records concerning an individual (whether living or dead) who can be identified from them and relating –

(a) to his physical or mental health;

(b) to spiritual counselling or assistance given or to be given to him; or

(c) to counselling or assistance given or to be given to him, for the purposes of his personal welfare, by any voluntary organisations or by any individual who –

(i) by reason of his office or occupation has responsibilities for his personal welfare; or

(ii) by reason of an order of a court has responsibilities for his supervision.

13 Meaning of 'journalistic material' [467]

(1) Subject to subsection (2) below, in this Act 'journalistic material' means material acquired or created for the purposes of journalism.

(2) Material is only journalistic material for the purposes of this Act if it is in the possession of a person who acquired or created it for the purposes of journalism.

(3) A person who receives material from someone who intends that the recipient shall use it for the purposes of journalism is to be taken to have acquired it for those purposes.

14 Meaning of 'special procedure material' [468]

(1) In this Act 'special procedure material' means –

(a) material to which subsection (2) below applies; and

(b) journalistic material, other than excluded material.

(2) Subject to the following provisions of this section, this subsection applies to material, other than items subject to legal privilege and excluded material, in the possession of a person who –

(a) acquired or created it in the course of any trade, business, profession or other occupation or for the purpose of any paid or unpaid office; and

(b) holds it subject –

(i) to an express or implied undertaking to hold it in confidence; or

(ii) to a restriction or obligation such as is mentioned in section 11(2)(b) above.

(3) Where material is acquired –

(a) by an employee from his employer and in the course of his employment; or

(b) by a company from an associated company,

it is only special procedure material if it was special procedure material immediately before the acquisition.

207

(4) Where material is created by an employee in the course of his employment, it is only special procedure material if it would have been special procedure material had his employer created it.

(5) Where material is created by a company on behalf of an associated company, it is only special procedure material if it would have been special procedure material had the associated company created it.

(6) A company is to be treated as another's associated company for the purposes of this section if it would be so treated under section 302 of the Income and Corporation Taxes Act 1970.

15 Search warrants – safeguards   [469]

(1) This section and section 16 below have effect in relation to the issue to constables under any enactment, including an enactment contained in an Act passed after this Act, of warrants to enter and search premises; and an entry on or search of premises under a warrant is unlawful unless it complies with this section and section 16 below.

(2) Where a constable applies for any such warrant, it shall be his duty –

    (a) to state –

        (i) the ground on which he makes the application; and
        (ii) the enactment under which the warrant would be issued;

    (b) to specify the premises which it is desired to enter and search; and
    (c) to identify, so far as is practicable, the articles or persons to be sought.

(3) An application for such a warrant shall be made ex parte and supported by an information in writing.

(4) The constable shall answer on oath any question that the justice of the peace or judge hearing the application asks him.

(5) A warrant shall authorise an entry on one occasion only.

(6) A warrant –

    (a) shall specify –

        (i) the name of the person who applies for it;
        (ii) the date on which it is issued;
        (iii) the enactment under which it is issued; and
        (iv) the premises to be searched; and

    (b) shall identify, so far as is practicable, the articles or persons to be sought.

(7) Two copies shall be made of a warrant.

(8) The copies shall be clearly certified as copies.

16 Execution of warrants   [470]

(1) A warrant to enter and search premises may be executed by any constable.

(2) Such a warrant may authorise persons to accompany any constable who is executing it.

(3) Entry and search under a warrant must be within one month from the date of its issue.

(4) Entry and search under a warrant must be at a reasonable hour unless it appears to the constable executing it that the purpose of a search may be frustrated on an entry at a reasonable hour.

(5) Where the occupier of premises which are to be entered and searched is

present at the time when a constable seeks to execute a warrant to enter and search them, the constable –

(a) shall identify himself to the occupier and, if not in uniform, shall produce to him documentary evidence that he is a constable;

(b) shall produce the warrant to him; and

(c) shall supply him with a copy of it.

(6) Where –

(a) the occupier of such premises is not present at the time when a constable seeks to execute such a warrant; but

(b) some other person who appears to the constable to be in charge of the premises is present,

subsection (5) above shall have effect as if any reference to the occupier were a reference to that other person.

(7) If there is no person present who appears to the constable to be in charge of the premises, he shall leave a copy of the warrant in a prominent place on the premises.

(8) A search under a warrant may only be a search to the extent required for the purpose for which the warrant was issued.

(9) A constable executing a warrant shall make an endorsement on it stating –

(a) whether the articles or persons sought were found; and

(b) whether any articles were seized, other than articles which were sought.,

(10) A warrant which –

(a) has been executed; or

(b) has not been executed within the time authorised for its execution,

shall be returned –

(i) if it was issued by a justice of the peace, to the clerk to the justices for the petty sessions area for which he acts; and

(ii) if it was issued by a judge, to the appropriate officer of the court from which he issued it.

(11) A warrant which is returned under subsection (10) above shall be retained for 12 months from its return –

(a) by the clerk to the justices, if it was returned under paragraph (i) of that subsection; and

(b) by the appropriate officer, if it was returned under paragraph (ii).

(12) If during the period for which a warrant is to be retained the occupier of the premises to which it relates asks to inspect it, he shall be allowed to do so.

17 Entry for purpose of arrest, etc   **[471]**

(1) Subject to the following provisions of this section, and without prejudice to any other enactment, a constable may enter and search any premises for the purpose –

(a) of executing –

(i) a warrant of arrest issued in connection with or arising out of criminal proceedings; or

(ii) a warrant of commitment issued under section 76 of the Magistrates' Courts Act 1980;

(b) of arresting a person for an arrestable offence;

(c) of arresting a person for an offence under –

(i) section 1 (prohibition of uniforms in connection with political objects) of the Public Order Act 1936;

(ii) any enactment contained in sections 6 to 8 or 10 of the Criminal Law Act 1977 (offences relating to entering and remaining on property);

(iii) section 4 of the Public Order Act 1986 (fear or provocation of violence);

(d) of recapturing a person who is unlawfully at large and whom he is pursuing; or

(e) of saving life or limb or preventing serious damage to property.

(2) Except for the purpose specified in paragraph (e) of subsection (1) above, the powers of entry and search conferred by this section –

(a) are only exercisable if the constable has reasonable grounds for believing that the person whom he is seeking is on the premises; and

(b) are limited, in relation to premises consisting of two or more separate dwellings, to powers to enter and search –

(i) any parts of the premises which the occupiers of any dwelling comprised in the premises use in common with the occupiers of any other such dwelling; and

(ii) any such dwelling in which the constable has reasonable grounds for believing that the person whom he is seeking may be.

(3) The powers of entry and search conferred by this section are only exercisable for the purposes specified in subsection (1)(c)(ii) above by a constable in uniform.

(4) The power of search conferred by this section is only a power to search to the extent that is reasonably required for the purpose for which the power of entry is exercised.

(5) Subject to subsection (6) below, all the rules of common law under which a constable has power to enter premises without a warrant are hereby abolished.

(6) Nothing in subsection (5) above affects any power of entry to deal with or prevent a breach of the peace.

18 Entry and search after arrest   [472]

(1) Subject to the following provisions of this section, a constable may enter and search any premises occupied or controlled by a person who is under arrest for an arrestable offence, if he has reasonable grounds for suspecting that there is on the premises evidence, other than items subject to legal privilege, that relates –

(a) to that offence; or

(b) to some other arrestable offence which is connected with or similar to that offence.

(2) A constable may seize and retain anything for which he may search under subsection (1) above.

(3) The power to search conferred by subsection (1) above is only a power to search to the extent that is reasonably required for the purpose of discovering such evidence.

(4) Subject to subsection (5) below, the powers conferred by this section may not be exercised unless an officer of the rank of inspector or above has authorised them in writing.

(5) A constable may conduct a search under subsection (1) above –

(a) before taking the person to a police station; and

(b) without obtaining an authorisation under subsection (4) above, if the presence of that person at a place other than a police station is necessary for the effective investigation of the offence.

(6) If a constable conducts a search by virtue of subsection (5) above, he shall inform an officer of the rank of inspector or above that he has made the search as soon as practicable after he has made it.

(7) An officer who –

(a) authorises a search; or

(b) is informed of a search under subsection (6) above, shall make a record in writing –

(i) of the grounds for the search; and

(ii) of the nature of the evidence that was sought.

(8) If the person who was in occupation or control of the premises at the time of the search is in police detention at the time the record is to be made, the officer shall make the record as part of his custody record.

19 General power of seizure, etc [473]

(1) The powers conferred by subsections (2), (3) and (4) below are exercisable by a constable who is lawfully on any premises.

(2) The constable may seize anything which is on the premises if he has reasonable grounds for believing –

(a) that it has been obtained in consequence of the commission of an offence; and

(b) that it is necessary to seize it in order to prevent it being concealed, lost, damaged, altered or destroyed.

(3) The constable may seize anything which is on the premises if he has reasonable grounds for believing –

(a) that it is evidence in relation to an offence which he is investigating or any other offence; and

(b) that it is necessary to seize it in order to prevent the evidence being concealed, lost, altered or destroyed.

(4) The constable may require any information which is contained in a computer and is accessible from the premises to be produced in a form in which it can be taken away and in which it is visible and legible if he has reasonable grounds for believing –

(a) that –

(i) it is evidence in relation to an offence which he is investigating or any other offence; or

(ii) it has been obtained in consequence of the commission of an offence; and

(b) that it is necessary to do so in order to prevent it being concealed, lost, tampered with or destroyed.

(5) The powers conferred by this section are in addition to any power otherwise conferred.

(6) No power of seizure conferred on a constable under any enactment (including an enactment contained in an Act passed after this Act) is to be taken to authorise the seizure of an item which the constable exercising the power has reasonable grounds for believing to be subject to legal privilege.

20 Extension of powers of seizure to computerised information   [474]

(1) Every power of seizure which is conferred by an enactment to which this section applies on a constable who has entered premises in the exercise of a power conferred by an enactment shall be construed as including a power to require any information contained in a computer and accessible from the premises to be produced in a form in which it can be taken away and in which it is visible and legible.

(2) This section applies –

(a) to any enactment contained in an Act passed before this Act;
(b) to sections 8 and 18 above;
(c) to paragraph 13 of Schedule 1 to this Act; and
(d) to any enactment contained in an Act passed after this Act.

21 Access and copying   [475]

(1) A constable who seizes anything in the exercise of a power conferred by any enactment, including an enactment contained in an Act passed after this Act, shall, if so requested by a person showing himself –

(a) to be the occupier of premises on which it was seized; or
(b) to have had custody or control of it immediately before the seizure,

provide that person with a record of what he seized.

(2) The officer shall provide the record within a reasonable time from the making of the request for it.

(3) Subject to subsection (8) below, if a request for permission to be granted access to anything which –

(a) has been seized by a constable; and
(b) is retained by the police for the purpose of investigating an offence,

is made to the officer in charge of the investigation by a person who had custody or control of the thing immediately before it was so seized or by someone acting on behalf of such a person, the officer shall allow the person who made the request access to it under the supervision of a constable.

(4) Subject to subsection (8) below, if a request for a photograph or copy of any such thing is made to the officer in charge of the investigation by a person who had custody or control of the thing immediately before it was so seized, or by someone acting on behalf of such a person, the officer shall –

(a) allow the person who made the request access to it under the supervision of a constable for the purpose of photographing or copying it; or
(b) photograph or copy it, or cause it to be photographed or copied.

(5) A constable may also photograph or copy, or have photographed or copied, anything which he has power to seize, without a request being made under subsection (4) above.

(6) Where anything is photographed or copied under subsection (4)(b) above, the photograph or copy shall be supplied to the person who made the request.

(7) The photograph or copy shall be so supplied within a reasonable time from the making of the request.

(8) There is no duty under this section to grant access to, or to supply a photograph or copy of, anything if the officer in charge of the investigation for the purposes of which it was seized has reasonable grounds for believing that to do so would prejudice –

(a) that investigation;

(b) the investigation of an offence other than the offence for the purposes of investigating which the thing was seized; or

(c) any criminal proceedings which may be brought as a result of –

(i) the investigation of which he is in charge; or

(ii) any such investigation as is mentioned in paragraph (b) above.

22 Retention [476]

(1) Subject to subsection (4) below, anything which has been seized by a constable or taken away by a constable following a requirement made by virtue of section 19 or 20 above may be retained so long as is necessary in all the circumstances.

(2) Without prejudice to the generality of subsection (1) above –

(a) anything seized for the purposes of a criminal investigation may be retained, except as provided by subsection (4) below –

(i) for use as evidence at a trial for an offence; or

(ii) for forensic examination or for investigation in connection with an offence; and

(b) anything may be retained in order to establish its lawful owner, where there are reasonable grounds for believing that it has been obtained in consequence of the commission of an offence.

(3) Nothing seized on the ground that it may be used –

(a) to cause physical injury to any person;

(b) to damage property;

(c) to interfere with evidence; or

(d) to assist in escape from police detention or lawful custody,

may be retained when the person from whom it was seized is no longer in police detention or the custody of a court or is in the custody of a court but has been released on bail.

(4) Nothing may be retained for either of the purposes mentioned in subsection (2)(a) above if a photograph or copy would be sufficient for that purpose.

(5) Nothing in this section affects any power of a court to make an order under section 1 of the Police (Property) Act 1897.

23 Meaning of 'premises', etc [477]

In this Act –

'premises' includes any place and, in particular, includes –

(a) any vehicle, vessel, aircraft or hovercraft;

(b) any offshore installation; and

(c) any tent or movable structure; and

'offshore installation' has the meaning given to it by section 1 of the Mineral Workings (Offshore Installations) Act 1971.

PART III

ARREST

24 Arrest without warrant for arrestable offences   [478]

(1) The powers of summary arrest conferred by the following subsections shall apply –

(a) to offences for which the sentence is fixed by law;

(b) to offences for which a person of 21 years of age or over (not previously convicted) may be sentenced to imprisonment for a term of five years (or might be so sentenced but for the restrictions imposed by section 33 of the Magistrates' Courts Act 1980); and

(c) to the offences to which subsection (2) below applies,

and in this Act 'arrestable offence' means any such offence.

(2) The offences to which this subsection applies are –

(a) offences for which a person may be arrested under the customs and excise Acts, as defined in section 1(1) of the Customs and Excise Management Act 1979;

(b) offences under the Official Secrets Act 1920 that are not arrestable offences by virtue of the term of imprisonment for which a person may be sentenced in respect of them;

(bb) offences under any provision of the Official Secrets Act 1989 except section 8(1), (4) or (5);

(c) offences under section 22 (causing prostitution of women) or 23 (procuration of girl under 21) of the Sexual Offences Act 1956;

(d) offences under section 12(1) (taking motor vehicle or other conveyance without authority, etc) or 25(1) (going equipped for stealing, etc) of the Theft Act 1968;

(e) any offence under the Football (Offences) Act 1991;

(h) an offence under section 166 of the Criminal Justice and Public Order Act 1994 (sale of tickets by unauthorised persons);

(j) an offence under section 167 of the Criminal Justice and Public Order Act 1994 (touting for hire car services).

(3) Without prejudice to section 2 of the Criminal Attempts Act 1981, the powers of summary arrest conferred by the following subsections shall also apply to the offences of –

(a) conspiring to commit any of the offences mentioned in subsection (2) above;

(b) attempting to commit any such offence other than an offence under s12(1) of the Theft Act 1968;

(c) inciting, aiding, abetting, counselling or procuring the commission of any such offence;

and such offences are also arrestable offences for the purposes of this Act.

(4) Any person may arrest without a warrant –

(a) anyone who is in the act of committing an arrestable offence;

(b) anyone whom he has reasonable grounds for suspecting to be committing such an offence.

(5) Where an arrestable offence has been committed, any person may arrest without a warrant –

(a) anyone who is guilty of the offence;

(b) anyone whom he has reasonable grounds for suspecting to be guilty of it.

(6) Where a constable has reasonable grounds for suspecting that an arrestable offence has been committed, he may arrest without a warrant anyone whom he has reasonable grounds for suspecting to be guilty of the offence.

(7) A constable may arrest without a warrant –

(a) anyone who is about to commit an arrestable offence;
(b) anyone whom he has reasonable grounds for suspecting to be about to commit an arrestable offence.

25 General arrest conditions   **[479]**

(1) Where a constable has reasonable grounds for suspecting that any offence which is not an arrestable offence has been committed or attempted, or is being committed or attempted, he may arrest the relevant person if it appears to him that service of a summons is impracticable or inappropriate because any of the general arrest conditions is satisfied.

(2) In this section 'the relevant person' means any person whom the constable has reasonable grounds to suspect of having committed or having attempted to commit the offence or of being in the course of committing or attempting to commit it.

(3) The general arrest conditions are –

(a) that the name of the relevant person is unknown to, and cannot be readily ascertained by, the constable;
(b) that the constable has reasonable grounds for doubting whether a name furnished by the relevant person as his name is his real name;
(c) that –

(i) the relevant person has failed to furnish a satisfactory address for service; or
(ii) the constable has reasonable grounds for doubting whether an address furnished by the relevant person is a satisfactory address for service;

(d) that the constable has reasonable grounds for believing that arrest is necessary to prevent the relevant person –

(i) causing physical injury to himself or any other person;
(ii) suffering physical injury;
(iii) causing loss of or damage to property;
(iv) committing an offence against public decency; or
(v) causing an unlawful obstruction of the highway;

(e) that the constable has reasonable grounds for believing that arrest is necessary to protect a child or other vulnerable person from the relevant person.

(4) For the purposes of subsection (3) above an address is a satisfactory address for service if it appears to the constable –

(a) that the relevant person will be at it for a sufficiently long period for it to be possible to serve him with a summons; or
(b) that some other person specified by the relevant person will accept service of a summons for the relevant person at it.

(5) Nothing in subsection (3)(d) above authorises the arrest of a person under sub-paragraph (iv) of that paragraph except where members of the public going about their normal business cannot reasonably be expected to avoid the person to be arrested.

(6) This section shall not prejudice any power of arrest conferred apart from this section.

27 Fingerprinting of certain offenders [480]

(1) If a person –

(a) has been convicted of a recordable offence;

(b) has not at any time been in police detention for the offence; and

(c) has not had his fingerprints taken –

(i) in the course of the investigation of the offence by the police; or

(ii) since the conviction,

any constable may at any time not later than one month after the date of the conviction require him to attend a police station in order that his fingerprints may be taken.

(2) A requirement under subsection (1) above –

(a) shall give the person a period of at least seven days within which he must so attend; and

(b) may direct him to so attend at a specified time of day or between specified times of day.

(3) Any constable may arrest without warrant a person who has failed to comply with a requirement under subsection (1) above.

(4) The Secretary of State may by regulations make provision for recording in national police records convictions for such offences as are specified in the regulations.

(5) Regulations under this section shall be made by statutory instrument and shall be subject to annulment in pursuance of a resolution of either House of Parliament.

28 Information to be given on arrest [481]

(1) Subject to subsection (5) below, where a person is arrested, otherwise than by being informed that he is under arrest, the arrest is not lawful unless the person arrested is informed that he is under arrest as soon as is practicable after his arrest.

(2) Where a person is arrested by a constable, subsection (1) above applies regardless of whether the fact of the arrest is obvious.

(3) Subject to subsection (5) below, no arrest is lawful unless the person arrested is informed of the ground for the arrest at the time of, or as soon as is practicable after, the arrest.

(4) Where a person is arrested by a constable, subsection (3) above applies regardless of whether the ground for the arrest is obvious.

(5) Nothing in this section is to be taken to require a person to be informed –

(a) that he is under arrest; or

(b) of the ground for the arrest,

if it was not reasonably practicable for him to be so informed by reason of his having escaped from arrest before the information could be given.

29 Voluntary attendance at police station, etc [482]

Where for the purpose of assisting with an investigation a person attends voluntarily at a police station or at any other place where a constable is present or accompanies a constable to a police station or any such other place without having been arrested –

(a) he shall be entitled to leave at will unless he is placed under arrest;

(b) he shall be informed at once that he is under arrest if a decision is taken by a constable to prevent him from leaving at will.

30 Arrest elsewhere than at police station [483]

(1) Subject to the following provisions of this section, where a person –

(a) is arrested by a constable for an offence; or
(b) is taken into custody by a constable after being arrested for an offence by a person other than a constable,

at any place other than a police station, he shall be taken to a police station by a constable as soon as practicable after the arrest.

(2) Subject to subsections (3) and (5) below, the police station to which an arrested person is taken under subsection (1) above shall be a designated police station.

(3) A constable to whom this subsection applies may take an arrested person to any police station unless it appears to the constable that it may be necessary to keep the arrested person in police detention for more than six hours.

(4) Subsection (3) above applies –

(a) to a constable who is working in a locality covered by a police station which is not a designated police station; and
(b) to a constable belonging to a body of constables maintained by an authority other than a police authority.

(5) Any constable may take an arrested person to any police station if –

(a) either of the following conditions is satisfied –

(i) the constable has arrested him without the assistance of any other constable and no other constable is available to assist him;
(ii) the constable has taken him into custody from a person other than a constable without the assistance of any other constable and no other constable is available to assist him; and

(b) it appears to the constable that he will be unable to take the arrested person to a designated police station without the arrested person injuring himself, the constable or some other person.

(6) If the first police station to which an arrested person is taken after his arrest is not a designated police station, he shall be taken to a designated police station not more than six hours after his arrival at the first police station unless he is released previously.

(7) A person arrested by a constable at a place other than a police station shall be released if a constable is satisfied, before the person arrested reaches a police station, that there are no grounds for keeping him under arrest.

(8) A constable who releases a person under subsection (7) above shall record the fact that he has done so.

(9) The constable shall make the record as soon as is practicable after the release.

(10) Nothing in subsection (1) above shall prevent a constable delaying taking a person who has been arrested to a police station if the presence of that person elsewhere is necessary in order to carry out such investigations as it is reasonable to carry out immediately.

(11) Where there is delay in taking a person who has been arrested to a police station after his arrest, the reasons for the delay shall be recorded when he first arrives at a police station.

(12) Nothing in subsection (1) above shall be taken to affect –

(a) paragraphs 16(3) or 18(1) of Schedule 2 to the Immigration Act 1971;

(b) section 34(1) of the Criminal Justice Act 1972; or

(c) section 15(6) and (9) of the Prevention of Terrorism (Temporary Provisions) Act 1989 and paragraphs 7(4) and 8(4) and (5) of Schedule 2 and paragraphs 6(6) and 7(4) and (5) of Schedule 5 to that Act.

(13) Nothing in subsection (10) above shall be taken to affect paragraph 18(3) of Schedule 2 to the Immigration Act 1971.

31 Arrest for further offence [484]

Where –

(a) a person –

(i) has been arrested for an offence; and

(ii) is at a police station in consequence of that arrest; and

(b) it appears to a constable that, if he were released from that arrest, he would be liable to arrest for some other offence,

he shall be arrested for that other offence.

32 Search upon arrest [485]

(1) A constable may search an arrested person, in any case where the person to be searched has been arrested at a place other than a police station, if the constable has reasonable grounds for believing that the arrested person may present a danger to himself or others.

(2) Subject to subsections (3) to (5) below, a constable shall also have power in any such case –

(a) to search the arrested person for anything –

(i) which he might use to assist him to escape from lawful custody; or

(ii) which might be evidence relating to an offence; and

(b) to enter and search any premises in which he was when arrested or immediately before he was arrested for evidence relating to the offence for which he has been arrested.

(3) The power to search conferred by subsection (2) above is only a power to search to the extent that is reasonably required for the purpose of discovering any such thing or any such evidence.

(4) The powers conferred by this section to search a person are not to be construed as authorising a constable to require a person to remove any of his clothing in public other than an outer coat, jacket or gloves.

(5) A constable may not search a person in the exercise of the power conferred by subsection (2)(a) above unless he has reasonable grounds for believing that the person to be searched may have concealed on him anything for which a search is permitted under that paragraph.

(6) A constable may not search premises in the exercise of the power conferred by subsection (2)(b) above unless he has reasonable grounds for believing that there is evidence for which a search is permitted under that paragraph on the premises.

(7) In so far as the power of search conferred by subsection (2)(b) above relates to premises consisting of two or more separate dwellings, it is limited to a power to search –

(a) any dwelling in which the arrest took place or in which the person arrested was immediately before his arrest; and

(b) any parts of the premises which the occupier of any such dwelling uses in common with the occupiers of any other dwellings comprised in the premises.

(8) A constable searching a person in the exercise of the power conferred by subsection (1) above may seize and retain anything he finds, if he has reasonable grounds for believing that the person searched might use it to cause physical injury to himself or to any other person.

(9) A constable searching a person in the exercise of the power conferred by subsection (2)(a) above may seize and retain anything he finds, other than an item subject to legal privilege, if he has reasonable grounds for believing –

(a) that he might use it to assist him to escape from lawful custody; or
(b) that it is evidence of an offence or has been obtained in consequence of the commission of an offence.

(10) Nothing in this section shall be taken to affect the power conferred by section 15(3), (4) and (5) of the Prevention of Terrorism (Temporary Provisions) Act 1989.

PART IV

DETENTION

34 Limitations on police detention [486]

(1) A person arrested for an offence shall not be kept in police detention except in accordance with the provisions of this Part of this Act.

(2) Subject to subsection (3) below, if at any time a custody officer –

(a) becomes aware, in relation to any person in police detention, that the grounds for the detention of that person have ceased to apply; and
(b) is not aware of any other grounds on which the continued detention of that person could be justified under the provisions of this Part of this Act,

it shall be the duty of the custody officer, subject to subsection (4) below, to order his immediate release from custody.

(3) No person in police detention shall be released except on the authority of a custody officer at the police station where his detention was authorised or, if it was authorised at more than one station, a custody officer at the station where it was last authorised.

(4) A person who appears to the custody officer to have been unlawfully at large when he was arrested is not to be released under subsection (2) above.

(5) A person whose release is ordered under subsection (2) above shall be released without bail unless it appears to the custody officer –

(a) that there is need for further investigation of any matter in connection with which he was detained at any time during the period of his detention; or
(b) that proceedings may be taken against him in respect of any such matter,

and, if it so appears, he shall be released on bail.

(6) For the purposes of this Part of this Act a person arrested under section 6(5) of the Road Traffic Act 1988 is arrested for an offence.

35 Designated police stations [487]

(1) The chief officer of police for each police area shall designate the police stations in his area which, subject to section 30(3) and (5) above, are to be the stations in that area to be used for the purpose of detaining arrested persons.

(2) A chief officer's duty under subsection (1) above is to designate police stations appearing to him to provide enough accommodation for that purpose.

(3) Without prejudice to section 12 of the Interpretation Act 1978 (continuity of duties) a chief officer –

(a) may designate a station which was not previously designated; and
(b) may direct that a designation of a station previously made shall cease to operate.

(4) In this Act 'designated police station' means a police station for the time being designated under this section.

36 Custody officers at police stations   [488]

(1) One or more custody officers shall be appointed for each designated police station.

(2) A custody officer for a designated police station shall be appointed –

(a) by the chief officer of police for the area in which the designated police station is situated; or
(b) by such other police officer as the chief officer of police for that area may direct.

(3) No officer may be appointed a custody officer unless he is of at least the rank of sergeant.

(4) An officer of any rank may perform the functions of a custody officer at a designated police station if a custody officer is not readily available to perform them.

(5) Subject to the following provisions of this section and to section 39(2) below, none of the functions of a custody officer in relation to a person shall be performed by an officer who at the time when the function falls to be performed is involved in the investigation of an offence for which that person is in police detention at that time.

(6) Nothing in subsection (5) above is to be taken to prevent a custody officer –

(a) performing any function assigned to custody officers –
(i) by this Act; or
(ii) by a code of practice issued under this Act;
(b) carrying out the duty imposed on custody officers by section 39 below;
(c) doing anything in connection with the identification of a suspect; or
(d) doing anything under sections 7 and 8 of the Road Traffic Act 1988.

(7) Where an arrested person is taken to a police station which is not a designated police station, the functions in relation to him which at a designated police station would be the functions of a custody officer shall be performed –

(a) by an officer who is not involved in the investigation of an offence for which he is in police detention, if such an officer is readily available; and
(b) if no such officer is readily available, by the officer who took him to the station or any other officer.

(8) References to a custody officer in the following provisions of this Act include references to an officer other than a custody officer who is performing the functions of a custody officer by virtue of subsection (4) or (7) above.

(9) Where by virtue of subsection (7) above an officer of a force maintained by a police authority who took an arrested person to a police station is to perform the functions of a custody officer in relation to him, the officer shall inform an officer who –

(a) is attached to a designated police station; and

(b) is of at least the rank of inspector,

that he is to do so.

(10) The duty imposed by subsection (9) above shall be performed as soon as it is practicable to perform it.

37 Duties of custody officer before charge　　　　　**[489]**

(1) Where –

(a) a person is arrested for an offence –

(i) without a warrant; or

(ii) under a warrant not endorsed for bail, or

(b) a person returns to a police station to answer to bail,

the custody officer at each police station where he is detained after his arrest shall determine whether he has before him sufficient evidence to charge that person with the offence for which he was arrested and may detain him at the police station for such period as is necessary to enable him to do so.

(2) If the custody officer determines that he does not have such evidence before him, the person arrested shall be released either on bail or without bail, unless the custody officer has reasonable grounds for believing that his detention without being charged is necessary to secure or preserve evidence relating to an offence for which he is under arrest or to obtain such evidence by questioning him.

(3) If the custody officer has reasonable grounds for so believing, he may authorise the person arrested to be kept in police detention.

(4) Where a custody officer authorises a person who has not been charged to be kept in police detention, he shall, as soon as is practicable, make a written record of the grounds for the detention.

(5) Subject to subsection (6) below, the written record shall be made in the presence of the person arrested who shall at that time be informed by the custody officer of the grounds for his detention.

(6) Subsection (5) above shall not apply where the person arrested is, at the time when the written record is made –

(a) incapable of understanding what is said to him;

(b) violent or likely to become violent; or

(c) in urgent need of medical attention.

(7) Subject to section 41(7) below, if the custody officer determines that he has before him sufficient evidence to charge the person arrested with the offence for which he was arrested, the person arrested –

(a) shall be charged; or

(b) shall be released without charge, either on bail or without bail.

(8) Where –

(a) a person is released under subsection (7)(b) above; and

(b) at the time of his release a decision whether he should be prosecuted for the offence for which he was arrested has not been taken,

it shall be the duty of the custody officer so to inform him.

(9) If the person arrested is not in a fit state to be dealt with under subsection (7) above, he may be kept in police detention until he is.

(10) The duty imposed on the custody officer under subsection (1) above shall be carried out by him as soon as practicable after the person arrested arrives at the

police station or, in the case of a person arrested at the police station, as soon as practicable after the arrest.

(15) In this Part of this Act –

'arrested juvenile' means a person arrested with or without a warrant who appears to be under the age of 17;
'endorsed for bail' means endorsed with a direction for bail in accordance with section 117(2) of the Magistrates' Courts Act 1980.

38 Duties of custody officer after charge   [490]

(1) Where a person arrested for an offence otherwise than under a warrant endorsed for bail is charged with an offence, the custody officer shall order his release from police detention, either on bail or without bail, unless –

(a) if the person arrested is not an arrested juvenile –

(i) his name or address cannot be ascertained or the custody officer has reasonable grounds for doubting whether a name or address furnished by him as his name or address is his real name or address;
(ii) the custody officer has reasonable grounds for believing that the detention of the person arrested is necessary for his own protection or to prevent him from causing physical injury to any other person or from causing loss of or damage to property; or
(iii) the custody officer has reasonable grounds for believing that the person arrested will fail to appear in court to answer to bail or that his detention is necessary to prevent him from interfering with the administration of justice or with the investigation of offences or of a particular offence;

(b) if he is an arrested juvenile –

(i) any of the requirements of paragraph (a) above is satisfied; or
(ii) the custody officer has reasonable grounds for believing that he ought to be detained in his own interests.

(2) If the release of a person arrested is not required by subsection (1) above, the custody officer may authorise him to be kept in police detention.

(3) Where a custody officer authorises a person who has been charged to be kept in police detention, he shall, as soon as practicable, make a written record of the grounds for the detention.

(4) Subject to subsection (5) below, the written record shall be made in the presence of the person charged who shall at that time be informed by the custody officer of the grounds for his detention.

(5) Subsection (4) above shall not apply where the person charged is, at the time when the written record is made –

(a) incapable of understanding what is said to him;
(b) violent or likely to become violent; or
(c) in urgent need of medical attention.

(6) Where a custody officer authorises an arrested juvenile to be kept in police detention under subsection (1) above, the custody officer shall, unless he certifies –

(a) that, by reason of such circumstances as are specified in the certificate, it is impracticable for him to do so; or
(b) in the case of an arrested juvenile who has attained the age of 15 years, that no secure accommodation is available and that keeping him in other local authority accommodation would not be adequate to protect the public from serious harm from him,

secure that the arrested juvenile is moved to local authority accommodation.

(6A) In this section –

'local authority accommodation' means accommodation provided by or on behalf of a local authority (within the meaning of the Children Act 1989);

'secure accommodation' means accommodation provided for the purposes of restricting liberty;

'sexual offence' and 'violent offence' have the same meanings as in Part I of the Criminal Justice Act 1991;

and any reference, in relation to an arrested juvenile charged with a violent or sexual offence, to protecting the public from serious harm from him shall be construed as a reference to protecting members of the public from death or serious personal injury, whether physical or psychological, occasioned by further such offences committed by him.

(6B) Where an arrested juvenile is moved to local authority accommodation under subsection (6) above, it shall be lawful for any person acting on behalf of the authority to detain him.

(7) A certificate made under subsection (6) above in respect of an arrested juvenile shall be produced to the court before which he is first brought thereafter.

(8) In this Part of this Act 'local authority' has the same meaning as in the Children Act 1989.

39 Responsibilities in relation to persons detained [491]

(1) Subject to subsections (2) and (4) below, it shall be the duty of the custody officer at a police station to ensure –

(a) that all persons in police detention at that station are treated in accordance with this Act and any code of practice issued under it and relating to the treatment of persons in police detention; and

(b) that all matters relating to such persons which are required by this Act or by such codes of practice to be recorded are recorded in the custody records relating to such persons.

(2) If the custody officer, in accordance with any code of practice issued under this Act, transfers or permits the transfer of a person in police detention –

(a) to the custody of a police officer investigating an offence for which that person is in police detention; or

(b) to the custody of an officer who has charge of that person outside the police station,

the custody officer shall cease in relation to that person to be subject to the duty imposed on him by subsection (1)(a) above; and it shall be the duty of the officer to whom the transfer is made to ensure that he is treated in accordance with the provisions of this Act and of any such codes of practice as are mentioned in subsection (1) above.

(3) If the person detained in subsequently returned to the custody of the custody officer, it shall be the duty of the officer investigating the offence to report to the custody officer as to the manner in which this section and the codes of practice have been complied with while that person was in his custody.

(4) If an arrested juvenile is moved to local authority accommodation in pursuance of arrangements made under section 38(6) above, the custody officer shall cease in relation to that person to be subject to the duty imposed on him by subsection (1) above.

## 40 Review of police detention	[492]

(1) Reviews of the detention of each person in police detention in connection with the investigation of an offence shall be carried out periodically in accordance with the following provisions of this section –

(a) in the case of a person who has been arrested and charged, by the custody officer; and

(b) in the case of a person who has been arrested but not charged, by an officer of at least the rank of inspector who has not been directly involved in the investigation.

(2) The officer to whom it falls to carry out a review is referred to in this section as a 'review officer'.

(3) Subject to subsection (4) below –

(a) the first review shall be not later than six hours after the detention was first authorised;

(b) the second review shall be not later than nine hours after the first;

(c) subsequent reviews shall be at intervals of not more than nine hours.

(4) A review may be postponed –

(a) if, having regard to all the circumstances prevailing at the latest time for it specified in subsection (3) above, it is not practicable to carry out the review at that time;

(b) without prejudice to the generality of paragraph (a) above –

(i) if at that time the person in detention is being questioned by a police officer and the review officer is satisfied that an interruption of the questioning for the purpose of carrying out the review would prejudice the investigation in connection with which he is being questioned; or

(ii) if at that time no review officer is readily available.

(5) If a review is postponed under subsection (4) above it shall be carried out as soon as practicable after the latest time specified for it in subsection (3) above.

(6) If a review is carried out after postponement under subsection (4) above, the fact that it was so carried out shall not affect any requirements of this section as to the time at which any subsequent review is to be carried out.

(7) The review officer shall record the reasons for any postponement of a review in the custody record.

(8) Subject to subsection (9) below, where the person whose detention is under review has not been charged before the time of the review, section 37(1) to (6) above shall have effect in relation to him, but with the substitution –

(a) of references to the person whose detention is under review for references to the person arrested; and

(b) of references to the review officer for references to the custody officer.

(9) Where a person has been kept in police detention by virtue of section 37(9) above, section 37(1) to (6) shall not have effect in relation to him but it shall be the duty of the review officer to determine whether he is yet in a fit state.

(10) Where the person whose detention is under review has been charged before the time of the review, section 38(1) to (6) above shall have effect in relation to him, but with the substitution of references to the person whose detention is under review for references to the person arrested.

(11) Where –

(a) an officer of higher rank than the review officer gives directions relating to a person in police detention; and

(b) the directions are at variance –

(i) with any decision made or action taken by the review officer in the performance of a duty imposed on him under this Part of this Act; or
(ii) with any decision or action which would but for the directions have been made or taken by him in the performance of such a duty,

the review officer shall refer the matter at once to an officer of the rank of superintendent or above who is responsible for the police station for which the review officer is acting as review officer in connection with the detention.

(12) Before determining whether to authorise a person's continued detention the review officer shall give –

(a) that person (unless he is asleep); or
(b) any solicitor representing him who is available at the time of the review,

an opportunity to make representations to him about the detention.

(13) Subject to subsection (14) below, the person whose detention is under review or his solicitor may make representations under subsection (12) above either orally or in writing.

(14) The review officer may refuse to hear oral representations from the person whose detention is under review if he considers that he is unfit to make such representations by reason of his condition or behaviour.

41 Limits on period of detention without charge [493]

(1) Subject to the following provisions of this section and to sections 42 and 43 below, a person shall not be kept in police detention for more than 24 hours without being charged.

(2) The time from which the period of detention of a person is to be calculated (in this Act referred to as 'the relevant time') –

(a) in the case of a person to whom this paragraph applies, shall be –

(i) the time at which that person arrives at the relevant police station; or
(ii) the time 24 hours after the time of that person's arrest,

whichever is the earlier;
(b) in the case of a person arrested outside England and Wales, shall be –

(i) the time at which that person arrives at the first police station to which he is taken in the police area in England or Wales in which the offence for which he was arrested is being investigated; or
(ii) the time 24 hours after the time of that person's entry into England and Wales,

whichever is the earlier;
(c) in the case of a person who –

(i) attends voluntarily at a police station; or
(ii) accompanies a constable to a police station without having been arrested,

and is arrested at the police station, the time of his arrest;
(d) in any other case, except where subsection (5) below applies, shall be the time at which the person arrested arrives at the first police station to which he is taken after his arrest.

(3) Subsection (2)(a) above applies to a person if –

(a) his arrest is sought in one police area in England and Wales;
(b) he is arrested in another police area; and
(c) he is not questioned in the area in which he is arrested in order to obtain evidence in relation to an offence for which he is arrested;

and in sub-paragraph (i) of that paragraph 'the relevant police station' means the first police station to which he is taken in the police area in which his arrest was sought.

(4) Subsection (2) above shall have effect in relation to a person arrested under section 31 above as if every reference in it to his arrest or his being arrested were a reference to his arrest or his being arrested for the offence for which he was originally arrested.

(5) If –

(a) a person is in police detention in a police area in England and Wales ('the first area'); and

(b) his arrest for an offence is sought in some other police area in England and Wales ('the second area'); and

(c) he is taken to the second area for the purposes of investigating that offence, without being questioned in the first area in order to obtain evidence in relation to it,

the relevant time shall be –

(i) the time 24 hours after he leaves the place where he is detained in the first area; or

(ii) the time at which he arrives at the first police station to which he is taken in the second area,

whichever is the earlier.

(6) When a person who is in police detention is removed to hospital because he is in need of medical treatment, any time during which he is being questioned in hospital or on the way there or back by a police officer for the purpose of obtaining evidence relating to an offence shall be included in any period which falls to be calculated for the purposes of this Part of this Act, but any other time while he is in hospital or on his way there or back shall not be so included.

(7) Subject to subsection (8) below, a person who at the expiry of 24 hours after the relevant time is in police detention and has not been charged shall be released at that time either on bail or without bail.

(8) Subsection (7) above does not apply to a person whose detention for more than 24 hours after the relevant time has been authorised or is otherwise permitted in accordance with section 42 or 43 below.

(9) A person released under subsection (7) above shall not be re-arrested without a warrant for the offence for which he was previously arrested unless new evidence justifying a further arrest has come to light since his release.

42 Authorisation of continued detention   [494]

(1) Where a police officer of the rank of superintendent or above who is responsible for the police station at which a person is detained has reasonable grounds for believing that –

(a) the detention of that person without charge is necessary to secure or preserve evidence relating to an offence for which he is under arrest or to obtain such evidence by questioning him;

(b) an offence for which he is under arrest is a serious arrestable offence; and

(c) the investigation is being conducted diligently and expeditiously,

he may authorise the keeping of that person in police detention for a period expiring at or before 36 hours after the relevant time.

(2) Where an officer such as is mentioned in subsection (1) above has authorised the keeping of a person in police detention for a period expiring less than 36

hours after the relevant time, such an officer may authorise the keeping of that person in police detention for a further period expiring not more than 36 hours after that time if the conditions specified in subsection (1) above are still satisfied when he gives the authorisation.

(3) If it is proposed to transfer a person in police detention to another police area, the officer determining whether or not to authorise keeping him in detention under subsection (1) above shall have regard to the distance and the time the journey would take.

(4) No authorisation under subsection (1) above shall be given in respect of any person –

(a) more than 24 hours after the relevant time; or
(b) before the second review of his detention under section 40 above has been carried out.

(5) Where an officer authorises the keeping of a person in police detention under subsection (1) above, it shall be his duty –

(a) to inform that person of the grounds for his continued detention; and
(b) to record the grounds in that person's custody record.

(6) Before determining whether to authorise the keeping of a person in detention under subsection (1) or (2) above, an officer shall give –

(a) that person; or
(b) any solicitor representing him who is available at the time when it falls to the officer to determine whether to give the authorisation,

an opportunity to make representations to him about the detention.

(7) Subject to subsection (8) below, the person in detention or his solicitor may make representations under subsection (6) above either orally or in writing.

(8) The officer to whom it falls to determine whether to give the authorisation may refuse to hear oral representations from the person in detention if he considers that he is unfit to make such representations by reason of his condition or behaviour.

(9) Where –

(a) an officer authorises the keeping of a person in detention under subsection (1) above; and
(b) at the time of the authorisation he has not yet exercised a right conferred on him by section 56 or 58 below,

the officer –

(i) shall inform him of that right;
(ii) shall decide whether he should be permitted to exercise it;
(iii) shall record the decision in his custody record; and
(iv) if the decision is to refuse to permit the exercise of the right, shall also record the grounds for the decision in that record.

(10) Where an officer has authorised the keeping of a person who has not been charged in detention under subsection (1) or (2) above, he shall be released from detention, either on bail or without bail, not later than 36 hours after the relevant time, unless –

(a) he has been charged with an offence; or
(b) his continued detention is authorised or otherwise permitted in accordance with section 43 below.

(11) A person released under subsection (10) above shall not be re-arrested without a warrant for the offence for which he was previously arrested unless new evidence justifying a further arrest has come to light since his release.

43 Warrants of further detention   [495]

(1) Where, on an application on oath made by a constable and supported by an information, a magistrates' court is satisfied that there are reasonable grounds for believing that the further detention of the person to whom the application relates is justified, it may issue a warrant of further detention authorising the keeping of that person in police detention.

(2) A court may not hear an application for a warrant of further detention unless the person to whom the application relates –

(a) has been furnished with a copy of the information; and
(b) has been brought before the court for the hearing.

(3) The person to whom the application relates shall be entitled to be legally represented at the hearing and, if he is not so represented but wishes to be so represented –

(a) the court shall adjourn the hearing to enable him to obtain representation; and
(b) he may be kept in police detention during the adjournment.

(4) A person's further detention is only justified for the purposes of this section or section 44 below if –

(a) his detention without charge is necessary to secure or preserve evidence relating to an offence for which he is under arrest or to obtain such evidence by questioning him;
(b) an offence for which he is under arrest is a serious arrestable offence; and
(c) the investigation is being conducted diligently and expeditiously.

(5) Subject to subsection (7) below, an application for a warrant of further detention may be made –

(a) at any time before the expiry of 36 hours after the relevant time; or
(b) in a case where –

(i) it is not practicable for the magistrates' court to which the application will be made to sit at the expiry of 36 hours after the relevant time; but
(ii) the court will sit during the six hours following the end of that period,

at any time before the expiry of the said six hours.

(6) In a case to which subsection (5)(b) above applies –

(a) the person to whom the application relates may be kept in police detention until the application is heard; and
(b) the custody officer shall make a note in that person's custody record –

(i) of the fact that he was kept in police detention for more than 36 hours after the relevant time; and
(ii) of the reason why he was so kept.

(7) If –

(a) an application for a warrant of further detention is made after the expiry of 36 hours after the relevant time; and
(b) it appears to the magistrates' court that it would have been reasonable for the police to make it before the expiry of that period,

the court shall dismiss the application.

(8) Where on an application such as is mentioned in subsection (1) above a magistrates' court is not satisfied that there are reasonable grounds for believing that the further detention of the person to whom the application relates is justified, it shall be its duty –

(a) to refuse the application; or

(b) to adjourn the hearing of it until a time not later than 36 hours after the relevant time.

(9) The person to whom the application relates may be kept in police detention during the adjournment.

(10) A warrant of further detention shall –

(a) state the time at which it is issued;
(b) authorise the keeping in police detention of the person to whom it relates for the period stated in it.

(11) Subject to subsection (12) below, the period stated in a warrant of further detention shall be such period as the magistrates' court thinks fit, having regard to the evidence before it.

(12) The period shall not be longer than 36 hours.

(13) If it is proposed to transfer a person in police detention to a police area other than that in which he is detained when the application for a warrant of further detention is made, the court hearing the application shall have regard to the distance and the time the journey would take.

(14) Any information submitted in support of an application under this section shall state –

(a) the nature of the offence for which the person to whom the application relates has been arrested;
(b) the general nature of the evidence on which that person was arrested;
(c) what inquiries relating to the offence have been made by the police and what further inquiries are proposed by them;
(d) the reasons for believing the continued detention of that person to be necessary for the purposes of such further inquiries.

(15) Where an application under this section is refused, the person to whom the application relates shall forthwith be charged or, subject to subsection (16) below, released, either on bail or without bail.

(16) A person need not be released under subsection (15) above –

(a) before the expiry of 24 hours after the relevant time; or
(b) before the expiry of any longer period for which his continued detention is or has been authorised under section 42 above.

(17) Where an application under this section is refused, no further application shall be made under this section in respect of the person to whom the refusal relates, unless supported by evidence which has come to light since the refusal.

(18) Where a warrant of further detention is issued, the person to whom it relates shall be released from police detention, either on bail or without bail, upon or before the expiry of the warrant unless he is charged.

(19) A person released under subsection (18) above shall not be re-arrested without a warrant for the offence for which he was previously arrested unless new evidence justifying a further arrest has come to light since his release.

44 Extension of warrants of further detention [496]

(1) On an application on oath made by a constable and supported by an information a magistrates' court may extend a warrant of further detention issued under section 43 above if it is satisfied that there are reasonable grounds for believing that the further detention of the person to whom the application relates is justified.

(2) Subject to subsection (3) below, the period for which a warrant of further

detention may be extended shall be such period as the court thinks fit, having regard to the evidence before it.

(3) The period shall not –

(a) be longer than 36 hours; or
(b) end later than 96 hours after the relevant time.

(4) Where a warrant of further detention has been extended under subsection (1) above, or further extended under this subsection, for a period ending before 96 hours after the relevant time, on an application such as is mentioned in that subsection a magistrates' court may further extend the warrant if it is satisfied as there mentioned; and subsections (2) and (3) above apply to such further extensions as they apply to extensions under subsection (1) above.

(5) A warrant of further detention shall, if extended or further extended under this section, be endorsed with a note of the period of the extension.

(6) Subsections (2), (3) and (14) of section 43 above shall apply to an application made under this section as they apply to an application made under that section.

(7) Where an application under this section is refused, the person to whom the application relates shall forthwith be charged or, subject to subsection (8) below, released, either on bail or without bail.

(8) A person need not be released under subsection (7) above before the expiry of any period for which a warrant of further detention issued in relation to him has been extended or further extended on an earlier application made under this section.

45 Detention before charge – supplementary   [497]

(1) In sections 43 and 44 of this Act 'magistrates' court' means a court consisting of two or more justices of the peace sitting otherwise than in open court.

(2) Any reference in this Part of this Act to a period of time or a time of day is to be treated as approximate only.

46 Detention after charge   [498]

(1) Where a person –

(a) is charged with an offence; and
(b) after being charged –

(i) is kept in police detention; or
(ii) is detained by a local authority in pursuance of arrangements made under section 38(6) above,

he shall be brought before a magistrates' court in accordance with the provisions of this section.

(2) If he is to be brought before a magistrates' court for the petty sessions area in which the police station at which he was charged is situated, he shall be brought before such a court as soon as is practicable and in any event not later than the first sitting after he is charged with the offence.

(3) If no magistrates' court for that area is due to sit either on the day on which he is charged or on the next day, the custody officer for the police station at which he was charged shall inform the clerk to the justices for the area that there is a person in the area to whom subsection (2) above applies.

(4) If the person charged is to be brought before a magistrates' court for a petty sessions area other than that in which the police station at which he was charged is situated, he shall be removed to that area as soon as is practicable and brought

before such a court as soon as is practicable after his arrival in the area and in any event not later than the first sitting of a magistrates' court for that area after his arrival in the area.

(5) If no magistrates' court for that area is due to sit either on the day on which he arrives in the area or on the next day –

(a) he shall be taken to a police station in the area; and
(b) the custody officer at that station shall inform the clerk to the justices for the area that there is a person in the area to whom subsection (4) applies.

(6) Subject to subsection (8) below, where a clerk to the justices for a petty sessions area has been informed –

(a) under subsection (3) above that there is a person in the area to whom subsection (2) above applies; or
(b) under subsection (5) above that there is a person in the area to whom subsection (4) above applies,

the clerk shall arrange for a magistrates' court to sit not later than the day next following the relevant day.

(7) In this section 'the relevant day' –

(a) in relation to a person who is to be brought before a magistrates' court for the petty sessions area in which the police station at which he was charged is situated, means the day on which he was charged; and
(b) in relation to a person who is to be brought before a magistrates' court for any other petty sessions area, means the day on which he arrives in the area.

(8) Where the day next following the relevant day is Christmas Day, Good Friday or a Sunday, the duty of the clerk under subsection (6) above is a duty to arrange for a magistrates' court to sit not later than the first day after the relevant day which is not one of those days.

(9) Nothing in this section requires a person who is in hospital to be brought before a court if he is not well enough.

47 Bail after arrest [499]

(1) Subject to subsection (2) below, a release on bail of a person under this Part of this Act shall be a release on bail granted in accordance with the Bail Act 1976.

(2) Nothing in the Bail Act 1976 shall prevent the re-arrest without warrant of a person released on bail subject to a duty to attend at a police station if new evidence justifying a further arrest has come to light since his release.

(3) Subject to subsection (4) below, in this Part of this Act references to 'bail' are references to bail subject to a duty –

(a) to appear before a magistrates' court at such time and such place; or
(b) to attend at such police station at such time,

as the custody officer may appoint.

(4) Where a custody officer has granted bail to a person subject to a duty to appear at a police station, the custody officer may give notice in writing to that person that his attendance at the police station is not required.

(5) Where a person arrested for an offence who was released on bail subject to a duty to attend at a police station so attends, he may be detained without charge in connection with that offence only if the custody officer at the police station has reasonable grounds for believing that his detention is necessary –

(a) to secure or preserve evidence relating to the offence; or
(b) to obtain such evidence by questioning him.

(6) Where a person is detained under subsection (5) above, any time during which he was in police detention prior to being granted bail shall be included as part of any period which falls to be calculated under this Part of this Act.

(7) Where a person who was released on bail subject to a duty to attend at a police station is re-arrested, the provisions of this Part of this Act shall apply to him as they apply to a person arrested for the first time.

51 Savings   [500]

Nothing in this Part of this Act shall affect –

(a) the powers conferred on immigration officers by section 4 of and Schedule 2 to the Immigration Act 1971 (administrative provisions as to control on entry, etc);

(b) the powers conferred by or by virtue of section 14 of the Prevention of Terrorism (Temporary Provisions) Act 1989 or Schedule 2 or 5 to that Act (powers of arrest and detention and control of entry and procedure for removal);

(c) any duty of a police officer under –

(i) sections 129, 190 or 202 of the Army Act 1955 (duties of governors of prisons and others to receive prisoners, deserters, absentees and persons under escort);

(ii) sections 129, 190 or 202 of the Air Force Act 1955 (duties of governors of prisons and others to receive prisoners, deserters, absentees and persons under escort);

(iii) section 107 of the Naval Discipline Act 1957 (duties of governors of civil prisons, etc); or

(iv) paragraph 5 of Schedule 5 to the Reserve Forces Act 1980 (duties of governors of civil prisons); or

(d) any right of a person in police detention to apply for a writ of habeas corpus or other prerogative remedy.

PART V

QUESTIONING AND TREATMENT OF PERSONS BY POLICE

53 Abolition of certain powers of constables   [501]
to search persons

(1) Subject to subsection (2) below, there shall cease to have effect any Act (including a local Act) passed before this Act in so far as it authorises –

(a) any search by a constable of a person in police detention at a police station; or

(b) an intimate search of a person by a constable;

and any rule of common law which authorises a search such as is mentioned in paragraph (a) or (b) above is abolished.

54 Searches of detained persons   [502]

(1) The custody officer at a police station shall ascertain and record or cause to be recorded everything which a person has with him when he is –

(a) brought to the station after being arrested elsewhere or after being committed to custody by an order or sentence of a court; or

(b) arrested at the station or detained there under section 47(5) above.

(2) In the case of an arrested person the record shall be made as part of his custody record.

(3) Subject to subsection (4) below, a custody officer may seize and retain any such thing or cause any such thing to be seized and retained.

(4) Clothes and personal effects may only be seized if the custody officer –

(a) believes that the person from whom they are seized may use them –

(i) to cause physical injury to himself or any other person;
(ii) to damage property;
(iii) to interfere with evidence; or
(iv) to assist him to escape; or

(b) has reasonable grounds for believing that they may be evidence relating to an offence.

(5) Where anything is seized, the person from whom it is seized shall be told the reason for the seizure unless he is –

(a) violent or likely to become violent; or
(b) incapable of understanding what is said to him.

(6) Subject to subsection (7) below, a person may be searched if the custody officer considers it necessary to enable him to carry out his duty under subsection (1) above and to the extent that the custody officer considers necessary for that purpose.

(6A) A person who is in custody at a police station or is in police detention otherwise than at a police station may at any time be searched in order to ascertain whether he has with him anything which he could use for the purposes specified in subsection (4)(a) above.

(6B) Subject to subsection (6C) below, a constable may seize and retain, or cause to be seized and retained, anything found on such a search.

(6C) A constable may only seize clothes and personal effects in the circumstances specified in subsection (4) above.

(7) An intimate search may not be conducted under this section.

(8) A search under this section shall be carried out by a constable.

(9) The constable carrying out a search shall be of the same sex as the person searched.

55 Intimate searches [503]

(1) Subject to the following provisions of this section, if an officer of at least the rank of superintendent has reasonable grounds for believing –

(a) that a person who has been arrested and is in police detention may have concealed on him anything which –

(i) he could use to cause physical injury to himself or others; and
(ii) he might so use while he is in police detention or in the custody of a court; or

(b) that such a person –

(i) may have a Class A drug concealed on him; and
(ii) was in possession of it with the appropriate criminal intent before his arrest,

he may authorise an intimate search of that person.

(2) An officer may not authorise an intimate search of a person for anything unless he has reasonable grounds for believing that it cannot be found without his being intimately searched.

(3) An officer may give an authorisation under subsection (1) above orally or in writing but, if he gives it orally, he shall confirm it in writing as soon as is practicable.

(4) An intimate search which is only a drug offence search shall be by way of examination by a suitably qualified person.

(5) Except as provided by subsection (4) above, an intimate search shall be by way of examination by a suitably qualified person unless an officer of at least the rank of superintendent considers that this is not practicable.

(6) An intimate search which is not carried out as mentioned in subsection (5) above shall be carried out by a constable.

(7) A constable may not carry out an intimate search of a person of the opposite sex.

(8) No intimate search may be carried out except –

(a) at a police station;
(b) at a hospital;
(c) at a registered medical practitioner's surgery; or
(d) at some other place used for medical purposes.

(9) An intimate search which is only a drug offence search may not be carried out at a police station.

(10) If an intimate search of a person is carried out, the custody record relating to him shall state –

(a) which parts of his body were searched; and
(b) why they were searched.

(11) The information required to be recorded by subsection (10) above shall be recorded as soon as practicable after the completion of the search.

(12) The custody officer at a police station may seize and retain anything which is found on an intimate search of a person, or cause any such thing to be seized and retained –

(a) if he believes that the person from whom it is seized may use it –

(i) to cause physical injury to himself or any other person;
(ii) to damage property;
(iii) to interfere with evidence; or
(iv) to assist him to escape; or

(b) if he has reasonable grounds for believing that it may be evidence relating to an offence.

(13) Where anything is seized under this section, the person from whom it is seized shall be told the reason for the seizure unless he is –

(a) violent or likely to become violent; or
(b) incapable of understanding what is said to him ...

(17) In this section –

'the appropriate criminal intent' means an intent to commit an offence under –

(a) section 5(3) of the Misuse of Drugs Act 1971 (possession of controlled drug with intent to supply to another); or
(b) section 68(2) of the Customs and Excise Management Act 1979 (exportation etc with intent to evade a prohibition of restriction);

'Class A drug' has the meaning assigned to it by section 2(1)(b) of the Misuse of Drugs Act 1971;

'drug offence search' means an intimate search for a Class A drug which an officer has authorised by virtue of subsection (1)(b) above; and 'suitably qualified person' means –

(a) a registered medical practitioner; or

(b) a registered nurse.

56 Right to have someone informed when arrested [504]

(1) Where a person has been arrested and is being held in custody in a police station or other premises, he shall be entitled, if he so requests, to have one friend or relative or other person who is known to him or who is likely to take an interest in his welfare told, as soon as is practicable except to the extent that delay is permitted by this section, that he has been arrested and is being detained there.

(2) Delay is only permitted –

(a) in the case of a person who is in police detention for a serious arrestable offence; and

(b) if an officer of at least the rank of superintendent authorises it.

(3) In any case the person in custody must be permitted to exercise the right conferred by subsection (1) above within 36 hours from the relevant time, as defined in section 41(2) above.

(4) An officer may give an authorisation under subsection (2) above orally or in writing but, if he gives it orally, he shall confirm it in writing as soon as is practicable.

(5) Subject to subsection (5A) below, an officer may only authorise delay where he has reasonable grounds for believing that telling the named person of the arrest –

(a) will lead to interference with or harm to evidence connected with a serious arrestable offence or interference with or physical injury to other persons; or

(b) will lead to the alerting of other persons suspected of having committed such an offence but not yet arrested for it; or

(c) will hinder the recovery of any property obtained as a result of such an offence.

(5A) An officer may also authorise delay where the serious arrestable offence is a drug trafficking offence or an offence to which Part VI of the Criminal Justice Act 1988 applies (offences in respect of which confiscation orders under that Part may be made) and the officer has reasonable grounds for believing –

(a) where the offence is a drug trafficking offence, that the detained person has benefited from drug trafficking and that the recovery of the value of that person's proceeds of drug trafficking will be hindered by telling the named person of the arrest; and

(b) where the offence is one to which Part VI of the Criminal Justice Act 1988 applies, that the detained person has benefited from the offence and that the recovery of the value of the property obtained by that person from or in connection with the offence or of the pecuniary advantage derived by him from or in connection with it will be hindered by telling the named person of the arrest.

(6) If a delay is authorised –

(a) the detained person shall be told the reason for it; and

(b) the reason shall be noted on his custody record.

(7) The duties imposed by subsection (6) above shall be performed as soon as is practicable.

(8) The rights conferred by this section on a person detained at a police station or other premises are exercisable whenever he is transferred from one place to

another; and this section applies to each subsequent occasion on which they are exercisable as it applies to the first such occasion.

(9) There may be no further delay in permitting the exercise of the right conferred by subsection (1) above once the reason for authorising delay ceases to subsist.

(10) In the foregoing provisions of this section references to a person who has been arrested include references to a person who has been detained under the terrorism provisions and 'arrest' includes detention under those provisions.

(11) In its application to a person who has been arrested or detained under the terrorism provisions –

(a) subsection (2)(a) above shall have effect as if for the words 'for a serious arrestable offence' there were substituted the words 'under the terrorism provisions';

(b) subsection (3) above shall have effect as if for the words from 'within' onwards there were substituted the words 'before the end of the period beyond which he may no longer be detained without the authority of the Secretary of State'; and

(c) subsection (5) above shall have effect as if at the end there were added 'or

(d) will lead to interference with the gathering of information about the commission, preparation or instigation of acts of terrorism; or

(e) by alerting any person, will make it more difficult –

(i) to prevent an act of terrorism; or

(ii) to secure the apprehension, prosecution or conviction of any person in connection with the commission, preparation or instigation of an act of terrorism.'.

58 Access to legal advice [505]

(1) A person arrested and held in custody in a police station or other premises shall be entitled, if he so requests, to consult a solicitor privately at any time.

(2) Subject to subsection (3) below, a request under subsection (1) above and the time at which it was made shall be recorded in the custody record.

(3) Such a request need not be recorded in the custody record of a person who makes it at a time while he is at a court after being charged with an offence.

(4) If a person makes such a request, he must be permitted to consult a solicitor as soon as is practicable except to the extent that delay is permitted by this section.

(5) In any case he must be permitted to consult a solicitor within 36 hours from the relevant time, as defined in section 41(2) above.

(6) Delay in compliance with a request is only permitted –

(a) in the case of a person who is in police detention for a serious arrestable offence; and

(b) if an officer of at least the rank of superintendent authorises it.

(7) An officer may give an authorisation under subsection (6) above orally or in writing but, if he gives it orally, he shall confirm it in writing as soon as is practicable.

(8) Subject to subsection (8A) below, an officer may only authorise delay where he has reasonable grounds for believing that the exercise of the right conferred by subsection (1) above at the time when the person detained desires to exercise it –

(a) will lead to interference with or harm to evidence connected with a serious arrestable offence or interference with or physical injury to other persons; or

(b) will lead to the alerting of other persons suspected of having committed such an offence but not yet arrested for it; or

(c) will hinder the recovery of any property obtained as a result of such an offence.

(8A) An officer may also authorise delay where the serious arrestable offence is a drug trafficking offence or an offence to which Part VI of the Criminal Justice Act 1988 applies and the officer has reasonable grounds for believing –

(a) where the offence is a drug trafficking offence, that the detained person has benefited from drug trafficking and that the recovery of the value of that person's proceeds of drug trafficking will be hindered by the exercise of the right conferred by subsection (1) above; and

(b) where the offence is one to which Part VI of the Criminal Justice Act 1988 applies, that the detained person has benefited from the offence and that the recovery of the value of the property obtained by that person from or in connection with the offence or of the pecuniary advantage derived by him from or in connection with it will be hindered by the exercise of the right conferred by subsection (1) above.

(9) If delay is authorised –

(a) the detained person shall be told the reason for it; and

(b) the reason shall be noted on his custody record.

(10) The duties imposed by subsection (9) above shall be performed as soon as is practicable.

(11) There may be no further delay in permitting the exercise of the right conferred by subsection (1) above once the reason for authorising delay ceases to subsist.

(12) The reference in subsection (1) above to a person arrested includes a reference to a person who has been detained under the terrorism provisions.

(13) In the application of this section to a person who has been arrested or detained under the terrorism provisions –

(a) subsection (5) above shall have effect as if for the words from 'within' onwards there were substituted the words 'before the end of the period beyond which he may no longer be detained without the authority of the Secretary of State';

(b) subsection (6)(a) above shall have effect as if for the words 'for a serious arrestable offence' there were substituted the words 'under the terrorism provisions'; and

(c) subsection (8) above shall have effect as if at the end there were added 'or

(d) will lead to interference with the gathering of information about the commission, preparation or instigation of acts of terrorism; or

(e) by alerting any person, will make it more difficult –

(i) to prevent an act of terrorism; or

(ii) to secure the apprehension, prosecution or conviction of any person in connection with the commission, preparation or instigation of an act of terrorism.'.

(14) If an officer of appropriate rank has reasonable grounds for believing that, unless he gives a direction under subsection (15) below, the exercise by a person arrested or detained under the terrorism provisions of the right conferred by subsection (1) above will have any of the consequences specified in subsection (8) above (as it has effect by virtue of subsection (13) above), he may give a direction under that subsection.

(15) A direction under this subsection is a direction that a person desiring to exercise the right conferred by subsection (1) above may only consult a solicitor in the sight and hearing of a qualified officer of the uniformed branch of the force of which the officer giving the direction is a member.

(16) An officer is qualified for the purpose of subsection (15) above if –

(a) he is of at least the rank of inspector; and
(b) in the opinion of the officer giving the direction he has no connection with the case.

(17) An officer is of appropriate rank to give a direction under subsection (15) above if he is of at least the rank of Commander or Assistant Chief Constable.

(18) A direction under subsection (15) above shall cease to have effect once the reason for giving it ceases to subsist.

61 Fingerprinting [506]

(1) Except as provided by this section no person's fingerprints may be taken without the appropriate consent.

(2) Consent to the taking of a person's fingerprints must be in writing if it is given at a time when he is at a police station.

(3) The fingerprints of a person detained at a police station may be taken without the appropriate consent –

(a) if an officer of at least the rank of superintendent authorises them to be taken; or
(b) if –

(i) he has been charged with a recordable offence or informed that he will be reported for such an offence; and
(ii) he has not had his fingerprints taken in the course of the investigation of the offence by the police.

(4) An officer may only give an authorisation under subsection (3)(a) above if he has reasonable grounds –

(a) for suspecting the involvement of the person whose fingerprints are to be taken in a criminal offence; and
(b) for believing that his fingerprints will tend to confirm or disprove his involvement.

(5) An officer may give an authorisation under subsection (3)(a) above orally or in writing but, if he gives it orally, he shall confirm it in writing as soon as is practicable.

(6) Any person's fingerprints may be taken without the appropriate consent if he has been convicted of a recordable offence.

(7) In a case where by virtue of subsection (3) or (6) above a person's fingerprints are taken without the appropriate consent –

(a) he shall be told the reason before his fingerprints are taken; and
(b) the reason shall be recorded as soon as is practicable after the fingerprints are taken.

(8) If he is detained at a police station when the fingerprints are taken, the reason for taking them shall be recorded on his custody record.

(9) Nothing in this section –

(a) affects any power conferred by paragraph 18(2) of Schedule 2 to the Immigration Act 1971; or
(b) except as provided in section 15(10) of, and paragraph 7(6) of Schedule 5 to, the Prevention of Terrorism (Temporary Provisions) Act 1989, applies to a person arrested or detained under the terrorism provisions.

62 **Intimate samples**

(1) An intimate sample may be taken from a person in police detention only –

(a) if a police officer of at least the rank of superintendent authorises it to be taken; and

(b) if the appropriate consent is given.

(2) An officer may only give an authorisation if he has reasonable grounds –

(a) for suspecting the involvement of the person from whom the sample is to be taken in a serious arrestable offence; and

(b) for believing that the sample will tend to confirm or disprove his involvement.

(3) An officer may give an authorisation under subsection (1) above orally or in writing but, if he gives it orally, he shall confirm it in writing as soon as is practicable.

(4) The appropriate consent must be given in writing.

(5) Where –

(a) an authorisation has been given; and

(b) it is proposed that an intimate sample shall be taken in pursuance of the authorisation,

an officer shall inform the person from whom the sample is to be taken –

(i) of the giving of the authorisation; and

(ii) of the grounds for giving it.

(6) The duty imposed by subsection (5)(ii) above includes a duty to state the nature of the offence in which it is suspected that the person from whom the sample is to be taken has been involved.

(7) If an intimate sample is taken from a person –

(a) the authorisation by virtue of which it was taken;

(b) the grounds for giving the authorisation; and

(c) the fact that the appropriate consent was given,

shall be recorded as soon as is practicable after the sample is taken.

(8) If an intimate sample is taken from a person detained at a police station, the matters required to be recorded by subsection (7) above shall be recorded in his custody record.

(9) An intimate sample, other than a sample of urine or saliva, may only be taken from a person by a registered medical practitioner.

(10) Where the appropriate consent to the taking of an intimate sample from a person was refused without good cause, in any proceedings against that person for an offence –

(a) the court, in determining –

(i) whether to commit that person for trial; or

(ii) whether there is a case to answer; and

(b) the court or jury, in determining whether that person is guilty of the offence charged,

may draw such inferences from the refusal as appear proper; and the refusal may, on the basis of such inferences, be treated as, or as capable of amounting to, corroboration of any evidence against the person in relation to which the refusal is material.

(11) Nothing in this section affects sections 4 to 11 of the Road Traffic Act 1988.

63 Other samples   [508]

(1) Except as provided by this section, a non-intimate sample may not be taken from a person without the appropriate consent.

(2) Consent to the taking of a non-intimate sample must be given in writing.

(3) A non-intimate sample may be taken from a person without the appropriate consent if –

> (a) he is in police detention or is being held in custody by the police on the authority of a court; and
> (b) an officer of at least the rank of superintendent authorises it to be taken without the appropriate consent.

(4) An officer may only give an authorisation under subsection (3) above if he has reasonable grounds –

> (a) for suspecting the involvement of the person from whom the sample is to be taken in a serious arrestable offence; and
> (b) for believing that the sample will tend to confirm or disprove his involvement.

(5) An officer may give an authorisation under subsection (3) above orally or in writing but, if he gives it orally, he shall confirm it in writing as soon as is practicable.

(6) Where –

> (a) an authorisation has been given; and
> (b) it is proposed that a non-intimate sample shall be taken in pursuance of the authorisation,

an officer shall inform the person from whom the sample is to be taken –

> (i) of the giving of the authorisation; and
> (ii) of the grounds for giving it.

(7) The duty imposed by subsection (6)(ii) above includes a duty to state the nature of the offence in which it is suspected that the person from whom the sample is to be taken has been involved.

(8) If a non-intimate sample is taken from a person by virtue of subsection (3) above –

> (a) the authorisation by virtue of which it was taken; and
> (b) the grounds for giving the authorisation,

shall be recorded as soon as is practicable after the sample is taken.

(9) If a non-intimate sample is taken from a person detained at a police station, the matters required to be recorded by subsection (8) above shall be recorded in his custody record.

64 Destruction of fingerprints and samples   [509]

(1) If –

> (a) fingerprints or samples are taken from a person in connection with the investigation of an offence; and
> (b) he is cleared of that offence,

they must be destroyed as soon as is practicable after the conclusion of the proceedings.

(2) If –

> (a) fingerprints or samples are taken from a person in connection with such an investigation; and

(b) it is decided that he shall not be prosecuted for the offence and he has not admitted it and been dealt with by way of being cautioned by a constable,

they must be destroyed as soon as is practicable after that decision is taken.

(3) If –

(a) fingerprints or samples are taken from a person in connection with the investigation of an offence; and
(b) that person is not suspected of having committed the offence,

they must be destroyed as soon as they have fulfilled the purpose for which they were taken.

(4) Proceedings which are discontinued are to be treated as concluded for the purposes of this section.

(5) If fingerprints are destroyed –

(a) any copies of the fingerprints shall also be destroyed; and
(b) any chief officer of police controlling access to computer data relating to the fingerprints shall make access to the data impossible, as soon as it is practicable to do so.

(6) A person who asks to be allowed to witness the destruction of his fingerprints or copies of them shall have a right to witness it.

(6A) If –

(a) subsection (5)(b) above falls to be complied with; and
(b) the person to whose fingerprints the data relate asks for a certificate that it has been complied with,

such a certificate shall be issued to him, not later than the end of the period of three months beginning with the day on which he asks for it, by the responsible chief officer of police or a person authorised by him or on his behalf for the purposes of this section.

(6B) In this section –

'chief officer of police' means the chief officer of police for an area mentioned in Schedule 8 to the Police Act 1964; and
'the responsible chief officer of police' means the chief officer of police in whose area the computer data were put on to the computer.

(7) Nothing in this section –

(a) affects any power conferred by paragraph 18(2) of Schedule 2 to the Immigration Act 1971; or
(b) applies to a person arrested or detained under the terrorism provisions.

65 Part V – supplementary   **[510]**

In this Part of this Act –

'appropriate consent' means –

(a) in relation to a person who has attained the age of 17 years, the consent of that person;
(b) in relation to a person who has not attained that age but has attained the age of 14 years, the consent of that person and his parent or guardian; and
(c) in relation to a person who has not attained the age of 14 years, the consent of his parent or guardian;

'drug trafficking' and 'drug trafficking offence' have the same meaning as in the Drug Trafficking Offences Act 1986;

'fingerprints' includes palm prints;
'intimate sample' means a sample of blood, semen or any other tissue fluid, urine, saliva or pubic hair, or a swab taken from a person's body orifices;
'non-intimate sample' means –

(a) a sample of hair other than pubic hair;
(b) a sample taken from a nail or from under a nail;
(c) a swab taken from any part of a person's body other than a body orifice;
(d) a footprint or a similar impression of any part of a person's body other than a part of his hand;

'the terrorism provisions' means section 14(1) of the Prevention of Terrorism (Temporary Provisions) Act 1989 and any provision of Schedule 2 or 5 to that Act conferring a power of arrest or detention; and
'terrorism' has the meaning assigned to it by section 20(1) of that Act.

References in this Part to any person's proceeds of drug trafficking are to be construed in accordance with the Drug Trafficking Offences Act 1986.

PART VI

CODES OF PRACTICE – GENERAL

66 Codes of practice   [511]

The Secretary of State shall issue codes of practice in connection with –

(a) the exercise by police officers of statutory powers –

(i) to search a person without first arresting him; or
(ii) to search a vehicle without making an arrest;

(b) the detention, treatment, questioning and identification of persons by police officers;
(c) searches of premises by police officers; and
(d) the seizure of property found by police officers on persons or premises.

67 Codes of practice – supplementary   [512]

(1) When the Secretary of State proposes to issue a code of practice to which this section applies, he shall prepare and publish a draft of that code, shall consider any representations made to him about the draft and may modify the draft accordingly.

(2) This section applies to a code of practice under section 60 or 66 above.

(3) The Secretary of State shall lay before both Houses of Parliament a draft of any code of practice prepared by him under this section.

(4) When the Secretary of State has laid the draft of a code before Parliament, he may bring the code into operation by order made by statutory instrument.

(5) No order under subsection (4) above shall have effect until approved by a resolution of each House of Parliament.

(6) An order bringing a code of practice into operation may contain such transitional provisions or savings as appear to the Secretary of State to be necessary or expedient in connection with the code of practice thereby brought into operation.

(7) The Secretary of State may from time to time revise the whole or any part of a code of practice to which this section applies and issue that revised code; and the

foregoing provisions of this section shall apply (with appropriate modifications) to such a revised code as they apply to the first issue of a code.

(8) A police officer shall be liable to disciplinary proceedings for a failure to comply with any provision of such a code, unless such proceedings are precluded by section 104 below.

(9) Persons other than police officers who are charged with the duty of investigating offences or charging offenders shall in the discharge of that duty have regard to any relevant provision of such a code.

(10) A failure on the part –

(a) of a police officer to comply with any provision of such a code; or
(b) of any person other than a police officer who is charged with the duty of investigating offences or charging offenders to have regard to any relevant provision of such a code in the discharge of that duty,

shall not of itself render him liable to any criminal or civil proceedings.

(11) In all criminal and civil proceedings any such code shall be admissible in evidence; and if any provision of such a code appears to the court or tribunal conducting the proceedings to be relevant to any question arising in the proceedings it shall be taken into account in determining that question.

(12) In this section 'criminal proceedings' includes –

(a) proceedings in the United Kingdom or elsewhere before a court-martial constituted under the Army Act 1955, the Air Force Act 1955 or the Naval Discipline Act 1957 or a disciplinary court constituted under section 50 of the said Act of 1957;
(b) proceedings before the Courts-Martial Appeal Court; and
(c) proceedings before a Standing Civilian Court.

PART VIII

EVIDENCE IN CRIMINAL PROCEEDINGS – GENERAL

76 Confessions   **[513]**

(1) In any proceedings a confession made by an accused person may be given in evidence against him in so far as it is relevant to any matter in issue in the proceedings and is not excluded by the court in pursuance of this section.

(2) If, in any proceedings where the prosecution proposes to give in evidence a confession made by an accused person, it is represented to the court that the confession was or may have been obtained –

(a) by oppression of the person who made it; or
(b) in consequence of anything said or done which was likely, in the circumstances existing at the time, to render unreliable any confession which might be made by him in consequence thereof,

the court shall not allow the confession to be given in evidence against him except in so far as the prosecution proves to the court beyond reasonable doubt that the confession (notwithstanding that it may be true) was not obtained as aforesaid.

(3) In any proceedings where the prosecution proposes to give in evidence a confession made by an accused person, the court may of its own motion require the prosecution, as a condition of allowing it to do so, to prove that the confession was not obtained as mentioned in subsection (2) above.

(4) The fact that a confession is wholly or partly excluded in pursuance of this section shall not affect the admissibility in evidence –

(a) of any facts discovered as a result of the confession; or

(b) where the confession is relevant as showing that the accused speaks, writes or expresses himself in a particular way, of so much of the confession as is necessary to show that he does so.

(5) Evidence that a fact to which this subsection applies was discovered as a result of a statement made by an accused person shall not be admissible unless evidence of how it was discovered is given by him or on his behalf.

(6) Subsection (5) above applies –

(a) to any fact discovered as a result of a confession which is wholly excluded in pursuance of this section; and

(b) to any fact discovered as a result of a confession which is partly so excluded, if the fact is discovered as a result of the excluded part of the confession.

(7) Nothing in Part VII of this Act shall prejudice the admissibility of a confession made by an accused person.

(8) In this section 'oppression' includes torture, inhuman or degrading treatment, and the use or threat of violence (whether or not amounting to torture).

77 Confessions by mentally handicapped persons [514]

(1) Without prejudice to the general duty of the court at a trial on indictment to direct the jury on any matter on which it appears to the court appropriate to do so, where at such a trial –

(a) the case against the accused depends wholly or substantially on a confession by him; and

(b) the court is satisfied –

(i) that he is mentally handicapped; and

(ii) that the confession was not made in the presence of an independent person,

the court shall warn the jury that there is special need for caution before convicting the accused in reliance on the confession, and shall explain that the need arises because of the circumstances mentioned in paragraphs (a) and (b) above.

(2) In any case where at the summary trial of a person for an offence it appears to the court that a warning under subsection (1) above would be required if the trial were on indictment, the court shall treat the case as one in which there is a special need for caution before convicting the accused on his confession.

(3) In this section –

'independent person' does not include a police officer or a person employed for, or engaged on, police purposes;

'mentally handicapped', in relation to a person, means that he is in a state of arrested or incomplete development of mind which includes significant impairment of intelligence and social functioning; and

'police purposes' has the meaning assigned to it by section 64 of the Police Act 1964.

78 Exclusion of unfair evidence [515]

(1) In any proceedings the court may refuse to allow evidence on which the prosecution proposes to rely to be given if it appears to the court that, having

regard to all the circumstances, including the circumstances in which the evidence was obtained, the admission of the evidence would have such an adverse effect on the fairness of the proceedings that the court ought not to admit it.

(2) Nothing in this section shall prejudice any rule of law requiring a court to exclude evidence.

82 Part VIII – interpretation   **[516]**

(1) In this Part of this Act –

'confession' includes any statement wholly or partly adverse to the person who made it, whether made to a person in authority or not and whether made in words or otherwise;

'court-martial' means a court-martial constituted under the Army Act 1955, the Air Force Act 1955 or the Naval Discipline Act 1957 or a disciplinary court constituted under section 50 of the said Act of 1957;

'proceedings' means criminal proceedings, including –

(a) proceedings in the United Kingdom or elsewhere before a court-martial constituted under the Army Act 1955 or the Air Force Act 1955;

(b) proceedings in the United Kingdom or elsewhere before the Courts-Martial Appeal Court –

(i) on an appeal from a court-martial so constituted or from a court-martial constituted under the Naval Discipline Act 1957; or

(ii) on a reference under section 34 of the Courts-Martial (Appeals) Act 1968; and

(b) proceedings before a Standing Civilian Court; and

'Service court' means a court-martial or a Standing Civilian Court.

(2) In this Part of this Act references to conviction before a Service court are references –

(a) as regards a court-martial constituted under the Army Act 1955 or the Air Force Act 1955, to a finding of guilty which is, or falls to be treated as, a finding of the court duly confirmed;

(b) as regards –

(i) a court-martial; or

(ii) a disciplinary court,

constituted under the Naval Discipline Act 1957, to a finding of guilty which is, or falls to be treated as, the finding of the court;

and 'convicted' shall be construed accordingly.

(3) Nothing in this Part of this Act shall prejudice any power of a court to exclude evidence (whether by preventing questions from being put or otherwise) at its discretion.

PART XI

MISCELLANEOUS AND SUPPLEMENTARY

116 Meaning of 'serious arrestable offence'   **[517]**

(1) This section has effect for determining whether an offence is a serious arrestable offence for the purposes of this Act.

(2) The following arrestable offences are always serious –

(a) an offence (whether at common law or under any enactment) specified in Part I of Schedule 5 to this Act; and

(aa) any of the offences mentioned in paragraphs (a) to (d) of the definition of 'drug trafficking offence' in section 38(1) of the Drug Trafficking Offences Act 1986; and

(b) an offence under an enactment specified in Part II of that Schedule.

(3) Subject to subsections (4) and (5) below, any other arrestable offence is serious only if its commission –

(a) has led to any of the consequences specified in subsection (6) below; or
(b) is intended or is likely to lead to any of those consequences.

(4) An arrestable offence which consists of making a threat is serious if carrying out the threat would be likely to lead to any of the consequences specified in subsection (6) below.

(5) An offence under section 2, 8, 9, 10 or 11 of the Prevention of Terrorism (Temporary Provisions) Act 1989 is always a serious arrestable offence for the purposes of section 56 or 58 above, and an attempt or conspiracy to commit any such offence is also always a serious arrestable offence for those purposes.

(6) The consequences mentioned in subsections (3) and (4) above are –

(a) serious harm to the security of the State or to public order;
(b) serious interference with the administration of justice or with the investigation of offences or of a particular offence;
(c) the death of any person;
(d) serious injury to any person;
(e) substantial financial gain to any person; and
(f) serious financial loss to any person.

(7) Loss is serious for the purposes of this section if, having regard to all the circumstances, it is serious for the person who suffers it.

(8) In this section 'injury' includes any disease and any impairment of a person's physical or mental condition.

117 Power of constable to use reasonable force   [518]

Where any provision of this Act –

(a) confers a power on a constable; and
(b) does not provide that the power may only be exercised with the consent of some person, other than a police officer,

the officer may use reasonable force, if necessary, in the exercise of the power.

118 General interpretation   [519]

(1) In this Act –

'arrestable offence' has the meaning assigned to it by section 24 above;
'designated police station' has the meaning assigned to it by section 35 above;
'document' has the same meaning as in Part I of the Civil Evidence Act 1968;
'intimate search' means a search which consists of the physical examination of a person's body orifices;
'item subject to legal privilege' has the meaning assigned to it by section 10 above;
'parent or guardian' means –

(a) in the case of a child or young person in the care of a local authority, that authority;

'premises' has the meaning assigned to it by section 23 above;
'recordable offence' means any offence to which regulations under section 27 above apply;
'vessel' includes any ship, boat, raft or other apparatus constructed or adapted for floating on water.

(2) A person is in police detention for the purposes of this Act if –

(a) he has been taken to a police station after being arrested for an offence or after being arrested under section 14 of the Prevention of Terrorism (Temporary Provisions) Act 1989 or under paragraph 6 of Schedule 5 to that Act by an examining officer who is a constable; or
(b) he is arrested at a police station after attending voluntarily at the station or accompanying a constable to it,

and is detained there or is detained elsewhere in the charge of a constable, except that a person who is at a court after being charged is not in police detention for those purposes.

SCHEDULE 1

SPECIAL PROCEDURE

1. If on an application made by a constable a circuit judge is satisfied that one or other of the sets of access conditions is fulfilled, he may make an order under paragraph 4 below.

2. The first set of access conditions is fulfilled if –

(a) there are reasonable grounds for believing –

(i) that a serious arrestable offence has been committed;
(ii) that there is material which consists of special procedure material or includes special procedure material and does not also include excluded material on premises specified in the application;
(iii) that the material is likely to be of substantial value (whether by itself or together with other material) to the investigation in connection with which the application is made; and
(iv) that the material is likely to be relevant evidence;

(b) other methods of obtaining the material –

(i) have been tried without success; or
(ii) have not been tried because it appeared that they were bound to fail; and

(c) it is in the public interest, having regard –

(i) to the benefit likely to accrue to the investigation if the material is obtained; and
(ii) to the circumstances under which the person in possession of the material holds it,

that the material should be produced or that access to it should be given.

3. The second set of access conditions is fulfilled if –

(a) there are reasonable grounds for believing that there is material which consists of or includes excluded material or special procedure material on premises specified in the application;
(b) but for section 9(2) above a search of the premises for that material could have been authorised by the issue of a warrant to a constable under an enactment other than this Schedule; and
(c) the issue of such a warrant would have been appropriate.

4. An order under this paragraph is an order that the person who appears to the circuit judge to be in possession of the material to which the application relates shall –

(a) produce it to a constable for him to take away; or
(b) give a constable access to it,

not later than the end of the period of seven days from the date of the order or the end of such longer period as the order may specify.

5. Where the material consists of information contained in a computer –

(a) an order under paragraph 4(a) above shall have effect as an order to produce the material in a form in which it can be taken away and in which it is visible and legible; and
(b) an order under paragraph 4(b) above shall have effect as an order to give a constable access to the material in a form in which it is visible and legible.

6. For the purposes of sections 21 and 22 above material produced in pursuance of an order under paragraph 4(a) above shall be treated as if it were material seized by a constable ...

11. Where notice of an application for an order under paragraph 4 above has been served on a person, he shall not conceal, destroy, alter or dispose of the material to which the application relates except –

(a) with the leave of a judge; or
(b) with the written permission of a constable,

until –

(i) the application is dismissed or abandoned; or
(ii) he has complied with an order under paragraph 4 above made on the application.

12. If on an application made by a constable a circuit judge –

(a) is satisfied –

(i) that either set of access conditions is fulfilled; and
(ii) that any of the further conditions set out in paragraph 14 below is also fulfilled; or

(b) is satisfied –

(i) that the second set of access conditions is fulfilled; and
(ii) that an order under paragraph 4 above relating to the material has not been complied with,

he may issue a warrant authorising a constable to enter and search the premises.

13. A constable may seize and retain anything for which a search has been authorised under paragraph 12 above.

14. The further conditions mentioned in paragraph 12(a)(ii) above are –

(a) that it is not practicable to communicate with any person entitled to grant entry to the premises to which the application relates;
(b) that it is practicable to communicate with a person entitled to grant entry to the premises but it is not practicable to communicate with any person entitled to grant access to the material;
(c) that the material contains information which –

(i) is subject to a restriction or obligation such as is mentioned in section 11(2)(b) above; and
(ii) is likely to be disclosed in breach of it if a warrant is not issued;

(d) that service of notice of an application for an order under paragraph 4 above may seriously prejudice the investigation.

15. (1) If a person fails to comply with an order under paragraph 4 above, a circuit judge may deal with him as if he had committed a contempt of the Crown Court.

(2) Any enactment relating to contempt of the Crown Court shall have effect in relation to such a failure as if it were such a contempt.

16. The costs of any application under this Schedule and of anything done or to be done in pursuance of an order made under it shall be in the discretion of the judge.

SCHEDULE 2

PRESERVED POWERS OF ARREST

Section 17(2) of the Military Lands Act 1892.

Section 12(1) of the Protection of Animals Act 1911.

Section 2 of the Emergency Powers Act 1920.

Section 7(3) of the Public Order Act 1936.

Section 49 of the Prison Act 1952.

Section 13 of the Visiting Forces Act 1952.

Sections 186 and 190B of the Army Act 1955.

Section 186 and 190B of the Air Force Act 1955.

Sections 104 and 105 of the Naval Discipline Act 1957.

Section 1(3) of the Street Offences Act 1959.

Section 32 of the Children and Young Persons Act 1969.

Section 24(2) of the Immigration Act 1971 and paragraphs 17, 24 and 33 of Schedule 2 and paragraph 7 of Schedule 3 to that Act.

Section 7 of the Bail Act 1976.

Sections 6(6), 7(11), 8(4), 9(7) and 10(5) of the Criminal Law Act 1977.

Schedule 5 to the Reserve Forces Act 1980.

Sections 60(5) and 61(1) of the Animal Health Act 1981.

Rule 36 in Schedule 1 to the Representation of the People Act 1983.

Sections 18, 35(10), 36(8), 38(7), 136(1) and 138 of the Mental Health Act 1983.

Section 5(5) of the Repatriation of Prisoners Act 1984.

SCHEDULE 5

SERIOUS ARRESTABLE OFFENCES

PART I

OFFENCES MENTIONED IN SECTION 116(2)(a)

1. Treason.

2. Murder.

3. Manslaughter.

4. Rape.

5. Kidnapping.

6. Incest with a girl under the age of 13.

7. Buggery with a person under the age of 16.

8. Indecent assault which constitutes an act of gross indecency.

PART II

OFFENCES MENTIONED IN SECTION 116(2)(b)

Explosive Substances Act 1883 (c 3)

Section 2 (causing explosion likely to endanger life or property).

Sexual Offences Act 1956 (c 69)

Section 5 (intercourse with a girl under the age of 13).

Firearms Act 1968 (c 27)

Section 16 (possession of firearms with intent to injure).

Section 17(1) (use of firearms and imitation firearms to resist arrest).

Section 18 (carrying firearms with criminal intent).

Taking of Hostages Act 1982 (c 28)

Section 1 (hostage-taking).

Aviation Security Act 1982 (c 36)

Section 1 (hi-jacking).

Road Traffic Act 1988 (c 52)

Section 1 (causing death by dangerous driving).

Section 3A (causing death by careless driving when under the influence of drink or drugs).

Criminal Justice Act 1988 (c 33)

Section 134 (torture).

Aviation and Maritime Security Act 1990 (c 31)

Section 1 (endangering safety at aerodromes).

Section 9 (hijacking of ships).

Section 10 (seizing or exercising control of fixed platforms).

Channel Tunnel (Security) Order 1994 No 570

Article 4 (hijacking of Channel Tunnel trains).

Article 5 (seizing or exercising control of the tunnel system).

[As amended by the Sexual Offences Act 1985, s5(3), Schedule; Representation of the People Act 1985, s25(1); Public Order Act 1986, s40(2), (3), Schedule 2, para 7, Schedule 3; Drug Trafficking Offences Act 1986, ss32(1), (3), 36; Criminal Justice Act 1988, ss99(1), (2), 140(1), 147, 148, 170, Schedule 15, paras 97, 98, 99, 100, 102, Schedule 16; Road Traffic (Consequential Provisions) Act 1988, ss3, 4, Schedules 1, 3, para 27(1), (3), (4), (5); Children Act 1989, s108(5), (7), Schedule 13, paras 53, 54, 55, Schedule 15; Official Secrets Act 1989, s11(1); Prevention of Terrorism (Temporary Provisions) Act 1989, s25(1), Schedule 8, para 6(1), (2), (3), (4), (5), (6), (7), (8); Aviation and Maritime Security Act 1990, s53(1), Schedule 3, para 8; Football (Offences) Act 1991, s5(1); Criminal Justice Act 1991, s59; Road Traffic Act 1991, s48, Schedule 4, para 39; Channel Tunnel (Security) Order 1994, art 38, Schedule 3, para 4; Criminal Justice and Public Order Act 1994, s166(4), 167(7), Schedule 10, para 59.]

PROSECUTION OF OFFENCES ACT 1985
(1985 c 23)

1 The Crown Prosecution Service [520]

(1) There shall be a prosecuting service for England and Wales (to be known as the 'Crown Prosecution Service'), consisting of –

(a) the Director of Public Prosecutions, who shall be head of the Service;

(b) the Chief Crown Prosecutors, designated under subsection (4) below, each of whom shall be the member of the Service responsible to the Director for supervising the operation of the Service in his area; and

(c) the other staff appointed by the Director under this section.

(2) The director shall appoint such staff for the Service as, with the approval of the Treasury as to numbers, remuneration and other terms and conditions of service, he considers necessary for the discharge of his functions.

(3) The Director may designate any member of the Service who has a general qualification (within the meaning of section 71 of the Courts and Legal Services Act 1990) for the purposes of this subsection, and any person so designated shall be known as a Crown Prosecutor.

(4) The Director shall divide England and Wales into areas and, for each of those areas, designate a Crown Prosecutor for the purposes of this subsection and any person so designated shall be known as a Chief Crown Prosecutor.

(5) The Director may, from time to time, vary the division of England and Wales made for the purposes of subsection (4) above.

(6) Without prejudice to any functions which may have been assigned to him in his capacity as a member of the Service, every Crown Prosecutor shall have all the

powers of the Director as to the institution and conduct of proceedings but shall exercise those powers under the direction of the Director.

(7) Where any enactment (whenever passed) –

(a) prevents any step from being taken without the consent of the Director or without his consent or the consent of another; or

(b) requires any step to be taken by or in relation to the Director;

any consent given by or, as the case may be, step taken by or in relation to, a Crown Prosecutor shall be treated, for the purposes of that enactment, as given by or, as the case may be, taken by or in relation to the Director.

2 The Director of Public Prosecutions   [521]

(1) The Director of Public Prosecutions shall be appointed by the Attorney General.

(2) The Director must be a person who has a ten year general qualification, within the meaning of section 71 of the Courts and Legal Services Act 1990.

(3) There shall be paid to the Director such remuneration as the Attorney General may, with the approval of the Treasury, determine.

3 Functions of the Director   [522]

(1) The Director shall discharge his functions under this or any other enactment under the superintendence of the Attorney General.

(2) It shall be the duty of the Director, subject to any provisions contained in the Criminal Justice Act 1987 –

(a) to take over the conduct of all criminal proceedings, other than specified proceedings, instituted on behalf of a police force (whether by a member of that force or by any other person);

(b) to institute and have the conduct of criminal proceedings in any case where it appears to him that –

(i) the importance or difficulty of the case makes it appropriate that proceedings should be instituted by him; or

(ii) it is otherwise appropriate for proceedings to be instituted by him;

(c) to take over the conduct of all binding over proceedings instituted on behalf of a police force (whether by a member of that force or by any other person);

(d) to take over the conduct of all proceedings begun by summons issued under section 3 of the Obscene Publications Act 1959 (forfeiture of obscene articles);

(e) to give, to such extent as he considers appropriate, advice to police forces on all matters relating to criminal offences;

(f) to appear for the prosecution, when directed by the court to do so, on any appeal under –

(i) section 1 of the Administration of Justice Act 1960 (appeal from the High Court in criminal cases);

(ii) Part I or Part II of the Criminal Appeal Act 1968 (appeals from the Crown Court to the criminal division of the Court of Appeal and thence to the House of Lords); or

(iii) section 108 of the Magistrates' Courts Act 1980 (right of appeal to Crown Court) as it applies, by virtue of subsection (5) of section 12 of the Contempt of Court Act 1981, to orders made under section 12 (contempt of magistrates' courts); and

(g) to discharge such other functions as may from time to time be assigned to him by the Attorney General in pursuance of this paragraph.

(3) In this section –

'the court' means –

(a) in the case of an appeal to or from the criminal division of the Court of Appeal, that division;

(b) in the case of an appeal from a Divisional Court of the Queen's Bench Division, the Divisional Court; and

(c) in the case of an appeal against an order of a magistrates' court, the Crown Court.

'police force' means any police force maintained by a police authority under the Police Act 1964 and any other body of constables for the time being specified by order made by the Secretary of State for the purposes of this section; and

'specified proceedings' means proceedings which fall within any category for the time being specified by order made by the Attorney General for the purposes of this section.

4 Crown Prosecutors [523]

(1) Crown Prosecutors shall continue to have the same rights of audience, in any court, as they had immediately before the coming into force of the Courts and Legal Services Act 1990.

(2) Subsection (1) is not to be taken as preventing those rights being varied or added to in accordance with the provisions of that Act.

(3) The Lord Chancellor may at any time direct, as respects one or more specified places where the Crown Court sits, that Crown Prosecutors, or such category of Crown Prosecutors as may be specified in the direction, may have rights of audience in the Crown Court.

(3A) Any such direction may be limited to apply only in relation to proceedings of a description specified in the direction.

(3B) In considering whether to exercise his powers under this section the Lord Chancellor shall have regard, in particular, to the need to secure the availability of persons with rights of audience in the court or proceedings in question.

(3C) Any direction under this section may be revoked by direction of the Lord Chancellor.

(3D) Any direction under this section may be subject to such conditions and restrictions as appear to the Lord Chancellor to be necessary or expedient.

(3E) Any exercise by the Lord Chancellor of his powers to give a direction under this section shall be with the concurrence of the Lord Chief Justice, the Master of the Rolls, the President of the Family Division and the Vice-Chancellor.

5 Conduct of prosecutions on behalf of the Service [524]

(1) The Director may at any time appoint a person who is not a Crown Prosecutor but who has a general qualification (within the meaning of section 71 of the Courts and Legal Services Act 1990) to institute or take over the conduct of such criminal proceedings as the Director may assign to him.

(2) Any person conducting proceedings assigned to him under this section shall have all the powers of a Crown Prosecutor but shall exercise those powers subject to any instructions given to him by a Crown Prosecutor.

6 Prosecutions instituted and conducted otherwise [525]
than by the Service

(1) Subject to subsection (2) below, nothing in this Part shall preclude any person from instituting any criminal proceedings or conducting any criminal proceedings to which the Director's duty to take over the conduct of proceedings does not apply.

(2) Where criminal proceedings are instituted in circumstances in which the Director is not under a duty to take over their conduct, he may nevertheless do so at any stage.

[As amended by the Criminal Justice Act 1987, s15, Schedule 2, para 13; Courts and Legal Services Act 1990, ss71(2), 125(3), Schedule 10, paras 60, 61(1), (2), Schedule 18, para 51.]

CORONERS ACT 1988
(1988 c 13)

2 Qualifications for appointment as coroner [526]

(1) No person shall be qualified to be appointed as coroner unless –

(a) he has a five year general qualification, within the meaning of section 71 of the Courts and Legal Services Act 1990; or
(b) he is a legally qualified medical practitioner of not less than five years' standing.

(2) A person shall, so long as he is a councillor of a metropolitan district or London borough, and for six months after he ceases to be one, be disqualified for being a coroner for a coroner's district which consists of, includes or is included in that metropolitan district or London borough.

(3) A person shall, so long as he is an alderman or a councillor of a non-metropolitan county, and for six months after he ceases to be one, be disqualified for being a coroner for that county.

(4) A person shall, so long as he is an alderman of the City or a common councillor, and for six months after he ceases to be one, be disqualified for being a coroner for the City.

8 Duty to hold inquest [527]

(1) Where a coroner is informed that the body of a person ('the deceased') is lying within his district and there is reasonable cause to suspect that the deceased –

(a) has died a violent or an unnatural death;
(b) has died a sudden death of which the cause is unknown; or
(c) has died in prison or in such a place or in such circumstances as to require an inquest under any other Act,

then, whether the cause of death arose within his district or not, the coroner shall as soon as practicable hold an inquest into the death of the deceased either with or, subject to subsection (3) below, without a jury.

(2) In the case of an inquest with a jury –

(a) the coroner shall summon by warrant not less than seven nor more than 11 persons to appear before him at a specified time and place, there to inquire as jurors into the death of the deceased; and
(b) when not less than seven jurors are assembled, they shall be sworn by or

before the coroner diligently to inquire into the death of the deceased and to give a true verdict according to the evidence.

(3) If it appears to a coroner, either before he proceeds to hold an inquest or in the course of an inquest begun without a jury, that there is reason to suspect –

(a) that the death occurred in prison or in such a place or in such circumstances as to require an inquest under any other Act;

(b) that the death occurred while the deceased was in police custody, or resulted from an injury caused by a police officer in the purported execution of his duty;

(c) that the death was caused by an accident, poisoning or disease notice of which is required to be given under any Act to a government department, to any inspector or other officer of a government department or to an inspector appointed under section 19 of the Health and Safety at Work, etc Act 1974; or

(d) that the death occurred in circumstances the continuance or possible recurrence of which is prejudicial to the health or safety of the public or any section of the public,

he shall proceed to summon a jury in the manner required by subsection (2) above.

(4) If it appears to a coroner, either before he proceeds to hold an inquest or in the course of an inquest begun without a jury, that there is any reason for summoning a jury, he may proceed to summon a jury in the manner required by subsection (2) above.

(5) In the case of an inquest or any part of an inquest held without a jury, anything done by or before the coroner alone shall be as validly done as if it had been done by or before the coroner and a jury.

(6) Where an inquest is held into the death of a prisoner who dies within a prison, neither a prisoner in the prison nor any person engaged in any sort of trade or dealing with the prison shall serve as a juror at the inquest.

9 Qualifications of jurors [528]

(1) A person shall not be qualified to serve as a juror at an inquest held by a coroner unless he is for the time being qualified to serve as a juror in the Crown Court, the High Court and county courts in accordance with section 1 of the Juries Act 1974 ...

12 Failure of jury to agree [529]

(1) This section applies where, in the case of an inquest held with a jury, the jury fails to agree on a verdict.

(2) If the minority consists of not more than two, the coroner may accept the verdict of the majority ...

(3) In any other case of disagreement the coroner may discharge the jury and issue a warrant for summoning another jury and, in that case, the inquest shall proceed in all respects as if the proceedings which terminated in the disagreement had not taken place.

30 Treasure trove [530]

A coroner shall continue to have jurisdiction –

(a) to inquire into any treasure which is found in his district; and

(b) to inquire who were, or are suspected of being, the finders;

and the provisions of this Act shall, so far as applicable, apply to every such inquest.

[As amended by the Courts and Legal Services Act 1990, ss71(2), 125(7), Schedule 10, para 70, Schedule 20.]

LEGAL AID ACT 1988
(1988 c 34)

PART I

PRELIMINARY

1 Purpose of this Act [531]

The purpose of this Act is to establish a framework for the provision under Parts II, III, IV, V and VI of advice, assistance and representation which is publicly funded with a view to helping persons who might otherwise be unable to obtain advice, assistance or representation on account of their means.

2 Interpretation [532]

(1) This section has effect for the interpretation of this Act.

(2) 'Advice' means oral or written advice on the application of English law to any particular circumstances that have arisen in relation to the person seeking advice and as to the steps which that person might appropriately take having regard to the application of English law to those circumstances.

(3) 'Assistance' means assistance in taking any of the steps which a person might take, including steps with respect to proceedings, having regard to the application of English law to any particular circumstances that have arisen in relation to him, whether by taking such steps on his behalf (including assistance by way of representation) or by assisting him in taking them on his own behalf.

(4) 'Representation' means representation for the purposes of proceeding and it includes –

(a) all such assistance as is usually given by a legal representative in the steps preliminary or incidental to any proceedings;
(b) all such assistance as is usually so given in civil proceedings in arriving at or giving effect to a compromise to avoid or bring to an end any proceedings; and
(c) in the case of criminal proceedings, advice and assistance to any appeal;

and related expressions have corresponding meanings.

(5) Regulations may specify what is, or is not, to be included in advice or assistance of any description, or representation for the purposes of proceedings of any description, to which any Part or provision of a Part of this Act applies and the regulations may provide for the inclusion, in prescribed circumstances, of advice or assistance given otherwise than under this Act.

(6) Advice, assistance and representation under this Act, except when made available under Part II, shall only be by legal representatives, but in the case of Part II, may be by other persons.

(7) Subject to section 59 of the Courts and Legal Services Act 1990, regulations –

(a) may prescribe the circumstances in which representation shall be only by one legal representative and may require him to be from a prescribed category;

(b) may regulate representation by more than one legal representative from any one or more prescribed categories.

(7A) If it is satisfied that the circumstances of a particular case in the Supreme Court or the House of Lords warrant a direction under this subsection, the Board or, in the case of criminal proceedings the competent authority, may direct that representation in that case shall be by one legal representative.

(7B) In subsection (7A), 'competent authority' shall be construed in accordance with section 20 ...

(10) In this Act 'person' does not include a body of persons corporate or unincorporate which is not concerned in a representative, fiduciary or official capacity so as to authorise advice, assistance or representation to be granted to such a body.

(11) In this Act 'legally assisted person' means any person who receives, under this Act, advice, assistance or representation and, in relation to proceedings, any reference to an assisted party or an unassisted party is to be construed accordingly.

PART II

LEGAL AID BOARD AND LEGAL AID

3 The Legal Aid Board   [533]

(1) There shall be established a body to be known as the Legal Aid Board (in this Act referred to as 'the Board').

(2) Subject to subsections (3) and (4) below, the Board shall have the general function of securing that advice, assistance and representation are available in accordance with this Act and of administering this Act.

(3) Subsection (2) above does not confer on the Board any functions with respect to the grant of representation under Part VI for the purposes of proceedings for contempt.

(4) Subsection (2) above does not confer on the Board any of the following functions unless the Lord Chancellor so directs by order and then only to the extent specified in the order.

The functions referred to are –

(a) determination of the costs of representation under Part IV;

(b) functions as respects representation under Part V other than determination of the costs of representation for the purposes of proceedings in magistrates' courts;

(d) determination of the financial resources of persons for the purposes of this Act.

(5) Subject to subsection (6) below, the Board shall consist of no fewer than 11 and no more than 17 members appointed by the Lord Chancellor; and the Lord Chancellor shall appoint one of the members to be chairman.

(6) The Lord Chancellor may, by order, substitute, for the number for the time being specified in subsection (5) above as the maximum or minimum membership of the Board, such other number as he thinks appropriate.

(7) The Board shall include at least two solicitors appointed after consultation with the Law Society.

(8) The Lord Chancellor shall consult the General Council of the Bar with a view to the inclusion on the Board of at least two barristers.

(9) In appointing persons to be members of the Board the Lord Chancellor shall have regard to the desirability of securing that the Board includes persons having expertise in or knowledge of –

(a) the provision of legal services;
(b) the work of the courts and social conditions; and
(c) management.

(10) Schedule 1 to this Act shall have effect with respect to the Board.

5 Duties of the Board [534]

(1) The Board shall, from time to time, publish information as to the discharge of its functions in relation to advice, assistance and representation including the forms and procedures and other matters connected therewith.

(2) The Board shall, from time to time, furnish to the Lord Chancellor such information as he may require relating to its property and to the discharge or proposed discharge of its functions.

(3) It shall be the duty of the Board to provide to the Lord Chancellor, as soon as possible after 31 March in each year, a report on the discharge of its functions during the preceding 12 months.

(4) The Board shall deal in any report under subsection (3) above with such matters as the Lord Chancellor may from time to time direct.

(5) The Board shall have regard, in discharging its functions, to such guidance as may from time to time be given by the Lord Chancellor.

(6) Guidance under subsection (5) above shall not relate to the consideration or disposal, in particular cases, of –

(a) applications for advice, assistance or representation;
(b) supplementary or incidental applications or requests to the Board in connection with any case where advice, assistance or representation has been made available

(7) For the purposes of subsection (2) above the Board shall permit any person authorised by the Lord Chancellor for the purpose to inspect and make copies of any accounts or documents of the Board and shall furnish such explanations of them as that person or the Lord Chancellor may require.

6 Board to have separate legal aid fund [535]

(1) The Board shall establish and maintain a separate legal aid fund.

(2) Subject to regulations, there shall be paid out of the fund –

(a) such sums as are, by virtue of any provision of or made under this Act, due from the Board in respect of remuneration and expenses properly incurred in connection with the provision, under this Act, of advice, assistance or representation;
(b) costs awarded to any unassisted party under section 13 or 18;
(c) any part of a contribution repayable by the Board under section 16(4) or 23(7); and
(d) such other payments for the purposes of this Act as the Lord Chancellor may, with the concurrence of the Treasury, determine.

(3) Subject to regulations, there shall be paid into the fund –

(a) any contribution payable to the Board by any person in respect of advice, assistance or representation under this Act;

(b) any sum awarded under an order of a court or agreement as to costs in any proceedings in favour of any legally assisted party which is payable to the Board;

(c) any sum which is to be paid out of property recovered or preserved for any legally assisted party to any proceedings;

(d) any sum in respect of the costs of an unassisted party awarded under section 13 or 18 which is repaid to the Board under that section;

(e) the sums to be paid by the Lord Chancellor in pursuance of section 42(1)(a); and

(f) such other receipts of the Board as the Lord Chancellor may, with the concurrence of the Treasury, determine.

PART III

ADVICE AND ASSISTANCE

8 Scope of this Part [536]

(1) Subject to the provisions of this section, this Part applies to any advice or assistance and advice and assistance under this Part shall be available to any person subject to and in accordance with the provisions of this section and sections 9, 10 and 11.

(2) This Part only applies to assistance by way of representation if, and to the extent that, regulations so provide; and regulations may make such provision in relation to representation for the purposes of any proceedings before a court or tribunal or at a statutory inquiry.

(3) Advice or assistance of all descriptions or advice or assistance of any prescribed description is excluded from this Part, or is so excluded as regards any area, if regulations so provide; and if regulations provide for all descriptions to be excluded as regards all areas then, so long as the regulations so provide, this Part (other than this subsection) shall not have effect.

(4) Advice or assistance of any prescribed description is restricted to its provision to prescribed descriptions or persons if regulations so provide.

(5) This Part does not apply to advice or assistance given to a person in connection with proceedings before a court or tribunal or at a statutory inquiry at a time when he is being represented in those proceedings under any other Part of this Act.

PART IV

CIVIL LEGAL AID

14 Scope of this Part [537]

(1) This Part applies to such proceedings before courts or tribunals or at statutory inquiries in England and Wales as –

(a) are proceedings of a description for the time being specified in Part I of Schedule 2 to this Act, except proceedings for the time being specified in Part II of that Schedule, and

(b) are not proceedings for which representation may be granted under Part V,

and representation under this Part shall be available to any person subject to and in accordance with sections 15 and 16.

(2) Subject to subsection (3) below, Schedule 2 may be varied by regulations so as to extend or restrict the categories of proceedings for the purposes of which representation is available under this Part, by reference to the court, tribunal or statutory inquiry, to the issues involved, to the capacity in which the person seeking representation is concerned or otherwise.

(3) Regulations under subsection (2) above may not have the effect of adding any proceedings before any court or tribunal or at any statutory inquiry before or at which persons have no right, and are not normally allowed, to be represented by a legal representative.

(4) Regulations under subsection (2) above which extend the categories of proceedings for the purposes of which representation is available under this Part shall not be made without the consent of the Treasury.

16 Reimbursement of Board by contributions and [538] out of costs or property recovered

(1) A legally assisted person shall, if his financial resources are such as, under regulations, make him liable to make such a contribution, pay to the Board a contribution in respect of the costs of his being represented under this Part.

(2) The contribution to be required of him by the Board shall be determined by the Board in accordance with the regulations and may take the form of periodical payments or one or more capital sums or both.

(3) The contribution required of a person may, in the case of periodical payments, be made payable by reference to the period during which he is represented under this Part or any shorter period and, in the case of a capital sum, be made payable by instalments.

(4) If the total contribution made by a person in respect of any proceedings exceeds the net liability of the Board on his account, the excess shall be repaid by him.

(5) Any sums recovered by virtue of an order or agreement for costs made in favour of a legally assisted person with respect to the proceedings shall be paid to the Board.

(6) Except so far as regulations otherwise provide –

(a) any sums remaining unpaid on account of a person's contribution in respect of the sums payable by the Board in respect of any proceedings, and
(b) a sum equal to any deficiency by reason of his total contribution being less than the net liability of the Board on his account,

shall be a first charge for the benefit of the Board on any property which is recovered or preserved for him in the proceedings.

(7) For the purposes of subsection (6) above it is immaterial what the nature of the property is and where it is situated and the property within the charge includes the rights of a person under any compromise or settlement arrived at to avoid the proceedings or bring them to an end and any sums recovered by virtue of an order for costs made in his favour in the proceedings (not being sums payable to the Board under subsection (5) above).

(8) The charge created by subsection (6) above on any damages or costs shall not prevent a court allowing them to be set off against other damages or costs in any case where a legal representative's lien for costs would not prevent it.

(9) In this section references to the net liability of the Board on a legally assisted person's account in relation to any proceedings are references to the aggregate amount of –

(a) the sums paid or payable to the Board on his account in respect of those proceedings to any legal representative, and

(b) any sums so paid or payable for any advice or assistance under Part III in connection with those proceedings or any matter to which those proceedings relate,

being sums not recouped by the Board by sums which are recoverable by virtue of an order or agreement for costs made in his favour with respect to those proceedings or by virtue of any right of his to be indemnified against expenses incurred by him in connection with those proceedings.

(10) Where a legally assisted person has been represented in any proceedings in pursuance of a contract made with the Board on terms which do not differentiate between the remuneration for his and other cases, the reference in subsection (9)(a) above to the sums paid or payable by the Board on his account in respect of the proceedings shall be construed as a reference to such part of the remuneration payable under the contract as may be specified in writing by the Board.

PART V

CRIMINAL LEGAL AID

19 Scope of this Part   [539]

(1) This Part applies to criminal proceedings before any of the following –

(a) a magistrates' court;

(b) the Crown Court;

(c) the criminal division of the Court of Appeal or the Courts-Martial Appeal Court; and

(d) the House of Lords in the exercise of its jurisdiction in relation to appeals from either of those courts;

and representation under this Part shall be available to any person subject to and in accordance with sections 21, 22, 23, 24 and 25.

(2) Representation under this Part for the purposes of the proceedings before any court extends to any proceedings preliminary or incidental to the proceedings including bail proceedings, whether before that or another court.

(3) Representation under this Part for the purposes of the proceedings before a magistrates' court extends to any proceedings before a youth court or other magistrates'. court to which the case is remitted.

(4) In subsection (2) above in its application to bail proceedings, 'court' has the same meaning as in the Bail Act 1976, but that subsection does not extend representation to bail proceedings before a judge of the High Court exercising the jurisdiction of that Court.

(5) In this Part –

'competent authority' is to be construed in accordance with section 20;

'Court of Appeal' means the criminal division of that Court;

'criminal proceedings' includes proceedings for dealing with an offender for an offence or in respect of a sentence or as a fugitive offender and also includes proceedings instituted under section 115 of the Magistrates' Courts Act 1980 (binding over) in respect of an actual or apprehended breach of the peace or other misbehaviour and proceedings for dealing with a person for a failure to comply with a condition of a recognizance to keep the peace or be of good behaviour and also includes proceedings under section 15 of the Children and Young Persons Act 1969 (variation and discharge of supervision orders) and section 16(8) of that Act (appeals in such proceedings);

'proceedings for dealing with an offender as a fugitive offender' means proceedings before a metropolitan stipendiary magistrate under section 9 of the Extradition Act 1870, section 7 of the Fugitive Offenders Act 1967 or section 6 of the Criminal Justice Act 1988; and

'remitted', in relation to a youth court, means remitted under section 56(1) of the Children and Young Persons Act 1933;

and any reference, in relation to representation for the purposes of any proceedings, to the proceedings before a court includes a reference to any proceedings to which representation under this Part extends by virtue of subsection (2) or (3) above.

PART VII

GENERAL AND SUPPLEMENTARY

31 Act not generally to affect position of legal [540]
representatives or other parties

(1) Except as expressly provided by this Act or regulations under it –

(a) the fact that the services of counsel or a solicitor are given under this Act shall not affect the relationship between or rights of the legal representative and client or any privilege arising out of such relationship; and

(b) the rights conferred by this Act on a person receiving advice, assistance or representation under it shall not affect the rights or liabilities of other parties to the proceedings or the principles on which the discretion of any court or tribunal is normally exercised.

(2) Without prejudice to the generality of subsection (1)(b) above, for the purpose of determining the costs of a legally assisted person in pursuance of an order for costs or an agreement for costs in his favour (other than an order under Part II of the Prosecution of Offences Act 1985) the services of his solicitor and counsel shall be treated as having been provided otherwise than under this Act and his legal representative shall be treated as having paid the fees of any additional legal representative instructed by him.

(3) A person who provides advice, assistance or representation under this Act shall not take any payment in respect of the advice, assistance or representation except such payment as is made by the Board or authorised by, or by regulations under, this Act.

(4) The revocation under this Act of a grant (or, in the case of Part III, of approval for a grant) of advice, assistance or representation to a legally assisted person shall not affect the rights of any legal representative of his, arising otherwise than under a contract, to remuneration for work done before the date of the revocation.

32 Selection and assignment of legal representatives [541]

(1) Subject to the provisions of this section, a person entitled to receive advice or assistance or representation may select the legal representative to advise, assist or act for him from among the legal representatives willing to provide advice, assistance or representation under this Act.

(2) Where the Board limits a grant of representation under Part IV to representation in pursuance of a contract made by the Board, it may, as it thinks fit, assign to the legally assisted person one or more legal representatives or direct

that he may only select a legal representative from among those with whom such a contract subsists.

(3) A person's right to select his legal representative is subject, in the case of representation under Part V, to regulations under subsection (8) below ...

(6) The selection by or assignment to a person of a legal representative shall not prejudice the law and practice relating to the conduct of proceedings by a legal representative or the circumstances in which a legal representative may refuse or give up a case or entrust it to another ...

(9) None of the following persons may be selected or assigned under this section –

(a) a solicitor who is for the time being excluded from legal aid work under section 47(2) of the Solicitors Act 1974 (powers of Solicitors Disciplinary Tribunal);

(b) a barrister excluded from such work under section 42 of the Administration of Justice Act 1985 (exclusion of barristers from legal aid work);

(c) any other legal representative excluded from such work for disciplinary reasons by an authorised body.

(10) Notwithstanding subsection (1) above, a legal representative who has been selected to act for a person under that subsection may himself select to act for that person, as a legal representative's agent, any other legal representative who is not for the time being excluded from selection.

SCHEDULE 2

CIVIL PROCEEDINGS: SCOPE OF PART IV REPRESENTATION

PART I

DESCRIPTION OF PROCEEDINGS

1.Proceedings in, or before any person to whom a case is referred in whole or in part by, any of the following courts, namely –

(a) the House of Lords in the exercise of its jurisdiction in relation to appeals from courts in England and Wales;

(b) the Court of Appeal;

(c) the High Court;

(d) any county court.

2. The following proceedings in a magistrates' court, namely –

(b) proceedings under section 43 of the National Assistance Act 1948, section 22 of the Maintenance Orders Act 1950, section 4 of the Maintenance Orders Act 1958, or section 18 of the Supplementary Benefits Act 1976;

(c) proceedings in relation to an application for leave of the court to remove a child from a person's custody under section 27 or 28 of the Adoption Act 1976 or proceedings in which the making of an order under Part II or section 29 or 55 of the Adoption Act 1976 is opposed by any party to the proceedings;

(d) proceedings under Part I of the Maintenance Orders (Reciprocal Enforcement) Act 1972 relating to a maintenance order made by a court of a country outside the United Kingdom;

(f) proceedings for or in relation to an order under Part I of the Domestic Proceedings and Magistrates' Courts Act 1978.

(g) proceedings under the Children Act 1989;

(h) appeals under section 20, where they are to be made to a magistrates' court, and proceedings under section 27 of the Child Support Act 1991.

3. Proceedings in the Employment Appeal Tribunal.

4. Proceedings in the Lands Tribunal.

5. Proceedings before a Commons Commissioner appointed under section 17(1) of the Commons Registration Act 1965.

6. Proceedings in the Restrictive Practices Court under Part III of the Fair Trading Act 1973, and any proceedings in that court in consequence of an order made, or undertaking given to the court, under that Part of the Act.

PART II

EXCEPTED PROCEEDINGS

1. Proceedings wholly or partly in respect of defamation, but so that the making of a counterclaim for defamation in proceedings for which representations may be granted shall not of itself affect any right of the defendant to the counterclaim to representation for the purposes of the proceedings and so that representation may be granted to enable him to defend the counterclaim.

2. Relator actions.

3. Proceedings for the recovery of a penalty where the proceedings may be taken by any person and the whole or part of the penalty is payable to the person taking the proceedings.

4. Election petitions under the Representation of the People Act 1983.

5. In a county court, proceedings for or consequent on the issue of a judgment summons and, in the case of a defendant, proceedings where the only question to be brought before the court is as to the time and mode of payment by him of a debt (including liquidated damages) and costs.

5A. Proceedings for a decree of divorce or judicial separation unless the cause is defended, or the petition is directed to be heard in open court, or it is not practicable by reason of physical or mental incapacity for the applicant to proceed without representation; except that representation shall be available for the purpose of making or opposing an application –

(a) for an injunction;
(b) for ancillary relief, excluding representation for the purpose only of inserting a prayer for ancillary relief in the petition;
(c) for an order relating to the custody of (or access to) a child, or the education or care or supervision of a child, excluding representation for the purpose only of making such an application where there is no reason to believe that the application will be opposed; or
(e) for the purpose of making or opposing any other application, or satisfying the courts on any other matter which raises a substantial question for determination by the court.

5B. Proceedings to the extent that they consist in, or arise out of, an application to the court under section 235A of the Trade Union and Labour Relations (Consolidation) Act 1992.

6. Proceedings incidental to any proceedings excepted by this Part of this Schedule.

[As amended by the Children Act 1989, ss99(3), 108(4), (7), Schedule 12, para 45, Schedule 15; Courts and Legal Services Act 1990, s125(3), Schedule 18, paras 59,

61, 62, 63(1)(a), (b), (2), (3)(a), (4); Criminal Justice Act 1991, s100, Schedule 11, para 40(1); Civil Legal Aid (Scope) Regulations 1993; Trade Union Reform and Employment Rights Act 1993, s49(2), Schedule 8, para 39.]

COURTS AND LEGAL SERVICES ACT 1990
(1990 c 41)

PART I

PROCEDURE, ETC IN CIVIL COURTS

1 Allocation of business between High Court   [542]
and county courts

(1) The Lord Chancellor may by order make provision –

(a) conferring jurisdiction on the High Court in relation to proceedings in which county courts have jurisdiction;
(b) conferring jurisdiction on county courts in relation to proceedings in which the High Court has jurisdiction;
(c) allocating proceedings to the High Court or to county courts;
(d) specifying proceedings which may be commenced only in the High Court;
(e) specifying proceedings which may be commenced only in a county court;
(f) specifying proceedings which may be taken only in the High Court;
(g) specifying proceedings which may be taken only in a county court.

(2) Without prejudice to the generality of section 120(2), any such order may differentiate between categories of proceedings by reference to such criteria as the Lord Chancellor sees fit to specify in the order.

(3) The criteria so specified may, in particular, relate to –

(a) the value of an action (as defined by the order);
(b) the nature of the proceedings;
(c) the parties to the proceedings;
(d) the degree of complexity likely to be involved in any aspect of the proceedings; and
(e) the importance of any question likely to be raised by, or in the course of, the proceedings.

(4) An order under subsection (1)(b), (e) or (g) may specify one or more particular county courts in relation to the proceedings so specified.

(5) Any jurisdiction exercisable by a county court, under any provision made by virtue of subsection (4), shall be exercisable throughout England and Wales.

(6) Rules of court may provide for a matter –

(a) which is pending in one county court; and
(b) over which that court has jurisdiction under any provision made by virtue of subsection (4),

to be heard and determined wholly or partly in another county court which also has jurisdiction in that matter under any such provision.

(7) Any such order may –

(a) amend or repeal any provision falling within subsection (8) and relating to –

(i) the jurisdiction, practice or procedure of the Supreme Court; or
(ii) the jurisdiction, practice or procedure of any county court,

so far as the Lord Chancellor considers it to be necessary, or expedient, in consequence of any provision made by the order; or

(b) make such incidental or transitional provision as the Lord Chancellor considers necessary, or expedient, in consequence of any provision made by the order.

(8) A provision falls within this subsection if it is made by any enactment other than this Act or made under any enactment.

(9) Before making any such order the Lord Chancellor shall consult the Lord Chief Justice, the Master of the Rolls, the President of the Family Division, the Vice-Chancellor and the Senior Presiding Judge (appointed under section 72).

(10) No such order shall be made so as to confer jurisdiction on any county court to hear any application for judicial review.

(11) For the purposes of this section the commencement of proceedings may include the making of any application in anticipation of any proceedings or in the course of any proceedings.

(12) The Lord Chancellor shall, within one year of the coming into force of the first order made under this section, and annually thereafter, prepare and lay before both Houses of Parliament a report as to the business of the Supreme Court and county courts.

8 Powers of Court of Appeal to award damages   [543]

(1) In this section 'case' means any case where the Court of Appeal has power to order a new trial on the ground that damages awarded by a jury are excessive or inadequate.

(2) Rules of court may provide for the Court of Appeal, in such classes of case as may be specified in the rules, to have power, in place of ordering a new trial, to substitute for the sum awarded by the jury such sum as appears to the court to be proper.

(3) This section is not to be read as prejudicing in any way any other power to make rules of court.

9 Allocation of family proceedings which are within the   [544]
jurisdiction of county courts

(1) The Lord Chancellor may, with the concurrence of the President of the Family Division, give directions that, in such circumstances as may be specified –

(a) any family proceedings which are within the jurisdiction of county courts; or

(b) any specified description of such proceedings,

shall be allocated to specified judges or to specified descriptions of judge.

(2) Any such direction shall have effect regardless of any rules of court.

(3) Where any directions have been given under this section allocating any proceedings to specified judges, the validity of anything done by a judge in, or in relation to, the proceedings shall not be called into question by reason only of the fact that he was not a specified judge.

(4) For the purposes of subsection (1) 'county court' includes the principal registry of the Family Division of the High Court in so far as it is treated as a county court.

(5) In this section –

'family proceedings' has the same meaning as in the Matrimonial and Family Proceedings Act 1984 and also includes any other proceedings which are family proceedings for the purposes of the Children Act 1989;

'judge' means any person who –

> (a) is capable of sitting as a judge for a county court district;
> (b) is a district judge, an assistant district judge or a deputy district judge; or
> (c) is a district judge of the principal registry of the Family Division of the High Court; and

'specified' means specified in the directions.

11 Representation in certain county court cases [545]

(1) The Lord Chancellor may by order provide that there shall be no restriction on the persons who may exercise rights of audience, or rights to conduct litigation, in relation to proceedings in a county court of such a kind as may be specified in the order.

(2) The power to make an order may only be exercised in relation to proceedings –

> (a) for the recovery of amounts due under contracts for the supply of goods or services;
> (b) for the enforcement of any judgment or order of any court or the recovery of any sum due under such judgment or order;
> (c) on any application under the Consumer Credit Act 1974;
> (d) in relation to domestic premises; or
> (e) referred to arbitration in accordance with county court rules made under section 64 of the County Court Act 1984 (small claims)

or any category (determined by reference to such criteria as the Lord Chancellor considers appropriate) of such proceedings.

(3) Where an order is made under this section, section 20 of the Solicitors Act 1974 (unqualified person not to act as solicitor) shall cease to apply in relation to proceedings of the kind specified in the order.

(4) Where a county court is of the opinion that a person who would otherwise have a right of audience by virtue of an order under this section is behaving in an unruly manner in any proceedings, it may refuse to hear him in those proceedings.

(5) Where a court exercises its power under subsection (4), it shall specify the conduct which warranted its refusal.

(6) Where, in any proceedings in a county court –

> (a) a person is exercising a right of audience or a right to conduct litigation;
> (b) he would not be entitled to do so were it not for an order under this section; and
> (c) the judge has reason to believe that (in those or any other proceedings in which he has exercised a right of audience or a right to conduct litigation) that person has intentionally misled the court, or otherwise demonstrated that he is unsuitable to exercise that right,

the judge may order that person's disqualification from exercising any right of audience or any right to conduct litigation in proceedings in any county court.

(7) Where a judge makes an order under subsection (6) he shall give his reasons for so doing.

(8) Any person against whom such an order is made may appeal to the Court of Appeal.

(9) Any such order may be revoked at any time by any judge of a county court.

(10) Before making any order under this section the Lord Chancellor shall consult the Senior Presiding Judge.

(11) In this section 'domestic premises' means any premises which are wholly or mainly used as a private dwelling.

PART II

LEGAL SERVICES

17 The statutory objective and the general principle [546]

(1) The general objective of this Part is the development of legal services in England and Wales (and in particular the development of advocacy, litigation, conveyancing and probate services) by making provision for new or better ways of providing such services and a wider choice of persons providing them, while maintaining the proper and efficient administration of justice.

(2) In this Act that objective is referred to as 'the statutory objective'.

(3) As a general principle the question whether a person should be granted a right of audience, or be granted a right to conduct litigation in relation to any court or proceedings, should be determined only by reference to –

(a) whether he is qualified in accordance with the educational and training requirements appropriate to the court or proceedings;
(b) whether he is a member of a professional or other body which –

(i) has rules of conduct (however described) governing the conduct of its members;
(ii) has an effective mechanism for enforcing the rules of conduct; and
(iii) is likely to enforce them;

(c) whether, in the case of a body whose members are or will be providing advocacy services, the rules of conduct make satisfactory provision in relation to the court or proceedings in question requiring any such member not to withhold those services –

(i) on the ground that the nature of the case is objectionable to him or to any section of the public;
(ii) on the ground that the conduct, opinions or beliefs of the prospective client are unacceptable to him or to any section of the public;
(iii) on any ground relating to the source of any financial support which may properly be given to the prospective client for the proceedings in question (for example, on the ground that such support will be available under the Legal Aid Act 1988); and

(d) whether the rules of conduct are, in relation to the court or proceedings, appropriate in the interest of the proper and efficient administration of justice.

(4) In this Act that principle is referred to as 'the general principle'.

(5) Rules of conduct which allow a member of the body in question to withhold his services if there are reasonable grounds for him to consider that, having regard to –

(a) the circumstances of the case;
(b) the nature of his practice; or
(c) his experience and standing,

he is not being offered a proper fee, are not on that account to be taken as being incompatible with the general principle.

18 The statutory duty [547]

(1) Where any person is called upon to exercise any functions which are conferred by this Part with respect to –

(a) the granting of rights of audience;
(b) the granting of rights to conduct litigation;
(c) the approval of qualification regulations or rules of conduct; or
(d) the giving of advice with respect to any matter mentioned in paragraphs (a) to (c),

it shall be the duty of that person to exercise those functions as soon as is reasonably practicable and consistent with the provisions of this Part.

(2) A person exercising any such functions shall act in accordance with the general principle and, subject to that, shall –

(a) so far as it is possible to do so in the circumstances of the case, act to further the statutory objective; and
(b) not act in any way which would be incompatible with the statutory objective.

19 The Lord Chancellor's Advisory Committee on Legal Education and Conduct [548]

(1) There shall be a body corporate to be known as the Lord Chancellor's Advisory Committee on Legal Education and Conduct (in this Act referred to as 'the Advisory Committee').

(2) The Advisory Committee shall consist of a Chairman, and 16 other members, appointed by the Lord Chancellor.

(3) The Chairman shall be a Lord of Appeal in Ordinary or a judge of the Supreme Court of England and Wales.

(4) Of the 16 other members of the Advisory Committee –

(a) one shall be a judge who is or has been a Circuit judge;
(b) two shall be practising barristers appointed after consultation with the General Council of the Bar;
(c) two shall be practising solicitors appointed after consultation with the Law Society;
(d) two shall be persons with experience in the teaching of law, appointed after consultation with such institutions concerned with the teaching of law and such persons representing teachers of law as the Lord Chancellor considers appropriate; and
(e) nine shall be persons other than –

(i) salaried judges of any court;
(ii) practising barristers;
(iii) practising solicitors; or
(iv) teachers of law,

appointed after consultation with such organisations as the Lord Chancellor considers appropriate.

(5) In appointing any member who falls within subsection (4)(e), the Lord Chancellor shall have regard to the desirability of appointing persons who have experience in, or knowledge of –

(a) the provision of legal services;
(b) civil or criminal proceedings and the working of the courts;
(c) the maintenance of professional standards among barristers or solicitors;
(d) social conditions;

(e) consumer affairs;

(f) commercial affairs; or

(g) the maintenance of professional standards in professions other than the legal profession.

(6) The Advisory Committee shall not be regarded as the servant or agent of the Crown, or as enjoying any status, immunity or privilege of the Crown.

(7) The Advisory Committee's property shall not be regarded as property of, or held on behalf of, the Crown.

(8) In this section 'practising' means –

(a) in relation to a barrister, one who is in independent practice or is employed wholly or mainly for the purpose of providing legal services to his employer;

(b) in relation to a solicitor, one who has a practising certificate in force or is employed wholly or mainly for the purpose of providing legal services to his employer.

(9) The provisions of Schedule 1 shall have effect with respect to the constitution, procedure and powers of the Advisory Committee and with respect to connected matters.

20 Duties of the Advisory Committee   [549]

(1) The Advisory Committee shall have the general duty of assisting in the maintenance and development of standards in the education, training and conduct of those offering legal services.

(2) The Advisory Committee shall carry out that general duty by performing the functions conferred on it by Schedule 2.

(3) In discharging its functions the Advisory Committee shall –

(a) where it considers it appropriate, have regard to the practices and procedures of other member States in relation to the provision of legal services;

(b) have regard to the desirability of equality of opportunity between persons seeking to practise any profession, pursue any career or take up any employment, in connection with the provision of legal services.

21 The Legal Services Ombudsman   [550]

(1) The Lord Chancellor shall appoint a person for the purpose of conducting investigations under this Act.

(2) The person appointed shall be known as 'the Legal Services Ombudsman'.

(3) The Legal Services Ombudsman –

(a) shall be appointed for a period of not more than three years; and

(b) shall hold and vacate office in accordance with the terms of his appointment.

(4) At the end of his term of appointment the Legal Services Ombudsman shall be eligible for re-appointment.

(5) The Legal Services Ombudsman shall not be an authorised advocate, authorised litigator, licensed conveyancer, authorised practitioner or notary.

(6) Schedule 3 shall have effect with respect to the Legal Services Ombudsman.

22 Ombudsman's functions [551]

(1) Subject to the provisions of this Act, the Legal Services Ombudsman may investigate any allegation which is properly made to him and which relates to the manner in which a complaint made to a professional body with respect to –

(a) a person who is or was an authorised advocate, authorised litigator, licensed conveyancer, registered foreign lawyer, recognised body or duly certificated notary public and a member of that professional body; or

(b) any employee of such a person,

has been dealt with by that professional body.

(2) If the Ombudsman investigates an allegation he may investigate the matter to which the complaint relates.

(3) If the Ombudsman begins to investigate an allegation he may at any time discontinue his investigation.

(4) If the Ombudsman decides not to investigate an allegation which he would be entitled to investigate, or discontinues an investigation which he has begun, he shall notify the following of the reason for his decision –

(a) the person making the allegation;

(b) any person with respect to whom the complaint was made; and

(c) the professional body concerned.

(5) The Ombudsman shall not investigate an allegation while –

(a) the complaint is being investigated by the professional body concerned;

(b) an appeal is pending against the determination of the complaint by that body; or

(c) the time within which such an appeal may be brought by any person has not expired.

(6) Subsection (5) does not apply if –

(a) the allegation is that the professional body –

(i) has acted unreasonably in failing to start an investigation into the complaint; or

(ii) having started such an investigation, has failed to complete it within a reasonable time; or

(b) the Ombudsman is satisfied that, even though the complaint is being investigated by the professional body concerned, an investigation by him is justified.

(7) The Ombudsman shall not investigate –

(a) any issue which is being or has been determined by –

(i) a court;

(ii) the Solicitors Disciplinary Tribunal;

(iii) the Disciplinary Tribunal of the Council of the Inns of Court; or

(iv) any tribunal specified in an order made by the Lord Chancellor for the purposes of this subsection; or

(b) any allegation relating to a complaint against any person which concerns an aspect of his conduct in relation to which he has immunity from any action in negligence or contract.

(8) The Ombudsman may –

(a) if so requested by the Scottish ombudsman, investigate an allegation relating to a complaint made to a professional body in Scotland; and

(b) arrange for the Scottish ombudsman to investigate an allegation relating to a complaint made to a professional body in England and Wales.

271

(9) For the purposes of this section, an allegation is properly made if it is made –

(a) in writing; and

(b) by any person affected by what is alleged in relation to the complaint concerned or, where that person has died or is unable to act for himself, by his personal representative or by any relative or other representative of his.

(10) The Ombudsman may investigate an allegation even though –

(a) the complaint relates to a matter which arose before the passing of this Act; or

(b) the person making the complaint may be entitled to bring proceedings in any court with respect to the matter complained of.

(11) In this section –

'professional body' means any body which, or the holder of any office who –

(a) has disciplinary powers in relation to any person mentioned in subsection (1)(a); and

(b) is specified in an order made by the Lord Chancellor for the purposes of this subsection;

'recognised body' means any body recognised under section 9 of the Administration of Justice Act 1985 (incorporated practices) or under section 32 of that Act (incorporated bodies carrying on business of provision of conveyancing services); and

'the Scottish ombudsman' means any person appointed to carry out functions in relation to the provision of legal services in Scotland which are similar to those of the Ombudsman.

23 Recommendations [552]

(1) Where the Legal Services Ombudsman has completed an investigation under this Act he shall send a written report of his conclusions to –

(a) the person making the allegation;

(b) the person with respect to whom the complaint was made;

(c) any other person with respect to whom the Ombudsman makes a recommendation under subsection (2); and

(d) the professional body concerned.

(2) In reporting his conclusions, the Ombudsman may recommend –

(a) that the complaint be reconsidered by the professional body concerned;

(b) that the professional body concerned or any other relevant disciplinary body consider exercising its powers in relation to –

(i) the person with respect to whom the complaint was made; or

(ii) any person who, at the material time, was connected with him;

(c) that –

(i) the person with respect to whom the complaint was made; or

(ii) any person who, at the material time, was connected with him,

pay compensation of an amount specified by the Ombudsman to the complainant for loss suffered by him, or inconvenience or distress caused to him, as a result of the matter complained of;

(d) that the professional body concerned pay compensation of an amount specified by the Ombudsman to the person making the complaint for loss suffered by him, or inconvenience or distress caused to him, as a result of the way in which the complaint was handled by that body;

(e) that the person or professional body to which a recomm-endation under paragraph (c) or (d) applies make a separate payment to the person making the allegation of an amount specified by the Ombudsman by way of reimbursement of the cost, or part of the cost, of making the allegation.

(3) More than one such recommendation may be included in a report under this section.

(4) Where the Ombudsman includes any recommendation in a report under this section, the report shall give his reasons for making the recommendation.

(5) For the purposes of the law of defamation the publication of any report of the Ombudsman under this section and any publicity given under subsection (9) shall be absolutely privileged.

(6) It shall be the duty of any person to whom a report is sent by the Ombudsman under subsection (1)(b) or (c) to have regard to the conclusions and recommendations set out in the report, so far as they concern that person.

(7) Where –

(a) a report is sent to any person under this section; and
(b) the report includes a recommendation directed at him,

he shall, before the end of the period of three months beginning with the date on which the report was sent, notify the Ombudsman of the action which he has taken, or proposes to take, to comply with the recommendation.

(8) Any person who fails to comply (whether wholly or in part) with a recommendation under subsection (2) shall publicise that failure, and the reasons for it, in such manner as the Ombudsman may specify.

(9) Where a person is required by subsection (8) to publicise any failure, the Ombudsman may take such steps as he considers reasonable to publicise that failure if –

(a) the period mentioned in subsection (7) has expired and that person has not complied with subsection (8); or
(b) the Ombudsman has reasonable cause for believing that that person will not comply with subsection (8) before the end of that period.

(10) Any reasonable expenses incurred by the Ombudsman under subsection (9) may be recovered by him (as a civil debt) from the person whose failure he has publicised.

(11) For the purposes of this section, the person with respect to whom a complaint is made ('the first person') and another person ('the second person') are connected if –

(a) the second person –

(i) employs the first person; and
(ii) is an authorised advocate, authorised litigator, duly certified notary public, licensed conveyancer or partnership;

(b) they are both partners in the same partnership; or
(c) the second person is a recognised body which employs the first person or of which the first person is an officer.

24 Advisory functions [553]

(1) The Legal Services Ombudsman may make recommendations to any professional body about the arrangements which that body has in force for the investigation of complaints made with respect to persons who are subject to that body's control.

(2) It shall be the duty of any professional body to whom a recommendation is made under this section to have regard to it.

(3) The Ombudsman may refer to the Advisory Committee any matters which come to his notice in the exercise of his functions and which appear to him to be relevant to the Committee's functions.

25 Procedure and offences   [554]

(1) Where the Legal Services Ombudsman is conducting an investigation under this Act he may require any person to furnish such information or produce such documents as he considers relevant to the investigation.

(2) For the purposes of any such investigation, the Ombudsman shall have the same powers as the High Court in respect of the attendance and examination of witnesses (including the administration of oaths or affirmations and the examination of witnesses abroad) and in respect of the production of documents.

(3) No person shall be compelled, by virtue of subsection (2), to give evidence or produce any document which he could not be compelled to give or produce in civil proceedings before the High Court.

(4) If any person is in contempt of the Ombudsman in relation to any investigation conducted under section 22, the Ombudsman may certify that contempt to the High Court.

(5) For the purposes of this section a person is in contempt of the Ombudsman if he acts, or fails to act, in any way which would constitute contempt if the investigation being conducted by the Ombudsman were civil proceedings in the High Court.

(6) Where a person's contempt is certified under subsection (4), the High Court may enquire into the matter.

(7) Where the High Court conducts an inquiry under subsection (6) it may, after –

  (a) hearing any witness produced against, or on behalf of, the person concerned; and
  (b) considering any statement offered in his defence,

deal with him in any manner that would be available to it had he been in contempt of the High Court.

26 Extension of Ombudsman's remit   [555]

(1) The Lord Chancellor may by regulation extend the jurisdiction of the Legal Services Ombudsman by providing for the provisions of sections 21 to 25 to have effect, with such modifications (if any) as he thinks fit, in relation to the investigation by the Ombudsman of allegations –

  (a) which relate to complaints of a prescribed kind concerned with the provision of probate services; and
  (b) which he would not otherwise be entitled to investigate.

(2) Without prejudice to the generality of the power given to the Lord Chancellor by subsection (1), the regulations may make provision for the investigation only of allegations relating to complaints –

  (a) made to prescribed bodies; or
  (b) with respect to prescribed categories of person.

27 Rights of audience   [556]

(1) The question whether a person has a right of audience before a court, or in relation to any proceedings, shall be determined solely in accordance with the provisions of this Part.

(2) A person shall have a right of audience before a court in relation to any proceedings only in the following cases –

(a) where –

(i) he has a right of audience before that court in relation to those proceedings granted by the appropriate authorised body; and

(ii) that body's qualification regulations and rules of conduct have been approved for the purposes of this section, in relation to the granting of that right;

(b) where paragraph (a) does not apply but he has a right of audience before that court in relation to those proceedings granted by or under any enactment;

(c) where paragraph (a) does not apply but he has a right of audience granted by that court in relation to those proceedings;

(d) where he is a party to those proceedings and would have had a right of audience, in his capacity as such a party, if this Act had not been passed; or

(e) where –

(i) he is employed (whether wholly or in part), or is otherwise engaged, to assist in the conduct of litigation and is doing so under instructions given (either generally or in relation to the proceedings) by a qualified litigator; and

(ii) the proceedings are being heard in chambers in the High Court or a county court and are not reserved family proceedings.

(3) No person shall have a right of audience as a barrister by virtue of subsection (2)(a) above unless he has been called to the Bar by one of the Inns of Court and has not been disbarred or temporarily suspended from practice by order of an Inn of Court.

(4) Nothing in this section affects the power of any court in any proceedings to refuse to hear a person (for reasons which apply to him as an individual) who would otherwise have a right of audience before the court in relation to those proceedings. •

(5) Where a court refuses to hear a person as mentioned in subsection (4) it shall give its reasons for refusing.

(6) Nothing in this section affects any provision made by or under any enactment which prevents a person from exercising a right of audience which he would otherwise be entitled to exercise.

(7) Where, immediately before the commencement of this section, no restriction was placed on the persons entitled to exercise any right of audience in relation to any particular court or in relation to particular proceedings, nothing in this section shall be taken to place any such restriction on any person.

(8) Where –

(a) immediately before the commencement of this section; or

(b) by virtue of any provision made by or under an enactment passed subsequently,

a court does not permit the appearance of advocates, or permits the appearance of advocates only with leave, no person shall have a right of audience before that court, in relation to any proceedings, solely by virtue of the provisions of this section.

(9) In this section –

'advocate', in relation to any proceedings, means any person exercising a right of audience as a representative of, or on behalf of, any party to the proceedings;

'authorised body' means –

(a) the General Council of the Bar;

(b) the Law Society; and

(c) any professional or other body which has been designated by Order in Council as an authorised body for the purposes of this section.

'appropriate authorised body', in relation to any person claiming to be entitled to any right of audience by virtue of subsection (2)(a), means the authorised body –

(a) granting that right; and

(b) of which that person is a member;

'family proceedings' has the same meaning as in the Matrimonial and Family Proceedings Act 1984 and also includes any other proceedings which are family proceedings for the purposes of the Children Act 1989;

'qualification regulations', in relation to an authorised body, means regulations (however they may be described) as to the education and training which members of that body must receive in order to be entitled to any right of audience granted by it;

'qualified litigator' means –

(i) any practising solicitor ('practising' having the same meaning as in section 19(8)(b));

(ii) any recognised body; and

(iii) any person who is exempt from the requirement to hold a practising certificate by virtue of section 88 of the Solicitors Act 1974 (saving for solicitors to public departments and the City of London);

'recognised body' means any body recognised under section 9 of the Administration of Justice Act 1985 (incorporated practices);

'reserved family proceedings' means such category of family proceedings as the Lord Chancellor may, after consulting the President of the Law Society and with the concurrence of the President of the Family Division, by order prescribe; and

'rules of conduct', in relation to an authorised body, means rules (however they may be described) as to the conduct required of members of that body in exercising any right of audience granted by it.

(10) Section 20 of the Solicitors Act 1974 (unqualified person not to act as a solicitor), section 22 of that Act (unqualified person not to prepare certain documents etc) and section 25 of that Act (costs where an unqualified person acts as a solicitor), shall not apply in relation to any act done in the exercise of a right of audience.

28 Rights to conduct litigation   [557]

(1) The question whether a person has a right to conduct litigation, or any category of litigation, shall be determined solely in accordance with the provisions of this Part.

(2) A person shall have a right to conduct litigation in relation to any proceedings only in the following cases –

(a) where –

(i) he has a right to conduct litigation in relation to those proceedings granted by the appropriate authorised body; and

(ii) that body's qualification regulations and rules of conduct have been approved for the purposes of this section, in relation to the granting of that right;

(b) where paragraph (a) does not apply but he has a right to conduct litigation in relation to those proceedings granted by or under any enactment;

(c) where paragraph (a) does not apply but he has a right to conduct litigation granted by that court in relation to those proceedings;

(d) where he is a party to those proceedings and would have had a right to conduct the litigation, in his capacity as such a party, if this Act had not been passed.

(3) Nothing in this section affects any provisions made by or under any enactment which prevents a person from exercising a right to conduct litigation which he would otherwise be entitled to exercise.

(4) Where, immediately before the commencement of this section, no restriction was placed on the persons entitled to exercise any right to conduct litigation in relation to a particular court, or in relation to particular proceedings, nothing in this section shall be taken to place any such restriction on any person.

(5) In this section –

'authorised body' means

(a) the Law Society; and

(b) any professional or other body which has been designated by Order in Council as an authorised body for the purposes of this section;

'appropriate authorised body', in relation to any person claiming to be entitled to any right to conduct litigation by virtue of subsection (2)(a), means the authorised body –

(a) granting that right; and

(b) of which that person is a member;

'qualification regulations', in relation to an authorised body, means regulations (however they may be described) as to the education and training which members of that body must receive in order to be entitled to any right to conduct litigation granted by it; and

'rules of conduct', in relation to any authorised body, means rules (however they may be described) as to the conduct required of members of that body in exercising any right to conduct litigation granted by it.

(6) Section 20 of the Solicitors Act 1974 (unqualified person not to act as a solicitor), section 22 of that Act (unqualified person not to prepare certain documents, etc) and section 25 of that Act (costs where unqualified person acts as a solicitor) shall not apply in relation to any act done in the exercise of a right to conduct litigation.

29 Authorised bodies: designation and approval of [558] regulations and rules

(1) In order to be designated as an authorised body for the purposes of section 27 or 28 a professional or other body must –

(a) apply to the Lord Chancellor under this section, specifying the purposes for which it is seeking authorisation; and

(b) comply with the provisions of Part I of Schedule 4 as to the approval of qualification regulations and rules of conduct and other matters.

(2) Where –

(a) an application has been made to the Lord Chancellor under this section;

(b) the requirements of Part I of Schedule 4 have been satisfied; and

(c) the application has not failed,

the Lord Chancellor may recommend to Her Majesty that an Order in Council be made designating that body as an authorised body for the purposes of section 27 or (as the case may be) section 28.

(3) Where an authorised body alters –

(a) any of its qualification regulations; or

(b) any of its rules of conduct,

those alterations shall not have effect, so far as they relate to any right of audience or any right to conduct litigation granted by that body, unless they have been approved under Part II of Schedule 4.

(4) Where an authorised body makes any alteration to the rights of audience or rights to conduct litigation granted by it (including the grant of a new right), the qualification regulations and rules of conduct of that body must be approved under Part II of Schedule 4.

(5) Where the Lord Chancellor or any of the designated judges considers that it might be appropriate for an authorised body to alter –

(a) any of its qualification regulations or rules of conduct; or

(b) any right of audience, or right to conduct litigation, which it is entitled to grant,

he may advise that body accordingly.

(6) Where –

(a) the Lord Chancellor gives any advice under subsection (5), he shall inform the designated judges; and

(b) where a designated judge gives any such advice, he shall inform the Lord Chancellor and the other designated judges.

(7) Where an authorised body has been given any such advice it shall, in the light of that advice, consider whether to make the recommended alteration.

30 Revocation of authorised body's designation [559]

(1) Where an Order in Council has been made under section 29 designating a body as an authorised body, the Lord Chancellor may recommend to Her Majesty that an Order in Council be made revoking that designation.

(2) An Order under this section may only be made if –

(a) the authorised body has made a written request to the Lord Chancellor asking for it to be made;

(b) that body has agreed (in writing) to its being made; or

(c) the Lord Chancellor is satisfied that the circumstances at the time when he is considering the question are such that, had that body then been applying to become an authorised body, its application would have failed.

(3) The provisions of Part III of Schedule 4 shall have effect with respect to the revocation of designations under this section.

(4) An Order made under this section may make such transitional and incidental provision as the Lord Chancellor considers necessary or expedient.

(5) Where such an order is made, any right of audience or right to conduct litigation granted to any person by the body with respect to whom the Order is made shall cease to have effect, subject to any transitional provision made by the Order.

(6) Where such an Order is made, the Lord Chancellor shall –

(a) give the body with respect to whom the Order is made written notice of the making of the Order;

(b) take such steps as are reasonably practicable to bring the making of the Order to the attention of the members of that body; and

(c) publish notice of the making of the Order in such manner as he considers appropriate for bringing it to the attention of persons (other than those members) who, in his opinion, are likely to be affected by the Order.

31 The General Council of the Bar [560]

(1) On the coming into force of section 27 –

(a) barristers shall be deemed to have been granted by the General Council of the Bar the rights of audience exercisable by barristers (in their capacity as such) immediately before 7 December 1989; and

(b) the General Council of the Bar shall be deemed to have in force qualification regulations and rules of conduct which have been properly approved for the purposes of section 27.

(2) Those qualification regulations and rules of conduct shall be deemed to have been approved only –

(a) in relation to the rights of audience mentioned in subsection (1)(a); and

(b) so far as they relate to those rights of audience.

(3) If any particular provision of those regulations or rules would not have been approved for the purposes of section 27 had it been submitted for approval under Part I of Schedule 4 it (but no other such provision) shall not be deemed to have been approved.

(4) In the event of any question arising as to whether any provision is deemed to have been approved, subsection (5) shall apply in relation to that question if the Lord Chancellor so directs.

(5) Where a direction is given under subsection (4) –

(a) the Lord Chancellor shall seek the advice of the Advisory Committee and the Director;

(b) the Lord Chancellor and each of the designated judges shall consider, in the light of that advice, whether the provision in question is deemed to have been so approved; and

(c) that provision shall not be deemed to have been so approved unless the Lord Chancellor and each of the designated judges are satisfied that it has been.

(6) In the event of any question arising as to whether any provision of the qualification regulations or rules of conduct of the General Council of the Bar requires to be approved by virtue of section 29(3) or (4), subsection (7) shall apply in relation to that question if the Lord Chancellor so directs.

(7) Where a direction is given under subsection (6) –

(a) the Lord Chancellor shall seek the advice of the Advisory Committee and the Director;

(b) the Lord Chancellor and each of the designated judges shall consider, in the light of that advice, whether the provision in question requires approval; and

(c) it shall require approval unless the Lord Chancellor and each of the designated judges are satisfied that it does not require approval.

(8) Where, by virtue of subsection (5)(c), any provision is not deemed to have been approved –

(a) it shall cease to have effect, so far as it relates to any right of audience deemed to have been granted by the General Council of the Bar; and

(b) the regulations and rules which are deemed, by virtue of subsection (1)(b), to have been properly approved shall be taken not to include that provision.

(9) Nothing in this section shall affect the validity of anything done in reliance on any provision of regulations or rules at any time before –

(a) it is determined in accordance with subsection (5)(c) that that provision is not deemed to have been approved; or

(b) it is determined in accordance with subsection (7)(c) that that provision requires approval.

32 The Law Society: rights of audience   [561]

(1) On the coming into force of section 27 –

(a) solicitors shall be deemed to have been granted by the Law Society the rights of audience exercisable by solicitors (in their capacity as such) immediately before 7 December 1989; and

(b) the Law Society shall be deemed to have in force qualification regulations and rules of conduct which have been properly approved for the purposes of section 27.

(2) Those qualification regulations and rules of conduct shall be deemed to have been approved only –

(a) in relation to the rights of audience mentioned in subsection (1)(a); and

(b) so far as they relate to those rights of audience.

(3) If any particular provision of those regulations or rules would not have been approved for the purposes of section 27 had it been submitted for approval under Part I of Schedule 4 it (but no other such provision) shall not be deemed to have been approved.

(4) In the event of any question arising as to whether any provision is deemed to have been approved, subsection (5) shall apply in relation to that question if the Lord Chancellor so directs.

(5) Where a direction is given under subsection (4) –

(a) the Lord Chancellor shall seek the advice of the Advisory Committee and the Director;

(b) the Lord Chancellor and each of the designated judges shall consider, in the light of that advice, whether the provision in question is deemed to have been so approved; and

(c) that provision shall not be deemed to have been so approved unless the Lord Chancellor and each of the designated judges are satisfied that it has been.

(6) In the event of any question arising as to whether any provision of the qualification regulations or rules of conduct of the Law Society requires to be approved by virtue of section 29(3) or (4), subsection (7) shall apply in relation to that question if the Lord Chancellor so directs.

(7) Where a direction is given under subsection (6) –

(a) the Lord Chancellor shall seek the advice of the Advisory Committee and the Director;

(b) the Lord Chancellor and each of the designated judges shall consider, in the light of that advice, whether the provision in question requires approval; and

(c) it shall require approval unless the Lord Chancellor and each of the designated judges are satisfied that it does not require approval.

(8) Where, by virtue of subsection (5)(c), any provision is not deemed to have been approved –

(a) it shall cease to have effect, so far as it relates to any right of audience deemed to have been granted by the Law Society; and

(b) the regulations and rules which are deemed, by virtue of subsection (1)(b), to have been properly approved shall be taken not to include that provision.

(9) Nothing in this section shall affect the validity of anything done in reliance on any provision of regulations or rules at any time before –

(a) it is determined in accordance with subsection (5)(c) that that provision is not deemed to have been approved; or

(b) it is determined in accordance with subsection (7)(c) that that provision requires approval.

33 The Law Society: rights to conduct litigation   [562]

(1) On the coming into force of section 28 –

(a) solicitors shall be deemed to have been granted by the Law Society the rights to conduct litigation exercisable by solicitors (in their capacity as such) immediately before 7 December 1989; and

(b) the Law Society shall be deemed to have in force qualification regulations and rules of conduct which have been properly approved for the purposes of section 28.

(2) Those qualification regulations and rules of conduct shall be deemed to have been approved only –

(a) in relation to the rights to conduct litigation mentioned in subsection (1)(a); and

(b) so far as they relate to those rights to conduct litigation.

(3) If any particular provision of those regulations or rules. would not have been approved for the purposes of section 28 had it been submitted for approval under Part I of Schedule 4 it (but no other such provision) shall not be deemed to have been approved.

(4) In the event of any question arising as to whether any provision is deemed to have been approved, subsection (5) shall apply in relation to that question if the Lord Chancellor so directs.

(5) Where a direction is given under subsection (4) –

(a) the Lord Chancellor shall seek the advice of the Advisory Committee and the Director;

(b) the Lord Chancellor and each of the designated judges shall consider, in the light of that advice, whether the provision in question is deemed to have been so approved; and

(c) that provision shall not be deemed to have been so approved unless the Lord Chancellor and each of the designated judges are satisfied that it has been.

(6) In the event of any question arising as to whether any provision requires to be approved by virtue of section 29(3) or (4), subsection (7) shall apply in relation to that question if the Lord Chancellor so directs.

(7) Where a direction is given under subsection (6) –

(a) the Lord Chancellor shall seek the advice of the Advisory Committee and the Director;

(b) the Lord Chancellor and each of the designated judges shall consider in the light of that advice, whether the provision in question requires approval; and

(c) it shall require approval unless the Lord Chancellor and each of the designated judges are satisfied that it does not require approval.

(8) Where, by virtue of subsection (5)(c), any provision is not deemed to have been approved –

> (a) it shall cease to have effect, so far as it relates to any right to conduct litigation deemed to have been granted by the Law Society; and
> (b) the regulations and rules which are deemed, by virtue of subsection (1)(b), to have been properly approved shall be taken not to include that provision.

(9) Nothing in this section shall affect the validity of anything done in reliance on any provision of regulations or rules at any time before –

> (a) it is determined in accordance with subsection (5)(c) that that provision is not deemed to have been approved; or
> (b) it is determined in accordance with subsection (7)(c) that that provision requires approval.

34 The Authorised Conveyancing Practitioners Board [563]

(1) There shall be a body corporate to be known as the Authorised Conveyancing Practitioners Board (in this Act referred to as 'the Board').

(2) The Board shall consist of a Chairman and at least four, and at most eight, other members appointed by the Lord Chancellor.

(3) In appointing any member, the Lord Chancellor shall have regard to the desirability of –

> (a) appointing persons who have experience in, or knowledge of –
>
>> (i) the provision of conveyancing services;
>> (ii) financial arrangements associated with conveyancing;
>> (iii) consumer affairs; or
>> (iv) commercial affairs; and
>
> (b) securing, so far as is reasonably practicable, that the composition of the Board is such as to provide a proper balance between the interests of authorised practitioners and those who make use of their services.

(4) The Board shall not be regarded as the servant or agent of the Crown, or as enjoying any status, immunity or privilege of the Crown.

(5) The Board's property shall not be regarded as property of, or held on behalf of, the Crown.

(6) Neither the Board nor any of its staff or members shall be liable in damages for anything done or omitted in the discharge or purported discharge of any of its functions.

(7) Subsection (6) does not apply where the act or omission is shown to have been in bad faith.

(8) The provisions of Schedule 5 shall have effect with respect to the constitution, procedure and powers of the Board and with respect to connected matters.

35 Functions of the Board and financial provisions [564]

(1) It shall be the general duty of the Board –

> (a) to seek to develop competition in the provision of conveyancing services;
> (b) to supervise the activities of authorised practitioners in connection with the provision by them of conveyancing services.

(2) In discharging the duty imposed on it by subsection (1)(b) the Board shall, in particular, make arrangements designed to enable it to ascertain whether authorised practitioners are complying with regulations made by the Lord Chancellor under section 40.

(3) The Board shall have the specific functions conferred on it by or under this Act.

(4) Where the Lord Chancellor refers to the Board any matter connected with –

(a) the provision of conveyancing services by authorised practitioners; or
(b) the organisation or practice of authorised practitioners,

it shall be the duty of the Board to consider the matter and to report its conclusions to the Lord Chancellor.

(5) Any report made under subsection (4) may be published by the Lord Chancellor in such manner as he thinks fit.

(6) A copy of any guidance for authorised practitioners issued by the Board shall be sent by the Board to the Lord Chancellor.

(7) Where it appears to the Lord Chancellor that there are grounds for believing that the Board has failed in any way to carry out any of its duties under this Act, he may give such directions to the Board as he considers appropriate ...

40 Regulations about competence and conduct, etc [565]
of authorised practitioners

(1) The Lord Chancellor may by regulation make such provision as he considers expedient with a view to securing –

(a) that authorised practitioners maintain satisfactory standards of competence and conduct in connection with the provision by them of conveyancing services;
(b) that in providing such services (and in particular in fixing their charges) they act in a manner which is consistent with the maintenance of fair competition between authorised practitioners and others providing conveyancing services; and
(c) that the interests of their clients are satisfactorily protected.

(2) The regulations may, in particular, make provisions –

(a) designed to –

(i) provide for the efficient transaction of business;
(ii) avoid unnecessary delays;

(b) as to the supervision, by persons with such qualifications as may be prescribed, of such descriptions of work as may be prescribed;
(c) requiring authorised practitioners to arrange, so far as is reasonably practicable, for each transaction to be under the overall control of one individual;
(d) designed to avoid conflicts of interest;
(e) as to the terms and conditions on which authorised practitioners may provide conveyancing services;
(f) as to the information to be given to prospective clients, the manner in which or person by whom it is to be given and the circumstances in which it is to be given free of charge;
(g) as to the handling by authorised practitioners of their clients' money;
(h) as to the disclosure of and accounting for commissions.

56 Administration of oaths, etc by justices in [566]
certain probate business

(1) Every justice shall have power to administer any oath or take any affidavit which is required for the purposes of an application for a grant of probate or letters of administration made in any non-contentious or common form probate business.

(2) A justice before whom any oath or affidavit is taken or made under this section shall state in the jurat or attestation at which place and on what date the oath or affidavit is taken or made.

(3) No justice shall exercise the powers conferred by this section in any proceedings in which he is interested.

(4) A document purporting to be signed by a justice administering an oath or taking an affidavit shall be admitted in evidence without proof of the signature and without proof that he is a justice.

(5) In this section –

'affidavit' has the same meaning as in the Commissioners for Oaths Act 1889;
'justice' means a justice of the peace;
'letters of administration' includes all letters of administration of the effects of deceased persons, whether with or without a will annexed, and whether granted for general, special or limited purposes; and
'non-contentious or common form probate business' has the same meaning as in section 128 of the Supreme Court Act 1981.

57 Notaries [567]

(1) Public notaries shall no longer be appointed to practise only within particular districts in England, or particular districts in Wales.

(2) It shall no longer be necessary to serve a period of apprenticeship before being admitted as a public notary ...

(4) The Master may by rules make provision –

(a) as to the educational and training qualifications which must be satisfied before a person may be granted a faculty to practise as a public notary;
(b) as to further training which public notaries are to be required to undergo;
(c) for regulating the practice, conduct and discipline of public notaries;
(d) supplementing the provision made by subsections (8) and (9);
(e) as to the keeping by public notaries of records and accounts;
(f) as to the handling by public notaries of clients' money;
(g) as to the indemnification of public notaries against losses arising from claims in respect of civil liability incurred by them;
(h) as to compensation payable for losses suffered by persons in respect of dishonesty on the part of public notaries or their employees; and
(i) requiring the payment, in such circumstances as may be prescribed, of such reasonable fees as may be prescribed, including in particular fees for –

(i) the grant of a faculty;
(ii) the issue of a practising certificate by the Court of Faculties of the Archbishop of Canterbury; or
(iii) the entering in that court of a practising certificate issued under the Solicitors Act 1974 ...

(8) With effect from the operative date, any restriction placed on a qualifying district notary, in terms of the district within which he may practise as a public notary, shall cease to apply.

(9) In this section –

'Master' means the Master of the Faculties;
'the operative date' means the date on which subsection (1) comes into force or, if on that date the notary concerned is not a qualifying district notary (having held his faculty for less than five years) –

(a) the date on which he becomes a qualifying district notary; or
(b) such earlier date, after the commencement of subsection (1), as the Master may by rules prescribe for the purpose of this subsection;

'prescribed' means prescribed by rules made under this section; and
'qualifying district notary' means a person who –

(a) holds a faculty as a notary appointed under section 2 of the Act of 1833 or section 37 of the Act of 1914; and

(b) has held it for a continuous period of at least five years ...

(11) Nothing in this section shall be taken –

(a) to authorise any public notary to practise as a notary or to perform or certify any notarial act within the jurisdiction of the Incorporated Company of Scriveners of London or to affect the jurisdiction or powers of the Company; or

(b) to restrict the power of the Company to require a person seeking to become a public notary within its jurisdiction to serve a period of apprenticeship.

58 Conditional fee agreements [568]

(1) In this section 'a conditional fee agreement' means an agreement in writing between a person providing advocacy or litigation services and his client which –

(a) does not relate to proceedings of a kind mentioned in subsection (10);

(b) provides for that person's fees and expenses, or any part of them, to be payable only in specified circumstances;

(c) complies with such requirements (if any) as may be prescribed by the Lord Chancellor; and

(d) is not a contentious business agreement (as defined by section 59 of the Solicitors Act 1974).

(2) Where a conditional fee agreement provides for the amount of any fees to which it applies to be increased, in specified circumstances, above the amount which would be payable if it were not a conditional fee agreement, it shall specify the percentage by which that amount is to be increased.

(3) Subject to subsection (6), a conditional fee agreement which relates to specified proceedings shall not be unenforceable by reason only of its being a conditional fee agreement.

(4) In this section 'specified proceedings' means proceedings of a description specified by order made by the Lord Chancellor for the purposes of subsection (3).

(5) Any such order shall prescribe the maximum permitted percentage for each description of specified proceedings.

(6) An agreement which falls within subsection (2) shall be unenforceable if, at the time when it is entered into, the percentage specified in the agreement exceeds the prescribed maximum permitted percentage for the description of proceedings to which it relates.

(7) Before making any order under this section the Lord Chancellor shall consult the designated judges, the General Council of the Bar, the Law Society and such other authorised bodies (if any) as he considers appropriate.

(8) Where a party to any proceedings has entered into a conditional fee agreement and a costs order is made in those proceedings in his favour, the costs payable to him shall not include any element which takes account of any percentage increase payable under the agreement.

(9) Rules of court may make provision with respect to the taxing of any costs which include fees payable under a conditional fee agreement.

(10) The proceedings mentioned in subsection (1)(a) are any criminal proceedings and any proceedings under –

(a) the Matrimonial Causes Act 1973;
(b) the Domestic Violence and Matrimonial Proceedings Act 1976;
(c) the Adoption Act 1976;
(d) the Domestic Proceedings and Magistrates' Courts Act 1978;
(e) sections 1 and 9 of the Matrimonial Homes Act 1983;
(f) Part III of the Matrimonial and Family Proceedings Act 1984;
(g) Parts I, II or IV of the Children Act 1989; or
(h) the inherent jurisdiction of the High Court in relation to children.

59 Representation under the Legal Aid Act 1988 [569]

(1) Nothing in this Part shall affect the right of a person who is represented in proceedings in the Supreme Court or the House of Lords under the Legal Aid Act 1988 to select his legal representative.

(2) The power to make regulations with respect to representation under section 2(7) or 32(8) of that Act shall not be exercised so as to provide that representation in any such proceedings may only be by a single barrister, solicitor or other legal representative (but that is not to be taken as restricting the power to make regulations under section 34(2)(e) of that Act).

61 Right of barrister to enter into contract for [570] the provision of his services

(1) Any rule of law which prevents a barrister from entering into a contract for the provision of his services as a barrister is hereby abolished.

(2) Nothing in subsection (1) prevents the General Council of the Bar from making rules (however described) which prohibit barristers from entering into contracts or restrict their right to do so.

62 Immunity of advocates from actions in negligence [571] and for breach of contract

(1) A person –
    (a) who is not a barrister; but
    (b) who lawfully provides any legal services in relation to any proceedings,

shall have the same immunity from liability for negligence in respect of his acts or omissions as he would have if he were a barrister lawfully providing those services.

(2) No act or omission on the part of any barrister or other person which is accorded immunity from liability for negligence shall give rise to an action for breach of any contract relating to the provision by him of the legal services in question.

63 Legal professional privilege [572]

(1) This section applies to any communication made to or by a person who is not a barrister or solicitor at any time when that person is –

    (a) providing advocacy or litigation services as an authorised advocate or authorised litigator; ...

(2) Any such communication shall in any legal proceedings be privileged from disclosure in like manner as if the person in question had at all material times been acting as his client's solicitor ...

66 Multi-disciplinary and multi-national practices [573]

(1) Section 39 of the Solicitors Act 1974 (which, in effect, prevents solicitors entering into partnership with persons who are not solicitors) shall cease to have effect.

(2) Nothing in subsection (1) prevents the Law Society making rules which prohibit solicitors from entering into any unincorporated association with persons who are not solicitors, or restrict the circumstances in which they may do so.

(3) Section 10 of the Public Notaries Act 1801 (which, in effect, prevents notaries entering into partnership with persons who are not notaries) shall cease to have effect.

(4) Nothing in subsection (3) prevents the Master of the Faculties making rules which prohibit notaries from entering into any unincorporated association with persons who are not notaries, or restrict the circumstances in which they may do so.

(5) It is hereby declared that no rule of common law prevents barristers from entering into any unincorporated association with persons who are not barristers.

(6) Nothing in subsection (5) prevents the General Council of the Bar from making rules which prohibit barristers from entering into any such unincorporated association, or restrict the circumstances in which they may do so.

69 Exemption from liability for damages, etc [574]

(1) Neither the Lord Chancellor nor any of the designated judges shall be liable in damages for anything done or omitted in the discharge or purported discharge of any of their functions under this Part.

(2) For the purposes of the law of defamation, the publication by the Lord Chancellor, a designated judge or the Director of any advice or reasons given by or to him in the exercise of functions under this Part shall be absolutely privileged.

70 Offences [575]

(1) If any person does any act in the purported exercise of a right of audience, or right to conduct litigation, in relation to any proceedings or contemplated proceedings when he is not entitled to exercise that right he shall be guilty of an offence ...

(6) A person guilty of an offence under this section, by virtue of subsection (1), shall also be guilty of contempt of the court concerned and may be punished accordingly ...

PART III

JUDICIAL AND OTHER OFFICES AND JUDICIAL PENSIONS

71 Qualification for judicial and certain [576]
other appointments

(3) For the purposes of this section, a person has –

(a) a 'Supreme Court qualification' if he has a right of audience in relation to all proceedings in the Supreme Court;
(b) a 'High Court qualification' if he has a right of audience in relation to all proceedings in the High Court;

(c) a 'general qualification' if he has a right of audience in relation to any class of proceedings in any part of the Supreme Court, or all proceedings in county courts or magistrates' courts;

(d) a 'Crown Court qualification' if he has a right of audience in relation to all proceedings in the Crown Court;

(e) a 'county court qualification' if he has a right of audience in relation to all proceedings in county courts;

(f) a 'magistrates' court qualification' if he has a right of audience in relation to all proceedings in magistrates' courts.

(4) References in subsection (3) to a right of audience are references to a right of audience granted by an authorised body.

(5) Any reference in any enactment, measure or statutory instrument to a person having such a qualification of a particular number of years' length shall be construed as a reference to a person who –

(a) for the time being has that qualification, and

(b) has had it for a period (which need not be continuous) of at least that number of years.

(6) Any period during which a person had a right of audience but was not entitled to exercise it shall count towards the period mentioned in subsection (5)(b) unless he was prevented by the authorised body concerned from exercising that right of audience as a result of disciplinary proceedings.

(7) For the purposes of subsection (5)(a), a solicitor who does not have a right of audience, by reason only of not having a practising certificate in force, shall be deemed to have such a right, unless his not having a practising certificate in force is the result of disciplinary proceedings.

(8) For the purposes of subsection (5)(b), any period during which a solicitor did not have a right of audience, by reason only of not having a practising certificate in force, shall be deemed to be a period during which he had such a right, unless his not having a practising certificate in force was the result of disciplinary proceedings.

72 Presiding Judges   [577]

(1) For each of the Circuits there shall be at least two Presiding Judges, appointed from among the puisne judges of the High Court.

(2) There shall be a Senior Presiding Judge for England and Wales, appointed from among the Lords Justices of Appeal.

(3) Any appointment under subsection (1) or (2) shall be made by the Lord Chief Justice with the agreement of the Lord Chancellor.

(4) In this section 'the Circuits' means –

(a) the Midland and Oxford Circuit;

(b) the North Eastern Circuit;

(c) the Northern Circuit;

(d) the South Eastern Circuit;

(e) the Western Circuit; and

(f) the Wales and Chester Circuit,

or such other areas of England and Wales as the Lord Chancellor may from time to time, after consulting the Lord Chief Justice, direct.

(5) A person appointed as a Presiding Judge or as the Senior Presiding Judge shall hold that office in accordance with the terms of his appointment ...

73 Delegation of certain administrative functions of [578] Master of the Rolls

(1) Where the Master of the Rolls expects to be absent at a time when it may be appropriate for any relevant functions of his to be exercised, he may appoint a judge of the Supreme Court to exercise those functions on his behalf.

(2) Where the Master of the Rolls considers that it would be inappropriate for him to exercise any such functions in connection with a particular matter (because of a possible conflict of interests or for any other reason), he may appoint a judge of the Supreme Court to exercise those functions on his behalf in connection with that matter.

(3) Where the Master of the Rolls is incapable of exercising his relevant functions, the Lord Chancellor may appoint a judge of the Supreme Court to exercise, on behalf of the Master of the Rolls, such of those functions as the Lord Chancellor considers appropriate ...

(5) In this section 'relevant functions' means any functions of the Master of the Rolls under –

(a) section 144A of the Law of Property Act 1922 (functions in relation to manorial documents);
(b) section 7(1) of the Public Records Act 1958 (power to determine where records of the Chancery of England are to be deposited);
(c) the Solicitors Act 1974 (which gives the Master of the Rolls various functions in relation to solicitors);
(d) section 9 of, and Schedule 2 to, the Administration of Justice Act 1985 (functions in relation to incorporated practices).

74 District judges [579]

(1) The offices of –

(a) registrar, assistant registrar and deputy registrar for each county court district; and
(b) district registrar, assistant district registrar and deputy district registrar for each district registry of the High Court,

shall become the offices of district judge, assistant district judge and deputy district judge respectively.

(2) The office of registrar of the principal registry of the Family Division of the High Court shall become the office of district judge of the principal registry of the Family Division ...

75 Judges, etc barred from legal practice [580]

No person holding as a full-time appointment any of the offices listed in Schedule 11 shall –

(a) provide any advocacy or litigation services (in any jurisdiction);
(b) provide any conveyancing or probate services;
(c) practise as a barrister, solicitor, public notary or licensed conveyancer, or be indirectly concerned in any such practice;
(d) practise as an advocate or solicitor in Scotland, or be indirectly concerned in any such practice; or
(e) act for any remuneration to himself as an arbitrator or umpire.

76 Judicial oaths   [581]

(1) A person holding any of the following offices –

(a) district judge, including district judge of the principal registry of the Family Division;
(b) Master of the Queen's Bench Division;
(c) Master of the Chancery Division;
(d) Registrar in Bankruptcy of the High Court;
(e) Taxing Master of the Supreme Court;
(f) Admiralty Registrar,

shall take the oath of allegiance and the judicial oath before a judge of the High Court or a Circuit judge ...

113 Administration of oaths and taking of affidavits   [582]

(1) In this section –

'authorised person' means –

(a) any authorised advocate or authorised litigator, other than one who is a solicitor (in relation to whom provision similar to that made by this section is made by section 81 of the Solicitors Act 1974); or
(b) any person who is a member of a professional or other body prescribed by the Lord Chancellor for the purposes of this section; and

'general notary' means any public notary other than –

(a) an ecclesiastical notary; or
(b) one who is a member of the Incorporated Company of Scriveners (in relation to whom provision similar to that made by this section is made by section 65 of the Administration of Justice Act 1985).

(2) Section 1(1) of the Commissioners for Oaths Act 1889 (appointment of commissioners by Lord Chancellor) shall cease to have effect.

(3) Subject to the provisions of this section, every authorised person shall have the powers conferred on a commissioner for oaths by the Commissioners for Oaths Acts 1889 and 1891 and section 24 of the Stamp Duties Management Act 1891; and any reference to such a commissioner in an enactment or instrument (including an enactment passed or instrument made after the commencement of this Act) shall include a reference to an authorised person unless the context otherwise requires.

(4) Subject to the provisions of this section, every general notary shall have the powers conferred on a commissioner for oaths by the Commissioners for Oaths Acts 1889 and 1891; and any reference to such a commissioner in an enactment or instrument (including an enactment passed or instrument made after the commencement of this Act) shall include a reference to a general notary unless the context otherwise requires.

(5) No person shall exercise the powers conferred by this section in any proceedings in which he is interested.

(6) A person exercising such powers and before whom any oath or affidavit is taken or made shall state in the jurat or attestation at which place and on what date the oath or affidavit is taken or made.

(7) A document containing such a statement and purporting to be sealed or signed by an authorised person or general notary shall be admitted in evidence without proof of the seal or signature, and without proof that he is an authorised person or general notary.

(8) The Lord Chancellor may, with the concurrence of the Lord Chief Justice and

the Master of the Rolls, by order prescribe the fees to be charged by authorised persons exercising the powers of commissioners for oaths by virtue of this section in respect of the administration of an oath or the taking of an affidavit.

(9) In this section 'affidavit' has the same meaning as in the Commissioners for Oaths Act 1889.

(10) Every –

(a) solicitor who holds a practising certificate which is in force;
(b) authorised person;
(c) general notary; and
(d) member of the Incorporated Company of Scriveners ('the Company') who has been admitted to practise as a public notary within the jurisdiction of the Company,

shall have the right to use the title 'Commissioner for Oaths'.

115 Law reports   [583]

A report of a case made by a person who is not a barrister but who is a solicitor or has a Supreme Court qualification (within the meaning of section 71) shall have the same authority as if it had been made by a barrister.

119 Interpretation   [584]

(1) In this Act –

'administration', in relation to letters of administration, has the same meaning as in section 128 of the Supreme Court Act 1981;
'advocacy services' means any services which it would be reasonable to expect a person who is exercising, or contemplating exercising, a right of audience in relation to any proceedings, or contemplated proceedings, to provide;
'authorised advocate' means any person (including a barrister or solicitor) who has a right of audience granted by an authorised body in accordance with the provisions of this Act;
'authorised body' and 'appropriate authorised body' –

(a) in relation to any right of audience or proposed right of audience, have the meanings given in section 27; and
(b) in relation to any right to conduct litigation or proposed right to conduct litigation, have the meanings given in section 28;

'authorised litigator' means any person (including a solicitor) who has a right to conduct litigation granted by an authorised body in accordance with the provisions of this Act;
'authorised practitioner' has the same meaning as in section 37;
'conveyancing services' means the preparation of transfers, conveyances, contracts and other documents in connection with, and other services ancillary to, the disposition or acquisition of estates or interests in land;
'court' includes –

(a) any tribunal which the Council on Tribunals is under a duty to keep under review;
(b) any court-martial; and
(c) a statutory inquiry within the meaning of section 16(1) of the Tribunals and Inquiries Act 1992;

'designated judge' means the Lord Chief Justice, the Master of the Rolls, the President of the Family Division or the Vice-Chancellor;
'the Director' means the Director General of Fair Trading;

'duly certificated notary public' has the same meaning as it has in the Solicitors
Act 1974 by virtue of section 87(1) of that Act;

'the general principle' has the meaning given in section 17(4);

'licensed conveyancer' has the same meaning as it has in the Administration of
Justice Act 1985 by virtue of section 11 of that Act;

'litigation services' means any services which it would be reasonable to expect
a person who is exercising, or contemplating exercising, a right to conduct
litigation in relation to any proceedings, or contemplated proceedings, to
provide;

'member', in relation to any professional or other body (other than any body
established by this Act), includes any person who is not a member of that
body but who may be subject to disciplinary sanctions for failure to comply
with any of that body's rules;

'multi-national partnership' has the meaning given by section 89(9);

'probate services' means the drawing or preparation of any papers on which to
found or oppose a grant of probate or a grant of letters of administration and
the administration of the estate of a deceased person;

'prescribed' means prescribed by regulations under this Act.

'proceedings' means proceedings in any court;

'qualification regulations' and 'rules of conduct' –

(a) in relation to any right of audience or proposed right of audience, have
the meanings given in section 27; and

(b) in relation to any right to conduct litigation or proposed right to conduct
litigation, have the meanings given in section 28;

'qualified person' has the meaning given in section 36(6);

'registered foreign lawyer' has the meaning given by section 89(9);

'right of audience' means the right to exercise any of the functions of
appearing before and addressing a court including the calling and examining
of witnesses;

'right to conduct litigation' means the right –

(a) to exercise all or any of the functions of issuing a writ or otherwise
commencing proceedings before any court; and

(b) to perform any ancillary functions in relation to proceedings (such as
entering appearances to actions);

'solicitor' means solicitor of the Supreme Court; and

'the statutory objective' has the meaning given in section 17(2).

(2) For the purposes of the definition of 'conveyancing services' in subsection (1)
–

'disposition'

(i) does not include a testamentary disposition or any disposition in the case
of such a lease as is referred to in section 54(2) of the Law of Property Act
1925 (short leases); but

(ii) subject to that, includes in the case of leases both their grant and their
assignment; and

'acquisition' has a corresponding meaning.

(3) In this Act any reference (including those in sections 27(9) and 28(5)) to rules
of conduct includes a reference to rules of practice.

120 Regulations and orders   **[585]**

(1) Any power to make orders or regulations conferred by this Act shall be
exercisable by statutory instrument.

(2) Any such regulations or order may make different provisions for different cases or classes of case.

(3) Any such regulations or order may contain such incidental, supplemental or transitional provisions or savings as the person making the regulations or order considers expedient.

(4) No instrument shall be made under section 1(1), 26(1), 37(10), 40(1), 58, 60, 89(5) or (7), 125(4) or paragraph 4 or 6 of Schedule 9 or paragraph 9(c) of Schedule 14 unless a draft of the instrument has been approved by both Houses of Parliament.

(5) An Order in Council shall not be made in pursuance of a recommendation made under section 29(2) or 30(1) unless a draft of the Order has been approved by both Houses of Parliament.

(6) Any other statutory instrument made under this Act other than one under section 124(3) shall be subject to annulment in pursuance of a resolution of either House of Parliament.

SCHEDULE 1

THE ADVISORY COMMITTEE

1. (1) Every member of the Advisory Committee –

(a) shall be appointed for such term, not exceeding five years, as the Lord Chancellor may specify; and

(b) shall hold and vacate office in accordance with the terms of his appointment.

(2) Any person who ceases to be a member of the Advisory Committee shall be eligible for re-appointment.

(3) A member of the Advisory Committee may at any time resign his office by giving notice in writing to the Lord Chancellor.

(4) The Lord Chancellor may remove a member of the Advisory Committee if satisfied –

(a) that he has been absent from meetings of the Advisory Committee for a period of more than six consecutive months without the permission of the Advisory Committee;

(b) that a bankruptcy order has been made against him or that this estate has been sequestrated or that he has made a composition or arrangement with, or granted a trust deed for, his creditors; or

(c) that he is otherwise unable or unfit to discharge the functions of a member of the Advisory Committee ...

12. For the purposes of the law of defamation, the publication of any advice or report by the Advisory Committee in the exercise of any of its functions shall be absolutely privileged ...

SCHEDULE 2

SPECIFIC FUNCTIONS OF THE ADVISORY COMMITTEE

1. (1) The Advisory Committee shall –

(a) keep under review the education and training of those who offer to provide legal services;

(b) consider the need for continuing education and training for such persons and the form it should take; and

(c) consider the steps which professional and other bodies should take to ensure that their members benefit from such continuing education and training.

(2) The Advisory Committee shall give such advice as it thinks appropriate with a view to ensuring that the education and training of those who offer to provide legal services is relevant to the needs of legal practice and to the efficient delivery of legal services to the public.

(3) The Advisory Committee's duties under this paragraph shall extend to all stages of legal education and training ...

7. In discharging its functions under this Schedule, the Advisory Committee shall have regard to the need for the efficient provision of legal services for persons who face special difficulties in making use of those services, including in particular special difficulties in expressing themselves or in understanding.

SCHEDULE 3

THE LEGAL SERVICES OMBUDSMAN

1. (1) The Lord Chancellor may give general directions concerning the discharge of the functions of the Legal Services Ombudsman ...

2. (1) The Ombudsman may delegate any of his functions to such members of his staff as he thinks fit.

(2) All recommendations and reports prepared by or on behalf of the Ombudsman must be signed by him ...

5. (1) The Ombudsman shall make an annual report to the Lord Chancellor on the discharge of his functions during the year to which the report relates.

(2) The Ombudsman may, in addition, report to the Lord Chancellor at any time on any matter relating to the discharge of the Ombudsman's functions.

(3) The Ombudsman shall provide the Lord Chancellor with such information relating to the discharge of his functions as the Lord Chancellor may see fit to require.

(4) The Lord Chancellor shall lay before each House of Parliament a copy of any annual report made to him under sub-paragraph (1) ...

SCHEDULE 4

AUTHORISATION AND APPROVAL

PART I

AUTHORISATION OF BODIES

1. (1) Any professional or other body which wishes to become an authorised body for the purposes of section 27 or 28 ('the applicant') shall send to the Advisory Committee –

(a) a draft of the qualification regulations which it proposes to apply to those of its members to whom it wishes to grant –

(i) any right of audience; or

(ii) any right to conduct litigation,

(b) a draft of the rules of conduct which it proposes to apply to those of its members exercising any such right granted by it; and

(c) a statement of the rights which it proposes to grant ('the proposed rights') and in relation to which it wishes to have those regulations and rules approved ...

(4) It shall be the duty of the Advisory Committee to consider the applicant's draft qualification regulations and rules of conduct in relation to the proposed rights.

(5) When it has completed its consideration, the Advisory Committee shall advise the applicant of the extent to which (if at all) the draft regulations or rules should, in the Committee's opinion, be amended in order to make them better designed –

(a) to further the statutory objective; or

(b) to comply with the general principle.

(6) In subsequently making its qualification regulations and rules of conduct, with a view to applying for authorisation for the purposes of section 27 or 28, the applicant shall have regard to any advice given to it by the Advisory Committee under this paragraph.

2. (1) Where the applicant has complied with paragraph 1 and wishes to proceed with its application for authorisation, it shall apply to the Lord Chancellor for its qualification regulations and rules of conduct to be approved in relation to the proposed rights ...

(4) On receipt of such an application, the Lord Chancellor shall –

(a) send a copy of the application and of any documents provided under sub-paragraph (2)(c) or (3) to the Advisory Committee and to each of the designated judges; and

(b) ask the Committee for advice as to whether the regulations and rules should be approved for the purposes of section 27 or 28.

3. (1) The Lord Chancellor shall also send copies of the documents mentioned in paragraph 2(4)(a) to the Director ...

5. (1) When he has received the advice of the Advisory Committee and that of the Director, the Lord Chancellor shall send a copy of the advice to the applicant.

(2) The applicant shall be allowed a period of 28 days, beginning with the day on which the copy is sent to him, to make representations about the advice –

(a) to the Lord Chancellor; or

(b) where the Lord Chancellor appoints a person for the purposes of this sub-paragraph, to that person.

(3) When the period of 28 days has expired the Lord Chancellor shall consider, in the light of the advice and of any representations duly made by the applicant under sub-paragraph (2) –

(a) whether the regulations and rules should be approved for the purposes of section 27 or 28; and

(b) whether the application should be approved.

(4) When the Lord Chancellor has complied with sub-paragraph (3) he shall –

(a) send to each designated judge a copy of –

(i) the advice; and

(ii) any representations duly made by the applicant under sub-paragraph (2); and

(b) inform each of those judges of the answers which he proposes to give to the questions which he has considered under sub-paragraph (3).

(5) It shall then be the duty of each designated judge to consider the regulations and rules and, in the light of the other material sent to him by the Lord Chancellor

under sub-paragraph (4), to consider the questions considered by the Lord Chancellor under sub-paragraph (3) ...

(10) If the Lord Chancellor or any of the designated judges has refused to approve the application it shall fail ...

PART II

APPROVAL REQUIRED BY SECTION 29

6. (1) Where an authorised body proposes to make any alterations to its qualification regulations or rules of conduct which is required by section 29(3) to be approved under this Part of this Schedule, it shall send to the Advisory Committee a copy of –

    (a) its qualification regulations;
    (b) its rules of conduct; and
    (c) the proposed amending regulations or rules.

(2) Where an authorised body proposes to make any alteration in the rights granted by it which calls for its qualification regulations and rules of conduct to be approved under section 29(4), it shall send to the Advisory Committee a copy of –

    (a) its qualification regulations;
    (b) its rules of conduct; and
    (c) a statement of the proposed alteration to the rights in question ...

7. (1) It shall be the duty of the Advisory Committee to consider the applicant's regulations and rules and the proposed alteration.

(2) When it has completed its consideration, the Advisory Committee shall advise the applicant of the extent to which (if at all) its qualification regulations or rules of conduct should, in the Committee's opinion, be amended in order better to –

    (a) further the statutory objective; or
    (b) comply with the general principle.

8. (1) If, after –

    (a) receiving the Advisory Committee's advice; and
    (b) making the alteration in question,

the applicant wishes the approval required by section 29(3) or (as the case may be) (4) to be given, it shall apply to the Lord Chancellor under this paragraph ...

(4) On receipt of such an application, the Lord Chancellor shall –

    (a) send a copy of the application and of any documents provided under sub-paragraph (2)(c) or (3) to the Advisory Committee and to each of the designated judges; and
    (b) refer the application to the Committee for advice.

9. (1) The Lord Chancellor shall also send a copy of the documents mentioned in paragraph 8(4)(a) to the Director ...

11. (1) When he has received the advice of the Advisory Committee and that of the Director, the Lord Chancellor shall send a copy of the advice to the applicant.

(2) The applicant shall be allowed a period of 28 days, beginning with the day on which the copy is sent to him, to make representations about the advice –

    (a) to the Lord Chancellor; or
    (b) where the Lord Chancellor appoints a person for the purposes of this sub-paragraph, to that person.

(3) When the period of 28 days has expired the Lord Chancellor shall consider, in the light of the advice and of any representations duly made by the applicant under sub-paragraph (2) whether the approval required by section 29(3) or (4) should be given.

(4) When the Lord Chancellor has complied with sub-paragraph (3) he shall –

(a) send to each designated judge a copy of –

(i) the advice; and

(ii) any representations duly made by the applicant under sub-paragraph (2);

(b) inform each designated judge as to whether he proposes to give the required approval; and

(c) where he proposes to withhold that approval, inform each designated judge of his reason for doing so.

(5) It shall then be the duty of each designated judge to consider, in the light of the material sent to him by the Lord Chancellor under sub-paragraph (4), whether the required approval should be given ...

(7) If the Lord Chancellor, or any of the designated judges, is satisfied that the alteration is incompatible with the statutory objective or the general principle, he shall refuse to give the required approval ...

PART III

REVOCATION OF DESIGNATION OF AUTHORISED BODY

12. (1) Where the Lord Chancellor is considering whether to recommend the making of a revoking Order by virtue of section 30(2)(c) or is advised by one or more of the designated judges that there are grounds for making such a recommendation, he shall seek the advice of the Advisory Committee.

(2) The Advisory Committee shall carry out such investigations with respect to the authorised body concerned as it considers appropriate.

(3) Where –

(a) the Lord Chancellor has not sought the advice of the Advisory Committee under sub-paragraph (1); but

(b) the Committee has reason to believe that there may be grounds for recommending that an Order be made under section 30(2)(c) with respect to an authorised body,

it may carry out such investigations with respect to the authorised body as it considers appropriate.

(4) On concluding any investigation carried out under sub-paragraph (2) or (3), the Advisory Committee shall –

(a) advise the Lord Chancellor as to whether or not there appear to be grounds for recommending the making of an Order under section 30 with respect to the authorised body concerned; and

(b) if its advice is that there appear to be such grounds, advise the Lord Chancellor as to the transitional and incidental provision (if any) which it considers should be made under section 30(4) with respect to the authorised body concerned ...

16. (4) No Order under section 30 shall be made with respect to the authorised body unless the Lord Chancellor and each of the designated judges have decided that it should be made.

SCHEDULE 5

THE AUTHORISED CONVEYANCING PRACTITIONERS BOARD

1. (1) Every member of the Board –

(a) shall be appointed for such term, not exceeding three years, as the Lord Chancellor may specify; and
(b) shall hold and vacate office in accordance with the terms of his appointment.

(2) Any person who ceases to be a member of the Board shall be eligible for re-appointment.

(3) A member of the Board may at any time resign his office by giving notice in writing to the Lord Chancellor.

(4) The Lord Chancellor may remove a member of the Board if satisfied –

(a) that he has failed to carry out his duties;
(b) that a bankruptcy order has been made against him or that his estate has been sequestrated or that he has made a composition or arrangement with, or granted a trust deed for, his creditors; or
(c) that he is otherwise unable or unfit to discharge the functions of a member of the Board ...

10. (1) The Board shall submit to the Lord Chancellor an annual report on the discharge of its functions.

(2) The Lord Chancellor shall lay the Board's annual report before Parliament ...

SCHEDULE 11

JUDGES, ETC BARRED FROM LEGAL PRACTICE

The following are the offices for the purposes of section 75 –

Lord of Appeal in Ordinary
Lord Justice of Appeal
Puisne judge of the High Court
Circuit judge
District judge, including district judge of the principal registry of the Family Division
Master of the Queen's Bench Division
Queen's Coroner and Attorney and Master of the Crown Office and Registrar of Criminal Appeals
Admiralty Registrar
Master of the Chancery Division
Registrar in Bankruptcy of the High Court
Taxing Master of the Supreme Court
Registrar of Civil Appeals
Master of the Court of Protection
District probate registrar
Judge Advocate General
Vice Judge Advocate General
Assistant or Deputy Judge Advocate General
Stipendiary Magistrate
Social Security Commissioner
President of social security appeal tribunals, medical appeal tribunals and

disability appeal tribunals or regional or other full-time chairman of such tribunals

President of Industrial Tribunals or chairman of such a tribunal appointed under the Industrial Tribunals (England and Wales) Regulations 1965

President or member of the Immigration Appeal Tribunal appointed under Schedule 5 to the Immigration Act 1971

Member of the Lands Tribunal appointed under section 2 of the Lands Tribunal Act 1949

President of Value Added Tax Tribunals or chairman of such a tribunal appointed under Schedule 8 to the Value Added Tax Act 1983

Special Commissioner appointed under section 4 of the Taxes Management Act 1970

Charity Commissioner appointed as provided in Schedule 1 to the Charities Act 1993

Coroner appointed under section 2 of the Coroners Act 1988.

[As amended by the Disability Living Allowance and Disability Working Allowance Act 1991, s4(2), Schedule 2, para 22; Tribunals and Inquiries Act 1992, s18(1), Schedule 3, para 35; Social Security (Consequential Provisions) Act 1992, s3(1), Schedule 1; Charities Act 1993, s98(1), Schedule 6, para 26.]

CHILD SUPPORT ACT 1991
(1991 c 48)

48 Right of audience [586]

(1) Any person authorised by the Secretary of State for the purposes of this section shall have, in relation to any proceedings under this Act before a magistrates' court, a right of audience and the right to conduct litigation.

(2) In this section 'right of audience' and 'right to conduct litigation' have the same meaning as in section 119 of the Courts and Legal Services Act 1990.

CRIMINAL JUSTICE ACT 1991
(1991 c 53)

1 Restrictions on imposing custodial sentences [587]

(1) This section applies where a person is convicted of an offence punishable with a custodial sentence other than one fixed by law.

(2) Subject to subsection (3) below, the court shall not pass a custodial sentence on the offender unless it is of the opinion –

(a) that the offence, or the combination of the offence and one or more offences associated with it, was so serious that only such a sentence can be justified for the offence; or
(b) where the offence is a violent or sexual offence, that only such a sentence would be adequate to protect the public from serious harm from him.

(3) Nothing in subsection (2) above shall prevent the court from passing a custodial sentence on the offender if he refuses to give his consent to a community sentence which is proposed by the court and requires that consent.

(4) Where a court passes a custodial sentence, it shall be its duty –

(a) in a case not falling within subsection (3) above, to state in open court that it is of the opinion that either or both of paragraphs (a) and (b) of subsection (2) above apply and why it is of that opinion; and

(b) in any case, to explain to the offender in open court and in ordinary language why it is passing a custodial sentence on him ...

2 Length of custodial sentences   [588]

(1) This section applies where a court passes a custodial sentence other than one fixed by law.

(2) The custodial sentence shall be –

(a) for such term (not exceeding the permitted maximum) as in the opinion of the court is commensurate with the seriousness of the offence, or the combination of the offence and one or more offences associated with it; or
(b) where the offence is a violent or sexual offence, for such longer term (not exceeding that maximum) as in the opinion of the court is necessary to protect the public from serious harm from the offender.

(3) Where the court passes a custodial sentence for a term longer than is commensurate with the seriousness of the offence, or the combination of the offence and one or more offences associated with it, the court shall –

(a) state in open court that it is of the opinion that subsection (2)(b) above applies and why it is of that opinion; and
(b) explain to the offender in open court and in ordinary language why the sentence is for such a term.

(4) A custodial sentence for an indeterminate period shall be regarded for the purposes of subsections (2) and (3) above as a custodial sentence for a term longer than any actual term.

53 Notices of transfer in certain cases involving children   [589]

(1) If a person has been charged with an offence to which section 32(2) of the [Criminal Justice Act 1988] applies (sexual offences and offences involving violence or cruelty) and the Director of Public Prosecutions is of the opinion –

(a) that the evidence of the offence would be sufficient for the person charged to be committed for trial;
(b) that a child who is alleged –

(i) to be a person against whom the offence was committed; or
(ii) to have witnessed the commission of the offence,

will be called as a witness at the trial; and

(c) that, for the purpose of avoiding any prejudice to the welfare of the child, the case should be taken over and proceeded with without delay by the Crown Court,

a notice ('notice of transfer') certifying that opinion may be served by or on behalf of the Director on the magistrates' court in whose jurisdiction the offence has been charged.

(2) A notice of transfer shall be served before the magistrates' court begins to inquire into the case as examining justices.

(3) On the service of a notice of transfer the functions of the magistrates' court shall cease in relation to the case except as provided by paragraphs 2 and 3 of Schedule 6 to this Act or by section 20(4) of the Legal Aid Act 1988.

(4) The decision to serve a notice of transfer shall not be subject to appeal or liable to be questioned in any court.

(5) Schedule 6 to this Act (which makes further provision in relation to notices of transfer) shall have effect.

(6) In this section 'child' means a person who –

(a) in the case of an offence falling within section 32(2)(a) or (b) of the 1988 Act, is under 14 years of age or, if he was under that age when any such video recording as is mentioned in section 32A(2) of that Act was made in respect of him, is under 15 years of age; or

(b) in the case of an offence falling within section 32(2)(c) of that Act, is under 17 years of age or, if he was under that age when any such video recording was made in respect of him, is under 18 years of age.

(7) Any reference in subsection (6) above to an offence falling within paragraph (a), (b) or (c) of section 32(2) of that Act includes a reference to an offence which consists of attempting or conspiring to commit, or of aiding, abetting, counselling, procuring or inciting the commission of, an offence falling within that paragraph.

[As amended by the Criminal Justice Act 1993, s69(1), (2), (9).]

BAIL (AMENDMENT) ACT 1993
(1993 c 26)

1 Prosecution right of appeal [590]

(1) Where a magistrates' court grants bail to a person who is charged with or convicted of –

(a) an offence punishable by a term of imprisonment of five years or more, or

(b) an offence under section 12 (taking a conveyance without authority) or 12A (aggravated vehicle taking) of the Theft Act 1968,

the prosecution may appeal to a judge of the Crown Court against the granting of bail.

(2) Subsection (1) above applies only where the prosecution is conducted –

(a) by or on behalf of the Director of Public Prosecutions; or

(b) by a person who falls within such class or description of person as may be prescribed for the purposes of this section by order made by the Secretary of State.

(3) Such an appeal may be made only if –

(a) the prosecution made representations that bail should not be granted; and

(b) the representations were made before it was granted.

(4) In the event of the prosecution wishing to exercise the right of appeal set out in subsection (1) above, oral notice of appeal shall be given to the magistrates' court at the conclusion of the proceedings in which such bail has been granted and before the release from custody of the person concerned.

(5) Written notice of appeal shall thereafter be served on the magistrates' court and the person concerned within two hours of the conclusion of such proceedings.

(6) Upon receipt from the prosecution of oral notice of appeal from its decision to grant bail the magistrates' court shall remand in custody the person concerned, until the appeal is determined or otherwise disposed of.

(7) Where the prosecution fails, within the period of two hours mentioned in subsection (5) above, to serve one or both of the notices required by that subsection, the appeal shall be deemed to have been disposed of.

(8) The hearing of an appeal under subsection (1) above against a decision of the magistrates' court to grant bail shall be commenced within 48 hours, excluding

weekends and any public holiday (that is to say, Christmas Day, Good Friday or a bank holiday), from the date on which oral notice of appeal is given.

(9) At the hearing of any appeal by the prosecution under this section, such appeal shall be by way of re-hearing, and the judge hearing any such appeal may remand the person concerned in custody or may grant bail subject to such conditions (if any) as he thinks fit.

(10) In relation to a child or young person (within the meaning of the Children and Young Persons Act 1969) –

(a) the reference in subsection (1) above to an offence punishable by a term of imprisonment is to be read as a reference to an offence which would be so punishable in the case of an adult; and
(b) the reference in subsection (5) above to remand in custody is to be read subject to the provisions of section 23 of the Act of 1969 (remands to local authority accommodation).

(11) The power to make an order under subsection (2) above shall be exercisable by statutory instrument and any instrument shall be subject to annulment in pursuance of a resolution of either House of Parliament.

Glossary
of Latin and other words and phrases

Ab extra. From outside.

Ab inconvenienti. *See* ARGUMENTUM

Ab initio. From the beginning.

Accessio. Addition; appendage. The combination of two chattels belonging to different persons into a single article.

Acta exteriora indicant interiora secreta. A man's outward actions are evidence of his innermost thoughts and intentions.

Actio personalis moritur cum persona. A personal right of action dies on the death of the person by or against whom it could be enforced.

Actus non facit reum, nisi mens sit rea. The act itself does not make a man guilty, unless he does it with a guilty intention.

Ad colligenda bona. To collect the goods.

Ad hoc. Arranged for this purpose; special.

Ad idem. *See* CONSENSUS.

Ad infinitum. To infinity; without limit; for ever.

Ad litem. For the purpose of the law suit.

Ad opus. For the benefit of: on behalf of.

Ad valorem. Calculated in proportion to the value or price of the property.

Adversus extraneos vitiosa possessio prodesse solet. Possession, though supported only by a defective title, will prevail over the claims of strangers other than the true owner.

A fortiori (ratione). For a stronger reason; by even more convincing reasoning.

Aliter. Otherwise; the result would be different, if ...; (also, used of a judge who thinks differently from his fellow judges).

Aliud est celare; aliud est tacere; neque enim id est celare quicquid reticeas. Mere silence is one thing but active concealment is quite another thing; for it is not disguising something when you say nothing about it.

Aliunde. From elsewhere; from other sources.

A mensa et thoro. A separation from the 'table and bed' of one's spouse.

Amicus curiae. A friend of the court.

Animo contrahendi. With the intention of contracting.

Animo revocandi. With the intention of revoking.

Animus deserendi. The intention of deserting.

Animus donandi. The intention of giving.

303

Animus possidendi. The intention of possessing.

Animus revertendi. The intention of returning.

Animus testandi. The intention of making a will.

Ante. Before; (also used of a case referred to earlier on a page or in a book).

A posteriori. From effect to cause; inductively; from subsequent conclusions.

A priori. From cause to effect; deductively; from previous assumptions or reasoning.

Argumentum ab inconvenienti. An argument devised because of the existence of an awkward problem so as to provide an explanation for it.

Asportatio. The act of carrying away.

Assensus. *See* CONSENSUS.

Assensus ad idem. Agreement as to the same terms.

Assumpsit (super se). He undertook.

Ats. (ad sectam). At the suit of. (The opposite of VERSUS.)

Autrefois acquit. Formerly acquitted.

Autrefois convict. Formerly convicted.

Bis dat qui cito dat. He gives doubly who gives swiftly; a quick gift is worth two slow ones.

Bona fide. In good faith; sincere.

Bona vacantia. Goods without an owner.

Brutum fulmen. A silent thunderbolt; an empty threat.

Cadit quaestio. The matter admits of no further argument.

Caeterorum. Of the things which are left.

Capias ad satisfaciendum. A writ commanding the sheriff to take the body of the defendant in order that he may make satisfaction for the plaintiff's claim.

Causa causans. The immediate cause of something; the last link in the chain of causation.

Causa proxima non remota spectatur. Regard is paid to the immediate, not to the remote cause.

Causa sine qua non. A preceding link in the chain of causation without which the causa causans could not be operative.

Caveat emptor. The buyer must look out for himself.

Cessante ratione legis, cessat lex ipsa. When the reason for its existence ceases, the law itself ceases to exist.

Cestui(s) que trust. A person (or persons) for whose benefit property is held on trust; a beneficiary (beneficiaries).

Cestui que vie. Person for the duration of whose life an estate is granted to another person.

Chose in action. Intangible personal property or rights, which can be enjoyed or enforced only by legal action, and not by taking physical possession (eg debts).

Chose jugée. Thing it is idle to discuss.

Coitus interruptus. Interrupted sexual intercourse, i.e. withdrawal before emission.

Colore officii. Under the pretext of a person's official position.

Commorientes. Persons who die at the same time.

Confusio. A mixture; union. The mixture of things of the same nature, but belonging to different persons so that identification of the original things becomes impossible.

Consensu. By general consent; unanimously.

Consensus ad idem. Agreement as to the same thing.

Consortium. Conjugal relations with and companionship of a spouse.

Contra. To the contrary. (Used of a case in which the decision was contrary to the doctrine or cases previously cited; also of a judge who delivers a dissenting judgment.)

Contra bonos mores. Contrary to good morals.

Contra mundum. Against the world.

Contra proferentem. Against the party who puts forward a clause in a document.

Cor. (coram). In the presence of; before (a judge).

Coram non judice. Before one who is not a judge. Corpus. Body; capital.

Corpus. Body; capital.

Coverture. Marriage.

Cri de coeur. Heartfelt cry.

Cujus est solum, ejus est usque ad coelum et ad inferos. Whosoever owns the soil also owns everything above it as far as the heavens and everything below it as far as the lower regions of the earth.

Culpa. Wrongful default.

Cum onere. Together with the burden.

Cum testamento annexo. With the will annexed.

Cur. adv. vult. (curia advisari vult). The court wishes time to consider the matter.

Cy-pres. For a purpose resembling as nearly as possible the purpose originally proposed.

Damage feasant. *See* DISTRESS.

Damnosa hereditas. An insolvent inheritance.

Damnum. Loss; damage.

Damnum absque injuria. *See* DAMNUM SINE INJURIA.

Damnum emergens. A loss which arises.

Damnum fatale. Damage resulting from the workings of fate for which human negligence is not to blame.

Damnum sine (or absque) injuria. Damage which is not the result of a legally remediable wrong.

De bene esse. Evidence or action which a court allows to be given or done provisionally, subject to further consideration at a later stage.

Debitor non praesumitur donare. A debtor is presumed to give a legacy to a creditor to discharge his debt and not as a gift.

Debitum in praesenti. A debt which is due at the present time.

Debitum in futuro solvendum. A debt which will be due to be paid at a future time.

De bonis asportatis. Of goods carried away.

De bonis non administratis. Of the assets which have not been administered .

De die in diem. From day to day.

De facto. In fact.

De futuro. Regarding the future; in the future; about something which will exist in the future.

Dehors. Outside (the document or matter in question); irrelevant.

De integro. As regards the whole; entirely.

De jure. By right; rightful.

Del credere agent. An agent who for an extra commission guarantees the due performance of contracts by persons whom he introduces to his principal.

Delegatus non potest delegare. A person who is entrusted with a duty has no right to appoint another person to perform it in his place.

De minimis non curat lex. The law does not concern itself with trifles.

De novo. Anew; starting afresh.

Deodand. A chattel which caused the death of a human being and was forfeited to the Crown.

De praerogativa regis. Concerning the royal prerogative.

De son tort. Of his wrong.

Deus est procurator fatuorum. God is the protector of the simpleminded.

Devastavit. Where an executor 'has squandered' the estate.

Dictum. Saying. *See* OBITER DICTUM.

Dies non (jurisdicus). Day on which no legal business can be transacted.

Dissentiente. Delivering a dissenting judgment.

Distress damage feasant. The detention by a landowner of an animal or chattel while it is doing damage on his land.

Distringas. That you may distrain.

Doli incapax. Incapable of crime.

Dolus qui dat locum contractui. A deception which clears the way for the other party to enter into a contract.

Dominium. Ownership.

Dominus litis. The principal in a suit.

Dominus pro tempore. The master for the time being.

Donatio mortis causa. A gift made in contemplation of death and conditional thereon.

Dubitante. Doubting the correctness of the decision.

Durante absentia. During an executor's absence abroad.

Durante minore aetate. While an executor remains an infant.

Durante viduitate. During widowhood.

Ei incumbit probatio qui dicit, non qui negat. The onus of proving a fact rests upon the man who asserts its truth, not upon the man who denies it.

Ejusdem generis. General words following a list of specific things are construed as relating to things 'of the same kind' as those specifically listed.

Enceinte. Pregnant.

En ventre sa mère. Conceived but not yet born.

Eodem modo quo oritur, eodem modo dissolvitur. What has been created by a certain method may be extinguished by the same method.

Eo instanti. At that instant.

Escrow. A document delivered subject to a condition which must be fulfilled before it becomes a deed.

Estoppel. A rule of evidence which applies in certain circumstances and stops a person from denying the truth of a statement previously made by him.

Et cetera. (Etc.) And other things of that sort.

Et seq. (et sequentes). And subsequent pages.

Ex. From; by virtue of.

Ex abundanti cautela. From an abundance of caution.

Ex acquo et bono. According to what is just and equitable.

Ex cathedra. From his seat of office: an authoritative statement made by someone in his official capacity.

Ex concessis. In view of what has already been accepted.

Ex contractu. Arising out of contract.

Ex converso. Conversely.

Ex debito justitiae. That which is due as of right; which the court has no discretion to refuse.

Ex delicto. Arising out of a wrongful act or tort.

Ex dolo malo non oritur actio. No right of action arises out of a fraud.

Ex facie. On the face of it; ostensibly.

Ex gratia. Out of the kindness. Gratuitous; voluntary.

Ex hypothesi. In view of what has already been assumed.

Ex improviso. Unexpectedly, without forethought.

Ex officio. By virtue of one's official position.

Ex pacto illicito non oritur actio. No action can be brought on an unlawful contract.

Ex parte. Proceedings brought on behalf of one interested party without notice to, and in the absence of, the other.

Ex post facto. By reason of a subsequent act; acting retrospectively.

Ex relatione. An action instituted by the Attorney-General on behalf of the Crown on the information of a member of the public who is interested in the matter (the relator).

Expressio unius est exclusio alterius. When one thing is expressly specified, then it prevents anything else being implied.

Expressum facit cessare tacitum. Where terms are expressed, no other terms can be implied.

Ex turpi causa non oritur actio. No action can be brought where the parties are guilty of illegal or immoral conduct.

Faciendum. Something which is to be done.

Factum. Deed; that which has been done; statement of facts or points in issue.

Fait accompli. An accomplished fact.

Falsa demonstratio non nocet cum de corpore constat. Where the substance of the property in question is clearly identified, the addition of an incorrect description of the property does no harm.

Falsus in ono, falsus in omnibus. False in one, false in all.

Fecundatio ab extra. Conception from outside, i.e. where there has been no penetration.

Feme covert. A married woman.

Feme sole. An unmarried woman.

Ferae naturae. Animals which are by nature dangerous to man.

Fieri facias. A writ addressed to the sheriff: 'that you cause to be made' from the defendant's goods the sum due to the plaintiff under the judgment.

Force majeure. Irresistible compulsion.

Fructus industriales. Cultivated crops.

Fructus naturales. Vegetation which grows naturally without cultivation.

Functus officio. Having discharged his duty; having exhausted its powers.

Genus numquam perit. Particular goods which have been identified may be destroyed, but 'a category or type of article can never perish'.

Habeas corpus (ad subjiciendum). A writ addressed to one who detains another in custody, requiring him 'that you produce the prisoner's body to answer' to the court.

Habitue. A frequent visitor to a place.

Ibid. (ibidem). In the same place, book, or source.

Id certum est quod certum reddi potest. That which is capable of being reduced to a certainty is already a certainty.

Idem. The same thing, or person.

Ideo consideratum est per. Therefore it is considered by the court.

Ignorantia juris haud (neminem) (non) excusat, ignorantia facti excusat. A man may be excused for mistaking facts, but not for mistaking the law.

Ignorantia juris non excusat. Ignorance of the law is no excuse.

Imperitia culpae adnumeratur. Lack of skill is accounted a fault.

In aequali jure melior est conditio possidentis. Where the legal rights of the parties are equal, the party with possession is in the stronger position.

In articulo mortis. On the point of death.

In bonis. In the goods (or estate) of a deceased person.

In capite. In chief; holding as tenant directly under the Crown.

In consimili casu. In a similar case.

In custodia legis. In the keeping of the law.

Indebitatus assumpsit. A form of action in which the plaintiff alleges the defendant 'being already indebted to the plaintiff undertook' to do something.

In delicto. At fault.

Indicia. Signs; marks.

Indicium. Indication; sign; mark.

In esse. In existence.

In expeditione. On actual military service.

In extenso. At full length.

In fieri. In the course of being performed or established.

In flagrante delicto. In the act of committing the offence.

In forma pauperis. In the character of a poor person.

Infra. Below; lower down on a page; later in a book. In futuro. In the future.

In futuro. In the future.

In hac re. In this matter; in this particular aspect.

In jure non remota causa sed proxima spectatur. In law it is the immediate and not the remote cause which is considered.

Injuria. A wrongful act for which the law provides a remedy.

Injuria sine damno. A wrongful act unaccompanied by any damage yet actionable at law.

In lieu of. In place of.

In limine. On the threshold; at the outset.

In loco parentis. In the place of a parent.

In minore delicto. A person who is 'less at fault'.

In omnibus. In every respect.

Inops consilii. Lacking facilities for legal advice.

In pari delicto, potior est conditio defendentis (or possidentis). Where both parties are equally at fault, the defendant (or the party in possession) is in the stronger position.

In pari materia. In an analogous case or position.

In personam. *See* JUS IN PERSONAM.

In pleno. In full.

In praesenti. At the present time.

In propria persona. In his own capacity. In re. In the matter of. In rem. *See* JUS IN REM.

In re. In the matter of.

In rem. *See* JUS IN REM.

In situ. In its place.

In specie. In its own form; not converted into anything else.

In statu quo ante. In the condition in which it, or a person, was before.

Inter alia. Amongst other things.

Inter alios. Amongst other persons.

Interest reipublicae ut sit finis litium. It is in the interests of the community that every law suit should reach a final conclusion (and not be reopened later).

Interim. In the meanwhile; temporary.

Inter partes. Between (the) parties.

In terrorem. As a warning; as a deterrent.

Inter se. Between themselves.

Inter vivos. Between persons who are alive.

In toto. In its entirety; completely.

In transitu. In passage from one place to another.

Intra vires. Within the powers recognised by law as belonging to the person or body in question.

In utero. In the womb.

In vacuo. In the abstract; without considering the circumstances.

In vitro. In glass; in a test tube.

Ipsissima verba. 'The very words' of a speaker.

Ipso facto. By that very fact.

Jura. Rights.

Jura mariti. By virtue of the right of a husband to the goods of his wife.

Jus. A right which is recognised in law.

Jus accrescendi. The right of survivorship; the right of joint tenants to have their interests in the joint property increased by inheriting the interests of the deceased joint tenants until the last survivor inherits the entire property.

Jus in personam. A right which can be enforced against a particular person only.

Jus in rem. A right which can be enforced over the property in question against all other persons.

Jus naturale. Natural justice.

Jus neque in re neque ad rem. A right which is enforceable neither over the property in question against all the world nor against specific persons only.

Jus quaesitum tertio. A right vested in a third party (who is not a party to the contract).

Jus tertii. *See* JUS QUAESITUM TERTIO

Laches. Slackness or delay in pursuing a legal remedy which disentitles a person from action at a later date.

Laesio fidei. Breach of faith.

Laissez faire. 'Let him do what he likes'; permissive.

Lapsus linguae. Slip of the tongue.

Lex domicilii. The law of domicile.

Lex fori. The law of the court in which the case is being heard.

Lex loci celebrationis. The law of the place where the marriage was celebrated.

Lex loci contractus. The law of the place where the contract was made.

Lex loci delicti. The law of the place where the wrong was committed.

Lex loci situs. *See* LEX SITUS.

Lex loci solutionis. The law of the place where the contract is to be performed.

Lex situs. The law of the place where the thing in question is situated.

Lien. The rights to retain possession of goods, deeds or other property belonging to another as security for payment of money.

Lis pendens. Pending action.

Loc. cit. (loco citato). In the passage previously mentioned.

Locus classicus. Authoritative passage in a book or judgment; the principal authority or source for the subject.

Locus in quo. Scene of the event.

Locus poenitentiae. Scope or opportunity for repentance.

Locus standi. Recognised position or standing; the right to appear in court.

Lucrum cessans. A benefit which is terminated.

Magnum opus. A great work of literature.

Mala fide(s). (In) bad faith.

Malitia supplet aetatem. Malice supplements the age of an infant wrongdoer who would (in the absence of malice) be too young to be responsible for his acts.

Malum in se. An act which in itself is morally wrong, e.g. murder.

Malum prohibitum. An act which is wrong because it is prohibited by human law but is not morally wrong.

Malus animus. Evil intent.

Mansuetae naturae. Animals which are normally of a domesticated disposition.

Mesne. Intermediate; middle; dividing.

Mesne profits. Profits of land lost by the plaintiff while the defendant remained wrongfully in possession.

Mobilia sequuntur personam. The domicile of movable property follows the owner's personal domicile.

Molliter manus imposuit. Gently laid his hand upon the other party.

Mutatis mutandis. With the necessary changes of detail being made.

Natura negotii. The nature of the transaction.

Negotiorum gestio. Handling of other people's affairs.

Nemo dat quod non habet. No one has power to transfer the ownership of that which he does not own.

Nemo debet bis vexari, si constat curiae quod sit pro una et eadem causa. No one ought to be harassed with proceedings twice, if it appears to the court that it is for one and the same cause.

Nemo est haeres viventis. No one can be the heir of a person who is still living.

Nexus. Connection; bond.

Nisi. Unless; (also used of a decree or order which will later be made absolute 'unless' good cause be shown to the contrary); provisional.

Nisi prius. Cases which were directed to be tried at Westminster only if the justices of assize should 'not' have tried them in the country 'previously'.

Nocumenta infinita sunt. There is no limit to the types of situations which constitute nuisances.

Nomen collectivum. A collective name, noun or description; a word descriptive of a class.

Non compos mentis. Not of sound mind and understanding.

Non constat. It is not certain.

Non est factum. That the document in question was not his deed.

Non haec in foedera veni. This is not the agreement which I came to sign.

Non omnibus dormio. I do not turn a blind eye on every instance of misconduct.

Non sequitur. It does not follow; an inconsistent statement.

Noscitur a sociis. The meaning of a word is known from the company it keeps (ie from its context).

Nova causa interveniens. An independent cause which intervenes between the alleged wrong and the damage in question.

Novus actus interveniens. A fresh act of someone other than the defendant which intervenes between the alleged wrong and the damage in question.

Nudum pactum. A bare agreement (unsupported by consideration).

Nullius filius. No man's son; a bastard.

Obiter dictum (dicta). Thing(s) said by the way; opinions expressed by judges in passing, on issues not essential for the decision in the case.

Obligatio quasi ex contractu. An obligation arising out of an act or event, as if from a contract, but independently of the consent of the person bound.

Omnia praesumuntur contra spoliatorem. Every presumption is raised against a wrongdoer.

Omnia praesumuntur rite et solemniter esse acta donec probetur in contrarium. All things are presumed to have been performed with all due formalities until it is proved to the contrary.

Omnis ratihabitio retrotrahitur et mandato priori aequiparatur. Every ratification of a previous act is carried back and made equivalent to a previous command to do it.

Onus probandi. The burden of proving.

Op. cit. (opere citato). In the book referred to previously.

Orse. Otherwise.

Par delictum. Equal fault.

Parens patriae. Parent of the nation.

Pari materia. With equal substance.

Pari passu. On an equal footing; equally; in step with.

Pari ratione. By an equivalent process of reasoning.

Parol. By word of mouth, or unsealed document.

Participes criminis. Accomplices in the crime.

Pater est quem nuptiae demonstrant. He is the father whom the marriage indicates to be so.

Passim. Generally; referred to throughout the book or source in question.

Patrimonium. Beneficial ownership.

Pendente lite. While a law suit is pending.

Per. By; through; in the opinion of a judge.

Per capita. Divided equally between all the persons filling the description.

Per curiam. In the opinion of the court.

Per formam doni. Through the form of wording of the gift or deed.

Per incuriam. Through carelessness or oversight.

Per quod. By reason of which.

Per quod consortium et servitium amisit. By reason of which he has lost the benefit of her company and services.

Per quod servitium amisit. By reason of which he has lost the benefit of his service.

Per se. By itself.

Persona(e) designata(e). A person(s) specified as an individual(s), not identified as a member(s) of a class nor as fulfilling a particular qualification.

Per stirpes. According to the stocks of descent; one share for each line of descendants; where the descendants of a deceased person (however many they may be) inherit between them only the one share which the deceased would have taken if alive.

Per subsequens matrimonium. Legitimation of a child 'by subsequent marriage' of the parents.

Plene administravit. A plea by an executor 'that he has fully administered' all the assets which have come into his hands and that no assets remain out of which the plaintiff's claim could be satisfied.

Plus quam tolerabile. More than can be endured.

Post. After; mentioned in a subsequent passage or page.

Post mortem. After death.

Post nuptial. Made after marriage.

Post obit bond. Agreement or bond by which a borrower agrees to pay the lender a sum larger than the loan on or after the death of a person on whose death he expects to inherit property.

Post obitum. After the death of a specified person.

Pour autrui. On behalf of another.

Prima facie. At first sight.

Primae impressionis. Of first impression.

Pro bono publico. For the public good.

Profit a prendre. The right to enter the land of another and take part of its produce.

Pro hac vice. For this occasion.

Pro privato commodo. For private benefit.

Pro rata. In proportion.

Pro rata itineris. At the same rate per mile as was agreed for the whole journey.

Pro tanto. So far; to that extent.

Pro tempore. For the time being.

Publici juris. Of public right.

Puisne. Inferior; lower in rank; not secured by deposit of deeds; of the High Court.

Punctum temporis. Moment, or point of time.

Pour autre vie. During the life of another person.

q.v. (quod vide). Which see.

Qua. As; in the capacity of.

Quaere. Consider whether it is correct.

Quaeritur. The question is raised.

Quantum. Amount; how much.

Quantum meruit. As much as he has earned.

Quantum valebant. As much as they were worth.

Quare clausum fregit. Because he broke into the plaintiff's enclosure.

Quasi. As if; seemingly.

Quasi ex contractu. *See* OBLIGATIO.

Quatenus. How far; in so far as; since.

Quia timet. Because he fears what he will suffer in the future.

Quicquid plantatur solo solo cedit. Whatever is planted in the soil belongs to the soil.

Quid pro quo. Something for something; consideration.

Qui facit per alium facit per se. He who employs another person to do something does it himself.

Qui prior est tempore potior est jure. He who is earlier in point of time is in the stronger position in law.

Quoad. Until; as far as; as to.

Quoad hoc. As far as this matter is concerned.

Quo animo. With what intention.

Quot judices tot sententiae. There were as many different opinions as there were judges.

Quousque. Until the time when.

Ratio decidendi. The reason for a decision; the principle on which a decision is based.

Ratione domicilii. By reason of a person's domicile.

Re. In the matter of; by the thing or transaction.

Renvoi. Reference to or application of the rules of a foreign legal system in a different country's courts.

Res. Thing; affair; matter; circumstance.

Res extincta. The thing which was intended to be the subject matter of a contract but had previously been destroyed.

Res gestae. Things done; the transaction.

Res integra. A point not covered by the authority of a decided case which must therefore be decided upon principle alone.

Res inter alios acta alteri nocere non debet. A man ought not to be prejudiced by what has taken place between other persons.

Res ipsa loquitur. The thing speaks for itself, i.e. is evidence of negligence in the absence of an explanation by the defendant.

Res judicata. A matter on which a court has previously reached a binding decision; a matter which cannot be questioned.

Res nova. A matter which has not previously been decided.

Res nullius. Nobody's property.

Respondeat superior. A principal must answer for the acts of his subordinates.

Res sua. Something which a man believes to belong to another when it in fact is 'his own property'.

Restitutio in integrum. Restoration of a party to his original position; full restitution.

Res vendita. The article which was sold.

Rex est procurator fatuorum. The King is the protector of the simple minded.

Rigor aequitatis. The inflexibility of equity.

Sc. *See* SCILICET.

Sciens. Knowing.

Scienter. Knowingly; with knowledge of an animal's dangerous disposition.

Scienti non fit injuria. A man who is aware of the existence of a danger has no remedy if it materialises.

Scilicet. To wit; namely; that is to say.

Scintilla. A spark; trace; or moment.

Scire facias. A writ; that you cause to know.

Scriptum praedictum non est factum suum. A plea that the aforesaid document is not his deed.

Secundum formam doni. In accordance with the form of wording in the gift or deed.

Secus. It is otherwise; the legal position is different.

Sed. But.

Sed quaere. But inquire; look into the matter; consider whether the statement is correct.

Semble. It appears; apparently.

Sentit commodum et periculum rei. He both enjoys the benefit of the thing and bears the risk of its loss.

Seriatim. In series; one by one; point by point.

Serivitium. Service.

Sic. So; in such a manner; (also used to emphasise wording copied or quoted from another source: 'such was the expression used in the original source').

Sic utere tuo ut alienum non laedas. So use your own property as not to injure the property of your neighbour.

Similiter. Similarly; in like manner.

Simplex commendatio non obligat. Mere praise of goods by the seller imposes no liability upon him.

Simpliciter. Simply; merely; alone; without any further action; without qualification.

Sine animo revertendi. Without the intention of returning.

Sine die. Without a day being appointed; indefinitely.

Solatium. Consolation; relief; compensation.

Sotto volce. In an undertone.

Specificatio. The making of a new article out of the chattel of one person by the labour of another.

Spes successionis. The hope of inheriting property on the death of another.

Spondes peritiam artis. If skill is inherent in your profession, you guarantee that you will display it.

Stare decisis. To stand by what has been dedided.

Status quo (ante). The previous position; the position in which things were before; unchanged position.

Stet. Let it stand; do not delete.

Stricto sensu. In the strict sense.

Sub colore officii. Under pretext of someone's official position.

Sub modo. Within limits; to a limited extent.

Sub nom. (sub nomine). Under the name of.

Sub silentio. In silence.

Sub tit. (sub titulo). Under the title of.

Suggestio falsi. The suggestion of something which is untrue.

Sui generis. Of its own special kind; unique.

Sui juris. Of his own right; possessed of full legal capacity.

Sup. *See* SUPRA.

Suppressio veri. The suppression of the truth.

Supra. (Sup.) Above; referred to higher up the page; previously.

Talis qualis. Such as it is.

Tam ... quam. As well ... as.

Toties quoties. As often as occasion shall require; as often as something happens.

Transit in rem judicatam. A right of action merges in the judgment recovered upon it.

Turpis causa. Immoral conduct which constitutes the subject matter of an action.

Uberrima fides. Most abundant good faith.

Ubi jus ibi remedium. Where there is a legally recognised right there is also a remedy.

Ubi supra. In the passage or reference mentioned previously.

Ultimus heres. The ultimate heir who is last in order of priority of those who may be entitled to claim the estate of an intestate.

Ultra vires. Outside the powers recognised by law as belonging to the person or body in question.

Uno flatu. With one breath; at the same moment.

Ut res magis valeat quam pereat. Words must be construed so as to support the validity of the contract rather than to destroy it.

v. (versus). Against.

Verba fortius accipiuntur contra proferentem. Ambiguous wording is construed adversely against the party who introduced it into the document.

Vera copula. True sexual unity.

Verbatim. Word by word; exactly; word for word.

Vice versa. The other way round; in turn.

Vide. See.

Vi et armis (et contra pacem domini regis). By force of arms (and in breach of the King's peace).

Vigilantibus et non dormientibus jura subveniunt (or jus succurrit). The law(s) assist(s) those who are vigilant, not those who doze over their rights.

Vinculum juris. Legal tie; that which binds the parties with mutual obligations.

Virgo intacta. A virgin with hymen intact.

Virtute officii. By virtue of a person's official position.

Vis-a-vis. Face to face; opposite to.

Vis major. Irresistible force.

Viva voce. Orally; oral examination.

Viz. (videlicet). Namely; that is to say.

Voir dire. Examination of a witness before he gives evidence, to ascertain whether he is competent to tell the truth on oath; trial within a trial.

Volens. Willing.

Volenti non fit injuria. In law no wrong is done to a man who consents to undergo it.

Index